From Medievalism to Early-Modernism

From Medievalism to Early-Modernism: Adapting the English Past is a collection of essays that both analyses the historical and cultural medieval and early modern past, and engages with the medievalism and early-modernism—a new term introduced in this collection—present in contemporary popular culture. By focusing on often overlooked uses of the past in contemporary culture—such as the allusions to John Webster's *The Duchess of Malfi* in J.K. Rowling's *Harry Potter* books, and the impact of intertextual references and internet fandom on the BBC's *The Hollow Crown: The Wars of the Roses*—the contributors illustrate how cinematic, televisual, artistic, and literary depictions of the historical and cultural past not only re-purpose the past in varying ways, but also build on a history of adaptations that audiences have come to know and expect. *From Medievalism to Early-Modernism: Adapting the English Past* analyses the way that the medieval and early modern periods are used in modern adaptations, and how these adaptations both reflect contemporary concerns and engage with a history of intertextuality and intervisuality.

Marina Gerzic works for the Centre for Medieval and Early Modern Studies at The University of Western Australia in both research and administrative roles. She also works as the Executive Administrator for the Australian and New Zealand Association for Medieval and Early Modern Studies, and as the editorial assistant for the academic journal *Parergon*. She has published articles on film and adaptation theory, Shakespeare, pedagogy, cinematic music, cultural studies, science fiction, comics and graphic novels, and children's literature.

Aidan Norrie is a historian of monarchy, and a Chancellor's International Scholar in the Centre for the Study of the Renaissance at The University of Warwick. He is the editor, with Lisa Hopkins, of *Women on the Edge in Early Modern Europe* (Amsterdam University Press), and, with Mark Houlahan, of *On the Edge of Early Modern English Drama* (MIP University Press).

Routledge Studies in Medieval Literature and Culture

4 Mary Magdalene in Medieval Culture
  Conflicted Roles
  Edited by Peter V. Loewen and Robin Waugh

5 The Signifying Power of Pearl
  Medieval Literacy and Cultural Contexts for the Transformation of Genre
  Jane Beal

6 Language and Community in Early England
  Imagining Distance in Medieval Literature
  Emily Butler

7 Storytelling as Plague Prevention in Medieval and Early Modern Italy
  The Decameron Tradition
  Martin Marafioti

8 Toleration and Tolerance in Medieval European Literature
  Albrecht Classen

9 Beowulf's Popular Afterlife in Literature, Comic Books, and Film
  Kathleen Forni

10 Disability and Knighthood in Malory's Morte Darthur
   Tory V. Pearman

11 From Medievalism to Early-Modernism
   Adapting the English Past
   Edited by Marina Gerzic and Aidan Norrie

For more information about this series, please visit: https://www.routledge.com

From Medievalism to Early-Modernism
Adapting the English Past

Edited by Marina Gerzic and
Aidan Norrie

First published 2019
by Routledge
52 Vanderbilt Avenue, New York, NY 10017

and by Routledge
2 Park Square, Milton Park, Abingdon, Oxon, OX14 4RN

First issued in paperback 2020

Routledge is an imprint of the Taylor & Francis Group, an Informa business

© 2019 Taylor & Francis

The right of Marina Gerzic and Aidan Norrie to be identified as the authors of the editorial material, and of the authors for their individual chapters, has been asserted in accordance with sections 77 and 78 of the Copyright, Designs and Patents Act 1988.

All rights reserved. No part of this book may be reprinted or reproduced or utilised in any form or by any electronic, mechanical, or other means, now known or hereafter invented, including photocopying and recording, or in any information storage or retrieval system, without permission in writing from the publishers.

Trademark notice: Product or corporate names may be trademarks or registered trademarks, and are used only for identification and explanation without intent to infringe.

Library of Congress Cataloging-in-Publication Data
Names: Gerzic, Marina, editor. | Norrie, Aidan, editor.
Title: From medievalism to early-modernism: adapting the English past / edited by Marina Gerziâc and Aidan Norrie.
Description: New York, NY: Routledge, 2019. | Series: Routledge studies in medieval literature and culture; 11 | Includes bibliographical references and index. |
Identifiers: LCCN 2018037042 (print) |
LCCN 2018046872 (ebook) | ISBN 9780429400544 (Master) |
ISBN 9780429683015 (Pdf) | ISBN 9780429683008 (Epub) |
ISBN 9780429682995 (Mobi) | ISBN 9781138366572 |
ISBN 9781138366572 (hardback) | ISBN 9780429400544 (ebk)
Subjects: LCSH: Literature, Modern—Medieval influences. | Medievalism in literature. | Middle Ages in literature. | Literature, Medieval—Appreciation. | Literature and history—England. | England—In literature.
Classification: LCC PN56.M534 (ebook) | LCC PN56.M534 F76 2019 (print) | DDC 809/.933582—dc23
LC record available at https://lccn.loc.gov/2018037042

ISBN 13: 978-0-367-66472-5 (pbk)
ISBN 13: 978-1-138-36657-2 (hbk)

Typeset in Sabon
by codeMantra

Printed in the United Kingdom
by Henry Ling Limited

For Ivanka Pribetic (1941–2015)

—M.G.

To John and Nurida, for everything.

—A.N.

Contents

List of Figures ix
Acknowledgements xi
Notes on Contributors xiii

1 Introduction: Medievalism and Early-Modernism in Adaptations of the English Past 1
MARINA GERZIC AND AIDAN NORRIE

SECTION I
Cultural Medievalism and Early-Modernism 19

2 Wonder Woman and the *Nine Ladies Worthy*: The Male Gaze and What It Takes to Be a 'Worthy Woman' 21
SIMONE CELINE MARSHALL

3 The King, the Sword, and the Stone: The Recent Afterlives of King Arthur 36
SARAH GORDON

4 Brand Chaucer: The Poet and the Nation 52
MARTIN LAIDLAW

5 Moving between Life and Death: Horror Films and the Medieval Walking Corpse 67
POLINA IGNATOVA

6 From *Cabaret* to *Gladiator*: Refiguring Masculinity in Julie Taymor's *Titus* 82
MARINA GERZIC

7 "There's My Exchange": The Hogarth Shakespeare   99
   SHEILA T. CAVANAGH

8 Bloody Brothers and Suffering Sisters: *The Duchess of
   Malfi* and Harry Potter   117
   LISA HOPKINS

SECTION II
Historical Medievalism and Early-Modernism   135

9 Playing in a Virtual Medieval World: Video Game
   Adaptations of England through Role-Play   137
   BEN REDDER

10 "I can piss on Calais from Dover": Adaptation and
   Medievalism in Graphic Novel Depictions of the
   Hundred Years' War (1337–1453)   154
   IAIN A. MACINNES

11 Beyond "tits and dragons": Medievalism, Medieval
   History, and Perceptions in *Game of Thrones*   171
   HILARY JANE LOCKE

12 Re-fashioning Richard III: Intertextuality, Fandom,
   and the (Mobile) Body in *The Hollow Crown:
   The Wars of the Roses*   188
   MARINA GERZIC

13 The Many Afterlives of Elizabeth Barton   207
   ANNIE BLACHLY

14 The Queen, the Bishop, the Virgin, and the Cross:
   Catholicism versus Protestantism in *Elizabeth*   226
   AIDAN NORRIE

15 "Unseen but very evident": Ghosts, Hauntings,
   and the Civil War Past   244
   MICHAEL DURRANT

   Index   261

List of Figures

6.1 Alan Cumming as Saturninus incites the crowd in *Titus*. Image courtesy of Clear Blue Sky Productions and Twentieth Century Fox ... 84
6.2 Angus MacFayden as Lucius, dressed in 'manly' armour in *Titus*. Image courtesy of Clear Blue Sky Productions and Twentieth Century Fox ... 91
12.1 Benedict Cumberbatch as Richard III addresses the camera in *The Hollow Crown: The Wars of the Roses*. Image courtesy of the British Broadcasting Corporation ... 191
12.2 Benedict Cumberbatch as Richard III plays chess in *The Hollow Crown: The Wars of the Roses*. Image courtesy of the British Broadcasting Corporation ... 192
12.3 Benedict Cumberbatch as Richard III in *The Hollow Crown: The Wars of the Roses*. Image courtesy of the British Broadcasting Corporation ... 196
13.1 A. [Henry] Tresham, *The Imposture of the Holy Maid of Kent*. c.1830. Print, 202 × 158 mm. The British Museum, London ... 212
14.1 The audience's first glimpse of Mary I (Kathy Burke) in *Elizabeth*. Image courtesy of PolyGram and Working Title Films ... 229
14.2 The first appearance of Elizabeth I (Cate Blanchett) in *Elizabeth*. Image courtesy of PolyGram and Working Title Films ... 231
14.3 The burning at the stake *Elizabeth* opens with. From top to bottom: the Protestants are led into the yard; the Catholic bishops look on without emotion; the guards have to hold the crowd back. Images courtesy of PolyGram and Working Title Films ... 235

Acknowledgements

The idea for this collection grew from a panel Marina convened at the 2017 Australian and New Zealand Association for Medieval and Early Modern Studies (ANZAMEMS) conference, in which we both read papers. We would like to thank the members of the audience for their helpful comments, and for sparking fruitful conversations.

We also acknowledge the advice and support of Louise D'Arcens (who also chaired our panel at the 2017 ANZAMEMS conference), Andrew Lynch, Claire McIlroy, Susan Broomhall, and Stephanie Trigg, whose input at various stages of the project's development was invaluable and much appreciated.

Finally, we thank Michelle Salyga, Tim Swenarton, and Bryony Reece at Routledge for their assistance with the collection's production.

Marina: I thank my parents, Silvia and Emilio, and brother Erik for their continual love and support, and my wonderful dog Rocky, whose cuddles and steadfast companionship got me through many a long day of working on this collection. I also thank my friends and colleagues for their helpful and constructive discussions about this collection. To my brother from another mother, Aidan, thank you for being an excellent collaborator and, more importantly, an amazing colleague and friend.

Aidan: I thank Robert Norrie, Mark Houlahan, Liam Lewis, Claire Macindoe, Joseph Massey, and Peter Sherlock for fruitful and encouraging discussions about the collection at various stages of its existence. I also acknowledge my long-suffering cat, Nathaniel, who sometimes had late dinners because I was distracted by working on this collection. Finally, and most especially, I thank my amazing friend and unflagging partner in crime, Marina, the James to my Jessie, for making the work that goes into shepherding an edited collection to publication a pleasurable experience.

Notes on Contributors

Annie Blachly is currently undertaking her PhD at Monash University. She holds a Bachelor of Arts (Honours) and a Diploma of Education (History and English) from Monash University. Prior to returning to her studies, Annie was a high school English teacher. Her thesis brings together a social and cultural history of Oxford with the burgeoning areas of the history of emotions, the history of violence, and digital mapping techniques.

Sheila T. Cavanagh is Professor of English at Emory University. Founding Director of the World Shakespeare Project (www.worldshakespeare project.org) and Director of Emory's Year of Shakespeare (2016–2017), she was recently Fulbright/Global Shakespeare Distinguished Chair in the UK. Author of *Wanton Eyes and Chaste Desires: Female Sexuality in the Faerie Queene* (Indiana University Press, 1994) and *Cherished Torment: the Emotional Geography of Lady Mary Wroth's Urania* (Duquesne University Press, 2001), she has published widely in the fields of pedagogy and Renaissance literature.

Michael Durrant is a Lecturer in Early Modern Literature at Bangor University. His first monograph, *The Dreadful Name of Henry Hills: The Lives, Transformations, and Afterlives of a Seventeenth Century Printer*, is due for publication with Manchester University Press in 2019, and focuses on the life and afterlives of the printer-publisher Henry Hills (c. 1625–1688/9).

Marina Gerzic works for the Centre for Medieval and Early Modern Studies at The University of Western Australia in both research and administrative roles. She also works as the Executive Administrator for the Australian and New Zealand Association for Medieval and Early Modern Studies and as the editorial assistant for the academic journal *Parergon*. She has published articles on film and adaptation theory, Shakespeare, pedagogy, cinematic music, cultural studies, science fiction, comics and graphic novels, and children's literature. Marina is currently developing a monograph on depictions of Richard III on stage, page, film, and other media, as well as an edited collection on the topic of irreverence and play in Shakespearean adaptations with Aidan Norrie.

Sarah Gordon is Associate Professor of French at Utah State University. She earned her PhD at Washington University in St Louis, and her MPhil at Oxford University. She is the author of *Culinary Comedy in Medieval French Literature* (Purdue University Press, 2007) and other interdisciplinary publications on Arthurian literature and medieval literature and culture. She has published in *Arthuriana* and *Arthurian Literature,* and regularly teaches in, and publishes on, film studies.

Lisa Hopkins is Professor of English at Sheffield Hallam University and co-editor of *Shakespeare*, of Arden Early Modern Drama Guides, and of Arden Studies in Early Modern Drama. She co-organises the annual *Othello's Island* conference on Cyprus (http://www.othellosisland.org). Her most recent monograph is *From the Romans to the Normans on the English Renaissance Stage* (ARC Humanities Press, 2017). She has published three articles on Harry Potter, and co-supervised a PhD on it.

Polina Ignatova has degrees in Diplomacy and Regional Studies from the Moscow State Institute of International Relations, and in Medieval History from King's College, London. She is currently completing her PhD at Lancaster University on the history of walking dead accounts, with particular focus on medieval England, Ireland, Scotland, and Wales.

Martin Laidlaw is currently under examination for a PhD thesis titled "Anticipating Reformist Agenda in the Literature of the Middle Ages" at the University of Dundee, and acts as tutor at Newcastle University. Awarded the Philippa Maddern Travel Prize in 2015 and a Scottish Graduate School for Arts and Humanities Cohort Development Grant in 2017, he is the founder of ScotMEMS, Scotland's Medieval and Early-Modern Postgraduate research network. His research interests include the Reformist agenda in medieval poetry, and poverty and poor relief in the Piers Plowman tradition.

Hilary Jane Locke is completing her Master of Philosophy in History at the University of Adelaide. Her thesis focuses on the presence of chivalry and courtly love in the courts of Henry VII and Henry VIII, and how this affected politics, performance, gender relations, and culture. Her other research interests include modern history, historical fiction, popular culture and public history, masculinity, and sexuality. Hilary also likes foxes, and is a keen tea drinker.

Iain A. MacInnes is Senior Lecturer in Scottish History at the University of the Highlands and Islands. His primary research focuses on fourteenth-century Scottish military history, and his monograph, *Scotland's Second War of Independence, 1332–1357* (Boydell Press,

2016), provides a detailed consideration of this conflict. He is currently exploring new areas of research, including graphic novel depictions of the Middle Ages, as well as the medieval-like world of *Game of Thrones*.

Simone Celine Marshall is an Associate Professor in the Department of English and Linguistics at the University of Otago, New Zealand. Her research focuses on later interpretations of medieval literature, especially the works of Geoffrey Chaucer. Currently, she is working on eighteenth- and nineteenth-century continuations of Chaucer's *The Squire's Tale*, arguing that they reveal a range of social, political, and cultural biases.

Aidan Norrie is a historian of monarchy, and is currently a Chancellor's International Scholar in the Centre for the Study of the Renaissance at The University of Warwick. He is the editor, with Lisa Hopkins, of *Women on the Edge in Early Modern Europe* (Amsterdam University Press), and, with Mark Houlahan, of *On the Edge of Early Modern English Drama* (MIP University Press). Aidan is working on a study of Elizabeth I's depiction in modern films and television series, and is currently developing a monograph that analyses Elizabeth's engagement with the Old Testament.

Ben Redder is a History PhD student at the University of Waikato, New Zealand, specialising in the representation of history through video games. He is currently writing his doctoral thesis on video game representation of the Middle Ages in several modern games. A key focus is how these medieval games apply new approaches towards historical research, historicity, game design, and forms of play that enable interactivity and immersion to be historically contextualised.

1 Introduction
Medievalism and Early-Modernism in Adaptations of the English Past

Marina Gerzic and Aidan Norrie[1]

Adaptation has a long history: the *Epic of Gilgamesh* likely inspired the Old Testament of the Bible;[2] Virgil's *Aeneid* adapted and expanded Homer's *Iliad*;[3] Lady Eleanor Hull's *Meditations Upon the Seven Days of the Week* drew on and adapted works by St Augustine, St Anselm, and St Bernard;[4] and Shakespeare's *Troilus and Cressida* adapted and reinterpreted Chaucer's *Troilus and Criseyde*, itself a retelling of Boccaccio's *Il Filostrato*, which was derived from Benoît de Sainte-Maure's *Le Roman de Troie*.[5] Throughout history, then, humans have drawn on influential texts—generally literary or historical, but not always—to enhance their own artistic endeavours: sometimes in homage, sometimes to expand on, sometimes to satirise or subvert, and sometimes for all of these reasons. While technologies have changed from the tablets that the *Epic of Gilgamesh* were inscribed on, the same basic concept—to tell a story relevant to the creator's audience using the stories, events, and accounts of the past—underpins most modern adaptations in whatever media form they take: from films and television series, to graphic novels and video games.

Medievalism and ?

This collection began with the question: why is there not an equivalent term like *medievalism* for early modern historical and cultural afterlives? Medievalism—that is, "the reception, interpretation or recreation of the European Middle Ages in post-medieval cultures"— emerged some 30 years ago and has spawned a number of critical studies.[6] The journals *Studies in Medievalism* (published since 1979), *The Year's Work in Medievalism* (since 1990), and *postmedieval* (since 2010) publish articles on the reception of medieval culture in postmedieval times.[7] Other foundational studies of medievalism, which have informed our own thinking about the subject, include: *Medievalism in the Modern World: Essays in Honour of Leslie J. Workman*, edited by Richard Utz and Tom Shippey; Angela J. Weisl's *The Persistence of Medievalism: Narrative Adventures in Contemporary Culture*; Michael

Alexander's *Medievalism: The Middle Ages in Modern England*; and Tison Pugh and Angela J. Weisl's *Medievalisms: Making the Past in the Present*.[8] More recent works that demonstrate the field's maturity, as well as its burgeoning place in the academy, include: *Medievalism: Key Critical Terms*, edited by Elizabeth Emery and Richard Utz; Louise D'Arcens's *Comic Medievalism: Laughing at the Middle Ages*; *International Medievalism and Popular Culture*, edited by Louise D'Arcens and Andrew Lynch; David Matthews's *Medievalism: A Critical Reader*; *Medieval Afterlives in Contemporary Culture*, edited by Gail Ashton; and *The Cambridge Companion to Medievalism*, edited by Louise D'Arcens.[9]

While this is not an exhaustive list of studies in medievalism, it does demonstrate both the increasing popularity of the field, and that defining what constitutes medievalism is not a simple task.[10] *Studies in Medievalism* devoted four consecutive volumes of scholarship to its definition (and that of the related concept of *neo-medievalism*, popularised by Umberto Eco in his 1973 essay "Dreaming in the Middle Ages").[11] As D'Arcens observes, the Middle Ages spans a millennium (generally the fifth to fifteenth centuries), with expanding and contracting geographic boundaries.[12] Nevertheless, there is certainly a much more coherent—if nebulous—idea of what constitutes the medieval in both the academic and popular conscious: generally, the period between the fall of the Western Roman Empire and the Protestant Reformation. In short, the lives of Charlemagne, William the Conqueror, and Joan of Arc, and the events of the Crusades, the Hundred Years' War, and the Wars of the Roses are all understood to be 'medieval'; perhaps it is the nebulous nature of the period—both geographically and chronologically—that makes it easier for medieval afterlives to be collected under the umbrella term 'medievalism.'

The same cannot be said, however, for the early modern period: no collective term exists for early modern cultural or historic afterlives. The concept of the 'early modern' is, arguably, far less established in the popular consciousness. This is partially because of the impact of the concept of the Renaissance (which we will turn to later) or even because of the problematic nature of the idea of 'modern'—for some reason, the events of the British Civil Wars feel closer to us than the events of the Wars of the Roses, even though they are closer to each other than to us. The early modern period, too, is hampered by Western-centrism but the term is increasingly being applied globally. Unlike the Middle Ages, the European early modern period is constrained to a much smaller time span— generally from the sixteenth century (and the Protestant Reformation) until the French Revolution; it also has to vie with other period classifications (such as the Enlightenment and the so-called 'Age of Discovery'), and has to contend with the complicating geographical shift caused by European colonisation and expansionism across the globe. Significantly, the survival of more literary and documentary evidence from the early modern period has also spurred the division of the period into smaller classifications; even more so than their medieval counterparts, these are often related to significant historical figures or dynasties, for example 'Shakespearean', and 'Tudorism.'[13] Afterlives of the early modern period thus have to contend with an unclear conception in popular culture, and indeed with a range of academic sub-disciplines that divide up periods or aspects of the period.

Early-Modernism

As a means to address this gap in classification, our collection offers the term *early-modernism*—defined as the reception, interpretation, or recreation of the early modern period in post-early modern cultures—as a means to address this gap in classification. The hyphen in the term 'early-modernism' is a calculated choice so that it is considered as a whole, not a sum of its parts, and to avoid confusion with the already existing term modernism. Another reason is that we do not view the terms early modern and Renaissance as interchangeable. 'Renaissance,' as a term in English, emerged in the 1830s and refers to a European cultural movement within the early modern period: specifically, the revival of the arts and high culture under the influence of classical models in specific geographical regions.[14] While both 'Renaissance' and 'early modern' are anachronistic labels applied retrospectively, the concept of the Renaissance is bound up with ideas of European exceptionalism (or even superiority), and has a distinct focus on high culture at the expense of a more rounded and inclusive view of the people who lived then. By using the term early-modernism (rather than the problematic, and indeed tongue-twisting, 'Renaissancism'), we hope this collection inspires scholars who interrogate important aspects such as race, gender, sexuality, and disability—and are working towards the decentralisation of medieval and early modern studies from a European focus—to investigate medievalism and early-modernism in non-European history and culture. While medievalism has generally been focused on the European Middle Ages, we hope that early-modernism will be embraced by scholars of the global early modern period, ensuring that the depictions of Edo Japan and the Tokugawa shogunate in manga, anime, and television shows are studied alongside comic book, graphic novel, and television series depictions of Shakespeare, his work, and Jacobean England generally.

Adaptations of the Medieval and Early Modern Past

This collection analyses medievalisms and early-modernisms present in modern adaptations of the cultural, literary, and historical English past—spanning from the eighth to the seventeenth centuries. As such, the collection is concerned with the intersection of these three fields. The term "adaptation," as Linda Hutcheon notes, may refer to either the process or the product of adaptation.[15] At the core of all of the chapters in this collection is the implicit acknowledgement that remembering the past—in virtually any form—is an adaptation.[16] For instance, Robert Stam reminds us—even if literary scholars might be inclined to disagree—that film, after all, "is a form of writing that borrows from other forms of writing."[17] Stam also points out the double standard that exists: "while filmic rewritings of novels are judged in terms of fidelity, literary rewritings of classical texts, such as Coetzee's rewriting of *Robinson Crusoe* are not so judged."[18] This understanding is central to this collection: the life of Elizabeth I of England is as worthy of academic study as her cinematic depictions; adaptations of the works of Chaucer are as important as the texts they adapt. Adaptations are not a lesser or an uncreative activity but are "about seeing things come back to us in as many forms as possible."[19]

By building on the foundation that adaptation theory offers us—as recently and expertly discussed in *The Oxford Handbook of Adaptation Studies*, edited by Thomas Leitch—this collection is ideally placed to introduce early-modernism to the scholarship.[20] In doing so, however, the collection builds on the understanding of the interconnected nature of medievalism and adaptation found in collections such as *Cinematic Illuminations: The Middle Ages on Film*, edited by Laurie A. Finke and Martin B. Shichtman, and more recently *The Medieval Motion Picture: The Politics of Adaptation*, edited by Andrew Johnston, Margitta Rouse, and Philipp Hinz.[21] These collections demonstrate that the study of medievalism relies—in varying degrees—on adaptation, whether in re-telling a medieval tale, or simply in the taking of inspiration from the fantasy of the Middle Ages.

Unlike the fields of medievalism and adaptation, there is not a depth of studies that look at early-modernism and adaptation beyond Shakespeare. As Jennifer Clement highlights in her analysis of early modern adaptation studies, "the field remains largely limited to two areas: Shakespeare and film."[22] Recent works that expand on this limited scope of Shakespeare-centric adaptation studies include Richard Burt's *Medieval and Early Modern Film and Media*; Pascale Aebischer's *Screening Early Modern Drama: Beyond Shakespeare*; the 2015 volume of the journal *Shakespeare* on "Adaptation and Early Modern Culture: Shakespeare and Beyond"; and *Premodern Rulers and Postmodern Viewers: Gender, Sex, and Power in Popular Culture*, edited by Janice North, Karl Alvestad, and Elena Woodacre.[23] While our collection includes adaptations of Shakespeare, it also features studies of non-Shakespeare adaptations—such as the inspiration J.K. Rowling's *Harry Potter* series took from John Webster's play *The Duchess of Malfi* and the literary and televisual afterlives of Elizabeth Barton, 'The Holy Maid of Kent' and later 'The Mad Maid of Kent.' It therefore fills a gap in scholarship, and we hope it inspires further studies of non-Shakespeare-related early modern adaptations.

Why Adapt? Fidelity versus Evaluation

While recent scholarship continues to demonstrate the way that the past is constantly being re-used and re-purposed for the present, and in spite of the excellent works already cited, historians and literary scholars still often focus on how 'accurately' adaptations depict the events (or text) they are re-telling.[24] This reductive engagement with popular culture does not acknowledge the fact that modern depictions of the past, like older ones, often say more about the time in which they were produced than about the event they are depicting. Indeed, modern adaptations of the past often serve as "a barometer that measures our own value and place in the world,"[25] and are thus deserving of attention because they "intersect with, comment upon, and add something to the larger discourse of history out of which they grow and to which they speak."[26]

As Deborah Cartmell and Imelda Whelehan note, "While fictional texts and their feature film adaptations remain at the subject's core, the study of adaptations has broadened to embrace 'literature' and the 'screen' in the broadest senses of each word."[27] This collection demonstrates that medievalism and early-modernism both find expression in many media adaptations, including cinematographic and literary works, as well as video games, practical performances/'living history,' and other related re-enactments (for example, the Society for Creative Anachronism). As Cartmell observes, "scholars are uncovering a wealth of material in the previously unchartered territories of what has normally been dismissed as merely 'entertainment'" because ultimately, "Video games, comic books, and popular cinema are all deserving objects of consideration."[28]

In analysing adaptations of the medieval and early modern English past, this collection focuses on evaluating the adaptation for its content and context, and rejects an analysis that emphasises fidelity to the source at all costs. As Linda Hutcheon argues, there are "many different possible intentions behind the act of adaptation: the urge to consume and erase the memory of the adapted text or to call it into question is as likely as the desire to pay tribute by copying."[29] Julie Sanders concurs with Hutcheon, stating that adaptation is "frequently involved in offering commentary on a sourcetext," something that is "achieved most often by offering a revised point of view from the 'original', adding hypothetical motivation, or voicing the silenced and marginalized."[30] Sanders adds that an adaptation "can also constitute a simpler attempt to make texts 'relevant' or easily comprehensible to new audiences and readerships via the processes of proximation and updating."[31] We suggested this focus on relevance at the beginning of this chapter, and do so again here: commentaries on and re-workings of original texts have been part of human culture for millennia, and modern media forms deserve the same attention that older re-workings, like Virgil's *Aeneid*, garner.

One of the hallmarks of adaptation studies is the field's movement away from fidelity and so-called 'accuracy,' to a focus on evaluation. Jørgen Bruhen, Anne Gjelsvik, and Eirik Frisvold Hanssen highlight fidelity's continued presence in the discussion of adaptations, stating, "fidelity, then, is questioned but not forgotten in current research, where it constantly resurfaces in the form of questions of medium specificity based on non-evaluative grounds."[32] Hutcheon argues against fidelity, insisting that an adaptation's "double nature," both as original work in its own right and as adaptation, does not mean that "proximity or fidelity to the adapted text should be the criterion of judgment or the focus of analysis."[33] Sanders highlights the positive aspects of looking beyond fidelity, noting that it is precisely "at the very point of infidelity that the most creative acts of adaptation and appropriation take place."[34] Jennifer Clement builds on Robert Stam's criticism of the double standard that exists when comparing book and film adaptations in her argument against considerations of fidelity in the study of adaptations, arguing that through a rejection of what she terms the "fidelity paradigm," scholars can "establish film adaptations as worthy of analysis in their own right, not necessarily shackled to a sense that the book is always better."[35] Gary R. Bortolotti and Hutcheon go even further, and strongly argue against the "continuing dominance of ... [the] 'fidelity discourse'":

> This common determination to judge an adaptation's 'success' only in relation to its faithfulness or closeness to the 'original' or 'source' text threatens to reinforce the current low estimation (in terms of cultural capital) of what is, in fact, a common and persistent way humans have always told and retold stories.[36]

Bortolotti and Hutcheon suggest that fidelity to the "original" is in fact "irrelevant to the actual evaluation of the 'success' of an adaptation" for two distinct reasons: an adaptation "stands on its own as an independent work, separate from the 'source,' and can be judged accordingly," and the "impact of an adaptation can far exceed anything measurable only by its degree of proximity to the adapted work. The story it retells is clearly significant, but not in this sense."[37] By focusing on the story told—whether that be in a graphic novel, a video game, or a film—this collection analyses the adaptation both as an "independent work," and as a way of making texts approachable and able to be engaged with.

It is fitting that the last word on fidelity should be given to seminal adaptation scholar Linda Hutcheon, who notes that it is "the (post-)Romantic valuing of the original creation and of the originating creative genius that is clearly one source of the denigration of adapters and adaptations."[38] Hutcheon rightly concludes that "this negative view is actually a late addition to Western culture's long and happy history of borrowing and stealing or, more accurately, sharing stories."[39] Imitation and invention were embedded in early modern culture. Rather than referring (as they do today) to making things up, the word 'invention' could also mean finding materials in existing sources.[40] Furthermore, as David Mayernik aptly argues, the system of imitation and invention was "derived from ancient rhetorical theory, a characteristic Renaissance importation of one kind of knowledge into another discipline."[41] Imitation and invention thus had a high status because they were an essential pedagogical method, and, as Dale L. Sullivan notes, they "remained a significant part of classicism until it was assaulted by the twin forces of science and Romanticism."[42] Nineteenth-century England's increasing industrialisation—accompanied by ever-increasing pollution and poverty—engendered a nostalgic longing for a return to a pastoral ideal. Victorians were concerned with not only reconstructing an idealised past, but also fully engaging with creating an idealised present. The Victorians looked back to the medieval and early modern past to create a sense of authority for their own ideas in areas such as art, literature, gender, religion, and national identity. While simultaneously looking back to the Middle Ages—the idealised chivalric stereotypes of romantic literature and the emergence of the Nazarene movement, for example—and embracing the medieval past—*Beowulf* was first translated into English in 1837—the nineteenth century saw a proliferation of universities and a much more academic focus on the past.[43] Likewise, (pseudo-)medieval symbols and imagery became part of monarchical trappings; in England, Magna Carta achieved its political and cultural zenith, and the concept of the Renaissance emerged in this (post-)Romantic period. Medievalism and early-modernism, to an extent (given the emergence of 'Bardolatry' in the nineteenth century),[44] thus emerged during the confluence of sometimes diverging movements, which sought to embrace the medieval and early modern past to reify nationalistic discourses and to use studies of the past as the basis for 'accurate'—indeed, fidelitous—artistic adaptations.

Medievalism, Early-Modernism, and Adapting the English Past

At its core, *From Medievalism to Early-Modernism: Adapting the English Past* interrogates the interplay between the past and the present. The collection is divided into two sections. Rather than perpetuate the reductive and unhelpful division between the medieval and the early modern periods, the chapters in each section focus on either (broadly defined) cultural or historical adaptations of the English past, although

8 *Marina Gerzic and Aidan Norrie*

the chapters are generally arranged chronologically. We do acknowledge that the collection focuses exclusively on adaptations of the English past. We do not claim that the English past alone is deserving of this attention, and we do not seek to perpetuate the English exceptionalism that characterised the Whiggish histories of the nineteenth and twentieth centuries; rather, as scholars of late medieval and early modern English history and literature, this geographical scope is within our sphere of specialisation.

Cultural Medievalism and Early-Modernism

In Section I, "Cultural Medievalism and Early-Modernism," the contributors analyse the modern adaptations that have their source (or take their inspiration) from cultural texts: for the most part, literary texts. As alluded to at the opening of this chapter, adaptations of literary texts have a history that spans millennia, and it is a history that is not confined to 'the West.' The seven chapters examine the literary inspiration for modern works—in a variety of media forms—that were produced between the eighth and seventeenth centuries, discussing both well-known and widely published works, and works that remain on the edge of popular culture.

Simone Marshall's chapter considers the relationship between the way that warrior-women are represented in the fifteenth-century poem known as "The Nine Ladies Worthy" (once attributed to Geoffrey Chaucer) and then transformed into the modern cinematic experience of *Wonder Woman* (2017). Marshall argues that in each work, the creators bring to the fore female strength as an abnormality that is sidelined and regarded with suspicion. The film and the poem are works concerned with how the reader or viewer engages with them; both are poignant examples of the complexities of how women are represented in literature and film, how women can participate in each art form, and how a woman can be worthy. Marshall examines recent reviews and responses to *Wonder Woman* that question to what extent the character of Wonder Woman herself—a warrior woman—is a feminist role model and a worthy woman.

The Arthurian legend has proved enduring and adaptable across temporal, geographic, and cultural borders for centuries. Sarah Gordon's chapter examines two recent Arthurian film adaptations, *King Arthur* (2004) and *King Arthur: Legend of the Sword* (2017): each re-writes Arthurian material, and highlights how medievalism in filmmaking is used as a tool for unpacking meaning in both the past and the present. For Gordon, the Arthurian story is so ubiquitous that it becomes a platform for filmmakers to tackle modern issues, such as social inequalities, socio-economic diversity, and multiculturalism. *King Arthur* speaks to the war in Iraq as much as it does to the early Britons' battles with the Romans, and *King Arthur: Legend of the Sword* is a postmodern mélange of *Game of Thrones*-inspired medievalism and British crime-caper that echoes debates about race and class in post-Brexit referendum Britain. As Gordon demonstrates, Arthurian themes remain material for filmmakers to adapt to the present moment.

The appropriation and employment of literary figures towards the creation or reflection upon concepts of a 'National Identity' is an enduring cultural paradigm. Martin Laidlaw's chapter tracks the adoption and manipulation of the works, image, and legacy of Geoffrey Chaucer towards the promotion of political aims—during the Reformation and the Restoration—and Chaucer's use in highlighting twenty-first-century issues. Laidlaw analyses several contemporary uses of Chaucer: Pasolini's *I Racconti di Canterbury* (1972), which employs the figure of Chaucer as quasi-narrator of the film; *A Knight's Tale* (2001), which subverts audience's expectations of Chaucer's appearance and character; Tacit Theatre's production of *The Canterbury Tales* (2011), which emphasises the text's humour, adding both music and song; and *Refugee Tales* (2016), which employs the frame setting of *The Canterbury Tales* to highlight the plight of refugees.

In medieval thought, the walking dead were figures deprived of mobility—of the ability to leave this world for the afterlife without assistance. Centuries later, the image of someone stuck between life and death remains appealing. Polina Ignatova's chapter explores the continuity between medieval tales of the walking dead and zombies featured in modern horror films. Ignatova demonstrates that the walking dead in these horror films have evolved to answer the concerns of modern society, while still preserving their medieval nature. While modern horror films now favour scientific explanations, rather than the use of religion and the supernatural to account for the undead, they share a basic plot structure with medieval narratives, where the committing of 'sin' leads to the appearance of walking dead. Ignatova concludes that while modern horror films reflect the anxieties of a modern man, they still largely draw on ideas and images found in medieval walking dead narratives.

Gender identity in Julie Taymor's film *Titus* (1999)—an adaptation of William Shakespeare's *Titus Andronicus*—is largely based on intertextual connections to historical events, figures, and popular cultural references. To demonstrate this observation, Marina Gerzic analyses the often-sidelined characters of Saturninus and Lucius, and reveals how Taymor uses popular culture tropes and Italy's Imperial and Fascist past to establish the men's masculinity in her film. Lucius's and Saturninus's masculinity is tied to Taymor's exploration of Rome's violent past. Through Taymor's selective use of imagery and editing of Shakespeare's text, Gerzic argues, Lucius's rugged, gladiator-like hero is presented as a redeeming force, arriving to cleanse and take over the corrupt Rome, led by the genderqueer and villainous Saturninus. These depictions, Gerzic demonstrates, suggest not only that violence and masculinity are linked, but also that only the "right" kind of masculinity—one that replicates violent Roman traditions—is an acceptable form of gender identity.

The *Hogarth Shakespeare Project*, a series of modern adaptations of William Shakespeare's plays, is the focus of Sheila Cavanagh's chapter. Cavanagh examines the novels published so far in this project—Jeannette Winterson's *The Gap of Time* (2015), Howard Jacobson's *Shylock Is My Name* (2016), Anne Tyler's *Vinegar Girl* (2016), Margaret Atwood's *Hag-Seed* (2016), Tracy Chevalier's *New Boy* (2017), Edward St Aubyn's *Dunbar* (2017), and Jo Nesbø's *Macbeth* (2018)—arguing that each of these works presents an updated "cover version" of Shakespeare's texts by presenting a variety of re-imagined settings and themes: for instance, *Vinegar Girl* introduces concerns about immigration into *The Taming of the Shrew*, and *Dunbar* relocates *King Lear* into the corporate world. For Cavanagh, these adaptations both emphasise and alter the central issues presented in Shakespeare's works for modern readers through their focus on the transactions of property, kinship, and power that infuse the stories.

The *Harry Potter* books by J.K. Rowling perhaps seem an unlikely example of adaptation. While Rowling has made clear that she has drawn on various aspects of the literary and cultural past to create the Potter-universe, Lisa Hopkins argues that an inspiration that is visible across the whole series has been overlooked: namely, the influence of John Webster's Jacobean tragedy *The Duchess of Malfi*. For Hopkins, siblings in the *Harry Potter* books are often a source of tension and trouble, and Webster's influence can be found in the way that sibling relationships in the books are often explicitly and emphatically pathologised. While Rowling does not hint at the play's presence—although she would do so later in her Cormoran Strike detective novels—she has taken a number of the play's central concerns, and re-worked them as an early-modernism, demonstrating how the early modern period continues to resonate and resurface in contemporary society.

Historical Medievalism and Early-Modernism

The chapters in Section II, "Historical Medievalism and Early-Modernism," analyse adaptations of the historical past, with particular emphasis on the way these adaptations re-purpose the past for modern concerns and to tell modern stories. While the seven chapters encompass a wide variety of media forms, they draw on decades of intertextual and intervisual references to discuss the various ways that a limited, and often erroneously clear-cut, vision of the past is both perpetuated by adaptors, and expected by their audiences.

Recent forms of medievalism have diverged from medieval high fantasy in favour of constructing narratives and themes in realist settings, and

Ben Redder's chapter examines this progression and development within recent video games. Redder argues that video games have unique characteristics compared to other media forms: they allow players to create their own narratives, meanings, and relationships within the spatial-temporal dimensions of medieval environments. In *Medieval 2: Total War – Kingdoms* (2007), the "Britannia campaign" relies on popular perceptions of the thirteenth-century British Isles to design its environment; *War of the Roses* (2012) follows conventions akin to medieval combat simulation to use the conflicts between the houses of York and Lancaster for competitive duelling and combat; and in *Expeditions: Vikings* (2017), environments are closely modelled on the real historical places and landscapes of late-ninth-century England. For Redder, these medieval environments create spatial-temporal configurations for the games' narratives that both are historically driven and allow for player agency.

The Hundred Years' War was the largest conflict of the medieval period. Iain MacInnes's chapter analyses the conflict's depiction in the modern graphic novels *Crécy* (Warren Ellis and Raulo Cáceres, 2007) and *Agincourt 1415* (Will Gill and Graeme Howard, 2015). Both are demonstrative of the growing popular interest in medieval and medieval-like worlds: while the two novels are quite different in approach, in tone, and in what is presented, they both deal with elements of medievalism that reflect what people of the present day think about the medieval past. Arguing that the novels themselves are an important medievalism that scholars need to engage with, MacInnes focuses on themes of class and national identity—and their representations—analysing how such elements are portrayed to a modern audience, and what they tell the reader about medieval—as well as modern—society.

Dramatic television serial *Game of Thrones* (HBO, 2011–present) has become the definition of event television set within a medieval inspired fantasy world. Hilary Jane Locke's chapter uses *Game of Thrones* as a case study to assess how audiences perceive medieval history as a setting and, in turn, how the representation of history affects viewers' perceptions of history. The chapter offers insight into the show's use and perception of medieval history for a popular audience, and demonstrates how the combination of epic, emotive story lines, visual effects, and use of historical contexts for fictional purposes situates it in a unique position. Crucially, Locke's chapter examines the reception of *Game of Thrones* in viewer reactions, as well as web and cultural commentary, concluding that while the show does not aim to present accurate medieval history, through the medievalism presented, it encourages the assumption that it represents historical events, aspects and, in some cases, accuracy.

Marina Gerzic's chapter analyses how Benedict Cumberbatch's performance as Richard III in the BBC adaptation of Shakespeare's history cycle *The Hollow Crown: The Wars of the Roses* (2016) is a creation of patchwork intertextual references that updates and adapts medieval and early modern ideas of disability. Gerzic argues that filming, editing, and costume choices recall recent media, which, when combined with Cumberbatch's own intertextuality from his previous roles and his celebrity status, are used to re-fashion Richard's disabled body and morally corrupt character for the small screen. The chapter examines the resulting reception of Cumberbatch's creation of a new (mobile) Richard, one that exists both inside the adaptation as a character and outside the adaptation in the realm of fandom. Recalling Richard Burbage's apparent fame for the role of Richard III, this 'new Richard' sees Cumberbatch's actor's body become an adaptive site where Shakespeare's Richard, as played by Benedict Cumberbatch, and 'Benedict Cumberbatch' the 'celebrity' conflate.

Elizabeth Barton—The Holy Maid of Kent, and later The Mad Maid of Kent—is the subject of Annie Blachly's chapter. Barton's condemnation of Henry VIII's divorce has taken on legendary status, but during the 1530s, her character underwent significant attack prior to, and following, her execution. Blachly analyses Barton's shifting identity through sixteenth-century county histories, eighteenth-century engravings, twenty-first-century television series, and a young adult fiction novel published in 2016, arguing that Barton becomes a vehicle through which to view evolving and contemporary ideas of deviance. Charting her transition from hypocrite and fraud in the sixteenth century, to her connection with the demonic in the Georgian era, and her depiction as being both physically and mentally unwell in the twentieth and twenty-first centuries, Blachly argues that Barton's changing afterlife is demonstrative of the society in which she is depicted.

As Aidan Norrie's contribution demonstrates, Shekhar Kapur's first film about Elizabeth I of England—*Elizabeth* (1998)—reflects and re-purposes contemporary religious tensions. While a film about Elizabethan England cannot avoid religion, Norrie demonstrates that Kapur made deliberate choices concerning the depictions of Catholics and Protestants: Mary's unflattering depiction ensures that she stands proxy for all Catholics; Elizabeth's overly flattering depiction exemplifies all of the rational and peaceable Protestants. Norrie also discusses two specific scenes—the burning of three Protestants at the film's opening, and the depiction of the passing of the *Act of Uniformity*—to demonstrate that Kapur inconsistently twists the historical reality to ensure that audiences (reductively) believe that the Protestant Elizabeth is 'good,' and that the Catholic Mary is 'bad.' Norrie concludes by discussing some of the criticisms of anti-Catholicism directed at the film, which, when combined with Kapur's own response to the criticisms, demonstrates that adapting the past to comment on the present is often fraught.

The figure of the ghost, and the metaphor of the haunting, can represent an uninhibited return of the past in the present, but the meanings that might be attached to the ghost and to the haunting are historically contingent and subject to variation. Michael Durrant's chapter analyses a selection of ghost stories set during, or written in response to, the events of the British Civil Wars (1642–1649): Ben Wheatley's psychedelic folk horror *A Field in England* (2013); Peter Young's military history *Edgehill 1642: The Campaign and the Battle* (1967); and two anonymous seventeenth-century ghost pamphlets, *A Great Wonder in Heaven* and *The New Yeares Wonder* (both published in 1642/1643). Durrant considers what narratives of the supernatural—specifically those involving ghosts and hauntings—can tell us about the period's subsequent appropriations, as well as alternative historical perspectives and pasts. The ghosts that emerge in these texts serve historically specific functions, calling attention to past sufferings, lost voices, and hidden stories that are often unduly thought of as part of history and therefore absent to us.

***

While the chapters in this collection discuss a variety of adaptation types, across a multitude of media forms, we do acknowledge the limits of our collection. For instance, space constraints mean we have not included discussions of the various forms of web-based medievalism and early-modernism that are increasing in popularity;[45] similarly, our collection includes limited engagement with historical re-enactment or the way science fiction and detective texts often present, or re-purpose, the medieval and early modern past.[46] Nevertheless, we hope that this collection—especially its offering of the concept of *early-modernism* to the scholarship—will encourage further study of adaptations of not only the English past, but also of cultures from around the world with histories of adaptation. Likewise, these future studies should emphasise the role of women as adaptors: Lady Eleanor Hull is not unique, and neither are the women who adapted Shakespeare's plays for the *Hogarth Shakespeare*. Finally, we hope that our collection will help future scholars to demonstrate the place that queer people, impaired people, and people of colour had in medieval and early modern Europe, despite current right-wing hysteria surrounding the perceived white, homogenous, heteronormative, and able-bodied view of the medieval and early modern past.[47]

Notes

1 We thank Andrew Lynch for his generous assistance in the preparation of this chapter.
2 Russell Gmirkin, *Berossus and Genesis, Manetho and Exodus: Hellenistic Histories and the Date of the Pentateuch* (New York: T & T Clark, 2006), 89–91, 103–114; and Karel Van der Toorn, "Did Ecclesiastes Copy Gilgamesh?," *Bible Review* 16, no. 1 (2000): 22–30.
3 Michael C.J. Putnam, "Virgil's *Aeneid*," in *A Companion to Ancient Epic*, ed. John Miles Foley (Malden, MA: Blackwell Publishing, 2005), 454–457. Similarly, echoes of the *Aeneid* can be found in medieval and early modern literature, including in Dante's *Divine Comedy*, Spenser's *Faerie Queene*, and Milton's *Paradise Lost*.

4 Alexandra Barratt, ed., *Women's Writing in Middle English: An Annotated Anthology*, 2nd ed. (London: Routledge, 2013), 233.
5 John Jowett, "Introduction: *Troilus and Cressida*," in *The New Oxford Shakespeare: Critical Reference Edition, Volume 2*, ed. Gary Taylor, John Jowett, Terri Bourus, and Gabriel Egan (Oxford: Oxford University Press, 2017), 3450. *Le Roman de Troie* itself drew on the two (potentially adapted or abridged, and possibly spurious) accounts of the Trojan War, Dictys Cretensis's *Ephemeris belli Troiani* and Dares Phrygius's *De excidio Trojae historia*; because both texts are in Latin, they are credited with bringing the story of the Trojan War to medieval Europe.
6 Louise D'Arcens, "Introduction: Medievalism; Scope and Complexity," in *The Cambridge Companion to Medievalism*, ed. Louise D'Arcens (Cambridge: Cambridge University Press, 2016), 1.
7 *Studies in Medievalism* and *The Year's Work in Medievalism* are both managed by the International Society for the Study of Medievalism. The society is based on the work of scholar Leslie J. Workman (1927–2001), who is recognised as the founder of the academic study of medievalism in the English-speaking world and was the editor of *Studies in Medievalism* from 1979 to 1999. The journal *postmedieval*, edited by Eileen Joy, Myra Seaman, and Lara Farina, supports the continuing development of historicist, materialist, comparatist, and theoretical approaches to subjects rooted in the Middle Ages.
8 Richard Utz and Tom Shippey, eds., *Medievalism in the Modern World: Essays in Honour of Leslie J. Workman* (Turnhout: Brepols, 1998); Angela J. Weisl, *The Persistence of Medievalism: Narrative Adventures in Contemporary Culture* (New York: Palgrave Macmillan, 2003); Michael Alexander, *Medievalism: The Middle Ages in Modern England* (New Haven, CT: Yale University Press, 2007); and Tison Pugh and Angela J. Weisl, *Medievalisms: Making the Past in the Present* (London: Routledge, 2012). See also: Allen J. Frantzen, ed., *Speaking Two Languages: Traditional Disciplines and Contemporary Theory in Medievalism Studies* (Albany: State University of New York Press, 1991); R. Howard Bloch and Stephen G. Nichols, eds., *Medievalism and the Modernist Temper* (Baltimore, MD: Johns Hopkins University Press, 1996); Kathleen Biddick, *The Shock of Medievalism* (Durham, NC: Duke University Press, 1998); Stephanie Trigg, *Medievalism and the Gothic in Australian Culture* (Turnhout: Brepols, 2005); Louise D'Arcens, Andrew Lynch, and Stephanie Trigg, eds., "Nationalism, Medievalism, Colonialism," special issue, *Australian Literary Studies* 26, no. 3–4 (2011); Helen Dell, Louise D'Arcens, and Andrew Lynch, eds., "The Medievalism of Nostalgia," special issue, *postmedieval* 2, no. 2 (2011); and Louise D'Arcens, *Old Songs in the Timeless Land: Medievalism in Australian Literature 1840–1910* (Crawley: UWA Publishing, 2012).
9 Elizabeth Emery and Richard Utz, eds., *Medievalism: Key Critical Terms* (Cambridge: D.S. Brewer, 2014); Louise D'Arcens, *Comic Medievalism: Laughing at the Middle Ages* (Cambridge: D.S. Brewer, 2014); Louise D'Arcens and Andrew Lynch, eds., *International Medievalism and Popular Culture* (Amherst, NY: Cambria Press, 2014); David Matthews, *Medievalism: A Critical Reader* (Cambridge: D.S. Brewer, 2015); Gail Ashton, ed., *Medieval Afterlives in Contemporary Culture* (London: Bloomsbury, 2015); and Louise D'Arcens, ed., *The Cambridge Companion to Medievalism* (Cambridge: Cambridge University Press, 2016). See also: Richard Utz, *Medievalism: A Manifesto* (Bradford: ARC Humanities Press, 2017); Bettina Bildhauer and Chris Jones, eds., *The Middle Ages in the Modern World* (Oxford: Oxford University Press, 2017); Andrew B.R. Elliott,

Medievalism, Politics and Mass Media: Appropriating the Middle Ages in the Twenty-First Century (Cambridge: D.S. Brewer, 2017); and Thomas A. Prendergast and Stephanie Trigg, *Affective Medievalism: Love, Abjection and Discontent* (Manchester: Manchester University Press, 2018). For an excellent discussion of the way medievalism is a form of *revisiting* the past, rather than simply *visiting*, see: Carolyn Dinshaw, "Nostalgia on My Mind," *postmedieval* 2, no. 2 (2011): 225–238.

10 This conundrum is discussed in Richard A. Marsden, "Medievalism: New Discipline or Scholarly No-man's Land?," *History Compass* 16, no. 2 (February 2018), doi:10.1111/hic3.12439.

11 Karl Fugelso, ed., "Defining Medievalism(s)," *Studies in Medievalism* XVII (2009); Karl Fugelso, ed., "Defining Medievalism(s) II," *Studies in Medievalism* XVIII (2009); Karl Fugelso, ed., "Defining Neomedievalism(s)," *Studies in Medievalism* XIX (2010); Karl Fugelso, ed., "Defining Neomedievalism(s) II," *Studies in Medievalism* XX (2011); and Umberto Eco, "Dreaming the Middle Ages," in *Travels in Hyperreality*, trans. William Weaver (New York: Harcourt, 1986), 61–72.

12 D'Arcens, "Introduction," 4. The difficulty in definition is perhaps best exemplified by the myriad of ways that the Middle Ages are broken down: it can be categorised by dynasties, centuries, or reigns of monarchs both secular and religious, or even in the problematic division of the Middle Ages into the Dark Ages, the High Middle Ages, and the late Middle Ages. Similarly, the division between the medieval and the early modern has always been a hotly contested concept. For a significant study of the impact of the medieval / modern divide, see: Margreta de Grazia, "The Modern Divide: From Either Side," *Journal of Medieval and Early Modern Studies* 37, no. 3 (2007): 453–467.

13 Recent examples include Jill L. Levenson and Robert Ormsby, eds., *The Shakespearean World* (London: Routledge, 2017); and Tatiana C. String and Marcus Bull, eds., *Tudorism: Historical Imagination and the Appropriation of the Sixteenth Century* (Oxford: Oxford University Press, 2011).

14 The *Oxford English Dictionary* cites W. Dyce and C.H. Wilson's "Letter to Lord Meadowbank" (1837)—"A style possessing many points of rude resemblance with the more elegant and refined character of the art of the renaissance in Italy"—and the following year in "Civil Engineer & Architect's Journal, 291/2": "Not that we consider the style of the Renaissance to be either pure or good *per se*." *Oxford English Dictionary*, s.v., "Renaissance, n."

15 Linda Hutcheon, *A Theory of Adaptation* (London: Routledge, 2006), 6–7.

16 We are indebted here to Linda Hutcheon's observations connecting memory and the act of remembering with adaptation: "Recognition and remembrance are part of the pleasure (and risk) of experiencing an adaptation; so too is change." Hutcheon, *A Theory of Adaptation*, 4.

17 Robert Stam, "Introduction: The Theory and Practice of Adaptation," in *Literature and Film: A Guide to the Theory and Practice of Film Adaptation*, ed. Robert Stam and Alessandra Raengo (Malden, MA: Blackwell, 2005), 1.

18 Stam, "Introduction," 15.

19 Julie Sanders, *Adaptation and Appropriation* (London: Routledge, 2006), 160.

20 Thomas Leitch, ed., *The Oxford Handbook of Adaptation Studies* (Oxford: Oxford University Press, 2017). See also the recent, and more specialised, collection: Dennis Cutchins, Katja Krebs, and Eckart Voigts, eds., *The Routledge Companion to Adaptation* (London: Routledge, 2018).

21 Laurie A. Finke and Martin B. Shichtman, eds., *Cinematic Illuminations: The Middle Ages on Film* (Baltimore, MD: Johns Hopkins University Press, 2010); and A. Johnston, M. Rouse, and Philipp Hinz, eds., *The Medieval Motion Picture: The Politics of Adaptation* (New York: Palgrave Macmillan, 2014).
22 Jennifer Clement, "Beyond Shakespeare: Early Modern Adaptation Studies and Its Potential," *Literature Compass* 10, no. 9 (2013): 677.
23 Richard Burt, *Medieval and Early Modern Film and Media* (New York: Palgrave Macmillan, 2008); Pascale Aebischer, *Screening Early Modern Drama: Beyond Shakespeare* (Cambridge: Cambridge University Press, 2013); Jennifer Clement, ed., "Adaptation and Early Modern Culture: Shakespeare and Beyond," special issue, *Shakespeare* 11, no. 1 (2015); and Janice North, Karl C. Alvestad, and Elena Woodacre, eds., *Premodern Rulers and Postmodern Viewers: Gender, Sex, and Power in Popular Culture* (New York: Palgrave Macmillan, 2018).
24 A recent example of this is William B. Robison, ed., *History, Fiction, and "The Tudors": Sex, Politics, and Artistic License in the Showtime Television Series* (New York: Palgrave Macmillan, 2016). The book's focus on accuracy is discussed in Aidan Norrie, review of *History, Fiction, and "The Tudors": Sex, Politics, and Artistic License in the Showtime Television Series*, ed. William B. Robison, *Royal Studies Journal* 4, no. 2 (2017): 258–262; the editor's unhelpful response to this critique was published in *Royal Studies Journal* 5, no. 1 (2018): 220–225.
25 Elizabeth A. Ford and Deborah C. Mitchell, *Royal Portraits in Hollywood: Filming the Lives of Queens* (Lexington: The University Press of Kentucky, 2009), 294.
26 Robert Rosenstone, *History on Film / Film on History* (New York: Pearson, 2006), 30.
27 Deborah Cartmell and Imelda Whelehan, "A Short History of Adaptation Studies in the Classroom," in *Teaching Adaptations*, ed. Deborah Cartmell and Imelda Whelehan (New York: Palgrave Macmillan, 2014), 1
28 Deborah Cartmell, "100+ Years of Adaptations, or, Adaptation as the Art Form of Democracy," in *A Companion to Literature, Film, and Adaptation*, ed. Deborah Cartmell (Malden, MA: Wiley Blackwell, 2012), 4.
29 Hutcheon, *A Theory of Adaptation*, 7.
30 Sanders, *Adaptation and Appropriation*, 18–19.
31 Sanders, *Adaptation and Appropriation*, 19.
32 Jørgen Bruhn, Anne Gjelsvik, and Eirik Frisvold Hanssen, "'There and Back Again': New Challenges and New Directions in Adaptation Studies," in *Adaptation Studies: New Challenges, New Directions*, ed. Jørgen Bruhn, Anne Gjelsvik, and Eirik Frisvold Hanssen (London: Bloomsbury, 2013), 6.
33 Hutcheon, *A Theory of Adaptation*, 6.
34 Sanders, *Adaptation and Appropriation*, 20.
35 Clement, "Beyond Shakespeare," 679. See also: David T. Johnson, "Adaptation and Fidelity," in *The Oxford Handbook of Adaptation Studies*, ed. Thomas Leitch (Oxford: Oxford University Press, 2017), 37–53.
36 Gary R. Bortolotti and Linda Hutcheon, "On the Origin of Adaptations: Rethinking Fidelity Discourse and 'Success'—Biologically," *New Literary History* 38, no. 3 (2007): 444.
37 Bortolotti and Hutcheon, "On the Origin of Adaptations," 444–445.
38 Hutcheon, *A Theory of Adaptation*, 3–4.
39 Hutcheon, *A Theory of Adaptation*, 4.
40 *Oxford English Dictionary*, s.v., "invention, n."

Introduction   17

41 David Mayernik, *The Challenge of Emulation in Art and Architecture* (London: Routledge, 2013), 2.
42 Dale L. Sullivan, "Attitudes toward Imitation: Classical Culture and the Modern Temper," *Rhetoric Review* 8, no. 1 (1989): 6.
43 John Kemble, *A Translation of the Anglo-Saxon Poem of "Beowulf"* (London, 1837). Kemble produced a close, literal English prose translation. The first complete (albeit imprecise) translation of *Beowulf* was into Latin, 1815, by Grímur Jónsson Thorkelin.
44 See: Gail Marshall, ed., *Shakespeare in the Nineteenth Century* (Cambridge: Cambridge University Press, 2012).
45 See, for example: Daniel T. Kline, ed., *Digital Gaming Re-Imagines the Middle Ages* (London: Routledge, 2013); Stephen O'Neill, *Shakespeare and YouTube: New Media Forms of the Bard* (London: Bloomsbury, 2014); Laura Estill, Diane K. Jakacki, and Michael Ullyot, eds., *Early Modern Studies After the Digital Turn* (Toronto, ON: Iter Press, 2016); Valerie M. Fazel and Louise Geddes, eds., *The Shakespeare User: Critical and Creative Appropriations in a Networked Culture* (New York: Palgrave Macmillan, 2017); Andrew B.R. Elliott, *Medievalism, Politics and Mass Media: Appropriating the Middle Ages in the Twenty-First Century* (Cambridge: D.S. Brewer, 2017); and Stephen O'Neill, ed., *Broadcast your Shakespeare: Continuity and Change Across Media* (London: Bloomsbury, 2018).
46 See, for example: Iain McCalman and Paul A. Pickering, eds., *Historical Reenactment: From Realism to the Affective Turn* (New York: Palgrave Macmillan, 2010); Kevin LaGrandeur, *Androids and Intelligent Networks in Early Modern Literature and Culture: Artificial Slaves* (London: Routledge, 2014); Helen Young, ed., *Fantasy and Science Fiction Medievalisms: From Isaac Asimov to A Game of Thrones* (Amherst, NY: Cambria Press, 2015); Carl Kears and James Paz, eds., *Medieval Science Fiction* (London: King's College London, Centre for Late Antique and Medieval Studies, 2016); Lisa Hopkins, *Shakespearean Allusion in Crime Fiction: DCI Shakespeare* (New York: Palgrave Macmillan, 2016); and Jerome de Groot, *Consuming History: Historians and Heritage in Contemporary Popular Culture*, 2nd ed. (London: Routledge, 2016), especially Chapter 6, "Historical re-enactment," 109–133.
47 This current right-wing hysteria is further discussed in Iain MacInnes's chapter, and is briefly touched on in Marina Gerzic's chapter on *Titus*. The historicity of a past that was not white, heterosexual, and able-bodied is routinely demonstrated in articles published by *The Public Medievalist* (https://publicmedievalist.com/). In addition, the following works—which represent a fraction of the excellent scholarship on these important subjects—have informed our own thinking of these topics: Helen Young, *Race and Popular Fantasy Literature: Habits of Whiteness* (London: Routledge, 2015); Miranda Kaufmann, *Black Tudors: The Untold Story* (London: Oneworld Publications, 2017); Glenn Burger and Steven F. Kruger, eds., *Queering the Middle Ages* (Minneapolis: University of Minnesota Press, 2001); Tom Betteridge, ed., *Sodomy in Early Modern Europe* (Manchester: Manchester University Press, 2002); Irina Metzler, *Disability in Medieval Europe: Thinking about Physical Impairment in the High Middle Ages, c. 1100–c. 1400* (London: Routledge, 2006); and Joshua R. Eyler, ed., *Disability in the Middle Ages: Reconsiderations and Reverberations* (Farnham: Ashgate, 2010).

Section I
Cultural Medievalism and Early-Modernism

2 Wonder Woman and the *Nine Ladies Worthy*
The Male Gaze and What It Takes to Be a 'Worthy Woman'

Simone Celine Marshall

The fifteenth-century English poem known commonly as the *Nine Ladies Worthy* is concerned with the representation of women warriors.[1] The figure is not unusual in literary history and in popular culture, and a recent redaction is that of the contemporary film *Wonder Woman* (2017).[2] This chapter concerns the dilemma that has come to light in recent reviews and responses to the 2017 film: to what extent is the character of Wonder Woman—a warrior woman—a feminist role model? The debate has resulted in numerous commentaries, not the least from the film's director, Patty Jenkins, and another Hollywood director, James Cameron.[3] However, in this chapter, I want to shed some additional light on this debate because it seems to me that both the film and the poem are works concerned with how the reader or viewer engages with them, and that Jenkins' and Cameron's debate seems to ignore the possibility that viewers' response to the film may well be part of its meaning. In other words, the impact of the male and female gaze may determine whether or not a text or film is a feminist role model.

The 2017 *Wonder Woman* film is the latest in a long line of iterations of the Wonder Woman character. From her beginnings as a comic strip character in 1941 in *All Star Comics* #8, followed by *Sensation Comics* #1 in 1942, Wonder Woman's backstory reveals her to be one of the legendary Amazon women from classical mythology. William Moulton Marston's superhero, who unleashes the Lasso of Truth,

> at once embodies the unrivalled force and supreme grace of a born warrior, and the genuine compassion and understanding of a true humanitarian. As a symbol of equality, power, and truth, her natural confidence and unmistakable intelligence made her unequalled.[4]

Wonder Woman's origins as an Amazon are of particular interest in this chapter, as the concerns of director of the 2017 film adaptation Patti Jenkins and fellow film director James Cameron use the spectre of earlier stories of the Amazons, and indicate that their concerns are not at all new. The DC Comics promotional material quoted earlier brings to the fore the dual concerns of how Wonder Woman can be both a powerful unrivalled force, and yet also show supreme grace and compassion. These apparent contradictions will be investigated in this chapter, focusing on the anonymous medieval poem, the *Nine Ladies Worthy*.

The earliest extant copy of the *Nine Ladies Worthy* is found in Trinity College MS R.3.19, a fifteenth-century manuscript that brings to the fore the topic of women and storytelling. The manuscript comprises 47 texts of courtly love literature, presented in a series of booklets that circulated independently for a short period of time, before being collected together, sometime in the fifteenth century.[5] The compiler, or compilers, of the manuscript clearly saw the manuscript as an opportunity to express an opinion about women, perhaps beyond the intentions of the authors of the various texts, as the selection and arrangement of the texts points to a deliberate effort at highlighting how women are frequently the subjects of literature, but rarely the authors of it.[6]

The majority of the texts in the manuscript are anonymously authored, while a few are written by well-known figures such as Geoffrey Chaucer and John Lydgate. The antiquarian John Stow at one time owned the manuscript, and it greatly influenced his edition of the works of Geoffrey Chaucer, which he published in 1561.[7] As a result of Stow's edition, many of the anonymously authored texts in R.3.19, including the *Nine Ladies Worthy*, were attributed to Chaucer, and remained circulating in editions of Chaucer's works until the end of the nineteenth century.[8]

Julia Boffey, considering the responses to Chaucer's *Legend of Good Women*, similarly notes that the compilation of R.3.19 points towards an interest in women. She says,

> At the very least, we seem to have some indications that London scribes and readers who knew Chaucer's *Legend* were probably also familiar with the tendency to group females in exemplary 'paks' of nine.[9]

Boffey's interest here is to show that the *Legend of Good Women*, a poem containing stories about nine women, sits in this manuscript alongside poems such as the *Nine Ladies Worthy*, and with other poems that group women together. She does not also note that *The Assembly of Ladies*, another poem contained in this manuscript, similarly concerns a group of nine women, although it contains a class division where they are divided into four gentlewomen and five ladies.

To shed more light on the compiler's purpose behind R.3.19, it is useful at this stage to consider the *Nine Ladies Worthy*, as this poem helps to reveal some of the overarching themes that are apparent in the manuscript as a whole.

The exact source for this poem is unknown, but it clearly draws on Eustace Deschamps's (1346–1406) ballade 403, which is generally credited as the first documented account of nine female 'worthies.'[10] The female worthies sat alongside their male counterparts, as Ann McMillan explains:

> The nine male worthies come to prominence first in Jacques de Longuyon's poem *Les Voeux du paon* (*The Vows of the Peacock*), around 1310. They epitomise chivalric virtues, and the nine men fall into three groups: the first three are pagan (Hector, Alexander, Julius Caesar), the next three are Jews (Joshua, David, Judas Maccabeus), and the final three are Christian (Arthur, Charlemagne, Godfrey of Bouillon) ... It seems fairly likely that Deschamps was responsible for the creation of the nine female worthies, set directly alongside the male worthies, as their counterpart. Others certainly wrote about famous women, but Deschamps' contribution is not that these women are written about at all, but that they are brought together as a group.[11]

As McMillian observes, "both groups of men and women are called 'worthies' in English, 'preux' and 'preuse' in French." This is an important definition because it presents a range of possibilities regarding the personalities and attributes of the worthies. In Old French, the word is often linked with other adjectives such as *sage* (wise, self-governing), *cortois* (courteous), and *vaillant* (strong, valiant), and the noun it most often modifies is *chevalier* (knight). In English, there are similar uses: Chaucer's Knight is made 'worthy' by his love of chivalry and its attendant virtues, and the Wife of Bath "was a worthy womman al hir lyve: / Housbondes at chirche dore she hadde five," here implying that she was worthy because she had had five husbands.[12]

The definition of 'worthy' is important for my argument, because 'worthiness' seems to underpin the related question that seems to have fuelled contemporary debates about the role of Wonder Woman: does being a warrior woman necessarily make her 'worthy'—that is, a feminist role model? Does her revealing clothing reduce or enhance the possibility of her being a role model?[13] Can Wonder Woman be a feminist role model when she is presented in a sexually provocative manner? These are among the topics that have arisen regarding the 2017 film, and these same questions apply equally to earlier representations of warrior women, such as those we see in the *Nine Ladies Worthy*.

Indeed, the topic of what a worthy woman is seems to pervade the entire manuscript in a range of ways, and it certainly challenges the reader to engage with the ambiguity of the concept. I have argued elsewhere that the contents of this manuscript suggest the compiler had an interest in the mechanics of medieval courtly love literature.[14] Much of the manuscript's contents are courtly love poems, but many also have a distinct sense of their own form. They parody the form, or draw attention to how it functions, and even its failings at times. All of this suggests that the compiler was particularly keen to reveal to the reader the 'literariness' of the compilation. An astute reader would come away from reading R.3.19 with a strong sense of the generic conventions of courtly love poetry, when those conventions were being adhered to and why, and when they were being usurped or contravened in some way. But in addition to this, the reader would have understood that attention to the literary conventions would throw into relief how women are presented in literature.

In this context, the *Nine Ladies Worthy* appears to be a simple poem that presents, in nine stanzas, descriptions of each warrior woman and the famous deeds she performed. The women, agreeing with Deschamps's poem, are Deipyle, Teuta, Semiramis, Penthesilea, Hippolyta, Thamyris, Lampedo/Marpesia, Menalippe, and Sinope. Immediately, a discrepancy is observable: there are, in fact, ten women discussed in the nine stanzas. Lampedo and her sister Marpesia are together the subject of the seventh stanza. Other versions of their story explain that they were Amazon queens who shared their rule. While one was at home governing, the other would be out fighting.[15] The mere fact of their interchangeability offers us the first indication that one characteristic of worthy women is that they are not always identifiable as individuals, but rather, are stereotypes. This is twice a feature of the women in the *Assembly of Ladies*. First, the narrator of the poem encounters a gentlewoman on her journey. Is she one of the gentlewomen who is part of the narrator's party? Or is she an additional tenth woman? This is never revealed, and is impossible to tell, because none of the women are identifiable as individuals.[16] Second, images of famous classical women, such as one might find in Giovanni Boccaccio's *De Claris Mulieribus* or Chaucer's *Legend of Good Women*, are presented on the internal walls of the castle in the *Assembly of Ladies*. Here, the women are identified by name, but conspicuously, their images are overlayed with a gauze:[17]

> And bicause the wallis shone so bright
> With fyne umple they were al over-spredde
> To that entent folk shuld nat hurt theyr sight,
> And thurgh that the storyes myght be redde.
>
> (470–473)

Apparently, the images on their own are damaging to the eye, so their intensity must be reduced for the viewer, thus effectively reducing their significance or importance, similar to the way the *Nine Ladies Worthy*, actually concerning ten women but stated as concerning only nine, reduces the significance of the women. As another comparison, Chaucer's *Legend of Good Women*, also containing nine tales, actually concerns ten women: Cleopatra, Thisbe, Dido, Hypsiple, Medea, Lucrece, Ariadne, Philomela, Phyllis, and Hypermnestra. The legends of Hypsiple and Medea are combined into a single legend. Advancing Boffey's suggestion, it seems plausible to me that the compiler of R.3.19 was alert to these discrepancies, particularly when they occur across three texts, and thus their presence together in this manuscript emphasises how the impact of women's actions and lives are frequently reduced in literature.

Looking more closely at the women in the *Nine Ladies Worthy*, we can see a similar pattern of reducing or undercutting the significance of the women. In the stanza concerning Lampedo and Marpesia, the emphasis is on Lampedo, giving the impression that she single-handedly extended Amazon influence throughout Europe and Asia, and built cities. Other versions credit Marpesia with these feats.[18] Yet, the narrator of the poem somewhat undercuts their achievements by beginning the stanza as follows:

The famous trumpe of gold forgyd so bryght
Hath blowyn so vp the fame and glory enuyron
Of thys lady Lampydo with hyr syster Masysy.[19]

The narrator suggests that the achievements of Lampedo and Marpesia have been overblown and exaggerated, despite concluding the stanza by acknowledging that the cities they built have lasted "perpetuelly," with "howge walles strong." It is difficult to discern clearly what a worthy woman might be from this stanza. Amazon queens seem to be an obvious choice: they are warriors; these particular ones captured large amounts of territory and were clearly set about increasing their impact by building cities. They are not dissimilar in their achievements from Alexander the Great or Julius Caesar. And yet, the narrator suggests, without justification, these achievements are exaggerations. Would Lampedo and Marpesia be worthy if the narrator felt their stories were true? Or is it that accepting these achievements would somehow undercut the achievements of their male counterparts? The narrator's description of Lampedo and Marpesia seems to raise questions about their worthiness, and in doing so, raises questions about how one should determine worthiness.

Five other women in the *Nine Ladies Worthy* are similarly mythological: Sinope, Hippolyta, Deipyle, Penthesilea, and Menalippe. Only Teuta, Semiramis, and Thamyris have historical backgrounds.[20] But it is difficult to determine if fiction or non-fiction seems to be a determining factor in their worthiness. Of the male worthies, there is a similar mixture of fiction and non-fiction, with the inclusion of Julius Caesar and Judas Maccabeus alongside Arthur and Hector. It is of course possible that medieval readers might not have recognised a distinction between fiction and non-fiction in the same way as readers today.

A significant feature that appears to extend through the entire poem is that the narrator is determined to praise each woman by referring to her feminine traits, in addition to her martial successes. The narrator describes Sinope, for instance, according to her "feymyne beryng"; of Hippolyta, he praises her "amorous chere" before she "smote [Hercules] to ground." Deipyle is described as first offering "releue and socour" to the Duke of Athens, before conquering Thebes. Teuta is described as "off all femyne most formous floure" before concluding

> O lady Tuca, muche was thy glory and honour,
> Yet moche more was to commend thy beauteuous benygnyte
> In thy perfyte lyuyng and virginall chastyte.
>
> (26–28)

Penthesilea is described as showing love to the Trojans "so pregnaunt and fertile," and Semiramis is described as the "most generrous gem and floure of louely fauour." Only Thamyris and Menalippe receive no feminine descriptions; the narrator explains only their prowess in battle. Does the narrator focus on the women's feminine qualities in order to undermine their warrior statuses? Or does the narrator present their femininity in order to suggest that a worthy woman can be both strong and feminine?[21] These are the same questions raised in relation to Wonder Woman, and the ones that James Cameron has so much difficulty with. How can Wonder Woman be a worthy woman when she is also attractive? For Cameron this is impossible, and one wonders if the narrator of the *Nine Ladies Worthy* is asking the same question.

Returning to Boffey's suggestion that perhaps the compiler of R.3.19 was keen to bring together texts that involved groups of women, the *Nine Ladies Worthy* certainly fits into this category. But what is the significance of groups of women? Are women collectives more worthy than women as individuals? Certainly, too, not all poems in this manuscript concern groups of women. One response to this question is to consider texts that might have influenced the authors of the texts in R.3.19.

The *Nine Ladies Worthies* draws its women mostly from classical mythology, although, as already noted, some of the women had an historical basis. Many of the fictional women are Amazons, and it pays to consider how this group of women has been depicted in texts, which will then, of course, throw light on how Diana Prince (also an Amazon) is presented in *Wonder Woman*. At this stage, it seems at least pertinent to acknowledge that Boffey's question about groups of women is partly answered: collectives of women, like the Amazons, generally exist outside of normal society. Thus, one can suggest that their role in fiction is to define socially acceptable behaviour by displaying its opposite.

The representation of Amazons as social outsiders is not a new concept. It has been investigated by many scholars and in relation to a range of different time periods.[22] While there are exceptions among different writers, it is frequently seen that Amazons are literary devices used to either challenge or reinforce social conventions. For instance, Priscilla Martin suggests Chaucer's use of Amazons in the *Knight's Tale* represents the end of a corrupt society:

> Theseus, in conquering the Amazons, asserts male supremacy over the unnatural race of warrior women. In marrying him, Hippolyta abandons her monstrous regiment in favour of the conventional role of wife. These mighty rulers from the mythical past are symbols of opposing ways of life now reconciled.[23]

Characteristically of Chaucer, he then challenges such stereotyping, as we see in the *Legend of Good Women*. Here, classical women—mostly from Ovid's *Heroides*—are described in a lacklustre manner by a reluctant narrator obliged to tell the tales of women who died for their love. The narrator clearly resents having to retell stories that imply a good woman is a dead one.

The Amazons, then, are frequently a convenient device used to show abnormality, but often this opposition is shown to be too simplistic. As an example, Dianne Dugaw shows how the Amazon myth is taken in an unexpected direction when it turns up in popular early modern ballads:

> Female Warrior ballads are success stories. Highly conventionalised, they sing of valiant "Nancys" and "Pollys" who defy oppressive parents, don men's clothing, sail the seas, and fight cruel wars. Inevitably their masquerading heroine – a model of bravery, beauty, and pluck – proves herself deserving in romance, able in war, and rewarded in both.[24]

Here, cross-dressing women are the norm, and are even valorised:

> The Female Warrior is a two-sided heroine. By way of her gender masquerade, she enacts both sides of the traditionally bifurcated ideal of Western heroism: female Lover and male Glory.[25]

In this instance, we see that the mythological idea of the Amazons as social outsiders is drawn on to respond to and explain contemporary behaviours, yet it is a fine line between rejecting Amazonian behaviour and celebrating it. Dugaw's Female Warrior is celebrated in song so long as her female identity is clear to the observer. A woman who successfully dupes the observer and passes for a man is still regarded as a threat to social order, thus the Female Warrior always ends in a heterosexual romance.

The depiction of Amazons in the *Nine Ladies Worthy* complies readily to these examples. They are no doubt excellent warriors, yet one never loses sight of their femininity, and thus correct social order is always retained. If we take up the possibility that this may well be an occasional poem intended to celebrate or complement a physical painting or sculpture, then the dual roles of the women become even more prominent. In such a scenario, the nine female worthies would very likely be depicted, literally, alongside the nine male worthies, and thus their roles as feminine versions of the nine male worthies would be clear to all. Surviving paintings and sculptures of the nine female worthies bear this out: the women are always shown in fashionable medieval dress, not armour, but with an accompanying sword or shield to indicate their warrior status. There is no doubt in these images that the women are socially acceptable depictions of female warriors. Their role is to not only balance the presence of the male worthies, but also to show that while their warrior status is accepted, it exists in a carefully defined space that does not disrupt social order.

A feature that is conspicuous in the *Nine Ladies Worthy* is that nearly every one of the women is described in relation to male figures. This is not the case on every occasion: Lampedo, for instance, is referred to, with her sister Marpesia, as bringing many lands into subjection and there is no specific mention of which rulers they conquered or comparison made with other warriors. Hippolyta, Deipyle, Thamyris, and Menalippe are all described as having personally beaten rulers: Diomedes, the Duke of Athens, Cyrus, and Duke Thesius, respectively. Teuta is described as conquering "the Romayns," Penthesilia, "the grekes," and Semiramis is presented as comparable to Alexander. Interestingly, Sinope and Penthesilia are presented in relation to an emotional attachment to Hercules and Hector, as a justification for their violent actions.

The selected information that is included in each stanza is also significant in terms of the impression that the author is attempting to present. The title suggests the intention is to present 'worthy' women, but is it possible to define what this means for the author? There is no doubt each woman is either a political leader or, in the case of Deipyle, had access to the leadership of a people, thus they are all from the ruling classes. Certainly, each is involved in a range of ways with violent acts against other people. It is not always clear the extent to which each participated in violent acts, but the association is there. Often, the women are praised for their femininity. When set beside the male worthies, there is no clear indication that the worthy women are especially exceptional. They are simply a convenient counterpoint to the male worthies. Together, they represent a ruling class, martial conquest, and violent behaviour. None of this is overridden by the fact that some of the men and women are fictional.

When seen separately from the male worthies, as in the case of R.3.19, the worthy women take on new meanings. In R.3.19, the women are set alongside texts that reveal women in a number of different ways. This, I believe, is the particular achievement of the compiler of the manuscript. It seems to me that this manuscript offers us a glimpse of a collection of texts with an intended female readership. This is not to say that only women read the manuscript, but that the point of view that is presented would have particular meaning for women that it might not have for a male readership. In this manuscript, the texts take on a new significance by their relationship with each other. Boffey gestures towards this when she notices the emphasis on groups of women, but I believe the intention is much more emphatic than this. The texts all point towards a well-educated and well-read female audience who would be familiar with the texts already, and thus recognise how their meanings have been altered by their new setting. Where previously the *Nine Ladies Worthy* was simple a counterpoint to the nine male worthies, in this manuscript, the reader is encouraged to consider seriously what a worthy woman is, and whether the poem accurately depicts this. With this focus, it is now possible to see the questioning nature of the narrator of the poem, which considers different ways of valuing women's achievements.

Wonder Woman as Feminist Role Model

Film director James Cameron caused considerable controversy following the release of the 2017 *Wonder Woman* film for his comments that the main character is not a feminist icon because she, played by Gal Gadot (former Miss Israel), is too beautiful.[26] There is a lot to unpack in this idea of Cameron's. Ostensibly, Cameron is suggesting, by directly contrasting Gal Gadot's Wonder Woman with his own female creation, Sarah Connor from the *Terminator* films,[27] that a woman can only be a feminist role model if she is not attractive. Less obviously, Cameron may be attempting to downplay the success of another film in order to promote his own.

The debate that has ensued between Cameron and *Wonder Woman*'s director, Patty Jenkins, reveals that at the heart of the matter is the similar question that my investigation of the *Nine Ladies Worthy* addressed: what does it mean to be a worthy woman? In addition to this, the films highlight another question, which also throws light on the medieval poem: who gets to determine what a worthy woman is? In the *Nine Ladies Worthy*, the author is anonymous and unknown, but with the *Wonder Woman* and *Terminator* films, we know exactly who their creators are, and their intentions.

Many of the concerns raised in the debate between Cameron and Jenkins are the same concerns raised by the *Nine Ladies Worthy*, and by the manuscript context of the poem. It seems to me that the compiler of the manuscript was engaged with attempting a response to the very same concerns that we see raised by *Wonder Woman*. How can a woman participate in literature (or film) in a credible way? Cameron asserts that his creation, Sarah Connor, is a better example of a feminist role model, yet this is disputed by Tricia Ennis on the grounds that "Cameron is not a woman," and thus has no authority to comment on what is or is not a worthy woman.[28] This, too, is a controversial stance. Why is it not credible for a man to make such a comment? Ennis does not explain, but assumes the reader understands already that his masculine presence undermines any claims about how a concept might be valued by women.

Of Sarah Connor, Cameron says, "She was strong, she was troubled, she was a terrible mother, and she earned the respect of the audience through pure grit."[29] These qualities, he claims, make Connor a feminist role model.[30] Wonder Woman, he says, is "absolutely drop-dead gorgeous. To me, that's not breaking ground."[31] Of course, whether Cameron realised this or not, he has cleverly deflected attention away from the detail of what Wonder Woman is by introducing a comparison. Why should we even begin to compare Wonder Woman and Sarah Connor? There is no reason aside from Cameron demanding that we do. Connor is a fictional character borne out of the *Terminator* films, and aside from subsequent spin-offs from the film franchise, such as the television series, the *Sarah Connor Chronicles* (2008–2009), she has a limited presence outside of the films; thus she is created solely for the roles she performs in those films.[32] Wonder Woman has a presence completely outside of the latest 2017 film. She has existed in a television series (played by Linda Carter) and in an animated television series,[33] and she was initially created as a comic strip character in 1941, appearing in *Sensation Comics* to document "the growth in the power of women."[34] Wonder Woman's image has been used in feminist iconography throughout the decades.[35] Thus, we can see that Sarah Connor and Wonder Woman have two vastly different trajectories and histories. By enforcing a comparison between the two, Cameron reduces the meanings of both to the simple concept that a woman cannot be a beautiful warrior.

Returning to Ennis's criticisms of Cameron, she states,

> What Cameron is—or at least, what he is supposed to be—is an ally; to feminists and to women on the whole whether in the audience or behind the camera ... [an ally is] about being quiet, opening doors (or breaking glass ceilings) and then stepping aside to allow someone else to walk through in front of you.[36]

The quietness that Ennis advocates is exactly what we see in anonymously authored and compiled medieval texts and manuscripts.

We do not know who wrote many of the poems in R.3.19, nor who compiled them into a single manuscript, and it is this absence that allows a reader to contemplate the texts and the women presented in them as worthy women. The *Nine Ladies Worthy* is a particular case in point. As mentioned, the existence of the nine female worthies relies on their male predecessors, and often, in other texts and paintings, the women are depicted alongside their male counterparts. In R.3.19, they are removed from their masculine origins and presented alongside other groups of women. The new association and contexts dramatically show the compiler's intention. In some ways, the compiler is doing what James Cameron's comments do: forces a comparison that otherwise might not be made. But the significant difference here is that we do not know the gender of the authors or the compiler; thus there is no male gaze to reduce the women to mere sexualised objects that exist solely in relation to men.

The issues here are not simple. Cameron takes issue with Wonder Woman's beauty, and Ennis criticises his right to comment. Yet, if we examine Wonder Woman's origins, she is indeed intended as a sexual object, although it was not at first realised. Noah Berlatsky states plainly, "[William] Marston meant for his Wonder Woman to be sexually appealing to men and women."[37] Tim Hanley notes, however, that Wonder Woman's first artist, H.G. Peter, who drew her in nearly every series from 1942 until 1958, conspicuously

> had a style that was notably different from the work of his younger peers at DC Comics ... Peter didn't much go for overstated figures or skimpy clothes, and his faces were pleasant instead of provocative. Because of Peter, when Wonder Woman debuted she looked unlike any other comic book woman on the newsstands.[38]

Much has been written about Marston's personal life, and his polyamorous relationship with Elizabeth Holloway Marston and partner Olive Byrne, who apparently contributed to the creation of the Wonder Woman character.[39] In a 1943 issue of *The American Scholar*, Marston wrote,

> Not even girls want to be girls so long as our feminine archetype lacks force, strength, and power. Not wanting to be girls, they don't want to be tender, submissive, peace-loving as good women are. Women's strong qualities have become despised because of their weakness. The obvious remedy is to create a feminine character with all the strength of Superman plus all the allure of a good and beautiful woman.[40]

Here, we can see Marston's attempts to describe a worthy woman. The *Nine Ladies Worthy* also seems to be attempting a similar duality.

This also causes me to return for a moment to Cameron's Sarah Connor. It seems to me naïve that Cameron would suggest Sarah Connor is not a sexualised object.[41] Clearly, all evidence shows that one of her appeals is her sexualised form. Cameron is disingenuous here, by hiding behind that reality that Sarah Connor, like Wonder Woman, is appealing to both men and women.[42]

For another point of view on Wonder Woman, Susannah Breslin says,

> what you see in "Wonder Woman," we all know that's not really feminism. That's the patriarchy's feminist icon, trussed up in feminist-themed marketing. In reality, she's a Playmate with a lasso, a girl pretending to be a woman. Don't worry, she's not *too* strong, she's not *too* tough, she's not *too* complicated. I mean, she's *empowered*, but not enough to scare you guys, right?[43]

Here, Breslin in some part agrees with Cameron's stance because she feels that Wonder Woman is not complex enough, unlike Sarah Connor, thus removing her from the realities of real women. There is no doubt this is true. Wonder Woman never questions her morality or judgement, and she is extremely limited in her knowledge of the world. We should not be surprised by this, because this is the role Amazons have always played. Diana Prince's naïvety about the world is a convenient narrative tool used as a contrast with the corruption of reality. There is even a direct female comparison in the film between Wonder Woman and Dr Poison. In case we hadn't figured out the contrast, these two female characters offer it to us on a plate: the naïvety of Wonder Woman, and the complex perversion of Dr Poison.

Isabel Maru—"Dr Poison"—is a sophisticated character who causes tension for the viewer because of her corrupt behaviour. Not only is she scheming to create a lethal gas to destroy millions, but she is also an intelligent woman chemist with a physical disability and little compassion or emotion. All of these characteristics clearly present her as an abomination of what a woman should be. She is a puzzling contrast with Wonder Woman, because the Amazons have traditionally taken on the role as social outcasts, yet here, Dr Poison's presence reinstates Wonder Woman to the position of normality within social boundaries.

It has been noted already that Amazons have always served as outsiders. Their role is frequently to emphasise and reinforce the cultural norm in a society. The Amazons are an all-women community, and they indulge in self-mutilation and infanticide; thus they represent a range of characteristics that a good society should not be.[44] That Wonder Woman is indeed a two-dimensional character should not surprise us. She is, after all, an Amazon who is designed for this purpose. In the film, she is presented as a pure and uncorrupted ideal who encounters a corrupt society, but this is soon remedied, and she settles in to life in the real world, emphasising that the real world, with its flaws and failings, is the ideal world, not her former world with the Amazons where life is a series of simple, but unhuman, truths.

As Zoe Williams explains in her article, "If you are still making the film for a male gaze, the female warrior becomes a sex object."[45] This, I feel, comes to heart of the matter for both *Wonder Woman* and the *Nine Ladies Worthy*. It's all about point of view: who is telling the story, and who is reading or viewing the story. In Trinity College Cambridge Manuscript R.3.19, we see a concerted attempt to reassign who the storyteller and reader might be. The removal of comparative male stories and the anonymity of the compiler come together to create a storytelling experience that brings to the fore the complexities of how women are represented in literature, how women can participate in literature, and how a woman can be worthy. In *Wonder Woman*, produced centuries later, we see the same concerns and debates raised, but we mustn't therefore think nothing has changed or improved for women. The complexities that are raised in both the film and the poem are not resolvable, but rather are integral to the realities of women. Cameron and Jenkins may not have realised, but the compiler of R.3.19 did: a worthy woman is, of course, a real woman.

Notes

1 The *Nine Ladies Worthy* is found in every edition of the works of Geoffrey Chaucer, from William Thynne's 1532 edition though until Alexander Chalmers's 1810 edition. The edition referred to here is Julia Boffey's transcription from Cambridge, Trinity College Manuscript R.3.19. Subsequent references will be in text and by line number.
2 *Wonder Woman*, dir. Patty Jenkins (Warner Bros Films, 2017).
3 Trent Moore, "James Cameron Calls Wonder Woman 'Step Backwards' for Female Heroes," *SyfyWire*, 24 August 2017, http://syfy.com/syfywire/james-cameron-calls-wonder-woman-%E2%80%98step-backwards%E2%80%99-for-female-heroes.
4 Tiras Buck, "Wonder Woman's Day Job Revealed in Batman V Superman!," *The Source*, 2 March 2016, https://source.superherostuff.com/movies/wonder-womans-day-job-revealed-in-batman-v-superman/.
5 Bradford Y. Fletcher, *Trinity R.3.19, Trinity College, Cambridge* (Norman, OK: Variorum Chaucer, 1987), xv–xxx.
6 Simone Celine Marshall, *The Anonymous Text: The 500-Year History of "The Assembly of Ladies"* (Bern: Peter Lang, 2011), 14–26.
7 John Stow, ed., *The Woorkes of Geffrey Chaucer Newlie Printed, with Divers Addicions, Which Were Never in Printed Before* (London, 1561). STC 5075, 5076, 5076.3.
8 It is beyond the scope of this chapter, but still interesting to note, that many anonymously authored texts were wrongly attributed to Chaucer, and as a result remained in circulation for many centuries. This points to the cultural preferences of male-authored texts.
9 Julia Boffey, "'Twenty Thousand More': Some Fifteenth- and Sixteenth-Century Responses to the Legend of Good Women," in *Middle English Poetry: Texts and Traditions*, ed. A.J. Minnis (York: York Medieval Press, 2001), 286.
10 Eustace Deschamps, *Oeuvres complètes de Eustache Deschamps*, ed. Gaston Raynaud and Henri Auguste Edouard, 11 vols. (Paris: Firmin-Didot, 1966–1994).

11 Ann McMillan, "Men's Weapons, Women's War: The Nine Female Worthies, 1400–1640," *Medievalia* 5 (1979): 113–115.
12 McMillan, "Men's Weapons," 113, 114.
13 Daisy Murray raised this issue in 2017 with a comparison of *Wonder Woman*'s costumes and those from the later *Justice League* (2017) film. She argues that the films show the difference between the male gaze and the female gaze. Daisy Murray, "'Justice League' Sparks Anger with 'Wonder Woman' Costume Change," *Elle*, 15 November 2017, https://elle.com/uk/life-and-culture/culture/news/a39944/justice-league-wonder-woman-amazon-outfit/.
14 Marshall, *The Anonymous Text*, 22.
15 Perhaps there is some similarity here with *Wonder Woman*'s presentation of Hippolyta and Antiope, sisters who go into battle together, although there is no evidence Jenkins is deliberately implying this connection.
16 Simone Celine Marshall, "Interiors, Exteriors, and the Veiling of Cupid's Martyrs: Gendered Space in *The Assembly of Ladies*," *Philological Quarterly* 84, no. 2 (2005): 161–187.
17 Julia Boffey, ed., *Fifteenth-Century English Dream Visions: An Anthology* (Oxford: Oxford University Press, 2003), 219.
18 Max Duncker, *The History of Antiquity, Volume I*, trans. Evelyn Abbott (London, 1877), 358n1.
19 Transcription is from Boffey, "'Twenty Thousand More,'" 297.
20 Teuta was the queen regent of the Ardiaei tribe in Illyria, who reigned from 231 BCE to 227 BCE; Semiramis (Shammuramat) was the Assyrian wife of Shamshi-Adad V (ruled 824 BCE–811 BCE); Thamyris (Tomyris) was a Massagetean ruler, an Iranian people from the Scythian pastoral-nomadic confederation of Central Asia, east of the Caspian Sea, c.520 BCE.
21 Conspicuously, the scribe of the manuscript has labelled each of the stanzas with each woman's name, sometimes entitling her as a "Quene," sometimes as a "Lady." It is not clear how this designation has been applied, as it does not always agree with classical titles traditionally attributed to the women.
22 See, in particular: William Blake Tyrrell, *Amazons: A Study in Athenian Mythmaking* (Baltimore, MD: Johns Hopkins University Press, 1984); Page DuBois, *Centaurs and Amazons: Women and the Pre-History of the Great Chain of Being* (Ann Arbor: University of Michigan Press, 1982); and Simon Shepherd, *Amazons and Warrior Women: Varieties of Feminism in Seventeenth-Century Drama* (Brighton: Harvester Press, 1981).
23 Priscilla Martin, *Chaucer's Women: Nuns, Wives, and Amazons* (London: Macmillan, 1990), 41.
24 Dianne Dugaw, *Warrior Women and Popular Balladry, 1650–1850* (Cambridge: Cambridge University Press, 1989), 1.
25 Dugaw, *Warrior Women*, 2.
26 Moore, "James Cameron."
27 The *Terminator* franchise comprises: *The Terminator* (1984); *Terminator 2: Judgment Day* (1991); *Terminator 3: Rise of the Machines* (2003); *Terminator Salvation* (2009); *Terminator Genisys* (2015); at the time of writing, a further Terminator film is projected for 2019.
28 Tricia Ennis, "James Cameron, Wonder Woman, and the Problem with Bad Feminist Allies," *SyfyWire*, 11 October 2017, http://syfy.com/syfywire/james-cameron-wonder-woman-and-the-problem-with-bad-feminist-allies.
29 Ennis, "James Cameron."

30 Cameron's suggestion that Connor's poor parenting makes her a feminist role model, while galling, is likely referring to the fact that she has a depth of human complexity, something that Wonder Woman does not have.
31 Ennis, "James Cameron."
32 *Terminator: The Sarah Connor Chronicles* (Warner Bros, 2008–2009).
33 *The New Adventures of Wonder Woman* (pilot movie 1974; series 1976–1979).
34 Michael Cavna, "A Look Back at Wonder Woman's Feminist (and Not-so-Feminist) History," *The Washington Post*, 26 May 2017, https://washingtonpost.com/news/comic-riffs/wp/2017/05/26/a-dive-into-wonder-womans-feminist-and-not-so-feminist-history/?noredirect=on&utm_term=.c864b36a31dd.
35 Ann Matsuuchi, "Wonder Woman Wears Pants: Wonder Woman, Feminism and the 1972 'Women's Lib' Issue," *Colloquy: Text Theory Critique* 24 (2012): 118–142.
36 Ennis, "James Cameron."
37 Noah Berlatsky, "James Cameron's Comments on Wonder Woman Completely Ignore Her History of Sex Appeal," *The Verge*, 25 August 2017, https://theverge.com/2017/8/25/16206496/james-cameron-wonder-woman-patty-jenkins-comics-sex-appeal.
38 Tim Hanley, *Wonder Woman Unbound: The Curious History of the World's Most Famous Heroine* (Chicago, IL: Chicago Review Press, 2014), 13.
39 Les Daniels, *Wonder Woman: The Complete History* (San Francisco, CA: Chronicle Books, 2000), 17.
40 William Mouton Marston, "Why 100,000,000 Americans Read Comics," *The American Scholar* 13, no. 1 (1943–1944): 35–44.
41 Although Cameron does not mention this, it is interesting to note that later actors who have played the part of Connor—Lena Headey and Emilia Clarke—undoubtedly gave their characters sexualised personas.
42 The character of Sameer in the 2017 film conspicuously says of Wonder Woman, after witnessing her fighting, "I am both frightened and aroused."
43 Susannah Breslin, "What James Cameron Gets Right About the 'Wonder Woman' Feminism Debate," *Forbes*, 26 August 2017, https://forbes.com/sites/susannahbreslin/2017/08/26/james-cameron-wonder-woman/#2ed816e240aa.
44 William Blake Tyrrell, *Amazons: A Study in Athenian Mythmaking* (Baltimore, MD: Johns Hopkins University Press, 1984), 40–44.
45 Zoe Williams, "Why Wonder Woman Is a Masterpiece of Subversive Feminism," *The Guardian*, 5 June 2017, https://theguardian.com/lifeandstyle/2017/jun/05/why-wonder-woman-is-a-masterpiece-of-subversive-feminism.

3 The King, the Sword, and the Stone
The Recent Afterlives of King Arthur

Sarah Gordon

Everything old is made new again in medieval-themed films, and nowhere is this adage as prevalent as in cinematic representations of the Arthurian legend. The Arthurian space has continued to grow over the centuries and across media. Hollywood's love affair with King Arthur needs no introduction here. The familiarity of the Arthurian legend, with its mythical characters, magical objects, and undying chivalric ethos, including King Arthur, Excalibur, the Knights of the Round Table, Merlin, Lancelot and Guenevere, and the Holy Grail, continues to feed our nostalgia for the Middle Ages.[1] Arthurian imagery often exposes audiences' particularly postmodern nostalgia for a past that never existed in history. The Arthurian legend has been told and re-told in different settings and time periods, even from its very beginnings in oral transmission and manuscript culture for medieval audiences—from the Roman occupation of Britain to the French twelfth-century Renaissance. This crossing of temporal, geographic, and generic borders has continued for centuries, in an ever-expanding corpus that still invites re-tellings adapted to new places and new times. Since the Middle Ages, the Arthurian legend has been steeped in authority and the possibility of truth. It can adapt to almost any ideology or cause with its universal themes, familiar story lines, enduring values, and archetypical characters and quests.[2] For audiences over the centuries—from manuscript culture to film pop culture—the question of Arthur being "real," with the narrative juxtaposition of the fictional and the historical, remains a compelling one.

All Arthurian literature and film is derivative. The unique nature and vast corpus of Arthurian literature (and other media) lends itself well to afterlives: medieval, early modern, and contemporary. Today, Arthur's character is so adaptable that we surprisingly see the future king reincarnated in recent films as a thieving urban gang member, or even embodied in a giggling high school girl through reincarnation.[3] This chapter explores how Arthurian material has endured for so long in so many different guises, focusing on the two very different re-writings of Arthurian origins in *King Arthur* (2004) and *King Arthur: Legend of the Sword* (2017)—films that scholars have not devoted proper attention to—in order to map the recent trajectory of this medieval material.

Many Arthurian films are hybrids, and are thus hard to define when it comes to genre. Most are characterised as in the fantasy drama category. Epic, action, comedy, historical (or even science fiction, thriller, and horror) all appear on Arthurian-themed official Motion Picture Association of America generic designation.[4] Directors from Steven Spielberg to Antoine Fuqua, and major studios from MGM to Disney, have all taken their turn in re-telling parts of the Arthurian saga. Storytelling itself appears as a motif in medieval narratives, often with Arthur waiting at a feast while news or a story of quests and adventures comes to court; such references to storytelling, or to knights living on through their fame, also appear in film.

Films featuring the eponymous medieval heroes, including Arthur and the Knights of the Round Table, Perceval, Gawain, Joan of Arc, Richard the Lionheart, Richard III, and Robin Hood, were popular from the 1950s to the 1980s in the USA, France, the UK, and beyond—Gorgievski's comprehensive study offers an overview of these earlier medievalist films.[5] The early 2000s saw significant resurgence in medieval and fantasy films in the USA and the UK, with Arthurian themes at the forefront. It becomes evident that the Arthurian material of the first two decades of the 2000s is primarily a postmodern pastiche, where often only familiar character names, place names, objects, and sometimes values, remain. The adaptable, formulaic, episodic, and familiar aspects of the King Arthur story make it one of the most enduring expressions of medievalism. Some of the aspects of Arthurian legend and literature that have been most repeated on screen are similar to those repeated in twentieth-century novels, but the two films discussed here concentrate more on Excalibur and Arthur's origin.

The wide range of Arthurian adaptations and their influence over the centuries are well known (Malory, Tennyson, Disney, Monty Python, and other well-known re-tellings have all left their mark).[6] Cinema lends itself particularly well to re-tellings of medieval romance and epic. In fact, Bettina Bildhauer explains that some current film theorists go so far as to see film as medieval in a sense, mostly because it is highly visual (like an illuminated manuscript or stained glass window), and liken the cinema to a cathedral.[7] There are over three-dozen full-length feature films that qualify as Arthurian.[8] It is not within the scope of this study (and has been attempted countless times) to make an exhaustive list of pop culture that contains medieval themes or Arthuriana (nor to delve into Arthurian allusions in the works of C.S. Lewis, Tolkien, or J.K. Rowling's *Harry Potter*), nor to trace the use or misuse of written source material or how closely any Arthurian stories were followed in screenplays.[9] This list grows longer every year.[10] However, some current trends in medievalist cinema emerge in this exploration of two recent films.

Episodic or cyclical literature is perhaps nowhere as prevalent as in the Arthurian corpus. The corpus includes the thirteenth- and fourteenth-century *Prose Lancelot*, *Prose Merlin*, and *Lancelot-Grail Cycle*, and the twelfth-century French Arthurian verse romances of Chrétien de Troyes; other popular medieval traditions, such as the *Roman de Renart* beast fables, were episodic as well. The preference for episodic or cyclical narratives in the medieval period stoked the fire of ever-growing popularity of insular and continental Arthurian material in literature and art. This phenomenon finds a near equivalent in modern-day film, in both large franchises and remakes. In the late twentieth-century and early twenty-first century, there was a resurgence of the tendency for episodic and formulaic storytelling in cinema, and episodes, sequels, and prequels again became a popular form of narrative: for example in Lucasfilm's *Star Wars* franchise, which spans decades, or in the online streaming partnership of Marvel Comics and Netflix, made popular by the practice of 'binge-watching.' To draw an (albeit anachronistic) comparison, medieval audiences of Arthurian romances and today's audiences of the *Star Wars* franchise, or Marvel super heroes franchise television series, expect to see familiar heroes and heroines in familiar settings, and the connection to a well-known fictional universe, its characters, repeated motifs, formulaic approach, and established ethos makes the Arthurian legend an enduring fictional force.

In each medium and genre, from early Celtic oral tradition to continental manuscript culture to print, to film and television and beyond, the story of Arthur, the sword, and the stone retains a revered status in our collective memory of medieval lore. In the Middle Ages, and particularly in Arthurian literature, originality was not as prized as authority and familiarity. Medieval manuscript culture was by nature fluid and variable, with each scribe and written version adding, changing, making (or correcting) errors, modifying, translating, or interpolating new material. As a character, Arthur is malleable, and as a legend, Arthurian material can be reformed into new stories, re-tellings, even media into the ever-growing corpus—seemingly endless repetition with variation. Thus, medieval storytelling was by its nature episodic, involving sequels, prequels, and what would be called today in the film, television, or comic book industries spin-offs, crossovers, and reboots in an endless stream of re-tellings and re-imaginings. Medieval romance was indeed highly formulaic, filled with recurring tropes and motifs and well-known characters. Audiences of medieval romance would have appreciated well-trodden ground and familiar patterns—the equivalent phenomenon today to knights with well-known quests, tourneys, and trysts would be perhaps the James Bond films or other highly formulaic franchises that play on audience familiarity and answer to audience expectations with regards to his missions, love affairs, gadgets, villains, and so on. Both film studies and adaptation studies have recently explored the phenomena of reboots and remakes.[11] This trend, especially in film and television, is a clear mirror of the way that medieval adaptations tend to value authority and (trope-like) familiarity over originality.

A measure of chivalry and courtly behaviour, the Arthurian court, wherever it may be located (often Camelot), has long acted as a benchmark of norms and expectations and a site of disruption and questioning of authority. Each story is a reflection of societal *moeurs* or political concerns of the time in which it is composed. Arthur does not always appear as the main character, as other characters and stories are drawn into the fictional universe with the authority and familiarity of the Arthurian name. Medieval romance, epic, and other genres were also highly formulaic, filled with repeating patterns and recurring motifs, tied together by the Arthurian court, the Round Table, or just Arthur's name as a unifying device. Norris J. Lacy was the first to tackle the question of, why so many (bad) Arthurian films continue to be made in the twentieth century in Hollywood and beyond. Lacy's answer was

> The same films may also be an example of their makers' apparent belief that the very name King Arthur will bring in the trade. But that attitude is anything but new: medieval romancers too understood that they could often turn a respectable non-Arthurian romance into a "best-seller" by inserting an Arthurian episode or by simply having the hero stop off at Arthur's court.[12]

Indeed, the King Arthur name sells, along with the blood and gore, noble quests, sword fights, and love triangles the name continues to imply. Characters, quests, places, objects all become attached to the central figure of Arthur, the Arthurian court and place names, and the Arthurian name today, just as they did by medieval authors and scribes. Camelot and the Round Table become a central place, and Arthur a central figure for other characters to rally around, providing structure and renown for later additions to the story or for later movie reboots (as they are commonly called in the film industry). Early swashbuckling action dramas, *film de cape et d'épée* films of the 1950s to the early 1970s, spotlighted action sequences and lavish costumes rather than the social themes raised in 2000s medievalist film, as seen in the two analysed later.[13] The Arthurian name—and be it Arthurian in name only—and the medieval images it conjures up are what matter in a twenty-first-century film adaptation. As seen in the following, it does not matter which era of castle serves as the set, which swords are swung in the choreographed battle scenes, or which cause the knights are said to be fighting for, for the Arthurian story to be made new again for new audiences.

King Arthur (2004)

African-American director Antoine Fuqua's *King Arthur* (2004) focuses on the quasi-historical Roman connections of the early Arthurian myth, and re-writes only a hint of the beginning of the

Arthur-Guenevere-Lancelot love triangle. The film's tagline implies truth, claiming it is "The Untold True Story that Inspired the Legend." Moreover, printed promotional materials and previews—in an appeal to authority that parallels a commonplace for medieval authors as well— make a bogus reference to a poem falsely attributed to sixth-century poet Taliesin:

> Let me sing with inspiration
> Of the man born of two nations,
> Of Rome and of Britain
> ... Arthur the blessed
> Led his assault from the Great Wall.

This poem is of course falsified, but it underlines the need for the quasi-historical feel as a quintessential aspect of most Arthurian adaptations. The film thus pretends to make (fake) literary and historic references to lend credibility to the legend, as authors of Arthurian literature in the Middle Ages would have made themselves (for example, Geoffrey of Monmouth, Chrétien de Troyes, and Thomas Malory all refer to prior textual sources, whether real or imaginary).[14]

King Arthur is an action-packed, bellicose imagining of a possible Arthurian Roman connection by a director known mostly for the quality of his action sequences. Fuqua is also known for socially conscious messages in his filmmaking. For instance, in his long career, he has treated themes from racism, crime, and law enforcement ethics in *Training Day* (2001), to social justice, poverty, and inequality in his remake of the western *The Magnificent Seven* (2016). These social themes also appear in *King Arthur*, where the Arthurian *mythos* provides a perfect platform for a narrative of defending the oppressed. In an interview, Fuqua explained he did not want to be limited to the contemporary urban subjects of his first films, and says of his own race-blind filmmaking, "In the process of making movies, I think that's my statement: color doesn't matter when it comes to storytelling."[15]

The sets of Stonehenge and Hadrian's Wall act as solid emblems of the anachronistic medievalism of this film, which picks and chooses from a patchwork of references to Roman Britain, Arthurian literature, and allusions to the 'Dark' Ages. They lend a sense of place (that never existed as such) and a nostalgic sense of the past (that never existed) in this postmodern rewrite. These sites also make reference to a multicultural past in Britain. This is an early King Arthur, based ostensibly on the earliest written texts to mention his name. Fuqua consulted with Arthurian specialist John Matthews on some of the historically and textually based aspects of the film. The film claims to be true, and leans on its verisimilitude, with references and historical imagery throughout. It begins in England circa 425 CE, with Arthurian knights in Roman military service.

Arthur, here called Artorios Castus, is described as part Sarmatian, part Roman, without the typical Celtic or English backgrounds typically given to him in most literary and cinematic adaptations. It is not difficult to find that Arthur is not only Sarmatian and Roman, but also somewhat American in his characterisation.

The film is one of the first Arthurian cinematic reinterpretations to foreground cultural and religious diversity. Arthur is a Christian, but his knights are not: they are pagans from around the Empire, from Celts to Sarmatia, with the knights' origins being in the East. Identity and diversity in the Arthurian canon are called into question in this film's approach. Arthur and the others show a tolerance for pagans and non-Christian cultures. In this film, there is no reference to the Holy Grail, and no allusion to any love triangle with Lancelot and Guenevere. Rather, in this mostly non-canonical story, after surviving several years of military conscription, just as the Roman occupying force is leaving Britain and the Saxons are arriving, the knights are sent on one last mission, to rescue the Pope's godson from enemy territory and barbarians. The Round Table appears but is also anachronistically, and quite comically, taken for a dance floor at first, before the concepts of unity, solidarity, and community come into focus. Familiar characters from elsewhere in the Arthurian canon (particularly from Malory and the English tradition) include Bors, Dagonet, Galahad, Gawain, Lancelot, and Tristan. They all appear with the same age and status, contrary to past centuries' re-tellings. The film ends with the saving of the Britons, and the wedding of Arthur and Guenevere. What is completely non-canonical is a rescue mission of the Pope's godson from the barbarians north of Hadrian's Wall, and the knights' desire for a return to a homeland in the Balkans.

As in the later Guy Ritchie *Arthur* film, here diversity is in the spotlight, with the multiculturalism and multilingualism of the Arthurian knights and Romans. This is a film with shades of postcolonialism, as it offers a contemporary take on a crumbling ancient empire and its relation to former occupied indigenous peoples. For example, Arthur and his companions are a multi-ethnic group, which Fuqua imagines as an elite unit of Sarmatian cavalry that was drafted from the eastern reaches of the empire and brought through Rome, to be sent to Britain as the Saxons arrive.[16] The film takes a sympathetic view of the indigenous peoples occupied by the Romans, particularly those living in what would become Britain, here embodied as the Woads (a made-up tribe of Britons), who are pagans (with references to a Druid-like religion) led by Merlin and represented by a young combatant named Guenevere. Arthur is shown as following Catholicism and Pelagianism. The Picts are represented as indigenous freedom fighters or insurgents, fighting against both the Romans and the Saxons. The film questions Rome's motivations and effectiveness in defending its colony against the invading barbarians. Incidentally, elements in this film, such as postcolonial imagery and multicultural themes, are, in turn, echoed later in HBO's *Rome* television series (2005–2007), popular in the same decade and sharing much of the same contemporary, action-packed portrayals of the end of Roman hegemony. In addition, questions are raised about xenophobia in religious institutions, through the Christian zealots in Britain shown enacting a violent sort of Inquisition aimed at forceful conversion of indigenous Pagans. The commentary on hegemony or religious fanaticism suggested by this film might have resonated with modern audiences.

This film makes use of a strong female lead, with Keira Knightley in the role of Guenevere, who fights back with arrows and with her powerful dialogue, and is anything but a damsel in distress or mere pretty face as in previous Hollywood incarnations. This characterisation of Guenevere plays upon Knightley's own intertext: at the time of *King Arthur*'s release she was known primarily for the roles of Jules Paxton (in *Bend in like Beckham*, 2002) and Elizabeth Swann (in the *Pirates of the Caribbean: The Curse of the Black Pearl*, 2003), both of which can also be described as strong female characters. This leads to a good amount of anachronistic banter, as when Lancelot cautions Guenevere as the warriors line up for battle with the invading Saxon army, warning, "There are a lot of lonely men over there," and she quips, "Don't worry. I won't let them rape you." Fuqua thus rewrites Arthurian gender roles, and the warrior-queen version of Guenevere dominates the second half of the film. Ideology, culture, religion, and gender are therefore all at play on Fuqua's unique battlefield.

The film was produced by action-film producer Jerry Bruckheimer of *Armageddon* (1998) and *Black Hawk Down* (2001), and *King Arthur* includes characteristically bloody battle scenes and acts of military heroism; the producer also had a hand in the editing. Arthurian scholar Kevin Harty attributes this portrayal of Arthur to the contemporary phenomenon that there are "no real heroes left" in 2004 cinema.[17] Anti-heroes with obvious flaws, moral ambiguity, or less than glamorous origins were becoming popular in the early 2000s through around 2010, appearing in media from television sitcoms to 'rom-coms' and action films. Instead of a more traditional historical or medieval action film, we have an anti-hero in a film that makes a stated attempt at historical realism. The Battle of Mount Badon is a lengthy action scene, re-enacting a brief textual allusion to the supposed historical Arthur in this tragic battle, in some of the first medieval texts to mention his name. The battle takes place on a frozen lake, perhaps a veiled reference to the Lady of the Lake and other Otherworld water imagery in medieval or medievalist Arthurian literature and art. Visually and thematically, this battle sets itself apart from any other Arthurian film battle. In this version, he is victorious and the Woads declare him their king—King of the Britons—and he is married to Guenevere. The Roman context and the concept of unifying barbarian Britain after the Roman occupation are Fuqua's focus, and this is because in part (as in Ritchie's 2017 film), leadership, public duty, and personal ambition are central themes. Leadership in this film is portrayed as an outsider helping not only to protect the Britons from another invasion, but also to help shepherd them into a new era and new form of unified government for a diverse indigenous and immigrant population.

In considering these recent re-tellings, it is clear that Arthurian material remains an enduring mythos adaptable to contemporary social concerns and individual creative choices. Why is the Arthurian legend so enduring? The elusive answer is in part because it is so adaptable. Haydock studies what he terms "the medieval imaginary," and explains this through a more psychoanalytical or affective lens, deeming that the Arthurian myth is "capable of embodying almost any desire."[18] Here, the desire is to tell a heroic story of freedom, and of liberation of the oppressed or benevolent imperialism. Alternatively, it could be calling into question these very notions in the twenty-first century.

As in medieval times, it is the re-telling and the familiarity of a story that counts, not the originality nor strict copying of previous tales; *King Arthur* is a postmodern patchwork of allusions to past texts, real or imagined, and draws on a collective memory of Arthurian legend, however vague it may be in the minds of the viewers. The film is infused with allusions to what was happening in Iraq (similarly to themes present in Ridley Scott's powerful 2005 film *Kingdom of Heaven*, which raised questions about US involvement in Iraq through the lens of the Crusades).[19] In addition, parallels to American imperialism are drawn by the Fuqua himself and by film critics, with the themes of liberation, occupation, and freedom being fairly obvious to modern-day spectators. There is a torture scene in a Roman torture chamber, as well as a scene about occupation, that mirrors the contemporary US conflict in Iraq in 2004. Even American foreign policy and military action (from Vietnam to Iraq) are echoed in the battle monologues of the Sarmatian-Roman mercenaries and their disillusionment with the government that sent them to fight. It is clear that they have little support from home in their mission to advance Rome's imperialism. Fuqua's representation of liberation and occupation is thus relevant, nuanced, and critical.

Freedom is a (particularly modern-day American) value that is key to the whole film.[20] Freedom was of course not explicitly addressed in works by Chrétien de Troyes, Malory, or other medieval Arthurian romances. This reverence for freedom, for liberation of the oppressed, and the dialogue devoted to liberty as a motivation for battle instead are in part what makes this a uniquely American, uniquely early 2000s vision of the Arthurian myth. As a leader from another culture, Arthur also calls into question the nature of Roman occupation and imperialism, in monologues about the freedom of his men that criticise Rome:

> For two hundred years knights had fought and died for a land not their own, but on that day on Badon Hill all who fought put their lives in service of a greater cause: freedom.

King Arthur also recalls previous American cinematic re-tellings of history and legend through creative fiction, such as the earlier quasi-historical drama *Braveheart* (1995), which resounds with the cry of "Freedom!" and deals with twentieth-century themes of imperialism, torture, and occupation in the thirteenth-century context of legendary hero William Wallace. It is interesting that *King Arthur*'s tag lines and the film's goals are to be 'true,' realistic, and historical in a story based on fiction and legend with only some quasi-historical references on which to base a screenplay. The final scene of the film makes reference to the continued narrative that is so characteristic of most Arthurian material, as Lancelot explains that the fallen knights will live on in future generations of storytelling.

King Arthur: Legend of the Sword (2017)

British director Guy Ritchie offers the most recent revision of the Arthurian story. The 2004 and 2017 Arthur movies endeavour to achieve a gritty, edgy, 'real-world' feel.[21] Strikingly, however medieval(ish) the costumes and weapons may be, the social issues and dialogue are the 'real-world' of 2017, rather than of any historic past. Both the 2004 and 2017 films have some echoes of their contemporary world—the 2017 version even more so. As Arthurian material has done for centuries, this re-telling grapples with today's issues, namely social inequalities; notably, classism and racism are addressed. Arthurian literature and film has long been a vehicle for social and political commentary.[22] It is the socio-cultural diversity in the landscape of this film that stands out from previous centuries of re-tellings. The 2017 version of the Arthurian legend was written within the context of the popularity of action-packed soap opera like fantasy medieval television such as *Game of Thrones* (2011–present) or *Vikings* (2013–present). The mix of ultra-violence in action sequences and soap-opera story arcs popularised by these series is echoed in this film.

"From Nothing Comes a King" was the concept behind the film, and this was used as the tagline on the movie poster and advertising that appeared notably on bus stops in poor urban areas in Los Angeles County and elsewhere. This rags-to-riches aspect of the Arthurian legend is exaggerated, playing on twenty-first-century concerns of classism and racism through a postmodern patchwork of vague references to Arthurian material. Cultural diversity, gender, age, and social class are all expressed in new ways in this film that calls into question both contemporary and medieval notions of identity. It disrupts audience expectations of traditional power relations and gender roles or class divisions. In doing so, the film makes a meta-commentary, and suggests how Arthurian re-tellings over time have been uniquely placed both within and without a canonical tradition, allowing them to either reinforce audience expectations or challenge dominant ideologies. Ritchie conveys an Everyman narrative of social mobility and the on-going struggle for equality.

King Arthur: Legend of the Sword (2017) is an action film that inscribes itself into an urban environment with a population that is culturally and socio-economically diverse. It departs from its titular Excalibur myth and makes itself relevant to today's audiences as it presents issues that face urban youth today, with images of poverty, crime (including theft, human trafficking, and fraud), and racism, within a medieval setting. Excalibur remains emblematic of the Arthurian tradition, but is a different symbol when wielded by the hands of British director Guy Ritchie—it becomes a symbol of the struggle of impoverished urban youth. In this latest iteration, the film makes a very different move, in that it removes most of the familiar elements that made the Arthurian material so popular through the centuries in the first place. This is a story of troubled urban youth; it is about rising up. Ritchie focuses on Arthur's origins, re-inscribing him into the harsh world of the streets, with clever young pickpockets in the marketplace and criminals running rampant. The film offers an alternative childhood story, playing on past traditions in which Arthur was a foster child and shows him raised by prostitutes, scrounging for food and saving up money he has earned through pandering and petty theft. The would-be king associates with a group of urban youths that is something akin to a gang today, and practices martial arts with a local Asian master in a neighbourhood dojo. Here, Guy Ritchie's postmodern pastiche of different cultures and time periods seems to be playing both with popular super hero origin stories (such as those popularised by recent Marvel franchises and television series) and with the gritty, edgy television medievalism of *Game of Thrones* or *Vikings*. This is a wily, self-made 2000s version of the young Arthur. Actor Charlie Hunnam (who played Arthur) explains the director's vision, saying Arthur

> has always been rendered as the noble man who goes on the noble journey to become the noble king ... But Ritchie had another take: he said, let's do the opposite. Let's make him ignoble and selfish with a heart of gold, but just a bit more rough around the edges.[23]

This is a cinematic Anglo-American Arthur who is a business-savvy entrepreneur, rather than a literary medieval nobleman. As an adolescent,

Arthur lives the life of a growing outlaw, almost more suggestive of a Robin Hood figure than any medieval or modern depiction of Arthur, as he steals food to help other street children. In a sense, this re-telling is all about community, but in a very different way from its medieval and early modern written tales. Cultural and socio-economic diversity are shown in the sets of the dirty streets of Londinium, showing poverty in the market place and Arthur's world as a rich fabric of diverse cultures, from European to Arab to Asian. Class consciousness is a mark of this production, more so than in some other twentieth-century medieval fantasy films, in part because it is a complete reimagining of the social context of the Arthurian origin myth.[24] The film develops the theme of the supposed young commoner who reveals his royal birth right. Diversity in the cast is also notable in this film, in particular with Beninese actor Djimon Hounsou in the supporting role of Arthur's companion Sir Bedivere (with even more diversity in the cast and extras than in Fuqua's 2004 film). The film also has a fresh take on gender in the Arthurian world, with a woman in the role of a wise mage. In this 2017 re-telling, we see that the names of central characters (Lancelot, Merlin, and Bedivere) and elements of the Excalibur origins story, as well as the values of justice, duty, honour, and loyalty, remain part of the Arthurian material, but audiences are exposed to a completely new sense of place and new story. As an origin story (similar to a superhero's origin story) intended to have the potential for sequels, this re-telling focuses on the origins and rise of King Arthur and does not deal with later material, such as the Lancelot/Guenevere relationship and the downfall of Arthur.

In multiple interviews, director Guy Ritchie credits his interest in the Arthurian story to seeing the knights in shining armour in the almost 'campy' Boorman's *Excalibur* (1981) as a youth. Hunnam also credits this film as a childhood inspiration. The screenplay is very loosely based on Arthurian material, both literary and cinematic. As a child, Arthur escapes the tyranny of his uncle Vortigern, who assassinates his parents and plans to execute him as heir to the throne. The young child Arthur escapes in a boat, perhaps an echo of the dead Arthur being sent by boat to the mythical island of Avalon, or a biblical allusion to the baby Moses. In a new imagining of how the sword Excalibur came to be lodged in the stone, as the uncle murders his father in front of his eyes, his father kneels and is killed with his own sword lodged in his back. Arthur is found by a group of prostitutes who raise him in their brothel, a new take on Arthur being a foster child raised by his relative Kay's family in Malory's *Morte D'Arthur*, or later adaptations. Later, Arthur is able to retrieve the magical sword from the stone, proving his royal lineage. As king, he institutes the equality of the Round Table and brokers a trade deal and unity with the Vikings. Ultimately, the film calls into question the nature/nurture dichotomy portrayed in so much of the medieval and early modern Arthurian tradition, showing that lineage and social class do not make the man, or the king.

Arthur is shown as upholding law and order, but within the context of organised crime and outlaws in his urban community. Renegade youth or organised crime boss, pimp, gambler, and thief, this is an unconventional medieval Arthur but a conventional modern Guy Ritchie gangster. *The Guardian* review calls this Arthur "a gonzo monarch, a death-metal warrior-king."[25] Countless online film critics have deemed Ritchie's Arthur a "bad boy." This new image for Arthur is magnified by the heavy metal music that defines the contemporary tone of the film. Arthur stops men from beating the prostitutes in the brothel where he lives. Arthurian values, such as fighting on the side of the weak, are echoed from medieval traditions but are given a new context. Values that are added from the twenty-first-century context are social mobility and resourcefulness. The dialogue is comic, sarcastic, and often tongue-in-cheek, and it pokes fun at the older versions of Arthur as a nobleman fulfilling an aristocratic destiny. Director Guy Ritchie, who is also one of the screenplay writers of *King Arthur*, is known for London crime dramas and comedies, full of action scenes and witty banter with dialogue between a group of criminals—such as in *Lock, Stock, and Two Smoking Barrels* (1998), *Snatch* (2000), *Revolver* (2005), *RocknRolla* (2008), and *Sherlock Holmes* (2009) and its sequel *Sherlock Holmes: A Game of Shadows* (2011)—and he has adapted a medieval story to this kind of storytelling, with light-hearted echoes of the contemporary London crime world in his other films. Now that the 'reboot' phenomenon is so popular in the film industry it is no wonder that Ritchie chose to start the possible beginnings of an Arthurian franchise. Thematically similar, revenge, social justice, individual integrity, individual recognition, and social mobility are present as central themes throughout Ritchie's films, and gritty characters and edgy scenes on the dirty streets of London feature in almost all his films. The story of the sword and the stone, with the unsuspecting youth proving himself worthy to be king, is once again ripe as a social commentary of upward mobility. These themes are all present in medieval Arthurian romance. The postmodern sense of place and time created by Ritchie and the dirty sets of Londinium also reveals parallels with the seedy underbelly of contemporary London shown in Ritchie's crime films, before turning to the action of the CGI battlefield. The pastiche not only recalls the modern London crime films and the director's own nostalgic Sherlock Holmes adaptations, but also perhaps reflects some other contemporary visual, verbal, and thematic elements of the popular and recent *Game of Thrones* and *Vikings* television series, including costuming and action sequences, along with more contemporary music and anachronistic dialogue. Ritchie's Sherlock Holmes and his Arthur are both gritty, flawed, national British heroes, both exhibiting integrity, ambition, and an over-developed sense of social justice.

Here again, Arthur is a creature of his time, and his sword, the tool of social justice.

Ritchie has modernised part of the Arthurian legend; by doing so he has 'medievalised' a modern rags-to-riches story. Once again, as in medieval romances, the name alone of Arthur and the powerful image of the sword Excalibur were enough to provide a familiar name and familiar frame and context. There is even a cameo appearance by the director himself, underlining once again that Ritchie has put his stamp on the Arthurian legend (just as we hear the voice of Malory or others in older Arthurian literature). As usual, this Arthurian rewriting is a reflection of the present moment, and here a reflection of the cultural forces at work in the film industry, and an echo of ongoing dialogue about Anglo-American social problems in 2017. In an interview, Hunman claimed, "the themes and issues of King Arthur feel very relevant."[26] The film may be viewed as an attempt to revive a national myth for Britain or as a reflection of recent growing expressions of nationalism in the UK and the USA; however, though it might be tempting for current audiences to reinterpret it in light of Brexit or even Trumpism,[27] in the aforementioned interview, Hunnam reminds us that the film was shot in 2016, prior to the Brexit referendum, the UK General Election, and the US elections that year.

This 2017 film was pitched as a reboot with a potential for money-making sequels. William Proctor defines the difference between a reboot and a remake as follows:

> a reboot attempts to forge a *series* of films, to begin a franchise anew from the ashes of an old or failed property. In other words, a remake is a reinterpretation of *one* film; a reboot 're-starts' a *series* of films that seek to disavow and render inert its predecessor's validity.[28]

However, due to the film's extremely poor showing at the global box office, it is unlikely that a series of sequels to this *King Arthur* film will be made. Many well-known Arthurian characters were intentionally left out of this film since it was initially intended to restart a potential Arthurian series: Merlin, for example, would have appeared in a planned sequel. The Arthurian legend has proven rebootable for over 1,300 years, with varying success among audiences. This most recent film turned out to be a box office flop (with some success in on-demand and streaming outlets), and perhaps this attempt to recast the Arthurian legend in a more contemporary light went too far; or, it may have failed with cinema-goers for other reasons.

Medievalism in filmmaking is a tool for unpacking meaning in both the past and the present.[29] With directors Fuqua and Ritchie, it becomes clear that it does not matter if each element of the story is true or not, because the story is valuable for both entertainment and socio-political commentary. The Arthurian name (be it Arthurian in name only) and the medieval images it conjures up are what matters in a twenty-first-century film adaptations. It does not matter which kind of castles are used for the set, which swords are swung in the battle scenes, or which cause the knights are said to be fighting for. Just like authors of medieval romance, film producers know that it is easier to sell stories that are already very familiar to a nostalgic public. Because the Arthurian story is already so well known and mined for storytelling, it becomes a solid platform on which the film industry may pile on the social issues of today. Again, the Arthurian legend has proved enduring and adaptable across temporal, geographic, generic—and cultural—borders for hundreds of years, and lends itself especially well to re-tellings within today's globalised environment. Socio-economic diversity and multiculturalism—especially in the most recent film *King Arthur: Legend of the Sword* as it completely re-writes Arthurian material and includes a multiracial cast and a class-inflected narrative—are now at the heart of Arthurian adaptations. The adaptable nature of Arthurian narrative continues to invite reboots for new contexts. Arthurian themes thus promise to remain material for once and future filmmakers to adapt to the present moment.

Notes

1 Pam Cook's work explores notions of nostalgic imagery in historical film or films with historical settings or biblical allusions, from westerns to melodramas: Pam Cook, *Screening the Past: Memory and Nostalgia in Cinema* (London: Routledge, 1995). Some more recent films even mock nostalgic audiences and the very nature of nostalgia for a time that never existed, such as in the recent independent comedy *Don Verdean* (2015), which is about a struggling charlatan biblical archaeologist pretending to find the Holy Grail for a wealthy client in the desert of Utah.
2 Many decades of medievalist films with political themes have been investigated in Andrew Johnston, Margitta Rouse, and Philipp Hinz, eds., *The Medieval Motion Picture: The Politics of Adaptation* (New York: Palgrave Macmillan, 2014).
3 This is the unique gender-bending, time-warping concept behind the television movie for the young adult audience, *Avalon High* (2010), directed by Stuart Gillard for the Disney Channel. For an exploration of older Disney medievalist productions, see Tison Pugh and Susan Aronstein, *The Disney Middle Ages: A Fairy-Tale and Fantasy Past* (New York: Palgrave Macmillan, 2012). *A Kid in King Arthur's Court* (1995) is another Arthurian film that is an adaptation for, and stars, children.
4 Hans Jürgen Scheuer, "Arthurian Myth and Cinematic Horror: M. Night Shyamalan's *The Sixth Sense*," in *The Medieval Motion Picture: The Politics of Adaptation*, ed. Andrew Johnston, Margitta Rouse, and Philipp Hinz (New York: Palgrave Macmillan, 2014), 171–191.
5 Sandra Gorgievski, *Le mythe d'Arthur: de l'imaginaire médiéval à la culture de masse: paralittérature, bande dessinée, cinéma, beaux-arts* (Paris: CEFAL, 2002). Gorgievski discusses earlier Arthurian film within the context of these medievalist movies, and also demonstrates the *Star Wars*

franchise's parallels with medieval and Arthurian characters and themes (49–50). Others have investigated Arthurian motifs in *Star Wars*, notably, Angela Weisl, *The Persistence of Medievalism: Narrative Adventures in Public Discourse* (New York: Palgrave Macmillan, 2003), 183–208. For a filmography of medievalist films up to 1999, see David John Williams, "Medieval Movies: A Filmography," *Film & History* 29, nos. 1–2 (1999): 20–32.

6 Thomas Malory, *Le Morte d'Arthur* (1485); Alfred Tennyson, "The Lady of Shalott" (1832), and *Idylls of the King* (1859); *The Sword in the Stone* (1963); *Monty Python and the Holy Grail* (1975).

7 Bettina Bildhauer, "Medievalism and Cinema," in *The Cambridge Companion to Medievalism*, ed. Louise D'Arcens (Cambridge: Cambridge University Press, 2016), 58.

8 Derek Pearsall provides an overview of major Arthurian films released prior to those analysed here: Derek Pearsall, *Arthurian Romance: A Short Introduction* (Malden, MA: Blackwell, 2003), 161–163. Similarly, Susan Aronstein explores Arthurian films over several decades: Susan Aronstein, *Hollywood Knights: Arthurian Cinema and the Politics of Nostalgia* (New York: Palgrave Macmillan, 2005).

9 Beatrice Groves, *Literary Allusion in Harry Potter* (London: Routledge, 2017), 38–50.

10 See, for example, the ever-expanding *Wikipedia* page, "List of works based on Arthurian legends": https://en.wikipedia.org/wiki/List_of_works_based_on_Arthurian_legends.

11 See: Constance Verevis, "Remakes, Sequels, Prequels," in *The Oxford Handbook of Adaptation Studies*, ed. Thomas Leitch (Oxford: Oxford University Press, 2017), 267–284; and Amanda Ann Klein and R. Barton Palmer, eds., *Cycles, Sequels, Spin-offs, Remakes, and Reboots: Multiplicities in Film and Television* (Austin: University of Texas Press, 2016).

12 Norris J. Lacy, "Arthurian Film and the Tyranny of Tradition," *Arthurian Interpretations* 4, no. 1 (1989): 75.

13 For example, later Hollywood blockbusters, such as *Beowulf* (2007) and *Robin Hood* (2010), were released during this same big-budget, major studio-distributed, medievalist action-fantasy vogue that called into question medieval and contemporary social inequalities. Needless to say, *Monty Python and the Holy Grail* (1975) (and its much later, successful Broadway theatre production of *Spamalot* [2005]) surprisingly follows a number of medieval sources closer than the recent films of the 2000s in its humorous and satirical take on the legends, which also briefly touches on social issues, such as through the Marxist peasant in the film who decries "the violence inherent in the system." Countless scholarly articles and popular reviews have provided interpretations of *Monty Python and the Holy Grail*, and more than one scholar has seen the Monty Python film as part of a larger trend of irony in Arthurian films: Raymond H. Thompson, "The Ironic Tradition in Four Arthurian Films," in *Cinema Arthuriana: Twenty Essay*, ed. Kevin J. Harty, rev. ed. (Jefferson, NC: McFarland, 2002), 110–117.

14 Geoffrey of Monmouth, *Historia Regum Britanniae* (History of the Kings of Britain) (c.1136); Chrétien de Troyes, *Yvain, the Knight of the Lion* (c.1170); and Malory, *Le Morte d'Arthur* (1485).

15 "Antoine Fuqua Fights for Self-Expression," *Today*, 22 March 2007, https://today.com/popculture/antoine-fuqua-fights-self-expression-wbna17742194.

16 Leslie Coote has also explored this pseudo-historical representation of Arthur as Sarmatian: Leslie Coote, "Brief Encounters: Arthur's Epic Journey in Antoine Fuqua's *King Arthur*," in *Medieval Afterlives in Popular Culture*,

ed. Gail Ashton and Daniel Kline (New York: Palgrave Macmillan, 2012), 159–172.
17 Kevin Harty, "*King Arthur*, Directed by Antoine Fuqua, Review," *Arthuriana* 14, no. 3 (2004): 121.
18 Nickolas Haydock, *Movie Medievalism: The Imaginary Middle Ages* (Jefferson, NC: McFarland, 2008), 165.
19 In his review of the film, critic Roger Ebert observes that Fuqua "tells a story with uncanny parallels to current events in Iraq." "King Arthur," *RogerEbert.com*, https://rogerebert.com/reviews/king-arthur-2004.
20 Aronstein also sees the film as very American, with a very Hollywood happy ending: Aronstein, *Hollywood Knights*, 211–212.
21 Somewhat similarly, *Kaamelot* is a French satirical television sitcom (2005–2009), in which Arthurian knights are not perfect, their own failings are the subject of humour, and the seven deadly sins, incompetence, and personality flaws prevent most quests of the Round Table from being achieved in each short episode. This series exhibited the early 2000s trend of the realistic, gritty Arthurian retelling that makes some attempt at historical accuracy, which, while taking place in the fifth century, still grappled with contemporary social issues.
22 Martin Shichtman and James Carley, eds., *Culture and the King: The Social Implications of the Arthurian Legend* (Albany: State University of New York Press, 1994). Finke and Shichtman's more recent volume also suggests throughout that there is a political and socio-cultural context to the cinematic production of medievalist films and that such films play into our own cultural fantasies of our own time: Laurie Finke and Martin Shichtman, eds., *Cinematic Illuminations: The Middle Ages on Film* (Baltimore, MD: Johns Hopkins University Press, 2009).
23 Andrea Mandell, "How Charlie Hunnam Horrified Guy Ritchie in the Early Days of *King Arthur*," *USA Today*, 12 April 2017, https://usatoday.com/story/life/movies/2017/04/12/how-charlie-hunnam-horrified-guy-ritchie-early-days-king-arthur/100339312/.
24 Issues of multiculturalism, social class, identity, gender roles, and even the status of animals have been explored in other medievalist films across the essays in: Lynn T. Ramey and Tison Pugh, eds., *Race, Class, and Gender in "Medieval" Cinema* (New York: Palgrave Macmillan, 2007).
25 Peter Bradshaw, "*King Arthur: Legend of the Sword* Review, Guy Ritchie's Cheerful Den of Medieval Dodginess," *The Guardian*, 9 May 2017, https://theguardian.com/film/2017/may/09/king-arthur-the-legend-of-the-sword-review-guy-ritchies-den-of-medieval-dodginess.
26 Adrian Lobb, "Interview with Charlie Hunnam," *The Big Issue*, 22 May 2017, https://bigissue.com/interviews/charlie-hunnam-themes-issues-king-arthur-feel-relevant/.
27 See, for example, Alissa Wilkson's review in *Vox*: "King Arthur: Legend of the Sword is surprisingly good, and surprisingly political," *Vox*, 11 May 2017, https://vox.com/culture/2017/5/11/15508278/king-arthur-review-charlie-hunnam-guy-ritchie-jude-law.
28 William Proctor, "Regeneration and Rebirth: Anatomy of the Franchise Reboot," *Scope: An Online Journal of Film and Television Studies* 22 (2012): 4.
29 See Anke Bernau and Bettina Bildhauer, eds., *Medieval Film* (Manchester: Manchester University Press, 2009).

4 Brand Chaucer
The Poet and the Nation

Martin Laidlaw[1]

The practice of appropriating the writings and characters of English canonical writers towards contemporary socio-political commentary has a well-established tradition in the works of adaptation. Shakespeare, in particular, has proven an effective vehicle for such analysis, with Orson Welles's 1937 Broadway stage adaptation of *Julius Caesar, Caesar*, being a stark example. Employing 'modern' dress and an aesthetic evocative of Fascist Germany, this production at the Mercury Theatre was heralded as a masterpiece in theatrical adaptation.[2] The work of Shakespeare's contemporaries has been employed towards similar commentary, something which can be seen in Derek Jarman's 1991 film adaptation of Christopher Marlowe's *Edward the Second*, which, through the transformation of Edward's forces to an army focused on gay rights, casts light on homophobic policy of the British government, particularly Section 28.[3] Traditionally, medieval writers have not, however, enjoyed such a varied system of adaptation and appropriation, although the last decade has seen a stage adaptation of *Piers Plowman*, called *Fair Field* (2017), which focused on poor relief and charity,[4] and *Marge and Jules* (2015)—a dramatisation of Margery Kempe's meeting with Julian of Norwich—comments on anti-feminist attitudes of the period.[5] One medieval poet who has experienced a system of adaptation and employment, however, is Geoffrey Chaucer. In particular, this chapter focuses on how the works and biography of Chaucer have been interpreted towards criticism of inequality and oppression in our contemporary society.

In focusing on both the life and works of Chaucer, this chapter analyses two different, but connected, forms of Chaucerian medievalism. Chaucer as a vehicle for explaining the medieval English past, and his role in transmitting its culture to us, is explored in *A Knight's Tale* (2001), which uses the name of Chaucer to construct a plausible plot, and in the Tacit Theatre's production of "The Canterbury Tales," which sought to emphasise similarities between medieval and modern-day senses of humour. On the other hand, Chaucer (and his works) is often used as a vehicle for social and political commentary, such as in Pier Paolo Pasolini's film, *I Racconti di Canterbury* (1972), and in *Refugee Tales*, a collection that juxtaposes the pilgrimage of *The Canterbury Tales* with the plight of modern refugees. No matter the reason for adapting Chaucer, these various interpretations all speak both to the poet's formative place in the English literary canon, and to the way that the concerns of the past have relevance today. As Hayden White has observed, "it is only the medium that differs, not the way in which the messages are produced."[6]

Medieval Afterlives of Chaucer

The notion that Geoffrey Chaucer plays a unique and formative role in the creation of an English national identity has endured since his lifetime, particularly the idea that it is through the labour of this author that the written language of the region was polished and articulated in a manner that allowed it to be viewed as a valid medium for public discourse. This can be seen in the *Ballade to Chaucer* of Eustache Deschamps (1346–1406) in which the poet appeals, in light of Chaucer's translation of *Roman de la Rose*, for a copy of his original works.[7] Deschamps praises Chaucer's use of the English language, and highlights the value of Chaucer providing translations that have "Sown the flowers and planted the rose-tree for those ignorant of the Grecian tongue."[8] In relation to Chaucer's improvement of the English language, Deschamps employs a metaphor in which the personification of Germanic English—"d'Angela Saxonne"—is seen to have been developed into a form more reflective of the French influence, becoming *Angleterre*.

Similar praise of Chaucer as the figure who has altered and improved the English language, and shifted it towards a fully developed written medium, may be seen in the first true literary 'afterlife' of the poet: the Proheme to William Caxton's second edition of *The Canterbury Tales* (1484). The print history of Geoffrey Chaucer acts to reflect the reverence with which he was treated in the century after his death. The first book printed in English, in England, was Chaucer's *Canterbury Tales*, and the fact that it was printed in the shadow of the south transept of Westminster Abbey where the poet lay buried is telling. The Proheme to Caxton's second edition contains praise similar to that of Deschamps, asserting that it is for the task in embellishing the English language that the poet deserves a privileged position. Caxton opens the Proheme by stating that "great thanks, laud, and honour ought to be given unto the clerks, poets, and historiographs" who have produced texts for the edification of the people.[9] He, however, states that a "singular laud," "especial before all others," must be given to "that noble and great philosopher Geoffrey Chaucer" for his services to written English.[10] Caxton outlines this process by claiming, "He by labour embellished, ornated, and made fair our English, in this realm was had rude speech and incongruous."[11] The Caxtonian position is thus one that valued Chaucer for this particular facet of his reputation.

Early Modern Afterlives of Chaucer

Chaucer's employment as a viable vehicle for propaganda may be seen in the printed editions of his works that appear in the sixteenth century.

One notable example of these attempts to form a 'collected works' of the author was made by William Thynne in 1532. Printed by Thomas Godfray, this text was the first to contain paratextual material exceeding that of Caxton's 1484 Proheme. The preface to Thynne's collected edition "not written by Thynne himself, but by his friend Sir Brian Tuke"[12] embellishes Caxton's praise of Chaucer in relation to the formation of English as a literary medium. The preface outlines the importance of language as being that which creates "a symylitude of man unto aungels,"[13] and, complimenting Chaucer's "swete and plesaunt sentences,"[14] Tuke notes that

> It ben a thyng right rare & straunge and worthy perpetuall laude yt any clerke by lernyng or wytte coulde than haue framed a tonge before so rude and imperfite to suche a sweete ornature and composycion.[15]

This employment of the Caxtonian position places Chaucer among the pantheon of writers such as Ennius and Dante who were viewed to be pivotal in the construction of a national language and identity. In this manner, the reprinting of Chaucer's works can be viewed as a matter of civic importance, as reflected in the 1532 Preface statement that it is out of "dewtie" and "loue to my countrey" that the edition was created.

From the sixteenth century, the literary reputation of Chaucer as a poet of extreme national importance to both the English language and heritage was thus asserted. One of the most striking visual representations of this reverence can be seen in Westminster Abbey, where the poet is buried. Although initially interred there for services within his working life, it is of note that the author "had a public tomb, and ca. 1556, following Nicholas Bringham's enhancement [and] worshippers could have seen a portrait of Chaucer between the sepulchre's arches."[16] The South Transept of Westminster Abbey has since been dubbed 'Poet's Corner,' and the visual implication present in the graves of Tennyson, Robert Browning, and Spenser surrounding the grave of the medieval poet is stark. Even more so is the positioning of the graves of Victorian poets Tennyson and Browning, which lie before the raised tomb of Chaucer as if prostrate in veneration.

A Knight's Tale

Contemporary adaptations of Geoffrey Chaucer can be broadly categorised into two types of medievalism: the use of the characters of Geoffrey Chaucer (primarily *The Canterbury Tales*), and the representation of Geoffrey Chaucer himself. The most prominent representation of the latter can be found in Brian Helgeland's 2001 film *A Knight's Tale*, starring Heath Ledger. Although presenting an anachronistic representation of medieval Europe, the film includes characters of the period, and central to the plot of the film is Chaucer himself, played by Paul Bettany. The film does, however, attempt to place the character within the late 1360s/1370s, accurately noting that Chaucer's most accomplished written work written while the Black Prince, who is also depicted in the film, was alive was *The Book of The Duchess*. Although the film does not aim to produce a 'faithful' depiction of the author, *A Knight's Tale* both adds to, and reflects, twenty-first-century conceptions of Geoffrey Chaucer, and he acts as a central figure in the narrative. The film focuses on the trials of the protagonist William Thatcher, and his attempts to win both a tournament and the heart of Lady Jocelyn, and through the representation of Chaucer's oratorical ability, knowledge of court practice, and skill at writing, he is aided in this quest.

The film begins with the protagonist discovering his master, Sir Ector, has died between jousting bouts, and endeavouring to take on his armour and compete in the final round of the contest. After succeeding in this William deduces that the best way to increase his fortune and to "change his stars" is to compete in further tournaments, something restricted for a man of his lowly social position. It is the figure of Geoffrey Chaucer who overcomes this problem and makes a startling entry to the film by walking naked towards the protagonist and his two companions. The literary ability of Chaucer is pronounced within the script; when it is inquired as to what he is doing ambling in the nude on a country path he replies, "trudging. You know, trudging? To trudge? To trudge the slow, weary, depressing, yet determined walk of a man who had nothing left except the impulse to simply soldier on." The character of Chaucer is also quick to assert his reputation, describing himself as "Lilium inter spinas," a lily amongst thorns. This learned introduction is, however, followed by the statement that "Geoffrey Chaucer's the name. Writing's the game," reflecting the film's use of a contemporary lexis in the medieval setting, and humorously undercutting any gravitas associated with the canonical figure buried in 'Poet's Corner.' Of central importance to Chaucer's function within the plot is his statement, "For a penny, I'll scribble anything. Summonses, decrees, edicts, warrants, patents of nobility." Chaucer is the character who has the relevant education and ability to facilitate William competing in further tournaments. Chaucer not only informs William that the tournament he seeks to enter will require proof of ennobled status—"patents of nobility must be provided"—but also forges a document declaring William to be Ulrich von Lichtenstein and have noble lineage tracing back six generations.

As well as providing the vital plot function of facilitating the entry of William to the tournaments central to the action, Chaucer acts as herald and introduces the knight before competition. In this regard, the figure of Chaucer is presented as an able and effective 'PR' man, demonstrating a great deal of oratorical ability. Within these statements, Chaucer appeals to the laity as well as the nobles present, and directly addresses the masses in his opening address with the comment, "My lords, my ladies and everybody else here not sitting on a cushion." The hyperbolic description of William's knightly exploits brings the crowd to a frenzy:

> I have the pride, the privilege, nay, the pleasure of introducing to you a knight sired by knights. A knight who can trace his lineage back beyond Charlemagne. I first met him atop a mountain near Jerusalem praying to God asking his forgiveness for the Saracen blood spilt by his sword. Next, he amazed me still further in Italy when he saved a fatherless beauty from the would-be ravishings of her dreadful Turkish uncle. In Greece he spent a year in silence just to better understand the sound of a whisper. So without further gilding the lily and with no more ado I give to you the Seeker of Serenity, the Protector of Italian Virginity, the Enforcer of our Lord God, the one, the only, Sir Ulrich von Lichtenstein!

Chaucer's personal acknowledgement of his oratorical abilities can be seen in his final, anachronistic, statement of this introduction, "Thank you! Thank you! I'll be here all week." His introduction of William is so effective that it draws applause from both the antagonist and the character of Wat, who is seen to be in conflict with Chaucer for much of the film.[17] Further examples of his oratorical prowess can be seen in his description of William as "The Lance that thrilled France. The Harasser of Paraser! He gave them hell at La Rochelle!" and his role in the proclamation of William's earned nobility at the end of the film. In this regard, *The Knight's Tale* can be seen to employ Chaucer's reputation as a writer towards the creation of a boisterous and capable public speaker.

As well as an able 'PR' co-ordinator, Chaucer plays the role of adviser to William, both in regards to courtly procedure and in his pursuits of Lady Jocelyn. When William is defeated in his first contest with Count Adhemar, the reaction of his other companions is one of anger towards the victor: Chaucer, who is aware of social expectations, congratulates Adhemar on his victory. Immediately following William's success in the sword-fighting contest, he urges his companions to leave. It is Chaucer who informs him that he "must go to the banquet. You'll dance and make an appearance." Further asserting his knowledge of courtly society, Chaucer attempts to teach William to dance in anticipation of this event. William's attendance at the dance plays a key function in the developing romance between himself and Jocelyn, and in the further encounters Chaucer guides his actions, drawing upon his literary prowess to provide fine words for the protagonist. On two occasions William demonstrates a keen ability to speak and write beautifully thanks to Chaucer's input. In one scene, William employs complex Biblical allusion towards Jocelyn's beauty, stating,

ULRICH: You remind me of the Bible, when God stopped the sun to give Joshua time to defeat the Amorites.
JOCELYN: I don't understand.
ULRICH: If I could ask God one thing it would be to stop the moon. Stop the moon and make this night and your beauty last forever.

Chaucer too aids William in the construction of a letter to Jocelyn in which he outlines his feelings, and his advice to look "towards the heavens" for inspiration impresses the recipient a great deal. So lost is William without Chaucer's aid in this area that, upon Jocelyn's request to "speak those words," he is only able to recite the conventional utterance of other wooing knights, "I will win this tournament for you." Further, William's attempts to create romantic sentiment of his own result in the farcical entreat "your beauty will be reflected in the power of my arm and my horse's flanks," angering his love interest considerably.

The role of Chaucer within the film is one of central importance, and it is only through the forging of the documents that William is able to compete. With the input of Chaucer in constructing romantic sentiment and in the instruction of courtly society, William is aided in succeeding his goals, and the successful conclusion of the film is realised. Faithful reference to the historical figure of Chaucer was rarely forthcoming within *A Knight's Tale*, and the author's literary ability is transformed into the depiction of an able forger and grandiloquent public speaker. There is, however, reference to *The Canterbury Tales*, which comes in regards to the Friar and the Summoner. One personality trait of note imagined by the writers of the film is that Chaucer suffers from a gambling addiction and becomes indebted to these figures, having engaged in betting. Having threatened him with death and extracted the funds needed from William to escape this fate, Chaucer is later confronted by the Friar and Summoner who attempt to goad him into another contest. This results in Chaucer promising to "eviscerate" them in fiction, anticipating the representation of these characters within *The Canterbury Tales*. This promise to "exact my revenge" foreshadows the author's most famous work, as do the closing lines of the film, which also function in this manner: "I'm going to write this story ... all of it. All human activity lies within the artist's scope."

Tacit Theatre's Production of "The Canterbury Tales"

Recent adaptations of Chaucer's works tend to focus on the bawdy tales, and to present the author as being a master humourist. That the characters of *The Canterbury Tales* are a successful vehicle for entertainment can be seen in several theatrical and commercial ventures, not least the interactive "The Canterbury Tales" theme park, which features animatronic pilgrims and has existed in Canterbury for 30 years. It is somewhat idiosyncratic that the work that features "The Prioress's Tale" and "The Second Nun's Tale" would be the focus of children's entertainment, but the characters of the poem are also employed towards the entertainment of adults. One example of this is Tacit Theatre's production of "The Canterbury Tales," a re-enactment of the bawdier sections of *The Canterbury Tales* which was first staged at the Southwark Playhouse in 2011, followed by a nationwide tour in 2012. This performance leans on the humour within the text to produce a well-received stage show peppered with jovial songs and audience participation.

In an interview conducted with Leo Steele, producer and founding member of Tacit Theatre, in January this year, I asked what considerations were paramount in these productions. Steele's response—that he "wanted to find a new way into the text that revealed not just the bawdy humour, but the sharp wit and surprisingly relatable characters"—echoes William Blake's nineteenth-century remark that *The Canterbury Tales* features "characters which compose all ages and nations."[18] The focus on lascivious elements of the text in order to produce an entertaining stage show was also referenced by Steele, and he states that "if you are presenting *The Canterbury Tales* as a theatrical performance, then there is an expectation of bawdy humour and you have to supply a certain amount of that," noting that "The Miller's and the Reeve's Tale were obvious choices." It was also discussed that "The Wife of Bath always got a strong reaction," and the performance of Rosalind Blessed in this role was particularly effective in drawing audience interaction, with the actress, in character, addressing the crowd on arrival.

In staging *The Canterbury Tales* for a modern audience, Tacit made some deviations from the original text. As well as the setting being transported to the Tabard Inn, as part of this modernising trend, 'Chaucer' does not appear as one of the characters; the role of narrator was granted to the Host (Harry Bailey, the publican), not to the Pilgrim-Chaucer who does not feature. Chaucer's absence in Tacit's stage adaptation is significant and is repeated in promotional material associated with the adaptation on the Company's website, where his name is glaringly absent.[19] This adaptation choice is perhaps an attempt to lessen any stigma associated with Chaucer (that is, the loss of interest due to Chaucer's being perceived as 'boring') by replacing him with a character more appropriate for the immersive 'Medieval Inn' experience of the show, the Tabard's publican. This decision is an implicit commentary on Chaucer's canonical status: Tacit was capitalising on the familiarity English audiences have with *The Canterbury Tales* to present the most famous of Chaucer's work *without* Chaucer himself. The show is an immersive experience set in the Tabbard Inn, which is the starting point for the pilgrim's journey in *The Canterbury Tales*: the show itself then is the pilgrimage. However, as one review notes, Tom Daplyn, who adapted the tales for the show, plays Tabard landlord Harry Bailey; Daplyn's

Bailey introduces each Tale with passages of Chaucer's original middle English before changing to modern English to accommodate the modern audience.[20] Thus, an unintended consequence is that Daplyn replaces Chaucer as the voice of authority in this production. This change has led to criticism in reviews, such as the Susannah Clapp in *The Guardian*, who derisively suggests, "The evening is hopeless for elucidating Chaucer, but successful as a medieval cabaret."[21] The inclusion of musical performances and singing pilgrims also provided an additional source of both bawdiness and entertainment, with fifteenth-century song such as "The Cuckoo's Nest" complimenting "The Reeve's Tale." Steele described how the production team "chose a selection of deliberately anachronistic folk songs in order to create the desired tavern atmosphere." What can be seen from the Tacit Theatre production of "The Canterbury Tales" is that the bawdier sections of the text can be seen to have a timeless humour that required little disruption of the original narrative in order to create this effect. In this adaptation of Chaucer then, the medievalism is *not* that the past is unfamiliar to us, but rather that the Caxtonian position hides the continuities between Chaucer's life and the twenty-first century. In short, Tacit Theatre's production served as reminder that humour—and in particular, the inherent humorous nature of flatulence—transcends the centuries.

Pier Paolo Pasolini's *I Racconti di Canterbury*

The tales selected by Tacit Theatre mirror those employed by Pier Paolo Pasolini in his 1972 film *I Racconti di Canterbury*, which was the controversial recipient of the Goldener Bär at the 22nd Berlin International Film Festival. The second film in Pasolini's "Trilogy of Life" series, his depiction of *The Canterbury Tales* also had a strong focus on the bawdier nature of the text. Although frequently heralded as an outrageous demonstration of sex and violence, the work does have a strong commitment to challenging social structures of Pasolini's contemporary Italy. The film too adapts the character of Geoffrey Chaucer, played by Pasolini, to make comment on the role of the creative artist. The film ultimately exceeds the notion that it is purely an outlet for the demonstration of sex and violence, and throughout employs the text in a manner that is both faithful to an imagined medieval aesthetic and able to cast commentary on the director's socio-political environment. Although incorporating a sumptuous staging of medieval England, Pasolini does make deviations from the text, most notably setting the film in Canterbury as the pilgrims arrive, and including additional scenes, such as an extended representation of "The Cook's Tale."

In regards to social commentary, Pasolini addresses the subject of both judicial bias and the discrimination of homosexuals in a prelude to "The Friar's Tale" that does not feature in the text. The scene presents, through use of a voyeuristically peering camera, the harrowing story of two different men found to have committed sodomy and at risk of receiving brutal repercussion. The scene is presented through the eyes of a seller of cakes, and creates juxtaposing depictions of the accused's interaction with officials that are reflective of judicial bias within Pasolini's contemporary society. The first man is observed through a firm door, and his sexual partner is hidden from view and silent. When confronted with the charge of sodomy, the rotund gentleman is able to produce a large quantity of gold with which to bribe the official, stating "do not denounce me for the sin of lust, for God's sake." The second figure accused of the same crime is presented in contrast to the one who is able to purchase absolution from the court, and whereas the larger, first, gentleman is clothed and of a large build, the second accused is presented naked and noticeably emaciated.

The means through which the exchange is witnessed is also presented in contrasting terms, with the soon-to-be condemned figure observed through a flimsy curtain and not a crack in a solid door. His sexual partner, too, juxtaposes the silent concubine of the first and laughs during the interrogation. Crucially, the second man has no money to pay for his release, with the official asking, "you swear by the body of God, that you have nothing to give me?" When he responds that he does not, he faints at the reply "Then you'll fry, friend." Pasolini's reflections of brutal, corrupt, judicial process can be further seen in the depiction of "The Pardoner's Tale." When the lone rioter returns to purchase poison, he observes a collection of enforcement officers who are strikingly attired in medieval-esque leather garb that is undeniably reflective of police riot gear. Here, Pasolini alludes to the spectre of Fascist Italy, a governmental paradigm that had existed but a generation before, and also the director's own conflict with bodies of censorship and control in relation to his own work.[22] This conflation of contemporary enforcement methods with the dress of medieval characters also further reflects the previous commentary on enduring tenets of judicial corruption highlighted in the introduction to "The Friar's Tale."

Pasolini's *I Racconti di Canterbury*, unlike Tacit Theatre's "The Canterbury Tales," employs the figure of Chaucer as a quasi-narrator, and the character is seen to observe his surroundings, and crucially his fellow pilgrims, while constructing the text that forms the basis of the film. In a vignette between "The Friar's Tale" and that of the Cook, Pasolini-as-Chaucer is seen to produce a collection of extravagant writing implements, reflecting his commitment to the craft and its accoutrement. Within this scene, which occurs in the lodgings of the Canterbury pilgrims, the author is seen to survey the entirety of the densely occupied space, with the camera employing a full pan of the area with specific focus on the final figure observed in this panorama, a young man (presumably anticipating the narrative of Pasolini's recreation of "The Cook's Tale").

In this manner, Pasolini depicts Chaucer as a figure for whom the text was closely rooted in the observance of his contemporary environment. In a section presented between "The Cook's Tale" and that of the Miller, Pasolini creates a fictional narrative in which Chaucer is scolded by his wife for sleeping at his desk, reflecting and isolating the ardour of the creative process. Important to this scene, however, is the employment of books as a marker for the author's commitment to his craft and the author is seen stacking multiple texts on the floor. The frictions caused by such dedication are expertly demonstrated in the shot that shows his wife scolding him, with a pile of books that can be seen to create a 'wall' between the two characters; the texts evocative of masonry in a fixed divide. Ultimately, Pasolini employs the characters of Chaucer to impart social commentary on judicial issues of his contemporary Italy, and also the character of Chaucer to make comment on the role of the artist. That Chaucer's works are a result of a keen observance of the characters of his age can be seen in the final shot, where Chaucer is seen to view a large assemblage of many figures, before writing "Aqui terminan los cuentos de Canterbury" ("here ends the Canterbury Tales"), a line that does not appear in the text.

Refugee Tales

The employment of Chaucer's characters and narrative form towards reflections upon contemporary issues seen in Pasolini's cinematic work may also be observed in the collection of stories published in 2016 under the title *Refugee Tales*. This work was originally formed around "A Walk in Solidarity with Refugees, Asylum Seekers, and Detainees, from Dover to Crawley via Canterbury," in which stories were performed in a manner reflective of the Canterbury pilgrimage itself, "in June, not April."[23] Editor David Herd described how

> the walk took nine days, punctuated at every stop, by the public telling of two tales; one, the tale of an asylum seeker, former immigration detainee or refugee; the other of a person—for instance a lawyer or interpreter—who works with people seeking asylum.[24]

The model of the project was such that "each tale was a collaboration between an established writer and the person whose tale was being told," and the collection features works by authors such as Ali Smith, Patience Agbabi, and Merina Lewycka. Drawing on the experience of the physical pilgrimage and its relevance in telling the narratives of detainees and asylum seekers, Herd writes, "the project thus had three fundamental elements: a culturally charged sense of space, the visible fact of human movement, and an exchange of information through the act of telling stories."[25] In this manner, *Refugee Tales* employs not just an appropriation of the narrative structure of the original text, but the notions of movement and travel so intrinsic to discussions of this subject.

References to both the character and contemporary environment of Chaucer are present within the text beyond the narrative structure of the telling of tales within a pilgrimage. The cover of the 2016 edition imitates a form of manuscript decoration, although refitted to suit the subject matter. Arabesque borders are replaced with barbed wire, and the initial of the title contained within a chain-link fence and not elaborate design. There is a prologue that, although strikingly different from the poetic form of the author on which the work is based, describes the manner in which the tenets of the project inherently reflect the medieval author. Announcing its central difference from the expected prologue form, the text centres the importance of its subject matter in the opening lines:

> This prologue is not a poem
> It is an act of welcome
> It announces
> That people present
> Reject the terms
> Of a debate that criminalises
> Human movement.[26]

Links between the Canterbury pilgrimage and that of the 2015 "Walk in Solidarity," as well as the ardour and danger of the crossings enacted by the migrants themselves, are highlighted through association with the dangers of medieval travel. Describing "the scale of the undertaking," the Prologue finds congruity between those seeking asylum in the West, and the destinations referenced in *The Canterbury Tales* of

> Chaucer's pilgrims crossing
> Palatye and Turkye and Ruce
> Across the Grete See.[27]

One of the central links between Chaucer and the focus of *Refugee Tales* is discussion of language and translation. Peppered throughout each tale are references to the confusions and pitfalls of language experienced by the migrants interviewed, in particular "The Interpreter's Tale," in which the subject mistranslates a term and finds that from that point, "word for word I am not believed."[28] The Prologue discusses Chaucer's role in the formation of a language that has been "rendered hostile by acts of law" and states "to make his English sweet, that's why Chaucer wrote his tales. How badly we need English to be made sweet again."[29] Ultimately, *Refugee Tales* seeks to "make a language that opens politics, establishes belongings," and the employment of both the legacy and structure of Chaucer and his works towards this shows congruity in these distant subjects.[30]

David Herd writes in his Afterword that "a number of writers became pre-occupied with ... 'The Man of Law's Tale', the events of which see an Italian Princess taken to Syria, from which regime she is banished," and a masterful conflation of this tale and the experience of one migrant is seen in "The Migrant's Tale" as told to Dragan Todorovic, which tells the narrative story of a Syrian migrant named Aziz.[31] Within the tale, a first person narrative of Todorovic's experience in meeting his subject, he describes how he set his mind to seeking asylum, and that "My plan was to reach England ... but every country had closed the door in our face. I found a number and contacted a smuggler."[32] The central focus of the narrative is the harrowing journey in which the subject is caught adrift and fearing for his life on a boat with over one hundred fellow migrants. The tale interjects translations by the author of "The Man of Law's Tale" to poignant effect, and the description of his traumatic voyage, for which he paid €3,700, is foreshadowed with the reference, "Custance was dragged to the port, put on a boat without rudder, told to learn how to sail and set on her way back to Italy."[33] Further description of the danger and hardship felt is punctuated with reference to the desperation of Custance in exile. Aziz recounts how his boat was "tied to a trawler," and how he had to change vessel and encounter "armed people" on board.[34] His experiences of how "the rope that tied our boat to the trawler snapped" and the feeling of the boat "rocking dangerously,"[35] with "75 of them plus 44 of us"[36] on board are coupled with the lament of Custance, "Oh feeble moon, unhappy your steps! You find yourself where you are not welcomed,"[37] and the description of how "for days, for years floated this creature across the eastern Mediterranean ... often she expected to die."[38]

This mirroring of Custance's plight with the biographic retelling of a recent and dangerous journey works to contextualise the emotive terror present in Chaucer's poem with the lived experience of marginalised, and often vilified, people today. Interactions with "The Man of Law's Tale" go further when Aziz describes how he was collected by the Italian coastguard and taken to the detention centre on Lampedusa. The joy at being saved from death upon the sea is coupled with the line from Chaucer's tale "who saved her from drowning in the sea." The experience of detention is told in a harrowing account of how the Italian officers tortured the migrants who refused to provide fingerprints for fear of being identified by Syrian officials and endangering their families. Aziz recounts how "for ten days we had no food, we were hungry, but we were told we wouldn't be given any food until we gave our fingerprints,"[39] and that an officer, "ordered his men to beat us and they took our fingerprints by force."[40] The presence of lines from the tale—"She would not talk of her rank, ready to die but not reveal anything" and

"Long was the sobbing and the bitter pain before their hearts could open again"—demonstrates the plight of the migrant in this desperate situation.[41] Although "The Man of Law's Tale" ends with the reuniting of Custance and King Alla, the realities of contemporary migrants are shown to occlude such happy endings. Aziz describes how his "story hasn't come to an end. His family is in Daraa and his wife is losing patience. He is now afraid that she would take their children and embark on one of the death boats," and the plight of this family is yet to see the much hoped for conclusion of "The Man of Law's Tale" that the central couple were "never parted" from the point of reunification.[42]

Refugee Tales is indicative of adaptations of Geoffrey Chaucer, a writer so intrinsically linked with the formation of English national identity, towards a shift in the paradigm which is so brutally exclusive of those who wish to be a part of it. Chaucer was appropriated in the Reformation by editors wishing to attach him to the Protestant cause; today, the "national author" makes the "crossing of a deeply national space by people whom the nation has organised itself in order that they be kept from view."[43] The legacy of Chaucer as a central figure in the creation of the English nation, both in the formation of language and his employment by Protestant editors to craft a new national faith, can be seen to fix the identities which work counterintuitively with notions of welcome and acceptance. In Pasolini's *I Racconti di Canterbury* and in *Refugee Tales*, we see an attempt to attach to the author a shift in the oppressive structures of our contemporary environment and craft a new language and attitude through characters and constructs of the old. David Herd's statement that *Refugee Tales* demands "national language be reread" rings true with the appropriation of Chaucer in a multitude of genre, towards many political purposes. In *A Knight's Tale*, we see Chaucer adapted as a figure whose fame can be used to facilitate a film's 'happy ending,' and in Tacit Theatre's production of "The Canterbury Tales," we see the humour and relevance of Chaucer brought to modern audiences. What emerges these four different adaptations of Chaucer and his works is not "the boring A-level set text they remember from school," but a flesh-and-blood character, who wrote about people from all economic and social classes, and tackled real-world issues.[44]

Notes

1 I thank both Aidan Norrie and Marina Gerzic for their assistance in the preparation of this chapter.
2 Michael T. Anderegg, "Orson Welles and After: Julius Caesar and the Twentieth Century Totalitarianism," in *Julius Caesar: New Critical Essays*, ed. Horst Zander (London: Routledge, 2005), 295–305.
3 Alexandra Parsons, "History, Activism, and the Queer Child in Derek Jarman's *Queer Edward II* (1991)," *Shakespeare Bulletin* 32, no. 3 (2014): 413–428.

4 *Fair Field* was conceived by arts company Penned in the Margins, and created with a collective of writers and performers including Breach Theatre, Francesca Millican-Slater, and The Society of Strange and Ancient Instruments, and performed in 2017. See the production's website: http://thisfairfield.com.
5 *Marge and Jules* is written and performed by the Queynte Laydies (Sarah Anson and Máirín O'Hagan), directed by Andrew Brock, and continues to be performed regularly since its premiere in 2015. See the production's website: http://queyntelaydies.com/marge-and-jules.
6 Hayden White, "Historiography and Historiophoty," *The American Historical Review* 93, no. 5 (December 1988): 1194.
7 T. Atkinson Jenkins, "Deschamps' Ballade to Chaucer," *Modern Language Notes* 33, no. 5 (May 1918): 268–278.
8 My own translation. Original French: "Semé les fleurs et planté le rosier, Aux ignorans de la langue pandras."
9 William Caxton, "Prohemye," to *Canterbury Tales*, by Geoffrey Chaucer (Westminster, 1485), fol. A2r.
10 Caxton, "Prohemye," fol. A2r.
11 Caxton, "Prohemye," fol. A2r.
12 *The Works of Geoffrey Chaucer and Others, Being a Reproduction in Facsimile of the First Collected Edition 1532* (London: Oxford University Press, 1905), xxi.
13 *Facsimile of the First Collected Edition 1532*, xxii.
14 *Facsimile of the First Collected Edition 1532*, xxiii.
15 *Facsimile of the First Collected Edition 1532*, xxiv.
16 Louise M. Bishop, "Father Chaucer and the Vivification of Print," *The Journal of English and Germanic Philology* 106, no. 3 (July 2007): 342.
17 The character of Wat is distrusting of Chaucer for much of the film, and frequently threatens him with violence should he attempt to deceive or hinder William's progress. One subplot is the cooling of hostilities and developing friendship between these two characters, which culminates in their embrace at the end of the film.
18 William Blake, "The Canterbury Pilgrims," in *English Critical Essays*, ed. E. Jones (London: Metheun, 1971), 73.
19 Tacit Theatre, "Portfolio: The Canterbury Tales – Southwark Production," http://tacittheatre.co.uk/portfolio_page/478; Tacit Theatre, "Portfolio: The Canterbury Tales – Touring Production," http://tacittheatre.co.uk/portfolio_page/the-canterbury-tales-touring-production.
20 Hugh Cadman, "REVIEW: Canterbury Tales," *Salisbury Journal*, 13 March 2014, http://salisburyjournal.co.uk/news/11073554.REVIEW__Canterbury_Tales.
21 Susannah Clapp, "Haunted Child; The Bollywood Trip; The Canterbury Tales–Review," *The Guardian*, 18 December 2011, https://theguardian.com/stage/2011/dec/18/haunted-child-bollywood-canterbury-review.
22 For more on how costumes are used to allude to Fascist Italy, see Marina Gerzic's chapter, "From *Cabaret* to *Gladiator*: Refiguring Masculinity in Julie Taymor's *Titus*," in this volume.
23 David Herd, "Prologue," in *Refugee Tales*, ed. David Herd and Anna Pincus (London: Comma Press, 2016), vi.
24 David Herd, "Afterword," in *Refugee Tales*, ed. David Herd and Anna Pincus (London: Comma Press, 2016), 132.
25 Herd, "Afterword," 133.
26 Herd, "Prologue," v.
27 Herd, "Prologue," viii.

28 Carol Watts, "The Interpreter's Tale," in *Refugee Tales*, ed. David Herd and Anna Pincus (London: Comma Press, 2016), 64.
29 Herd, "Prologue," ix.
30 Herd, "Prologue," v.
31 Herd, "Afterword," 139.
32 Dragan Todorovic, "The Migrant's Tale," in *Refugee Tales*, ed. David Herd and Anna Pincus (London: Comma Press, 2016), 1–3, 5.
33 Todorovic, "The Migrant's Tale," 5.
34 Todorovic, "The Migrant's Tale," 6.
35 Todorovic, "The Migrant's Tale," 6.
36 Todorovic, "The Migrant's Tale," 7.
37 Todorovic, "The Migrant's Tale," 6.
38 Todorovic, "The Migrant's Tale," 7.
39 Todorovic, "The Migrant's Tale," 9.
40 Todorovic, "The Migrant's Tale," 10.
41 Todorovic, "The Migrant's Tale," 11.
42 Todorovic, "The Migrant's Tale," 12.
43 Herd, "Afterword," 138.
44 James Tillitt, "Right of Reply: The People's Tale," *Independent*, 27 July 1994, https://independent.co.uk/arts-entertainment/right-of-reply-the-peoples-tale-1416720.html.

5   Moving between Life and Death
Horror Films and the Medieval Walking Corpse
Polina Ignatova

The walking dead—or zombies—are mysterious creatures stuck between life and death, who terrify, and are dangerous to, the living. According to Wikipedia, there are at least 467 films about zombies, and this list expands every year.[1] The origins of zombie stories are somewhat nebulous. Kyle Bishop argues that in contrast to other monsters—such as werewolves, vampires, or ghosts—zombies do not originate from a written narrative.[2] Álvaro Hattnher similarly claims that zombie films, together with their appearance in written fiction, video games, and comic books, constitute variations of a motif first introduced by George A. Romero.[3] That different zombie narratives from the twentieth and the twenty-first centuries indeed seem to follow the patterns established in Romero's films is undeniable. This chapter demonstrates, however, that these patterns drew on a much older history that stretches back millennia.

While the word *zombie* originated in West Africa, and subsequently entered European culture in the nineteenth century, the concept of a reanimated corpse that comes back to haunt the living can be traced back to Antiquity. Pliny the Elder recounts the story of a man called Gabienus, who returned after his execution during the Sicilian War in order to convey a message to Sextus Pompeius from the gods.[4] Similarly, Lucan's *Pharsalia* describes how the witch Erichto revived a dead soldier in order to learn the future from him.[5] So, while Hattnher claims Romero's films to be the "patient zero" of zombie studies, the actual "patient zero" does not seem possible to trace, since evidence of potential beliefs in walking dead occurs even in Ancient Mesopotamian sources.[6]

Throughout the Middle Ages, restless corpses continued to appear in written sources, including those created in the British Isles.[7] Modern zombie films thus engage in medievalism, and their appearance largely adheres to the same patterns as their medieval precursors. From the outset, it is worth noting that the modern idea of zombies, while certainly having a long history, may not be drawn from the medieval sources. However, contrary to Winston Black's assertion that walking dead stories ceased to exist after the thirteenth century, stories about restless corpses continued to appear throughout the early modern and modern periods.[8] Likewise, Romero's filmography also includes *Knightriders* (1981), a film that contains allusions to King Arthur: thus, the possibility that Romero consciously included medieval elements in his zombie films should not be dismissed. While we cannot be certain that modern horror films consciously engage with medieval (and even older) depictions of zombies, their very existence in modern adaptations demonstrates the deep permeation of zombie stories into the popular conscious: a historical medievalism that has been perpetuated for centuries. Without claiming to have identified the exact reasons why medieval motifs appear in modern horror films, this chapter analyses the various elements of modern zombie films that have been borrowed from medieval texts. I compare the best-known zombie films with medieval British stories of the walking dead, and focus on parallels in the circumstances in which the protagonists find themselves, before turning to the reasons for the appearance of zombies, the nature of walking dead, the reanimating of cadavers, the roles assigned to authorities, and the apotropaics—that is, the measures that the living take to put the corpse to (final) rest.[9]

The General Framework of a Walking Dead Story

The circumstances in which authors position their characters play an important role in defining how the plot develops. It is useful, therefore, to begin this chapter by comparing medieval narratives and horror films in terms of the framework of events within which authors place their protagonists. In classical sources, walking dead were portrayed as peaceful (or at least not causing a large-scale disaster); medieval texts, however, start to describe something similar to the zombie 'apocalypses' featured in modern horror films, since their restless corpses spread pestilence, but without turning their victims into walking dead themselves.

Consider the following story from Geoffrey of Burton's early twelfth-century account of the life and miracles of St Modwenna, whose relics resided at the monastery of Burton-on-Trent. Two peasants from Stapenhill, the village that was under the jurisdiction of Burton Abbey, escaped to the village of Drakelaw, which was under the authority of Count Roger the Poitevin. In response to the peasants' disobedience, the abbot ordered that their crops be taken to the abbey's barns. Meanwhile, the peasants persuaded Roger to attack the abbey in order to get their crops back. During the battle, the monks placed the relics of St Modwenna on the floor and begged her for help. The monks won the battle, and on the following day both of the fugitive peasants were suddenly struck dead, and were buried in a churchyard in Stapenhill. On the evening of the same day they appeared on the streets of Drakelaw carrying their coffins on their shoulders. They wandered around the village, sometimes in the shape of humans, other times in the shape of

Moving between Life and Death 69

dogs, bears, and other animals, banging on the walls of the houses and shouting, "Move, faster, move! Move, move and come!"[10] This continued for several nights. In addition, the village was afflicted by a pestilence that soon killed almost the entire population. Seeing this, Roger repented and made a double restitution for the damages he caused. The activity of the revenants, however, did not cease until two peasants, with permission from the bishop, dug up the corpses—in medieval texts, walking dead usually take 'breaks' in their wanderings and return to their graves—severed their heads (placing them between the cadavers' legs), tore out their hearts and buried the bodies again. The locals set the hearts on fire, and as they burned, they cracked letting out an evil spirit in the form of a raven. The pestilence immediately ceased, and those who were ill recovered.[11]

A similar tale was narrated by Walter Map in his *Courtiers' Trifles*, a collection of stories, compiled in the late twelfth century. Here, an "evil"[12] Welshman, who died "unchristianly,"[13] kept exiting his grave, coming back to his village, and calling the locals by their names. Those whose names he shouted fell ill and died within three days. Attempting to stop the revenant, an English knight named William Laudun asked Gilbert Foliot, the Bishop of Hereford, for advice. Gilbert suggested exhuming the body, cutting the neck with a spade, sprinkling the body and the grave with holy water, and re-burying the corpse. After this was done the cadaver continued walking. Eventually, when the revenant called out William's own name, the knight chased him to his grave and cleaved the corpse's head with a sword. After that, the wanderings ceased.[14]

William of Newburgh's *Historia rerum Anglicarum* (from the late twelfth century) contains four walking dead stories; in two of them, the restless corpses spread pestilence.[15] A revenant from Berwick, described as "a rich man, but very evil, as it became obvious later," started a plague because its decomposing flesh was polluting the air.[16] The cadaver's wanderings ceased after ten brave young men dug the corpse up, cut it limb from limb, and burnt it. In the fourth tale, a man fled Yorkshire—evading either his enemies or the law—and settled down at the castle of Anantis, serving the local lord. Suspecting his wife of adultery, he pretended to leave for a journey and hid on a beam above her chamber.[17] Seeing his wife with a lover he fell down and was badly injured. As the lover fled, the woman tried to persuade her husband that what he thought he had seen was an illusion caused by his injury. When visited by a priest on his sickbed, he refused to confess his sins and receive the Eucharist, being still enraged by his wife's unfaithfulness. He agreed to do the confession the following day, but did not live to it. After death, he started leaving his grave every night, putrefying the air with his decomposing flesh. The neighbourhood soon became deserted as those who did not die fled from the plague. On Palm Sunday, the priest who had visited the man before his death held a council to discuss the problem, but the council soon descended into a feast. Meanwhile, two brothers, whose father was killed by the pestilence, decided to solve the problem by themselves. The men took the corpse out of the village and were about to burn it when one of them said that the body would not burn unless the heart was removed, so they extracted the heart and tore it into pieces. After the body was consumed by fire, the air purified.

While modern horror films often show hordes of zombies invading cities, medieval British narratives generally only contain one or two revenants causing trouble. In keeping with contemporary ideas about the transmission of disease, medieval walking dead spread plague either through air or by summoning people by name; the modern zombie, in contrast, spreads infection by biting its victims. This means that, on the one hand, the pestilence appears harder to catch, as one remains safe as long as one does not come in contact with a zombie. On the other hand, a larger number of restless corpses threaten the living. The number and persistence of the zombies often forces the protagonists to keep moving around in search of a safe refuge. In *Dawn of the Dead* (1978), the four main characters travel by helicopter in search of a safe shelter, and the film concludes with the two survivors setting out on another journey, their shelter rendered unsafe not by the zombies, but by bikers, who also travel around searching for loot. Likewise, in the remake of 2004, the protagonists end up in a mall, having left their homes after the walking dead invade their neighbourhoods. Despite an abundance of food and water inside the mall, they attempt to escape to an island, which is supposedly free of zombies. Similarly, the protagonists of *28 Days Later* (2002) head to Manchester to join a group of survivors; in *Zombieland* (2009) the main characters attempt to reach various destinations, and in *World War Z* (2010) one of the protagonists states that the "people who moved survived."

In contrast, the main characters in the medieval narratives rarely resort to flight; instead, they stay and attempt to put the walking corpse(s) to rest. Thus, in Geoffrey of Burton's account the only people fleeing are Roger the Poitevin and Drogo, the 'villains' of the story. William of Newburgh mentions people escaping the pestilence in just one of his four tales, and his plots focus on those who stay behind to defeat the revenant.[18] Thus, while in modern horror films the protagonists run away, their medieval counterparts chose to stay and face the problem. This can be explained by the fact that in the Middle Ages an individual was more closely tied to their place of living, their parish, and their priest, and for many migration was an intimidating option. Meanwhile, horror films have adapted to the modern increasingly mobile lifestyle, and large hordes of zombies serve to create a situation, when the protagonists cannot avoid interacting with the undead, as it was the case in medieval sources.

Sin and the Beginning of a Zombie 'Apocalypse'

Where do zombies come from? In texts produced in the medieval Britain there are only one or two walking dead, thus making it possible for the narrators to provide details about their lives. In the four narratives discussed earlier, the authors cast the individuals who turn into restless corpses as sinners, and their crimes explain why they become wandering cadavers. The same trend appears in other walking-dead texts created in medieval England, Wales, and Scotland. For example, in the early twelfth-century *Life of Kenelm*, attributed to Goscelin of St Bertin, St Kenelm's wicked sister Cwoenthryth plots his murder, usurps power in Mercia, terrorises her own people, and attempts to use black magic, before dying and turning into a walking corpse.[19] In the *Miracles of Edmund*, Herman the Archdeacon includes an account of how a saint punished the evil sheriff Leofstan for attempting to violate his shrine.[20] One of William of Newburgh's walking dead is a monk from the Melrose monastery, who was absorbed by worldly joys, such as hunting. So too was James Tankerlay, an undead priest, appearing in the anonymous *Byland Collection* (early fifteenth century), who during his lifetime kept a concubine.[21]

In addition, before returning as revenants, the sinners often die a bad death. In the Middle Ages, deaths were prone to being read negatively, as evidence of divine retribution if they were caused by violence,[22] if they were sudden,[23] or if they took place before the victim could repent their sins.[24] Thus, the aforementioned Cwoenthryth died after suffering an act of divine vengeance, her eyes being plucked from their sockets as she attempted to use sorcery; Leofstan was driven mad and was possessed by a demon; Geoffrey of Burton's peasants, and the Anantis revenant, died without confessing their sins.

In horror films, similarly, zombie epidemics are often attributed to both collective and individual 'sins.' For example, the opening scene of *Resident Evil* (2002) describes how the Umbrella Corporation had been conducting illegal and dangerous genetics experiments, which eventually led to the discovery of a T-virus, which was able to turn people into zombies. The 'apocalypse' starts with one of the protagonists' sin of stealing the T-virus. Likewise, in *28 Days Later*, the lethal zombie virus was created in a laboratory, and the epidemic starts when an environmental activist lets out an infected chimpanzee, breaking rules established to protect society at large. *World War Z* opens with reports about environmental change, which implies that humanity as a whole is guilty of causing the zombifying plague that follows. Furthermore, the protagonists manage to trace the spread of infection to a single soldier, who caught it mysteriously while being on unauthorised leave—again, breaking the rules. In the Middle Ages, religion (to a large extent) served to regulate the life of society. While religious rules have largely been replaced by secular ones, the 'sinners' of modern horror films still seem to be punished for their transgressions.

Dawn of the Dead and the 2004 remake contain numerous hints at humanity's collective guilt. In the 1978 version, one of the protagonists suggests that zombies coming to the shopping mall are drawn there by the instinct, for "this was an important place in their lives." This idea reappears in the remake. The clumsy comedic wanderings of zombies inside the mall clearly parody living shoppers. Their behaviour in this case is similar to the activities of Melrose monk and James Tankerlay, who in their revenant forms keep visiting the women they associated with during their lifetime: the former was haunting his patron, the latter rose from the grave to poke out the eye of his concubine. Just as William of Newburgh criticised the monk for leading too secular a lifestyle, both *Dawn of the Dead* films indirectly blame zombies for wasting time shopping while alive. The 1978 version reinforces this impression when one of the protagonists says of the zombies, "They are us, that is all. There is no more room in hell." The remake, again, repeats the same words. In addition to that, *Dawn of the Dead* (2004) emphasises this idea of humanity's collective guilt by demonstrating that the undead only show interest in eating human flesh—for instance, they ignore a dog. In some films animals are zombified,[25] and the undead feed on animals as well,[26] but zombie films never show restless corpses eating each other: a pattern that implies that they represent a punishment for the living.

Just like their medieval counterparts, the guilty occasionally die a bad death in zombie films. In *Resident Evil*, for example, the scientists involved in the creation of the T-virus are trapped inside an underground research facility and become zombies. The protagonist who has stolen the virus and started the epidemic gets attacked by a mutant monster and also turns into a walking corpse. In *28 Days Later*, the environmental activist who lets the infected chimpanzee out becomes the first victim of the pestilence. At the same time, together with the shift from individual to collective punishment, bad death becomes collective as well, as numerous people, whose particular sins we do not know, get torn to pieces by hordes of zombies, and join them afterwards. This, again, can be explained by the overall larger scale of disaster that occurs in modern horror films.

Medieval walking dead narratives generally develop in the following way: an individual commits an offence, and, as the result, dies a horrible death and returns as a restless corpse. It is noteworthy that there is no particular sin that leads to becoming a revenant, as the protagonists commit diverse crimes ranging from homicide to spying on one's wife, which all fall into the category of breaking the rules established by the society. Horror films adhere to the same pattern, as zombie 'apocalypses' often start because of someone's sin, but the emphasis shifts to collective rather than individual guilt, and in many cases humanity as a whole carries the blame for the appearance of zombies. This difference, however, can be explained through a larger scale of disaster in zombie films in comparison to medieval narratives in general. Both a medieval story and a walking dead film seem to convey the same message: anyone could be responsible for starting a 'zombie apocalypse.'

The Nature and Activities of a Restless Corpse

A walking corpse constitutes a dead body with some of the characteristics of a living person, the first (and the most obvious) being its ability to move around. Although a dead corpse is supposed to decompose, medieval writers handle the issue of putrefaction in opposing ways. For example, in William of Newburgh's accounts, the walking corpses are decomposing.[27] Conversely, Geoffrey of Burton describes the exhumed bodies as intact.[28] At the same time, the majority of walking dead stories created in Britain, as well as the classical sources and medieval European texts, generally ignore the idea of decay. In horror films, the protagonists do not worry about decomposing corpses, except in one scene in *Dawn of the Dead* (1978) where the men store the 'neutralised' zombies in a fridge. Overall, the extent to which zombies putrefy in horror films seems to depend only on how far a particular director is willing to go regarding the make-up or digital graphics.

The main aim of a typical walking corpse in a horror film is to eat humans and to spread the zombie virus. The most detailed explanation for this phenomenon appears in *Resident Evil*: the half-dead brain of a revenant cares only for the most basic need, which is hunger. Just like modern horror films, medieval British narrators emphasise the revenants' spreading plagues, but in most cases they are not eating the living, but are beating or simply terrifying them instead. Still, there are at least two episodes that can suggest the walking dead could indeed feed on the living. In Geoffrey of Burton's tale, when the two survivors open the tombs containing the undead peasants, they discover that the linen covering the faces of the exhumed corpses is stained with blood. William of Newburgh, similarly, calls the walking corpse terrorising Anantis "a leech."[29] The same idea may be implied in the account of the Melrose cadaver, for it lets out a large amount of gore when it is wounded.[30]

Some medieval revenants could talk to the living: thus, Agamund explains why he has become a walking corpse. The Berwick revenant told the people he met during his wanderings that he needed to be burned. The corpse of Robert of Killeburne, another undead from the *Byland Collection*, haunted the village in order to get attention of the living, and when the local priest finally asked him for his cause, he confessed his sins.[31] At the same time, a number of medieval British revenants—such as Geoffrey of Burton's peasants and Walter Map's Welshman—possess a limited ability to communicate to the living, and in a number of tales the walking dead remain silent or produce indistinct sounds, such as groans or murmurs.[32] Horror films also portray the revenants mainly as screaming and growling, although in *Day of the Dead* (1985), Dr Logan manages to train a zombie to say simple words. Therefore, while some medieval narratives allow the living and the dead to negotiate with one another, in most horror films effective communication is unattainable, which can be, again, explained through a more scientific approach taken in films. While in medieval sources there is a soul or a demon speaking from inside a dead body, in modern horror films it should be the body that speaks, which is impossible for decomposing or damaged cadavers.[33]

Finally, in some medieval British narratives, the walking dead possess additional supernatural powers. Thus, one of William of Newburgh's restless corpses can become invisible, and Geoffrey of Burton's peasants are able to change shapes.[34] The late twelfth- to early thirteenth-century *Lanercost Chronicle* contains a story about a walking corpse that could reduce to ashes any objects the living drove into his body in an attempt to 'kill' him.[35] In modern films, however, zombies seldom have additional powers, with the exception of some films that portray zombies as able to run very fast.[36] Since medieval writers explain the occurrence of walking dead by referring to divine or diabolical agency, their narratives can easily accommodate supernatural powers. With their preference for modern scientific explanations, zombie films stopped featuring abilities that cannot be easily explained in terms of science, such as invisibility or shape-shifting. At the same time, the ability to move faster can be described as another consequence of the infection. Thus, modern zombies were not stripped of their additional powers altogether, but they were accommodated to fit in the new, science-based narrative.

The medieval revenant and the modern zombie are equipped, broadly speaking, with similar attributes: they move around, spread infection, produce sounds, and feed on human flesh or blood. However, while medieval texts portray the walking dead as individuals, suffering punishment and requiring help, horror films tend to emphasise the violent and dangerous aspects of zombies, portraying them as harder to reason with and, consequently, as less human.

Agent

In both medieval narratives and modern horror films, restless cadavers need to be revived by some sort of agent. Medieval writers often explain that the corpse is moved around either by the soul, stuck inside the dead body, or by a demon, which enters the corpse and uses it like a puppet. Examples of corpses inhabited by a soul include Agamund, a reanimated cadaver from Goscelin's *Life of St Edith*, and Robert of Killeburne. The walking cadavers with the devil inside are Herman's and Goscelin's Leofstan, Geoffrey of Burton's peasants, William of Newburgh's Berwick, and Anantis corpses.

In horror films, the remaining brain activity and memories sometimes replace the soul as the cause of the zombie's behavioural patterns. The brain activity, like a soul, represents something defining one's personality and, consequently, can constitute a modern secular analogue of a soul. Occasionally, the undead behave similarly to the living; thus, a zombie in *Dawn of the Dead* (1978) covers his eyes to protect them from fire. Modern revenants appear to retain some intellect, as one of them successfully breaks the window of a truck with a heavy object. The living protagonists of the remake expect zombies to feel pain, for they attempt to protect their bus with barbed wire, and, contrary to logic, zombies indeed scream of pain when cut with a chainsaw. Dr Logan's favourite zombie, Bub, remembers how to use different objects, such as a razor, a telephone, and a gun, and exhibits some signs of sorrow upon seeing his master dead. Overall, horror films often show zombies retaining parts of the personalities they had while alive, a practice that roughly equates to the medieval notion of a soul, which, remaining inside a dead body, also determined the revenant's activities.

At the same time, the role of the devil in a horror film has been replaced with something more topical and more formidable for modern humans: usually, a virus that turns its victims into zombies. *Resident Evil* provides one of the most detailed explanations of how one becomes a restless corpse: the T-virus partially reverses the process of dying. In *28 Days Later*, the scientist simply states that the chimpanzee is infected with "rage," and in *World War Z*, the infection is referred to as rabies. Just as the nature of devilish powers remains unclear, and, therefore, more frightening for a medieval individual, the nature of a virus is ambiguous for an average moviegoer. The diverse list of sins that medieval writers portrayed as turning people into restless dead suggests that almost anyone could end up becoming a revenant but for God's grace. Similarly, horror films imply that no one can be absolutely protected from the lethal virus.

In some medieval narratives, however, a soul or a devil does not get inside one's corpse by accident. Often a saint, in order to punish a sinner, prevents their soul proceeding to the afterlife, or lets an evil spirit enter their cadaver. For example, St Edmund allows a demon to possess Leofstan, the evil sheriff who has violated his shrine, and Geoffrey of Burton's peasants are punished by St Modwenna. In some narratives, saints or church figures can also stop a revenant's activity. Thus, Cwoenthryth's corpse is dumped in a remote gully when the living are directed to this solution by a dazzling child (apparently St Kenelm) who has appeared to one of them in a dream.[37] William of Newburgh described a wandering cadaver whose activity ceased after a letter of absolution written by Hugh of Lincoln was placed in his tomb.[38] In modern horror films, the scientist replaces the saint, because both figures possess knowledge and skills that are incomprehensible to most people. Just as the saint is portrayed using his or her intercession to control demonic activity, so too is the scientist shown using equally arcane and inaccessible technical skills to constrain the undead. In some instances, the scientist(s) create(s) a virus (for example, the research groups in *Resident Evil* and *28 Days Later*); in some, they understand its effects (for instance, the virologist Dr Andrew Fassbach in *World War Z*, who was expected to find the cure for the zombifying plague); or in others they study, manage, and tame zombie behaviour (like Dr Logan in both *Day of the Dead* films).

Both medieval narratives and horror films show two agents involved in the reanimation of a dead corpse: first, there is an entity that creeps inside a cadaver, and, second, there is a figure that controls this entity. While in the modern zombie film, these agents have evolved to become more comprehensible and secular, their core nature remains the same.

The Authorities and the 'Good' Hero

Although in medieval British narratives saints are often responsible for turning people into revenants, and, along with some particularly advanced churchmen, seem to know how to put them to rest, they prefer not to do so. Moreover, local authorities are also often unwilling or unable to save the situation. For example, St Modwenna does not intervene to stop the undead peasants' activity, even after Roger the Poitevin makes efforts to resolve his conflict with the Burton Abbey and assuage Modwenna's wrath. That done, Roger departs from the neighbourhood along with the reeve of the village, leaving it for the locals to deal with the revenants. In Map's story about the restless Welshman, Bishop Gilbert Foliot does try to help, but his proposed remedy fails to work. A local "religious man" from William of Newburgh's Anantis story is not so considerate.[39] The council that he gathers in order to discuss the problem fails to provide any solution, and soon turns into a feast that is hardly appropriate, given that the village is struggling against a deadly plague.

While the authorities prove to be useless, ordinary people have to save themselves. Two surviving laymen defeat the restless peasants, a local knight puts to rest the evil Welshman, and two villagers destroy the Anantis corpse. Even when a writer does not emphasise the authorities' ineffectiveness, the plot still focuses on ordinary heroes. Thus, the locals burn the Berwick revenant, two monks and two laymen destroy the Melrose walking corpse, and two brave youths catch the undead Roger of Killeburne and call the priest to absolve him.

Horror films also demonstrate the inability of authorities to help. In *Dawn of the Dead* (1978), scientists ramble on TV, proposing unrealistic solutions, while in the remake, a military helicopter ignores the protagonists gathered on the roof of the shopping mall. Later, the survivors learn that the zombies have destroyed St Verbena, advertised on the radio as a safe place, as well as the allegedly safe Fort Pastor. *Resident Evil* concludes with the Umbrella Corporation losing control of its T-virus by opening a previously sealed underground facility that is full of zombies. In *28 Days Later*, a unit of soldiers who could protect the remaining survivors establish a manic dictatorship, becoming a threat to the protagonists' survival as grave as the zombies themselves. In *World War Z*, the US government, unable to help all its citizens, picks those it deems worthy of saving. The Israeli army appears similarly incompetent, as it misses the moment when the zombies start climbing over the wall, bringing the infection into Jerusalem. The virologist who was expected to find the cure dies ridiculously by accidently shooting himself. In *Maggie* (2015), the government's control over zombies is shown as inefficient, and its way of putting to death infected individuals is extremely cruel. Consequently, just like in the medieval narratives, the plot in these films focuses on the efforts of ordinary heroes to fight zombies, in spite of being ill equipped with the necessary skills and knowledge. Consider, for example, the survivors hiding in the mall in *Dawn of the Dead* (1978) and its remake; the group of people trapped inside the underground research facility in *Resident Evil*; the former UN beemployee with no knowledge of virology who attempts to find a cure for the plague in *World War Z*; and the father protecting his infected daughter from the government in *Maggie*.

Apotropaics

In medieval British narratives, where there are typically just one or two walking corpses, and the protagonists remain in the area plagued by the revenant's activity, putting the restless cadaver to rest seems to be the only logical conclusion of the story. Medieval sources contain different approaches towards dealing with walking dead. The first approach was a procedure associated with Christianity and the Church. Thus, the Buckinghamshire revenant, Walter Map's excommunicate, and Robert of Killeburne, all calm down after their sins are absolved.[40] Alternatively, in the stories about Cwoenthryth, Leofstan, and James Tankerlay, the living carry the restless cadavers to remote places.[41] Another common cure in medieval British texts is mutilating or burning a walking corpse. This is how the problem is resolved for Walter Map's restless Welshman, for Geoffrey of Burton's peasants, and for William of Newburgh's Berwick, Melrose, and Anantis revenants.

Because horror films normally feature hordes of zombies, it is not logical for the protagonists to try and 'kill' all the revenants. Consequently, people often attempt to isolate themselves from the walking dead: such as the survivors in *Dawn of the Dead* (1978) and the remake, who hide in a shopping mall; like the people barricading themselves inside a house in *Night of the Living Dead* (1968) and its 1990 remake; and like both the Israeli government, creating a zombie-free zone in Jerusalem, and the American government, evacuating people on ships and setting up refugee camps in *World War Z*. This solution seems to parallel the medieval idea of taking an allegedly dangerous corpse to a remote area where it can walk without disturbing people, the only difference being that in horror films, due to a larger number of zombies, it is harder for the living to isolate themselves.

When the protagonists cannot escape zombies, they attempt to physically destroy them, and in most zombie films the walking corpse 'dies' after its head is injured or separated from the body. In a similar manner to the medieval narratives, *Night of the Living Dead* (1990), *Dawn of the Dead* (2004), and *World War Z* portray protagonists burning the 'killed' zombies, although no particular explanation is provided as to why this should be an effective solution. In medieval sources, the protagonists were burning the restless dead not only to destroy them, but also to facilitate their translation to the afterlife, for this was the purpose of burning dead bodies and objects in classical sources.[42] Consequently, it is possible that modern horror films picked up this trope. Finally, some films present sophisticated solutions, which can potentially curb a zombie 'apocalypse.' For example, *Resident Evil* features an antivirus that can revert the process of zombification at an early stage, while *World War Z* concludes with the discovery of a vaccine that makes the living 'invisible' to zombies.

The apotropaics appearing in both medieval sources and in modern films can be divided into two groups: those directed at the cause of the corpse's restlessness, and those targeting the revenant itself. Both medieval letters of absolution and modern vaccines affect the entity inhabiting the dead body, the devil, or the virus. At the same time, the idea of mutilation and burning is based on the logic that the agent moving the corpse cannot do it if the cadaver is badly damaged. Although Hattnher has argued that the idea of zombies being "neutralised" by destroying their heads was also introduced by Romero, this motif often appears in medieval sources.[43] It is not clear, however, why the revenants cannot walk without their heads in medieval texts. This belief could exist owing to the fact that the head was regarded as particularly significant in early medieval society.[44] Also, since a walking corpse constitutes a dead body that bears some of the characteristics of the living, these characteristics may include the possibility of being 'killed' by beheading.

In the *Life and Miracles of St Modwenna*, the burned hearts of the undead peasants let out an evil spirit. In the Anantis story, the survivors similarly carve out the revenant's heart and tear it to pieces. It is possible to assume that the living extracted and destroyed the body part that they believed contained the entity responsible for moving the corpse around. The same logic can possibly explain why in horror films the living attack the zombies' heads. In *Resident Evil*, the protagonists learn that revenants are active due to the remaining impulses in the brain, and a number of films hint at the possibility of walking dead preserving some memories that influence their behaviour. Consequently, the head appears to be the container of the zombies' 'personality,' without which it will not be able to function. Broadly speaking, and in an interesting use of medievalism, horror films do not offer much in the way of new solutions to the problem of the walking dead.

Conclusion

Modern zombie films and their medieval counterparts generally share a common plot structure: an individual or a group of people commit a sin, which causes the appearance of walking dead, spreading pestilence, and posing danger to the living; the actions taken by local authorities are ineffective, forcing ordinary people to rescue themselves. Neither the medieval walking dead story nor the modern zombie film ever fully explains the nature of the restless corpse, but the reader or the viewer often learns that there is some sort of entity inside the dead body moving it around and that some individual knows how to control this entity. The apotropaics employed include ways of affecting directly the cause of restlessness (namely, the being inside a walking corpse) or the cadaver itself. The main differences between the structure of the medieval walking-dead narrative and the zombie film owe much to the long-term decline of religion and influence of modern science. Thus, while medieval narratives use religion and the supernatural to account for the undead, modern films favour scientific explanations. In other respects, however, there is an overwhelming continuity. I began by observing that the zombie is a creature deprived of mobility, stuck between life and death; one could argue that the zombie story is as constrained as its subjects, with the same plots being recycled again and again.

Notes

1 "List of Zombie Films," *Wikipedia*, accessed 21 January 2018, https://en.wikipedia.org/wiki/List_of_zombie_films. For horror films studies, see: Carlos Clarens, *Horror Movies: An Illustrated Survey* (London: HarperCollins, 1968); Peter Hutchings, *Hammer and Beyond: The British Horror Film* (Manchester: Manchester University Press, 1993); Mark Jancovich, ed., *Horror: The Film Reader* (London: Routledge, 2002); Sarah Juliet Lauro, ed., *Zombie Theory: A Reader* (Minneapolis: University of Minnesota Press, 2017); Siegbert Salomon Prawer, *Caligaris' Children: The Film as Tale of Terror* (Oxford: Da Capo Press, 1980); and David Roche, *Making and Remaking Horror in the 1970s and 2000s: Why Don't They Do It Like They Used To?* (Jackson: University Press of Mississippi, 2014).
2 Kyle Bishop, *American Zombie Gothic: The Rise and Fall (and Rise) of the Walking Dead in Popular Culture* (Jefferson, NC: McFarland, 2010), 12–13.
3 Álvaro Hattnher, "Zombies Are Everywhere: The Many Adaptations of a Subgenre," in *The Oxford Handbook of Adaptation Studies*, ed. Thomas Leitch (Oxford: Oxford University Press, 2015), 370–373.
4 C. Mayhoff, ed., *C. Plini Secundi Naturalis Historiae Libri XXXVII* (Leipzig, 1875), 7.52, 44–45.
5 Lucan, *Pharsalia*, ed. C.E. Haskins (New York: Georg Olms Verlag, 1971), 209–226.

6 Hattnher, "Zombies," 370. See also R.C. Thompson, ed., *The Devils and Evil Spirits of Babylonia*, 2 vols. (London, Luzac and Co, 1903).
7 See, for example: John Blair, "The Dangerous Dead in Early Medieval England," in *Early Medieval Studies in Memory of Patrick Wormald*, ed. Stephen Baxter (Farnham: Ashgate, 2009), 539–560; Nancy Caciola, "Wraiths, Revenants and Ritual in Medieval Culture," *Past and Present* 152 (1996): 3–45; Stephen Gordon, "Disease, Sin and the Walking Dead in Medieval England, c.1100–1350: A Note on the Documentary and Archaeological Evidence," in *Medicine, Healing and Performance*, ed. Effie Gemi-Iordanau and Stephen Gordon (Oxford: Oxbow Books, 2014), 55–70; Stephen Gordon, "Domestic Magic and the Walking Dead in Medieval England: A Diachronic Approach," in *The Materiality of Magic: An Artifactual Investigation into Ritual Practices and Popular Beliefs*, ed. Ceri Houlbrook and Natalie Armitage (Oxford: Oxbow Books, 2015), 65–84; Stephen Gordon, "Medical Condition, Demon or Undead Corpse? Sleep Paralysis and the Nightmare in Medieval Europe," *Social History of Medicine* 28, no. 3 (2015): 425–444; Stephen Gordon, "Monstrous Words, Monstrous Bodies: Irony and the Walking Dead in Walter Map's De Nugis Curialium," *English Studies* 96, no. 4 (2015): 379–402; Stephen Gordon, "Social Monsters and Walking Dead in William of Newburgh's Historia Rerum Anglicarum," *Journal of Medieval History* 41, no. 4 (2015): 446–465; Jean-Claude Schmitt, *Ghosts in the Middle Ages: The Living and the Dead in Medieval Society*, trans. Teresa Lavender Fagan (Chicago, IL: University of Chicago Press, 1998); Jacqueline Simpson, "Repentant Soul or Walking Corpse? Debatable Apparitions in Medieval England," *Folklore* 114, no. 3 (2003): 389–402; and Carl Watkins, *History and the Supernatural in Medieval England* (Cambridge: Cambridge University Press, 2007).
8 Winston Black, "Animated Corpses and Bodies with Power in the Scholastic Age," in *Death in Medieval Europe: Death Scripted and Death Choreographed*, ed. Joelle Rollo-Koster (London: Routledge, 2017), 71–92. For early modern and modern walking dead stories, see: Marie Balfour, "Legends of the Cars," *Folk–Lore* 2 (1891): 145–170, 257–283, 401–418; Paul Barber, *Vampires, Burial and Death: Folklore and Reality* (New Haven, CT: Yale University Press, 2010); Sabine Baring-Gould, *A Book of Folk* (London: Collins, 1928); Richard Blum and Eva Blum, *The Dangerous Hour: The Lore of Crisis and Mystery in Rural Greece* (London, Scribner & Co, 1970); Richard Dorson, ed., *Peasant Customs and Savage Myths, Volume I* (London: Routledge & Kegan Paul, 1968); Ella Mary Leather, *The Folklore and Witchcraft of Herefordshire* (Hereford: Oakmagic Publications, 1912); and Montague Summers, *The Vampire in Europe* (Wellingborough: The Aquarian Press Ltd, 1980).
9 Throughout this chapter, the word *zombie* will not be used in reference to the walking dead in medieval British narratives, because their narrators did not, for obvious reasons, use the term. At the same time, words such as *corpse, cadaver, dead body,* and *revenant* will all be used interchangeably to refer to walking dead.
10 "Promovete, citius promovete! Agite, agite et venite!" Geoffrey of Burton, *Life and Miracles of St Modwenna*, ed. and trans. Robert Bartlett (Oxford: Clarendon Press, 2002), 194–196.
11 Geoffrey of Burton, *Life*, 192–198.
12 "maleficus." Walter Map, *De Nugis Curialium: Courtiers' Trifles*, ed. and trans. M.R. James, C.N.L. Brooke, and R.A.B. Mynors (Oxford: Clarendon Press, 1983), 202.
13 "infideliter." Map, *De Nugis*, 202.

14 Map, *De Nugis*, 202–204.
15 William of Newburgh, "Historia rerum Anglicarum," in *Chronicles of the Reigns of Stephen, Henry II, and Richard I*, ed. Richard Howlett, 4 vols. (London, 1884–1889), 2:474–482.
16 "vir pecuniosus, sed pessimus, ut postea plenius claruit." William of Newburgh, "Historia," 476.
17 Joseph Stevenson identifies Anantis as Annan or Annand in Dumfriesshire, and Stephen Gordon as Alnwick in Northumbria. Joseph Stevenson, ed. and trans., *The History of William of Newburgh*, (London: Llanerch Publishers, 1996), 660; Gordon, "Social Monsters," 454.
18 William of Newburgh, "Historia," 481.
19 Rosalind Love, ed. and trans., *Three Eleventh-Century Anglo-Latin Saints' Lives* (Oxford: Clarendon Press, 1996), 50–72.
20 Herman the Archdeacon and Goscelin of St Bertin, *Miracles of St Edmund*, ed. and trans. T. Licence, with the assistance of L. Lockyer (Oxford: Clarendon Press, 2014), 10–14. The story also appears in the revised version of the text that has recently been attributed to Goscelin of Saint-Bertin, in Love, *Three Eleventh-Century Anglo-Latin Saints' Lives*, 142–144.
21 Montague Rhodes James, "Twelve Medieval Ghost Stories," *The English Historical Review* 37, no. 147 (July 1922): 418.
22 Caciola, "Wraiths," 28–29.
23 Christopher Daniell, *Death and Burial in Medieval England, 1066–1550* (London: Routledge, 1996), 29; Rosemary Horrox, "Purgatory, Prayer and Plague, 1150–1380," in *Death in England: An Illustrated History*, ed. Peter Jupp and Clare Gittings (Manchester: Manchester University Press, 1999), 95.
24 Horrox, "Purgatory," 98.
25 For example, *Resident Evil* and *28 Days Later*.
26 For example, *Maggie*.
27 William of Newburgh, "Historia," 476, 481.
28 Geoffrey of Burton, *Life*, 196.
29 "sanguisuga." William of Newburgh, "Historia," 482.
30 William of Newburgh, "Historia," 479.
31 James, "Twelve Medieval Ghost Stories," 418.
32 For example, the Melrose monk (William of Newburgh, "Historia," 479).
33 For example, Robert of Killeburne spoke without using his tongue: "quo coniurato loquebatur in interioribus visceribus et non cum lingua sed quasi in vacuo dolio." James, "Twelve Medieval Ghost Stories," 418.
34 William of Newburgh, "Historia," 475.
35 Joseph Stephenson, ed., *Chronicon de Lanercost 1201–1346. E codice Cottoniano nunc primum typis mandatum* (Edinburgh, 1839), 163–164.
36 See "The 22+ Best Fast Moving Zombie Movies" for examples: https://ranker.com/list/fast-moving-zombie-movies/ranker-film.
37 Love, *Three Eleventh-Century Anglo-Latin Saints' Lives*, 72.
38 William of Newburgh, "Historia," 475.
39 "sene religioso." William of Newburgh, "Historia," 479.
40 William of Newburgh, "Historia," 475; Map, *De Nugis*, 206; James, "Twelve Medieval Ghost Stories," 418.
41 Herman the Archdeacon, *Miracles of St Edmund*, 12, 144; James, "Twelve Medieval Ghost Stories," 418.
42 See, for example, Lucan, *Pharsalia*, 226.
43 Hattnher, "Zombies," 375.
44 Andrew Reynolds, *Anglo-Saxon Deviant Burial Customs* (Oxford: Oxford University Press, 2009), 91.

6 From *Cabaret* to *Gladiator*
Refiguring Masculinity in Julie Taymor's *Titus*

Marina Gerzic[1]

Capitalising on the Shakespeare-on-screen boom of the 1990s, Julie Taymor's *Titus* (1999) is the first feature-length film adaptation of *Titus Andronicus*. Taymor draws on numerous cultural and iconographic references in order to create a complex network of meanings in which past and present reflect on each other, allowing her to explore the play's violence from a great variety of perspectives.[2] This chapter explores how references to figures and images from popular culture and Italy's Imperial and Fascist historical past are used by Taymor to establish the masculine and moral identity of the characters Saturninus and Lucius. While I acknowledge that Taymor uses similar techniques in her representation of other male characters featured in the film, a detailed examination of how the masculinity of these other characters is defined is outside the scope of my specific analysis in this chapter.[3] The characters of Saturninus and Lucius have been often overlooked in the abundant critical reception the film's release has generated, and this chapter is the first close study focused entirely on their comparative masculinities.

Taymor's *Titus* is set in an undetermined time and setting. Through a stylised mise-en-scène and amalgamation of genres, times, and setting, the world created in Taymor's film is a visual extravaganza of epic proportions that is both ancient and modern. Taymor's approach to adapting Shakespeare for the screen is not to rewrite the words, but what I term as filling them out visually. This visual "filling out" of Shakespeare is achieved through the numerous references to historical events, periods, and figures, as well as popular cultural references. As Elsie Walker aptly surmises, Taymor "self-consciously translates Shakespeare's play for a modern audience and medium using contemporary as well as classical myths to tell the story."[4] The various references in *Titus* are not deliberate attempts to situate the audience in a specific time and place, but instead work thematically to help the audience to engage with the film, and draw parallels with their own lives and culture.

This chapter demonstrates how the various references in *Titus* are fundamentally important to Taymor's construction of characters' gender identity, particularly masculinity. Alan Cumming's portrayal of Saturninus draws upon the film history of grandiose and camp emperors from sword-and-sandal epics, Fascist imagery, and most significantly his previous renowned performance of the Emcee in Sam Mendes's 1998 stage revival of the musical *Cabaret*. These references signal that Saturninus is a sinister, corrupt, weak, and effeminate antecedent to Angus MacFayden's Lucius. Lucius's portrayal references both the sword-and-sandal and gladiatorial film genres, in an attempt to present him as a hero-like warrior and exemplary manly leader. What troubles me about Taymor's *Titus* is how she goes out of her way to tie the moral identity of Lucius and Saturninus to their gender identity. Through Taymor's selective use of imagery and editing of Shakespeare's text, Lucius's rugged gladiator-like hero is presented as a redeeming force, arriving to cleanse and take over the corrupt Rome, led by the genderqueer Fascist villain Saturninus. Thus, Taymor seems to suggest not only that violence and masculinity are linked—in order to be masculine, you must be violent and represent violence—but also that only the 'right' kind of masculinity—one that replicates violent Roman traditions—is an acceptable form of gender identity.

David Frederick has offered a detailed examination of the influence of sword-and-sandal films on the design of Taymor's *Titus*.[5] In particular, Frederick connects Alan Cumming's Saturninus's effeminate appearance and extravagant mannerisms with the history of how emperors are portrayed in Roman-themed films, such as *Quo Vadis* (1951) and *The Robe* (1953). I acknowledge that these films have influenced Taymor's production design, and her film includes many motifs from Roman epic film; I will examine such "sword-and-sandal" epics later in this chapter in reference to the gladiatorial-inspired masculinity of the character Lucius. However, Cumming's portrayal of Saturninus also owes much to references to figures such as Benito Mussolini and Adolf Hitler, as well as Cumming's own intertext, drawn from a history of playing morally questionable and repugnant characters around the time *Titus* was made, both on film and on stage. I refer here in particular to social climber Mr Elton in *Emma* (1996), villain Boris "Mr Invincible" Ivanovich Grishenko in *Golden Eye* (1995), creepy lizard-like Sean Walsh in *Circle of Friends* (1995), and most significantly the Master of Ceremonies—or "Emcee"—in the Sam Mendes-directed 1998 Broadway revival of *Cabaret*. All of these characters inform Cumming's performance in some way, and are particularly important in terms of how his Saturninus, in bodily terms, is feminised, infantilised, and demonised in the film.

Saturninus and the Fascist Aesthetic in *Titus*

From the very first moment the audience sees Alan Cumming's Saturninus on-screen, he is coded as sinister, villainous, and childish. As acknowledged by Taymor in the screenplay for the film, costumes in *Titus* "were conceived to express the nature of a character, the personality of people and of events rather than to maintain a specific time period."[6]

84 *Marina Gerzic*

Figure 6.1 Alan Cumming as Saturninus incites the crowd in *Titus*. Image courtesy of Clear Blue Sky Productions and Twentieth Century Fox.

Slight and pale in a Gestapo-like red-fringed black leather overcoat, Saturninus's jet-black hair is cut like that of Hitler. His bearing and delivery of lines as he provokes his supporters and demands to be the next emperor are reminiscent of the fiery speeches delivered by both Mussolini and Hitler (see Figure 6.1). This reading of Saturninus is acknowledged by various critics and reviewers, including Rob Blackwelder, who characterises Cumming's interpretation of his role as "Hitler-esque."[7] Taymor combines this interpretation of Saturninus with other overt Fascist symbolism. The centrepiece of Taymor's film is the Palazzo della Civiltà Italiana, which serves as Saturninus's Roman court. The Palazzo is part of the Esposizione Universale Roma (also known as the EUR): an enormous complex built by Mussolini as a celebration of Fascism in Italy. Alberto Zambenedetti, while critical of Taymor's use of the EUR complex in her film—he bemoans her lack of directorial sophistication in using the complex as simply "a stage and … a backdrop" used to create "a generic Fascist urban landscape"[8]—concedes that the EUR in *Titus* also acts as a sophisticated architectural signifier of Fascism that "prestages Saturninus' upcoming, unjust leadership."[9] Taymor explains in the screenplay to her 2010 film adaptation of *The Tempest* that, as in her adaptation of *Titus*, "location is metaphor and represents the essence of the scene in a visual ideograph."[10] The presence of the EUR in Taymor's film thus alludes to Fascism and to Mussolini's brutal regime; the Fascist aesthetic of the EUR, combined with Saturninus's costuming and performance, suggests his eventual 'dictator' status in running Rome.[11]

Watching Taymor's film in 2018, our current engagement with the film must take note of a further (unintentional) allusion to an ultra-right-wing aesthetic: the presence of the name "Stephen K. Bannon" in the film's credits. Bannon is now known primarily as the founder and former executive chairman of online alt-right news, opinion, and commentary website *Breitbart News*, and for his roles as chief executive of Donald Trump's 2016 Presidential Campaign, as well as serving as Trump's White House Chief Strategist in 2017. In the 1990s, Bannon, a former investment banker, also served as an executive producer on a number of films, including Taymor's *Titus*. While there are conflicting accounts as to how much Bannon was involved in producing Taymor's 1999 film,[12] his name in the credits now draws uncomfortable parallels with the alt-right *Breitbart*; Charlottesville's violent "Unite the Right" rally held by white nationalists, neo-Nazis, and alt-right activists;[13] the appropriation of faux-medieval/Renaissance culture by the alt-right;[14] and his own unproduced screenplays (co-written with Julia Jones), *Andronicus*, an adaptation of *Titus Andronicus* set in space, and *Coriolanus*, a rap musical set in South Central Los Angeles during the Rodney King riots. These screenplays are defined as much by their violence and controversial gender and racial politics as they are by their "dreadful" dialogue.[15]

Early-Modernism and Saturninus's Problematic Masculinity

Combining with the film's ultra-right-wing aesthetic, including his fantastical Fascist-like appearance, Alan Cumming delivers an over-the-top performance that is both "comical and sinister."[16] His portrayal is frightening in its fluidity: one moment megalomaniacal, mad, and power hungry; the next, almost childlike in his insecurity. Russell Jackson neatly sums up Cumming's portrayal of Saturninus, through his description of him as a "hysterical ninny."[17] Taymor uses contrasting examples of behaviour as a way to show Saturninus's unsuitability for the crown. Bassianus, his brother, offers a diplomatic and measured response to the news that the tribunes have elected Titus as the new Emperor of Rome. Saturninus, on the other hand, is childlike and petulant in his desire that his birthright, the crown of Rome, be immediately bestowed upon him. He stands with arms crossed and behaves "like an impulsive, spoiled child."[18] Taymor literally presents him as childlike, ill-prepared, and incapable of running Rome. Once he does become emperor, Saturninus reclines frailly within an oversized metal throne, designed to look like a giant armchair. His legs dangle over the edge, like a child sitting in adult chair that is too big for him.

Saturninus is drawn to queen of the Goths, Tamora, in an uncomfortable blend of sexual lust and the psychological need for a mother figure. Tamora seizes the opportunity to rise to a position of power and exercises both physical and emotional influence over her infantile husband. She urges Saturninus to "Be ruled by me" (I.i.447),[19] and he instantly is, forgiving apparent transgressions at the insistence of his new wife. Taymor visualises Tamora's domination over the childlike emperor in imagery that conflates the idea of her as both mother and lover. Tamora cradles a sleeping

Saturninus in bed, his head resting childlike on her naked breast, his hand clutching the other breast. Dorothea Kehler argues that Saturninus's relationship with Tamora—he is his own man in public, but led by his wife in private—is a vital characteristic in differentiating Lucius and Saturninus, their rule of Rome, and ultimately their masculinity.[20] Elements of Taymor's film engage in early-modernism by adapting early modern traditions. For example, early modern conduct books and military manuals warn men against the effeminizing effect of women's erotic power.[21] Eugene Giddens notes that these conduct books "served as 'how to' manuals for the performance of appropriate masculinity, and thus othered inappropriate male behaviour."[22] Kehler adds that "Tudor ideology can tolerate Lucius's leading the Goths into Rome," despite it looking like a foreign takeover, as a Rome ruled by Saturninus is "a Rome ruled by a 'child' who is ruled by his 'mother.'"[23] Tamora's transgressive behaviour embodies early modern male anxieties over effeminacy and erotic transgressions, in particular the "popular belief that most women are deceitful" and are "quick to take advantage of men's sexual vulnerability."[24] Surprisingly, Saturninus, as cuckold, never seems jealous, even though his wife's infidelities (according to Lavinia) "have made him noted long" (II.iii.86). Giddens notes that the phrase "No greater shame to a man than to be a cuckold" was proverbial in Shakespeare's time.[25] If a man was cuckolded, it was seen as a sign that he had failed to maintain order in his household. For example, Count Romei's 1598 conduct book *The Courtiers Academie* places the blame of a wife's adultery squarely on her husband:

> The wife ... being in her husbands power, and vnder his gouernment, it appeareth she cannot offend, without some fault in her husband, as he that either by con-sent, or euill gouernment, hath beene the occasion of such a defect: and therefore it cannot bee that the adulterous wife, should not in some part offend her husbands honour, because such a man, cannot bee in that good opinion hee first was, with them who haue notice of his offence, or they iudge him ignorant, of final worth, and worthy of that contempt his wife and adulterer procure him.[26]

Adulterous wives thus only strayed because their husbands could not control their wives and households sufficiently. That the Emperor of Rome has been cuckolded shows a shocking breakdown in law and order and a concerning deficit in (masculine) leadership.

Rome Is a *Cabaret:* Sexual and Gender Ambivalence and Fascist Symbolism

In order to appear in *Titus*, Alan Cumming took time off from his Tony award-winning performance as the Master of Ceremonies in

Sam Mendes's 1998 Broadway revival of *Cabaret*, a musical written by John Kander and Fred Ebb, and set in Fascist Germany of the 1930s. Joel Grey initially played the role of the "Emcee" in Bob Fosse's 1972 film *Cabaret*, reprising his role from the West End and Broadway stage productions. While there are many differences between Fosse's film and Mendes's stage revival, the most significant is the characterisation of the Emcee. Cumming's portrayal of the Emcee is more overtly sexual and queer in both appearance and performance. His costume consists of white suspenders that weave their way around his body and crotch, and red paint on his nipples. The cabaret number "Two Ladies" offers valuable insight into the difference between the two productions. In Fosse's film version, Grey's Emcee and two cabaret girls perform in a style reminiscent of the burlesque comedy of vaudeville. To borrow a phrase from *Monty Python*, the performance never goes beyond "wink wink, nudge nudge, say no more." In Mendes's revival, the number is staged with Cumming's Emcee, a cabaret girl, and a cabaret boy in drag, all dressed in lingerie, dancing in an explicitly suggestive manner, and includes a shadow play simulating various sexual positions. By making the Emcee bisexual, Mendes subtly refers to Alan Cumming's openness about his own bisexuality,[27] but also troublingly plays into the "evil bisexual stereotype"[28] by having the Emcee dressed (at times) in a black leather coat reminiscent of those worn by the Gestapo in Nazi Germany. Keith Garebian reads this (and other Nazi symbolism) as primarily "a tocsin of the impending doom" and as the Emcee "mocking the encroaching Nazi movement."[29] The same cannot be said of Cumming's turn as Saturninus.

Much like Cumming's Emcee, Saturninus is also "played with [a] camp flamboyance" that combines sexual ambivalence with Fascist symbolism.[30] Cynthia Fuchs highlights the visual similarity of both characters in her review of *Titus*; she describes Saturninus as like Cumming's portrayal of the Emcee, "done up with Fuhrer-bangs and psycho eye shadow."[31] This Nazi-inspired costume choice is most obvious in the scene where Saturninus and his brother Bassianus battle over who should be appointed the next Emperor of Rome: Saturninus wears a long ankle-length leather jacket, and matching black leather gloves, reminiscent of those worn by officers in the Gestapo. Parallels between Saturninus and the Emcee go beyond simply visual similarity. Like the Emcee, Saturninus is happy to have "two ladies" of his own—Lavinia and Tamora—and suggests such an unscrupulous arrangement in the first act. Once he is crowned Rome's new Emperor, Saturninus's camp sensibility is increasingly emphasised through both appearance and performance. His emperorship is celebrated by a raucous and flamboyant feast, and his court later plays host to a decadent orgy scene, which puts the scantily clad Kit Kat Club dancers from *Cabaret* to shame. In a visual amalgam of masculine and feminine identity, Saturninus is often dressed in a pristine military uniform and wears visible make-up, including golden eyeshadow, mascara, and dark lipstick.

Saturninus's androgynous "New Romantic" look visually contrasts him with the brutal, war-like Romans, especially Lucius, who is presented as more rugged and conventionally masculine. Unlike Lucius, Saturninus is effeminate and extravagant in his facial expressions and other mannerisms. David Frederick aptly refers to Saturninus as a "screamer," adding that his use of "mascara and lipstick, a flip haircut, and a petulant strut" marks him as "highly effeminate."[32] During his hysterical outburst in front of the senate, Saturninus displays his emotions with abandon: he screams and flails wildly before bursting into tears. Fragile and weak, he is incapable of handling his own problems, and instead needs to be comforted by his wife, Tamora. Stephen Orgel notes that the early moderns considered women dangerous to men, precisely "because sexual passion for women renders men effeminate."[33] In another instance of early-modernism then, Saturninus's lack of control over his emotions further demonstrates Tamora's bad influence on him: he has been rendered a passive and weak vessel due to his lust for her. Thus, the gender and power dynamics here reflect the film's overt engagement with early-modernism.

While Saturninus is set up as sinister and amoral through both Cumming's intertext and Milena Canonero's costume design, through most of *Titus*, his actions do not justify being presented in such a villainous way. Saturninus is undeniably spoiled, insecure, pompous, and lacks the strength, direction, and authority of a great leader. I am not, however, completely convinced of his role as representative of a corrupt Rome where formal justice has given way to personal revenge, nor that he violates the ethics of kingship by sentencing Martius and Quintus to death, for the apparent murder of his brother Bassianus, without a trial. It is important to note that the new Roman regime that replaces him, led by Lucius, is also guilty of being led by personal revenge.[34] Jeannette S. White goes so far as to describe Lucius as "just another vindictive character."[35] I am inclined to side with Alan Hughes's defence of Saturninus's actions against Titus's sons as justified under Roman law, as "he acts in the belief that they are guilty of Bassianus's murder."[36] Saturninus also demonstrates belief in justice, and not simply revenge for crimes committed, when he demands Chiron and Demetrius be brought to him when Titus reveals what they have done to Lavinia (V.iii.58). Taymor further exonerates Saturninus of guilt through eliminating the crime that he clearly does commit in Shakespeare's play: his order, delivered in a fit of rage, that the Clown, who delivers a letter from Titus, be hanged (IV.iv.44).[37] Taymor instead includes only one instance on-screen in which Saturninus clearly commits a crime—his attack and murder of Titus in retaliation for the murder of his wife, Tamora. To use Taymor's own words in defence of Lucius (which I will come to again shortly), "surely everybody would understand his violent response because he is so greatly provoked?"[38] Certainly not Lucius, who immediately kills Saturninus with a spoon in a fairly grotesque manner and becomes the new leader of Rome.

How Do You Solve a Problem Like Lucius?: Early-Modernism, Honour, and Masculinity

Taymor's characterisation of Saturninus as sinister and corrupt, and as a physical and moral opposite to Angus MacFadyen's Lucius in *Titus* is problematic precisely because Lucius begins the cycle of violent revenge, and also brings bloodshed and death into the play.[39] Both the opening and the closing of the film are dominated by Lucius's call for revenge, first in the guise of institutionalised justice and, by the end, simply bloodthirsty retribution. Lucius's first words in the film are an insistence on a ritualistic sacrifice as a tribute to his dead brothers. He demands and relishes in the sacrifice of Alarbus. His report of the event is disturbing in the language he uses to describe the violent event and the pride with which he says it. In front of Alarbus's grieving family, Lucius equates the smell of his burning flesh with a sweet-smelling perfume that should be enjoyed:

> See, lord, father, how we have performed
> Our Roman rites: Alarbus' limbs lopped,
> And entrails feed the sacrificing fire,
> Whose *smoke like incense doth perfume* the sky.
> (I.i.142–145; emphasis mine)

Taymor punctuates the brutal and disturbing way that Lucius relishes in the sacrifice of Alarbus with the reaction of his son Young Lucius. Taymor does not show the actual sacrifice, and instead focuses on Young Lucius's shocked expression as he witnesses the gruesome image, and the sizzling sound of entrails being thrown into the fire by his blood-splattered father. Giddens argues that the slaying of Alarbus represents "one of the greatest crimes against early modern honour," as early modern military theorists universally condemned killing the captured.[40] In addition to Sir John Ferne's *The Blazon of Gentrie* (1586),[41] a further example can be seen in Hugo Grotius's seminal work *On the Law of War and Peace* (1625), which instructs readers that "Captives, and They that yield, are not to be killed."[42] Giddens further notes that as with Henry V's killing of prisoners at Agincourt, Lucius's sacrifice of Alarbus affects his "heroic stature" and, furthermore, "offers a telling contrast between models of dealing with prisoners within Roman society."[43] While Saturninus offers a gentler treatment to the Goths taken prisoner by Rome, stating that "Princely shall be thy usage every way" (I.i.270), Lucius relishes in the killing of a prisoner; this overt early-modernism complicates Roman ethics in the play and makes Lucius's role as leader of the military campaign against Saturninus, and eventual crowning as the new Emperor of Rome, problematic.

While Taymor is critical of the cruel and pointless ritualistic violence of this scene, she later characterises Lucius as justified in his violent actions against Aaron. When Aaron is captured at the Goth army base, Lucius stands over him and cruelly gloats with a menacing grin, and also threatens to murder Aaron's infant son. Only after Aaron revels in his description of the rape of Lavinia does Lucius explode into action and senselessly beats him as he kneels on the ground, helpless, defenceless, and with arms bound. Taymor excuses the depiction of violence with the explanation that "everybody would understand his violent response because he is so greatly provoked."[44] Her defence of Lucius is at odds with how the violent act is presented on-screen. Lucius's attack on Aaron is brutal. The sound of Lucius's fists and boot making contact with Aaron is harsh and loud, all the more noticeable by the absence of the musical score during the scene.

A further significant example of Taymor's attempts to cleanse Lucius's character is her elimination of lines from Act IV, where Shakespeare gives insight into Lucius's behaviour while he was a soldier at war. His son, Young Lucius, is extremely upset at the rape and butchering of his aunt Lavinia at the hands of Chiron and Demetrius, and angrily threatens to revenge rape with rape:

> I say, my lord, that if I were a man
> Their mother's bedchamber should not be safe
> For these base bondmen to the yoke of Rome.
> (IV.i.107–109)

In a horrifying lesson of corrupt manliness and violence, Young Lucius is not reprimanded by his uncle; instead, Marcus congratulates him:

> Ay, that's my boy! *Thy father hath* full oft
> For this ungrateful country *done the like*.
> (IV.I.110–111; emphasis mine)

Marcus implies that during the long war with the Goths, Lucius raped women and should be congratulated for the deed. Coppelia Kahn notes that for Marcus, certain types of "rape is manly, Roman and in warfare, surely, a component of *virtus*."[45] Thus, if Young Lucius wants to live up to his father's valour and manliness, he should do the same. Lesson learnt, Young Lucius responds with "And, uncle, *so will I*, and if I live" (IV.i.112; emphasis mine), before setting off to deliver presents of weapons—literal manifestations of violence and war—to Chiron and Demetrius at the behest of his grandfather.[46] Thus, all of the masculine figures in Young Lucius's life guide him to replicate violent behaviour.

Taymor further exonerates Lucius in her revelation in her director's commentary on the DVD release of the film that actor Angus Mac-Fayden, who plays Lucius, insisted his character not kill Aaron's infant son because his character would not break his word.[47] This differs from Taymor's earlier 1994 stage production of *Titus Andronicus*, where Aaron's son is represented onstage in the final moments of the play by a tiny black coffin, suggesting to the audience that Lucius has indeed murdered the infant. Virginia Mason Vaughn aptly outlines the problematic nature of Taymor's interpretation and edits:

> In choices that seem inconsistent with the rest of the film, Mac-Fayden and Taymor clearly want their Lucius to be a "good guy" in a play where there are no good guys.[48]

Taymor's attempt to acquit Lucius of blame for the violence he engages in sends the message that violence becomes acceptable when justifiably provoked against a character who is a figure of empathy and is presented as a 'hero.'

As I have shown is the case with Saturninus, costuming in *Titus* serves to express the nature of a character. Vaughn describes MacFayden's Lucius as a "manly man, a warrior garbed in dark and austere uniforms, or leather garnished with metal"[49] (see Figure 6.2). Sixteenth-century notions of gender fused manhood and masculinity with arms and armour. Etiquette manuals, conduct books, and advice literature from the early modern period link masculinity to military prowess. For example, Baldassare Castiglione's *The Courtier* (1528) instructs men to be "skilfull in all kynd of marciall feates both on horsbacke and a foote, and well practised in them" and to "undertake his bould feates and couragious

Figure 6.2 Angus MacFayden as Lucius, dressed in 'manly' armour in *Titus*. Image courtesy of Clear Blue Sky Productions and Twentieth Century Fox.

enterprises in war."[50] Taymor's conception of Lucius is thus influenced by early-modernism and replicates both its gendering of military prowess as masculine and its connection of masculinity (and honour) with military apparel.

"Honour" is achieved mainly through martial combat and is the badge of elite masculinity. When Lucius tells the Romans in his final speech that "My scars can witness, dumb although they are, / That my report is just and full of truth" (V.iii.113–114), his battle scars are offered not only as guarantees of his truthfulness, but also as visible symbols of his masculinity and honour. Jeffrey R. Wilson highlights that on the early English stage, wounds "signify the highest virtue," adding that "in the Corpus Christi cycles [of Mystery Plays], the resurrected Christ displays his divinity by showing his stigmata to a doubting Thomas."[51] As Giddens aptly notes, "honour, as a marker of gender, has an especially prominent place in *Titus Andronicus*, where the word is mentioned 45 times."[52] Lucius as armed warrior turned statesman is presented as a manly and honourable substitute for Saturninus's corrupt gender-fluid politician. However, as Giddens rightly criticises, this type of "Roman honour" in *Titus Andronicus* is both "confused and at odds with Renaissance ideologies," and "alien not only to the early modern, but also to the more identifiably Roman traditions of masculinity that Shakespeare stages later in his career."[53] While Taymor's early-modernism is, in some ways, a direct response to Shakespeare's own medievalism, she plays it up for her contemporary audiences, allowing 'honour' to serve as a shorthand for Lucius's masculinity in ways that move beyond the original text.

Lucius the "Survivor": *Titus* and the Heroic "Sword-and-Sandal" Aesthetic

Lucius's appearance is also reminiscent of the past heroes of sword-and-sandal epics—such as Kirk Douglas in *Spartacus* (1960) and Charlton Heston in *Ben-Hur* (1959)—and prefigures the popularity of sword-and-sandal films with problematic heroes, such as Maximus in Ridley Scott's *Gladiator* (2000) (who, like Shakespeare's Lucius, is also an amalgamation of various historical figures), Brad Pitt's Achilles in *Troy* (2004), Colin Farrell's Alexander the Great in *Alexander* (2004) (which also stars Anthony Hopkins as Ptolemy, the father-like figure and general to Alexander), and Gerard Butler's Leonidas in *300* (2006).[54] The dramatic parallels between *Titus* and *Gladiator* are particularly seen in the similarity of the characters Saturninus and Commodus, who are presented as villainous symbols of a Fascist Imperial Rome, as well as the characters Lucius and Maximus, who are the heroic cleansing force who end the villains' tyranny.[55] The audience is therefore encouraged to read Lucius as a 'heroic' gladiator, who emerges from the battle victorious and is 'rightly' awarded the rule of Rome. Lisa Hopkins draws on this 'heroic' intertext in her examination of MacFayden's portrayal of Lucius, and notes a similarity with MacFayden's role of Robert the Bruce in Mel Gibson's film *Braveheart* (1995). Hopkins argues that both characters are "survivors," who emerge as rulers in the end because of the "death of the other contenders."[56] Hopkins's use of the word "survivors" is problematic, however, in that it suggests that the audience overlooks each man's flaws and instead focuses on their great will and determination to overcome the obstacles in their lives, consequences be damned.

After the brutal massacre of Act V, Lucius emerges as a figure of authority and responsibility to restore order to Rome. Now leader of Rome, Lucius's final judgements replicate his father's earlier violent Roman traditions, and as Thomas Betteridge rightly points out, "*Titus Andronicus* ends as it began with a failure of pity":[57]

> As for that ravenous tiger, Tamora,
> No funeral rite, nor man in mourning weed,
> No mournful bell shall ring her burial,
> But throw her forth to beasts and birds to prey:
> Her life was beastly and *devoid of pity*,
> And being dead, let birds on her *take pity*.
> (V.iii.194–199; emphasis mine)

While the play and film end with the repetition of the word pity, Lucius is guilty of that which he accuses Tamora of: being "devoid of pity" (V.iii.198). In his questioning of both why Tamora is singled out in this way and the motives for Lucius's hate of her, Betteridge acknowledges the dramatic parallels between Tamora's fate and that of Antigone in the eponymous play by Sophocles.[58] While Betteridge's allusion is valid, Tamora is more like the power-hungry Polynices than the martyr Antigone (who are both improperly buried), and thus Lucius becomes a stand-in for Creon, the cruel figure doling out harsh institutional punishment. Lucius implies in his final orders that his actions stem from Tamora's apparent cruelty and pitilessness. Mary Villeponteaux argues that in Shakespeare's plays, "cruel women are repeatedly characterized as monstrous, their lack of pity a violation of nature itself."[59] Tamora's excessive cruelty and lack of pity leads Lavinia to characterise her as a "beastly creature" (II.ii.182) (Lucius also re-emphasises her beastliness in his epilogue); thus, Tamora is a monster who not only denies pity, but also makes it clear that it is not even part of her understanding, shown when she tells Lavinia "I know not what it [pity] means" (II.ii.157), and by defining herself by the self-ascribed term "pitiless" (II.ii.162). Through Lucius's connection with Roman gladiatorial imagery, Taymor frames Lucius's lack of pity as forgivable due to his *virtus* and masculinity. However, Tamora can never achieve this forgiveness due to the excessive cruelty that corrupts her nature and is thus 'justifiably' denied proper burial rites. Betteridge also situates Tamora's punishment in historical terms, arguing that it recalls the violent and disturbing treatment of religious enemies during the Reformation.[60] Yet, along with his own lack of pity, Lucius does not attempt to disguise his words behind notions of institutionalised forms of justice or religious piety. Rather than merely dispensing justice, he is "once again inflicting pain and agony with calculated relish."[61] In sentencing Aaron and Tamora, "vengeance remains the governing motivation for violence."[62] These savage words and exaction of brutal revenge are what Lucius leaves with his son and the audience at film's end. I find it frightening that in view of Lucius's "fearful brutality ... we are expected to applaud" his role as victorious and noble gladiator turned statesman and saviour of Rome.[63]

The ending of *Titus* leaves the audience at the point where one of Shakespeare's other Roman plays, *Coriolanus*, starts: with a decorated and victorious soldier shifting to a political role of influence, power, and leadership. While *Titus Andronicus* and *Coriolanus* stand at opposite ends of both Shakespeare's career and of Roman history, John Cox draws noticeable parallels between the figures of Lucius and Coriolanus, which are evident in Lucius's Act V speech where he addresses the Goths (V.i.5–8). Cox rightly argues that Lucius's "appeal to patrician sentiment, his determination to support Titus's heroic honour in the face of every adversity, his expressed need to compete vengefully with Saturninus" all anticipate the character Coriolanus.[64] Aemilius, on informing Saturninus of Lucius's return to Rome with the support of the Goths, makes this connection to Coriolanus explicit (IV.iv.66–67). Unsurprisingly, Taymor does not include this line in her film adaptation. This falls in line with her attempts throughout the film to rehabilitate Lucius's character, and to present him as a viable alternative power at film's end. Although motivated by different reasons—Lucius by revenge and Coriolanus by his pride—both men are very much soldiers who believe in the myth of Rome and replicate violent Roman traditions. Shakespeare ends *Titus Andronicus* before we see if Lucius will be able to shift to be a political man in a suit or if, like Coriolanus, he fails dramatically in this new role and once again brings Rome to its knees. Similarly, Taymor's film does not give us a glimpse into what Rome will be like under the stewardship of Lucius's rule. She instead cuts to a scene of Young Lucius carrying Aaron's infant son into the sunset, the fate of both left purposely ambiguous.[65] In spite of Lucius's brutality and final words of revenge, Taymor's film offers up Lucius as a suitable masculine and supposedly honourable replacement for the ostensibly corrupt, feminised, and Fascist-like Saturninus. So, at film's end, Rome may gain a more decisive 'masculine' leader but also one who is just as—if not more—vengeful, brutal, and violent.

Notes

1. I thank Aidan Norrie, Bríd Phillips, and Michael Barbezat for their assistance during the preparation of this chapter. Earlier versions of this chapter were presented at both the Cambridge Shakespeare Conference – Shakespeare: Sources and Adaptation in 2011, and Gender Worlds, 500–1800: New Perspectives (the Centre for Medieval and Early Modern Studies & Perth Medieval and Renaissance Group Annual Conference in 2016), and I thank the participants at both these events for their helpful feedback.
2. Anne-Kathrin Marquardt, *The Spectacle of Violence in Julie Taymor's "Titus": Ethics and Aesthetics* (Berlin: Trafo, 2010), 9–16.
3. For more on how masculinity is explored and defined in Julie Taymor's *Titus*, see Pascale Aebischer, "Shakespeare, Sex, and Violence: Negotiating Masculinities in Branagh's *Henry V* and Taymor's *Titus*," in *A Concise Companion to Shakespeare on Screen*, ed. Diana Henderson (Malden, MA: Blackwell, 2006), 112–132; and Marina Gerzic, "The Intersection of Shakespeare and Popular Culture: An Intertextual Examination of Some Millennial Shakespearean Film Adaptations (1999–2001), with Special Reference to Music" (PhD thesis, The University of Western Australia, 2008), 148–161.
4. Elsie Walker, "'Now Is a Time to Storm': Julie Taymor's *Titus* (2000)," *Literature/Film Quarterly* 30, no.3 (2002): 196.
5. David Frederick, "Titus Androgynous: Foul Mouths and Troubled Masculinity," *Arethusa* 41, no. 1 (2008): 205–233.
6. Julie Taymor, *Titus: The Illustrated Screenplay* (New York: Newmarket Press, 2000), 180.
7. Rob Blackwelder, "A Graphic Feast of Brilliance," *SPLICEDwire*, 1999, http://splicedwire.com/99reviews/titus.html.
8. Alberto Zambenedetti, "Filming in Stone: Palazzo della Civiltà Italiana and Fascist Signification in Cinema," *Annali d'Italianistica* 28 (2010): 209.
9. Zambenedetti, "Filming in Stone," 208.
10. Julie Taymor, *The Tempest: Adapted from the Play by William Shakespeare* (New York: Abrams, 2010), 18.
11. For more on how Julie Taymor re-deploys Fascist iconography in *Titus*, see Richard Burt, "Shakespeare and the Holocaust: Julie Taymor's *Titus* Is Beautiful, or Shakesploi Meets (the) Camp," *Colby Quarterly* 37, no. 1 (March 2001): 78–106.
12. Rex Weiner writes in the *Paris Review* that Bannon optioned Taymor's 1994 off-Broadway adaptation of *Titus Andronicus*, the basis for her 1999 film. Rex Weiner, "Titus in Space," *The Paris Review*, 29 November 2016, https://theparisreview.org/blog/2016/11/29/titus-in-space; Jonathan Bate repeats this claim in his introduction to his revised edition of *Titus Andronicus* (London: Arden Shakespeare, 2018), 159–160. However, Taymor has distanced herself and her work from any connection with Bannon, stating that although Bannon "is listed as one of the executive producers of the [1999] film, he had nothing to do with the actual producing or financing of it" (Taymor, quoted in Adam White, "Shakespeare in Space, with 'ectoplasmic sex': The Bizarre Story of Donald Trump Strategist Steve Bannon's Titus Andronicus Script," *The Telegraph*, 5 December 2016, http://telegraph.co.uk/films/2016/12/05/shakespeare-space-featuring-ectoplasmic-sex-bizarre-story-donald).
13. Glenn Thrush and Maggie Haberman reported in *The New York Times* that Trump "was the only national political figure to spread blame for the 'hatred, bigotry and violence' that resulted in the death of one person to 'many sides.'" Glenn Thrush and Maggie Haberman, "Trump Is Criticized for Not Calling

Out White Supremacists," *The New York Times*, 12 August 2017, https://nytimes.com/2017/08/12/us/trump-charlottesville-protest-nationalist-riot.html. Haberman and Thrush add that this decision was reported to have come from Bannon. Maggie Haberman and Glenn Thrush, "Bannon in Limbo as Trump Faces Growing Calls for the Strategist's Ouster," *The New York Times*, 14 August 2017, https://nytimes.com/2017/08/14/us/politics/steve-bannon-trump-white-house.html.

14   For more on the rise of the far right across the world, and their fascination with, and increased use of medieval and Renaissance imagery, see Iain A. MacInnes's chapter in this volume.
15   Julia Jones, quoted in White, "Shakespeare in Space." For more on Bannon and Jones's adaptation, *Andronicus*, see Weiner, "Titus in Space"; and Asawin Suebsaeng, "How Donald Trump's Top Guy Steve Bannon Wrote a Hollywood Sex Scene Set in Outer Space," *Daily Beast*, 3 December 2016, https://thedailybeast.com/how-donald-trumps-top-guy-steve-bannon-wrote-a-hollywood-sex-scene-set-in-outer-space. For more on Bannon and Jones's adaptation of *Coriolanus*, see: Daniel Pollack-Pelznerdec, "Behold, Steve Bannon's Hip-Hop Shakespeare Rewrite: 'Coriolanus,'" *The New York Times*, 17 December 2016, https://nytimes.com/2016/12/17/opinion/sunday/steve-bannon-hip-hop-shakespeare-rewrite-coriolanus.html.
16   Michael A. Anderegg, *Cinematic Shakespeare* (Lanham, MD: Rowman & Littlefield, 2004), 185.
17   Russell Jackson, *Shakespeare and the English-speaking Cinema* (Oxford: Oxford University Press, 2014), 101.
18   Alan A. Stone, "Shakespeare's Tarantino Play," *Boston Review*, 1 April 2000, https://bostonreview.net/film/alan-stone-shakespeares-tarantino-play.
19   All quotations from *Titus Andronicus* are taken from William Shakespeare, *Titus Andronicus*, ed. Jonathan Bate (London: Arden Shakespeare, 1995).
20   Dorothea Kehler, "That Ravenous Tiger Tamora: *Titus Andronicus*'s Lusty Widow, Wife and M/Other," in *Titus Andronicus: Critical Essays*, ed. Phillip C. Kolin (New York: Garland, 1995), 323.
21   See, for example: Alexander Niccholes, *A Discourse, of Marriage and Wiving and of the Greatest Mystery Therein Contained* (London, 1615), 8–11; and Robert Ward, *Anima'dversions of vvarre* (London, 1639), 179.
22   Eugene Giddens, "Masculinity and Barbarism in Titus Andronicus," *Early Modern Literary Studies* 15, no. 2 (2010–2011): 20. Giddens also adds that "controlling female sexuality is overwhelmingly the most important issue in conduct manuals for women" (21).
23   Kehler, "That Ravenous Tiger Tamora," 323. A similar situation emerged during England's 'Glorious Revolution,' where England was invaded (and James II deposed) by a Dutch fleet and army led by his son-in-law William III, Prince of Orange. For more on this see Lisa Jardine, *Going Dutch: How England Plundered Holland's Glory* (London: HarperPress, 2008).
24   Kehler, "That Ravenous Tiger Tamora," 323.
25   Giddens, "Masculinity and Barbarism," 18.
26   Annibale Romei, *The courtiers academie comprehending seuen seuerall dayes discourses* (London, 1598), 126–127.
27   Alan Cumming has been outspoken about his own sexuality (he famously appeared on the cover of American gay lifestyle magazine *Out* in November 1999 and gave an interview where he discussed his sexuality) and is a renowned activist for LGBTIQA+ rights.
28   For more on this, see Wayne Bryant's survey of negative representations of male bisexuality in Hollywood and foreign films, in "Is That Me Up There?," *Journal of Bisexuality* 5 (2005): 305–312.

From Cabaret to Gladiator 97

29 Keith Garebian, *The Making of Cabaret*, 2nd ed. (Oxford: Oxford University Press, 2011), 174. Other examples mentioned by Garebian include the end of the first act that infamously ends with the Emcee bending over and whipping up his coat to reveal a swastika tattooed on his buttocks (174), and the final image of the Emcee is of him in a concentration camp uniform adorned with both a yellow star and pink triangle (175).
30 Anderegg, *Cinematic Shakespeare*, 185.
31 Cynthia Fuchs, "Meltdown," *Pop Matters*, 3 August 2004, http://popmatters.com/film/reviews/t/titus.shtml.
32 Frederick, "Titus Androgynous," 215, 216.
33 Stephen Orgel, *Impersonations: The Performance of Gender in Shakespeare's England* (Cambridge: Cambridge University Press, 2000), 26.
34 See Lucius's line, "to be revenged on Rome and Saturnine" (III.i.301), as well as his pitiless attitude at play's end.
35 Jeanette S. White. "'Is black so base a hue?': Shakespeare's Aaron and the Politics and Poetics of Race," *CLA Journal* 40, no. 3 (1997): 360.
36 William Shakespeare, *Titus Andronicus*, ed. Alan Hughes (Cambridge: Cambridge University Press, 1994), 38.
37 Both Peter Brook (1955) and Deborah Warner (1987) include this scene in their respective stage productions of *Titus Andronicus* for the Royal Shakespeare Company. Jane Howell also includes this scene in her filmed BBC television adaptation of the play (1985). All three productions, especially Howell's, influenced the artistic and thematic conceptions of both Taymor's stage and film adaptations of *Titus Andronicus*, and therefore the scene's absence is all the more noticeable. For more on the influence of Howell of Taymor's adaptations of *Titus Andronicus*, see: Gerzic, "Intersection of Shakespeare and Popular Culture," 137–138; and Lucian Ghita, "Reality and Metaphor in Jane Howell's and Julie Taymor's Productions of Shakespeare's *Titus Andronicus*," *CLCWeb: Comparative Literature and Culture* 6, no. 1 (2004), doi:10.7771/1481-4374.1215.
38 Quotations from director Julie Taymor's "Director's Commentary" are my own transcription based on the DVD release of the film. *Titus* [two-disc special edition], dir. Julie Taymor (Clear Blue Sky Productions/Fox Searchlight Pictures/Twentieth Century Fox Film Corporation, 1999).
39 Anthony Brian Taylor, "Lucius, the Severely Flawed Redeemer of *Titus Andronicus*," *Connotations* 6, no. 2 (1996–1997): 141.
40 Giddens, "Masculinity and Barbarism," 9.
41 John Ferne, *The Blazon of Gentrie* (London, 1586), 96–97, cited in Giddens, "Masculinity and Barbarism," 9, and n20.
42 Hugo Grotius, *The Illustrious Hugo Grotius of the Law of Warre and Peace with Annotations* (London, 1655), Book 3, section XLVI, 594–597.
43 Giddens, "Masculinity and Barbarism," 9.
44 Taymor, "Director's Commentary."
45 Coppelia Kahn, *Roman Shakespeare: Warriors, Wounds and Women* (London: Routledge, 1997), 68.
46 Taymor cuts all these lines except for Titus's instructions to Young Lucius to deliver the weapons to Chiron and Demetrius. Unlike Julie Taymor, Jane Howell includes these lines from Act IV in her 1985 BBC television production. This falls into her line with her critical reading of Lucius's new Roman leadership as "worse than the regime that went before." Michael Billington, "Shaping a Gory Classic for TV," *New York Times*, 14 April 1985, sec. 2: 29.
47 Taymor, "Director's Commentary."
48 Virginia Mason Vaughn, "Looking at the 'Other' in Julie Taymor's *Titus*," *Shakespeare Bulletin* 21, no. 3 (2003): 78.

49 Vaughn, "Looking at the 'Other,'" 78.
50 Baldassare Castiglione, *The Courtyer of Count Baldessar Castilio divided into foure bookes* (London, 1561), sigs Pp6v, Pp7r. For more on the models of masculinity (and femininity) proffered in conduct books and other such works, and their relation to gender in Shakespeare's plays, see, for example: Coppélia Kahn, *Man's Estate: Masculine Identity in Shakespeare* (Berkeley: University of California Press, 1981); Mark Breitenberg, *Anxious Masculinity in Early Modern England* (Cambridge: Cambridge University Press, 2003); Bruce R. Smith, *Shakespeare and Masculinity* (Oxford: Oxford University Press, 2012); and Jennifer Feather and Catherine E. Thomas, eds., *Violent Masculinities: Male Aggression in Early Modern Texts and Culture* (New York: Palgrave Macmillan, 2013).
51 Jeffrey R. Wilson, "Coriolanus's Wounds," *Stigma in Shakespeare*, 2017, https://wilson.fas.harvard.edu/stigma-in-shakespeare/coriolanus%E2%80%99s-wounds. Lucius's battle scars are one of many parallels we may draw between him and the character Coriolanus. Like Lucius, Coriolanus seeks public office, but unlike Lucius he refuses to perform the Roman custom of showing the public the wounds and scars he received in his years of wartime service. These scars signify Coriolanus's Roman valour and Christian virtue, but unseen they instead become symbols of his untrustworthiness, contempt for the people, and his pride, the sin that gets him banished from Rome and sets forth the tragic action of the play.
52 Giddens, "Masculinity and Barbarism," 5.
53 Giddens, "Masculinity and Barbarism," 14, 13.
54 For more on the rise and decline of each successive cycle of sword-and-sandal epics, see: Jeffrey Richards, *Hollywood's Ancient Worlds* (New York: Continuum, 2008), especially Chapter 6, "The Ancient World Revival"; and Martin M. Winkler, ed., *Gladiator: Film and History* (Oxford: Blackwell, 2004), especially Martin M. Winkler, "*Gladiator* and the Traditions of Historical Cinema," 87–110.
55 For more on Fascist imagery in *Gladiator*, see: Arthur J. Pomeroy, "The Vision of a Fascist Rome in *Gladiator*," in *Gladiator: Film and History*, ed. Martin M. Winkler (Oxford: Blackwell, 2004), 111–123.
56 Lisa Hopkins, "'A Tiger's Heart Wrapped in a Player's Hide': Julie Taymor's War Dances," *Shakespeare Bulletin* 21, no. 3 (2003): 63.
57 Thomas Betteridge, "The Most Lamentable Roman Tragedy of *Titus Andronicus*: Shakespeare and Tudor Theatre," in *The Oxford Handbook of Tudor Drama*, ed. Thomas Betteridge and Greg Walker (Oxford: Oxford University Press, 2012), 667.
58 Betteridge, "*The Most Lamentable Roman Tragedy*," 667.
59 Mary Villeponteaux, *The Queen's Mercy: Gender and Judgment in Representations of Elizabeth I* (New York: Palgrave Macmillan, 2014), 15.
60 Betteridge, "*The Most Lamentable Roman Tragedy*," 667. Not being buried properly was also a concern during the plague/s.
61 Taylor, "Lucius, the Severely Flawed Redeemer," 144.
62 Brecken Rose Hancock, "Roman or Revenger?: The Definition and Distortion of Masculine Identity in *Titus Andronicus*," *Early Modern Literary Studies* 10, no. 1 (2004): 6.
63 R.F. Hill, "The Composition of *Titus Andronicus*," *Shakespeare Survey* 10 (1957): 62.
64 John D. Cox, *Seeming Knowledge: Shakespeare and Skeptical Faith* (Waco, TX: Baylor University Press, 2007), 176.
65 Richard Burt argues that the film's "shlocky" ending subverts Taymor's criticism of Fascism, and instead offers a "Fascist romanticisation of the child" (Burt, "Shakespeare and the Holocaust," 94, 83).

7 "There's My Exchange"
The Hogarth Shakespeare

Sheila T. Cavanagh

In anticipation of the commemorative events surrounding the 400th anniversary of Shakespeare's death in 2016, Hogarth Press commissioned a series of well-regarded fiction writers to create modern adaptations of Shakespeare's plays. So far, the published novels include Jeanette Winterson's *The Gap of Time* (*Winter's Tale*),[1] Howard Jacobson's *Shylock Is My Name* (*The Merchant of Venice*),[2] Anne Tyler's *Vinegar Girl* (*The Taming of the Shrew*),[3] Margaret Atwood's *Hag-Seed* (*The Tempest*),[4] Tracy Chevalier's *New Boy* (*Othello*),[5] Edward St Aubyn's *Dunbar* (*King Lear*),[6] and Jo Nesbø's "thriller" *Macbeth*.[7] As *The Washington Post*'s Ron Charles notes, *Hamlet* will not appear for several years: "If you can keep from shuffling off this mortal coil for a few more years, Hogarth is promising Gillian Flynn's retelling of 'Hamlet' in 2021."[8] Each of these works presents an updated "cover version" of Shakespeare's texts, with a variety of re-imagined settings. *The Gap of Time*, for example, alternates between London after the financial crisis and "New Bohemia." *Vinegar Girl* introduces immigration concerns into *Shrew*. *Dunbar* highlights international business networks. *New Boy* relocates *Othello* to Washington, DC. *Hag-Seed* brings *The Tempest* into a Canadian prison environment, and *Shylock Is My Name* moves Shakespeare's play from Venice to England. *Macbeth* offers a gritty urban reimagining of the original story. This publishing endeavour demonstrates the veracity of Laurie Osborne's observation that "Shakespearean performance is so deeply implicated in popular fiction."[9] These texts continue a lengthy history of Shakespearean reconceptualisations. As Douglas Lanier notes, moreover, given the novels' styles and the reputations of their authors, "the series provides a 'literary' alternative to Shakespeare adaptation in mass media."[10]

The literary pedigrees of the commissioned authors are unassailable, but the quality of the texts presented varies widely. The novels introduce modern topics into these classic works, which require substantial alterations in plot and characterisation. They work best when they retain the challenging issues confronted in Shakespeare's early modern works. This assertion does not emanate from an insistence on what Thomas Leitch calls "the notion of fidelity," or "the responsibility of adaptations to communicate or evoke some essential features associated with the texts they are adapting."[11] Rather, this response reflects the occasional tendency for these adaptations to diminish the complexity offered in the earlier texts. Some of these works shy away from the controversial or ambiguous elements found in their predecessors, and these omissions weaken the reimagined narratives. As Lanier comments, for instance, the novels tend to present "literary realism": "Elements of magic or intrusions of the divine are naturalized."[12] Some of the pieces introduce new settings or altered characterisations that contribute to powerful modern texts, but others fall flat. This chapter investigates significant ways these distinguished authors reconceptualise Shakespearean drama, with a particular focus on the distinctive roles played in the narratives by shifts in prominent geographical spaces and by potentially disruptive socio-political perspectives. As Kamilla Elliott rightly remarks, adaptations can be "scintillating, surprising, immensely creative, subtle, innovative, and absolutely cutting edge."[13] They can also, in her formulation, be "dull, obvious, banal, gauche, clichéd, and unfashionable."[14] The Hogarth series encompasses many of these evaluative categories, offering readers and scholars of adaptation studies much to contemplate and assess.

Margaret Atwood's *Hag-Seed* appears to be modelled, at least obliquely, on the growing number of modern 'Shakespeare in Prison' programmes in the USA and other countries, although the story as it is written suggests that the author did not visit any of these endeavours herself. Her acknowledgements reference a couple of relevant texts, but are silent on whether she personally interacted with any incarcerated Shakespearean performers. Given how many such programmes exist in North America, this failure to undertake research 'inside' is both surprising and unfortunate. As the biannual "Shakespeare in Prison" conferences indicate,[15] such undertakings are thriving and accessible for those who are interested. Atwood's apparent decision not to take advantage of these resources undermines her ability to present a level of literary achievement in the text commensurate with her recognised talents. This absence is surprising, since, as Fiona Tolan comments, "Atwood's fictions [often] betray her preoccupation with pressing contemporary concerns."[16] Nevertheless, some reviewers praise *Hag-Seed*, despite its weaknesses. Viv Groscop, for example, is exuberant in her 2016 *Guardian* review:

> This is written with such gusto and mischief that it feels so much like something Atwood would have written anyway. The joy and hilarity of it just sing off the page. It's a magical eulogy to Shakespeare, leading the reader through a fantastical reworking of the original but infusing it with ironic nods to contemporary culture, thrilling to anyone who knows *The Tempest* intimately, but equally compelling to anyone not overly familiar with the work.[17]

Similarly, Sofía Muñoz-Valdivieso maintains that this novel "imaginatively transforms its ostensible source text."[18] Such enthusiasm notwithstanding, this novel is unlikely to achieve a prominent place within Atwood's literary legacy.

Shakespeare in Prison

Hag-Seed offers a number of promising narrative elements, however, despite its ultimate failure. Felix, the protagonist, seems appropriately distracted from his professional responsibilities in the Makeshiweg Festival and completely unprepared for the ouster organised by his ambitious colleague Tony.[19] In *The Tempest*, Prospero neglects his primary ducal tasks in order to further his expertise in the mystical arts: "The government I cast upon my brother and to my state grew stranger, being transported and rapt in secret studies."[20] Felix similarly declines to attend key professional events, instead focusing on the development of increasingly unconventional productions of Shakespeare's plays, including *The Tempest*:

> His Ariel, he'd decided, would be played by a transvestite on stilts who'd transform into a giant firefly at significant moments. His Caliban would be a scabby street person—black or maybe Native—and a paraplegic as well, pushing himself around the stage on an oversized skateboard. Stephano and Trinculo? He hadn't worked them out, but bowler hats and codpieces would be involved. And juggling: Trinculo could juggle some things he might pick up on the beach of the magic island, such as squids.[21]

While Atwood's adaptation alters the familial relationship involved in Prospero's abandonment on the unidentified island in Shakespeare's rendition, *Hag-Seed* creates a plausible scenario that depicts a circumstance similar enough for readers to recognise the correspondences, whether or not they value 'fidelity' when approaching this kind of reconceptualisation. The novel also introduces a number of modern technological references, as Coral Howells notes: "she adds a whole new dimension to the narrative with her use of digital media."[22] In this way, Howells remarks, Atwood underscores thematic associations between her work and her model's creations: "Like Shakespeare, Atwood exploits the tricksy relationship between reality and fantasy that theatre provides."[23]

When Felix is removed as Festival artistic director, he isolates himself in a remote cabin relatively nearby, unlike his literary forebear, who is forcibly sent away from his dukedom and ends up on a remote island with no means of escape: "There they hoist us, to cry to th' sea that roared to us" (1.2.149–150). During the initial period of Felix's isolation, *Hag-Seed* offers its most evocative sections of the narrative. Felix spends considerable time ruminating over his situation and poignantly interacts with a spectral version of his deceased daughter Miranda:

> Miranda's fifteen now, a lovely girl. All grown up from the cherub on the swing who's still enclosed in her silver frame beside his bedside.

> The fifteen-year-old version is slender and kind, though a bit pale. She needs to get out more, run around in the fields and woods the way she used to. Bring some roses to her cheeks. Of course it's winter, there's snow, but that never used to bother her; she could skim above drifts, light as a bird.[24]

Although Felix seems not to have moved far enough away for his adoption of the alternate identity, "Mr. Duke," to be successful, this self-imposed solitude offers readers an opportunity to experience this director turned hermit in depth. Since he is the only well-developed character in the book, this extended focus is crucial for whatever compelling features this novel ultimately presents.

The ghostly Miranda, who appears most prominently in this section, offers a masterfully depicted representation of a daughter whom Felix can control, since she only exists in his imagination:

> If she'd lived, she would have been at the awkward teenager stage: making dismissive comments, rolling her eyes at him, dying her hair, tattooing her arms. Hanging out in bars or worse. He's heard the stories. But none of that has happened. She remains simple, she remains innocent. She's such a comfort.[25]

Prospero exerts significant authority over his daughter in *The Tempest*, much to the chagrin of many critics, as Muñoz-Valdivieso notes.[26] Nevertheless, Shakespeare's Miranda shows signs of growing consciousness and a desire for comparative autonomy as she expresses her unbridled thoughts to Ferdinand: "But I prattle something too wildly, and my father's precepts I therein do forget" (3.1.56–59). Felix's daughter, however, largely offers insight into this protagonist's mental state, which includes periodic moments of recognition that this growing young girl is not actually still alive: "Miranda might have been on a school bus once, if she'd ever reached that age."[27]

The narrative derails, however, when Felix decides to start bringing his Shakespearean expertise into a local correctional facility, aptly called "Fletcher" in honour of Shakespeare's contemporary playwriting colleague. The problems in this portion of the novel overcome the merit contained in its earlier sections. Some missteps could have been avoided through a closer affiliation with the themes presented in Shakespeare's play. Others could be alleviated if Atwood had spent time with incarcerated Shakespearean actors. Unlike the prisoners described in countless first-hand accounts of 'Shakespeare in Prison' programmes by Rob Pensalfini,[28] Jonathan Shailor,[29] and others, Atwood's incarcerated thespians are not crafted as realistic, multifaceted characters. In the award-winning documentary, *Shakespeare Behind Bars*, a group of prisoners, under the direction of Curt Tofteland, prepare a production of *The Tempest*.[30] During a series of 2018 screenings at Emory University, which included conversations with a former inmate who features prominently in the film, students expressed common reactions to this documentary: they cared deeply about the men they encountered on-screen, and they felt devastated upon learning the mixed fates facing these figures after the documentary was released. Sammie Byron, for example, seemed poised for parole when the film was made, but spent an additional eleven years in prison.[31] Viewers regularly become invested sufficiently in the lives they see portrayed on the screen that they want to know what has happened since. In response, *Shakespeare Behind Bars* includes an update on its website.

It is unlikely that Atwood's incarcerated characters would attract similar concern, since they do not resonate as living, human beings engaged in a compelling life journey. Felix is the sole character with any depth, so readers only experience the prisoners through his eyes, and that vision lacks veracity and compassion. The story veers completely away from verisimilitude when Felix uses the prisoners in order to wreak revenge on those who caused his professional downfall. Here, in an elaborate ruse, complete with blackmail, Felix enlists his incarcerated actors into an outlandish manoeuvre that threatens to eliminate any chance they would have for eventual freedom. Emily St John Mandel, herself a talented novelist, notes this plot deficiency in her *New York Times* review of the novel:

> But the prison production of "The Tempest" leads to some of the book's clunkiest elements. At least some of the prisoners are in on Felix's plot. But to break the enchantment for a moment: These are inmates in a medium-security prison, who are being asked to menace two federal ministers. They've been told the literacy program is in peril, but this alone can't explain why they'd risk longer sentences, deferred parole or transfer to maximum security for such a harebrained scheme.[32]

This part of the plot seems more appropriate for a screwball comedy than for an even marginally serious reinterpretation of *The Tempest*. Ron Charles, in the *Washington Post*, suggests, for instance, "The prisoners are goofy fun."[33] "Goofy" can clearly be an authorial choice, but it does not serve Atwood's narrative well.

Atwood's far-fetched denouement not only defies logic, but also undermines her novel and distances it in disappointing ways from her model. Unlike Prospero in *The Tempest*, or the performers in *Shakespeare Behind Bars*, Felix does not appear to value forgiveness or redemption. Although Lanier maintains that Atwood creates a tale "of redemption," Felix's choices seem starkly different from Prospero's.[34] Shakespeare's character ultimately decides not to punish his brother, despite originally engineering the opportunity to make this occur. Instead, he chooses reconciliation: "since I have my dukedom got and pardoned the deceiver" (Epilogue, 7–8). While audiences might not always understand this narrative turn, *The Tempest* offers this path without equivocation. Tofteland's prison actors speak at length about the centrality of forgiveness and redemption in their conceptualisation of the play. While it makes sense that prisoners, many of whom have committed horrendous crimes, would gravitate towards stories supporting forgiveness, this emphasis comes directly from Shakespeare's text. Prospero decides to forgive, even though there is little evidence suggesting that his brother has earned such beneficence. In the play and in the documentary, reconciliation is possible, even when there is ample reason not to expect it.

Atwood's decision to keep Felix on a path for revenge weakens the novel. Even the absurdity of a group of prisoners jeopardising their own lives in favour of a man who has done nothing to warrant their self-sacrifice pales in comparison to *Hag-Seed*'s decision to shield its protagonist and those around him from the harder task of offering forgiveness, even when it may not be deserved. As the many publications detailing modern 'Shakespeare in Prison' programmes suggest, these endeavours do not take the path of least resistance. They are not designed to reinforce the kinds of impulses that helped subvert the lives of those incarcerated. Margaret Atwood is an esteemed writer, for many good reasons. It is unfortunate that she did not bring her formidable talents as a fiction writer to bear on this project.

The Shrew in Baltimore

Anne Tyler does better with *Vinegar Girl*, but she would also have been well advised to engage with the complexities of the text, even when they appear to fly in the face of modern sensibilities. Like Atwood, who set *Hag-Seed* in her home territory of Canada, Tyler relocates *Shrew* to Baltimore, the site where she typically places her novels, although there is no apparent reason for this story to occur there. There are more interesting characters in Tyler's Hogarth project than one encounters in Atwood's, but the story remains much more bland than the one Shakespeare offers. Here, Kate works in a day-care centre, having been ejected from university for questioning one of her instructors. Her prospects of continued employment remain uncertain, since she does little to placate the demanding parents served in this environment. At home, she helps look after her beautiful and rebellious younger sister, while her widowed father spends most of his time in his lab. Given the distance in social conditions between Shakespeare's time and our own, Tyler was inevitably challenged to find an appropriate modern parallel for Kate's marital circumstances, particularly since creating a character in an environment containing an arranged marriage could easily raise questions about cultural appropriation.

Tyler's answer is not ideal, but largely works. Kate's father belatedly emerges from his absent-minded research focus to realise that his lab assistant, Pyotr, is about to lose his legal ability to work in the USA. Since this problem is not noticed in sufficient time to address it through normal, official channels, a plan is concocted to keep Pyotr in the USA through marriage with the beautiful but unattached "vinegar girl" Kate. Predictably, she initially resists, then relents when told that she would be entering a sham marriage, carefully designed to deter unwanted questions from immigration officials. Kate is initially assured that she would retain her own room in her father's house. When she is subsequently encouraged to move into Pyotr's apartment, she is also promised separate accommodation. By the end of the novel, she and her husband have clearly been cohabiting for several years, since they leave a young son at home while travelling to receive a horticultural award granted to Kate, who has always been most at home in the botanical world.

There is nothing inherently objectionable to the story Tyler presents, but it suffers through the author's determination to ameliorate some of the interpretive challenges associated with *Shrew*. While socially awkward, Kate here lacks the vituperativeness that makes Shakespeare's character so challenging. Thus, in their first meeting in the play, Katherine warns Petruchio "If I be waspish, best beware my sting" (2.1.210). Tyler's Kate, in contrast, is supportive of her quirky family and does not engage in the outbursts linking her to the sobriquet "shrew" in Shakespeare's play. Similarly, Pyotr's Petruchio does not display the harsh treatment that often disconcerts Shakespeare's audiences. While films typically portray the story as a romantic comedy,[35] staged productions frequently have to contend with Petruchio's apparently abusive behaviour when he starves Kate and keeps her from sleeping: "She ate no meat today, nor none shall eat. Last night she slept not, nor tonight she shall not" (4.1.185–186). In some renditions, Kate and Petruchio are well matched; in others, Kate is partnered with someone who will clearly make her life a misery. From either perspective, Kate's final speech, with its seeming capitulation to the idea of Petruchio's supremacy, typically makes modern audiences angry or uncomfortable: "And place your hands below your husband's foot, in token of which duty, if he please, my hand is ready, may it do him ease" (5.2.181–183).

Pyotr's lapses into cluelessness do not equate with Petruchio's evident cruelty, however. While the often-hapless lab assistant regularly commits social faux pas, he seems to genuinely care for Kate:

> He flung an arm exuberantly around her waist and pulled her close and kissed her cheek. For a moment, she didn't resist; his arm enclosed her so securely and his fresh-hay smell was quite pleasant.[36]

Kate initially appears disconcerted by her father's clumsy plan to save his lab at her expense, but there is no real evident bite in this inelegant manoeuvre. Kate's passive crush on a fellow teacher evaporates quickly, and the marriage is solemnised with little apparent angst. Jane Smiley, who has successfully transformed Shakespearean drama into modern fiction, offers a plausible explanation for Tyler's shift in focus here in her *New York Times* review:

> The tamer of Kate is not Pyotr (in the play, Petruchio's use of reverse psychology to disorient but also amuse Katherina wins and subdues her at the same time). Appropriately for a modern shrew, it is Kate who tames herself by coming to understand what is going on (and there is a somewhat sinister climactic event), to acknowledge that change and growth and acceptance are to be welcomed.[37]

Smiley's generous reading may well be accurate, but this choice nevertheless diminishes the novel. Lanier makes a similar point about Kate taming herself, suggesting that "Portraying Pyotr as comically inept rather than misogynistically motivated allows Tyler to sidestep the problem of Petruccio's shrew-taming project for modern readers."[38]

Tyler's decision to eliminate the complexities fuelling Shakespeare's drama leaves the narrative without sufficient challenges to merit lasting attention. Like many of its cinematic predecessors, *Vinegar Girl* presents a pleasant, albeit saccharine, happy ending. Instead of Shakespeare's often disturbing tale, this novel offers a mildly eccentric array of people. Unlike *The Taming of the Shrew*, *Vinegar Girl* employs standard romantic comedy manoeuvres that ignore the sharp edges that keep its dramatic counterpart so timely and controversial. As suggested by John Fletcher's 1611 *The Woman's Prize, or the Tamer Tamed*, which offers a reimagined female response to Shakespeare's play that in its own way is an early-modernism, *Shrew* has unsettled viewers throughout its long history. *Vinegar Girl*, however, merely neutralises many of the problems introduced in *The Taming of the Shrew*.

Cover Versions across the Genres

Other books in the Hogarth Series, however, take on the kind of textual challenges that *Hag-Seed* and *Vinegar Girl* decline. *The Gap of Time*, *Shylock Is My Name*, and *Dunbar* each confront difficult issues raised in Shakespeare's drama. *Macbeth* and *New Boy* will be considered separately, but Nesbø's thriller is much stronger in this regard than Chevalier's disappointing attempt at modernising *Othello*. Jeanette Winterson offered *The Gap of Time* as Hogarth's first entry into this revisioning of key texts in the Shakespearean canon. While *The Winter's Tale* is not as well known as the other plays in this series, this novel sets a high standard for its successors to meet.

The Gap of Time transforms the monarchs presented in Shakespeare's plays into prominent business and entertainment figures. Like *Hag-Seed's* Felix, however, who creates the pseudonym "Duke" when he goes into hiding, Winterson presents her Leontes with a name signalling his royal heritage: "Leo Kaiser." Set alternately between London after the economic meltdown in the early twenty-first century and "New Bohemia" (presumably New Orleans), *The Gap of Time* succeeds as a novel on its own merits. While *The Winter's Tale's* shift from tragedy to pastoral romance often defeats efforts for a coherent production, the novel takes advantage of modern transportation and video game technology to create a narrative that plausibly depicts the emotional twists and turns of its characters' lives. As Joanna Kavenna notes, Winterson's introduction of Xeno's (Polixenes) "Gap of Time" game "supplies a parallel world in which sorrowful mortals are potentially redeemed. It's a lovely, poignant concept,"[39] even though, as Paul Joseph Zajac comments, "against the sense of alienation exacerbated by modern technologies, several of Winterson's characters long for a less mediated form of existence."[40]

The novel is consistently savvy about the implications associated with the "gap of time" signalled in its title. In Shakespeare's play, that phrase denotes the lengthy hiatus of many years separating the first and second sections of the play. Here, the story also includes a space during which Perdita can mature, but the narrative concurrently deftly incorporates a lengthy, unexplained period where the fate of Mamillius/Milo is unknown. He vanishes during the chaos following Leo's jealous rage, but there is no information provided about him for over 100 pages, and no explanation is offered for this obvious but perplexing narrative omission. This striking textual representation of the narrative's title demonstrates why Winterson's novel is so powerful. Readers are likely to think that they missed some important information that has not, in fact, yet been offered. They could easily be unsettled as the story continues without conscious acknowledgement that a character has vanished without comment. Mamillius's loss in *The Winter's Tale* is reported fairly abruptly but he then disappears from the text: "The Prince your son, with mere conceit and fear of the Queen's speed, is gone ... is dead" (3.2.144–145).

Winterson's unexpected reintroduction of Milo and the lengthy period where his fate is uncertain strengthens the child's conceptual power in the narrative. Milo/Mamillius's death undercuts any unequivocal possibility that this story can claim a 'happy ending,' as Winterson's narrative manoeuvre makes unavoidably clear:

> After the nuclear wastes of Leontes's fallout, there is nothing that can be done until the next generation is ready to remedy it—and they too must first escape the necrotic longings of the past, as Perdita avoids death for a second time.[41]

The Gap of Time is a more compelling contribution to this series than *Vinegar Girl* or *Hag-Seed* not because Winterson is more 'faithful' to Shakespeare's text, but because she does not shy away from unpleasant aspects of the plot or characters that might prove difficult for modern audiences. However unbelievable Hermione's extended absence might be in Shakespeare's version, for example, here, Hermione/MiMi's disappearance from public view provides a meaningful and appropriate, though less mystical, analogue. Winterson does not attempt to recreate all of the qualities inherent in the early modern genre of 'romance,' but she does fashion a narrative that correlates closely both with modern sensibilities and with the issues driving *The Winter's Tale*. Her use of a "baby hatch" and video games to correspond to the abandoned child and mystical elements found in Shakespeare's version works well. Although Kavenna finds much to admire in the text, she argues that Winterson offers too many answers for the questions introduced in the dramatic version:

> Where Winterson furnishes us with interpretations of the characters' behaviour, Shakespeare leaves spaces; baffling blanks into which we're obliged to project our own reckonings. Ultimately, the provision of concrete explanations is reductive: they close the play's possibilities down.[42]

This kind of aversion to ambiguity is common in modern renditions of Shakespearean drama but seems less prevalent in Winterson's novel than Kavenna suggests. *The Gap of Time* tackles difficult questions with rigour and grace. As the first book in this ambitious series, it sets the bar quite high. As noted, however, not all of the novels that follow meet the high standard Winterson establishes.

Howard Jacobson's *Shylock Is My Name*, however, draws from its author's considerable Shakespearean knowledge in order to present an impressive novel that mirrors, reflects, and deflects the original. *Shylock Is My Name* does not purport to be a modernised version of *The Merchant of Venice* so much as a realistic, yet phantasmagoric, variation on a series of related characters and themes. The novel frequently cites its predecessor to great effect, while the reimagined characters resemble and refract aspects of those presented in the early modern text. Here, Shylock appears but in concert with Simon Strulovitch, who also figures as a joint avatar of Shakespeare's moneylender. This duality fits well within many scholarly interpretations of the text, including Barbara Estrin's remark that "There are endless 'turnings' in the play, most notably characterized by Antonio, the merchant of the title, who slides in and out of parallels and chiasms to Lancelot, Bassanio, and Shylock."[43] As Lanier notes, however, the presentation of both Strulovich and Shylock is largely unexplained, "In Jacobson's novel, Shakespeare's Shylock, inexplicably alive in modern Manchester, becomes the companion of Simon Strulovitch, a rich Jewish philanthropist whose faith in Judaism has lapsed—but not his commitment to a Jewish cultural heritage."[44] Many of the other characters also carry multiple meanings. In a move illustrating Jacobson's adept use of language, the heiress Portia transforms into a TV star known by the literarily resonant names of "Plurabelle" or "Anna Livia Plurabelle Cleopatra A Thing of Beauty is a Joy Forever Christine." This delightfully absurd moniker demonstrates Jacobson's superlative ability to present this problematic Shakespearean "comedy" from a perspective that calls every character and situation into question. Just as modern productions of the play often criticise Portia and the other Christians, while keeping the Jewish characters under scrutiny, this version of the text keeps no one immune from sardonic investigation. At the same time, *Shylock Is My Name* does not devolve into parody. The characters and issues presented reward close attention and cannot be dismissed as allusive gimmickry. Jacobson offers a serious and insightful narrative that appropriately, yet surprisingly, adopts absurdist aspects of modern celebrity culture in order to highlight the emotional complexity permeating this text. As James Lasdun indicates, Jacobson's literary talents and Shakespearean background serve him well throughout this novel:

> the most enjoyable thing about *Shylock Is My Name* is, fittingly, the astute way in which it reads and rereads the play it was commissioned to retell. It does this explicitly, with Strulovich, for example, pressing Shylock to tell him exactly what was going on in his head when he came up with his ill-omened forfeit. But it also does so at a structural level, building on ideas latently present in *The Merchant of Venice* to bring Shylock's own story to a surprising but strangely satisfying resolution.[45]

Jacobson's re-telling offers a compelling route towards re-examining a controversial play. As Lanier notes, some of these changes offer thought-provoking revisions: "By engineering a do-over of the trial scene, Shylock frees himself from the ancient blood libel and restores his fundamental humanity."[46] Splitting Shylock into two figures succeeds because this device keeps the reader appropriately engaged and off balance. The text demands close attention from its audience and, like Shakespeare's play, does not offer easy answers to the moral and literary questions presented.

Edward St Aubyn's *Dunbar* offers a similarly complex rendering of *King Lear*. As Sophie Gilbert states in *The Atlantic*, "St. Aubyn writes like a fencer fences—so elegantly that it disguises the sharpness of his strike."[47] Like several of the other volumes, *Dunbar* relocates Henry Dunbar/King Lear from the monarchy into the corporate world, where the title character has built a massive empire that he now plans to leave to the management of his children, with the exception of Florence (Cordelia), whom he has disinherited. St Aubyn offers fewer overtly self-conscious references to *King Lear* than Jacobson includes regarding *Merchant of Venice*, but he still demonstrates considerable attention to the themes, issues, and problems of Shakespeare's text. The figure of Dunbar is more sympathetic than many portrayals of King Lear, but that characterisation emerges partially because of the immediacy presented through the currently familiar story of children putting their parents into an institution. Many who do so clearly have the best interests of their relatives in mind, but Abby and Megan—the novel's stand-ins for Goneril and Regan—are every bit as cruel, sinister, and bloodthirsty as their literary predecessors, with sadistic sexual demands and no indication of human empathy:

> In her (Megan) view, pain was the gold standard to which the paper currency of love needed to be pegged. Pain could be measured, whereas love often couldn't even be located. Why not gradually exchange something that was not much better than a rumor for something real?[48]

St Aubyn's recreation of the characters from *King Lear* is especially masterful when he transforms the Fool into an ageing, alcoholic comedian who joins Dunbar in the institution where his children are hiding him until they can complete their takeover of his business interests. Peter/The Fool was a well-known performer in his prime. Now, he helps Dunbar escape in order to score a few drinks. The poignant partnering of these two formerly powerful figures highlights how much they each have lost and makes it clear that redemption is not forthcoming. Peter's eventual suicide, resulting in part from his being tortured by Dunbar's malicious daughters, strikes Dunbar (and the reader) deeply. Upon hearing news of Peter's death, Dunbar is "temporarily emptied by the surfeit of horror, as if there was no room left for thought or speech, or any specific grief."[49] Audiences may not know exactly what has happened to the Fool in *King Lear* when the monarch announces, "My poor fool is hanged" (5.3.311). The graphic description of what drives Peter to his death, however, matches the viciousness of Gloucester's blinding in Shakespeare's tale:

> Peter's arms were twisted over the back of the bench and held in place by Jesus. Kevin unscrewed the tops from two bottles of whisky and started to pour them over Peter's head. The whiskey soaked his hair, streamed down his face, and drenched his shirt and the lapels of his jacket. As soon as they were empty, Kevin replaced the bottles and got out two more full ones.[50]

"There's My Exchange" 111

When Peter is completely covered with whiskey, Abby pulls out "a Hurricane Lighter designed to work in just these sorts of conditions" and sets him on fire.[51] This incident leads to an overwhelming sense of despair at the end of the novel. Dunbar's mammoth grief at the death of his daughter and the suicide of his companion create a mixture of sympathy and horror at the tragedy that makes this an impressive rendition of a powerful, sad story.

Dunbar and most of the volumes in this series are modestly sized, but Jo Nesbø's *Macbeth,* translated from the Norwegian by Don Bartlett, runs over 500 pages long, which *Publishers Weekly* suggests is "bloated."[52] The last in the series currently scheduled, except for Gillian Flynn's *Hamlet,* this novel demonstrates why Nesbø reigns as a major figure in Scandinavian crime fiction. Like the other successful texts in the Hogarth Shakespeare, *Macbeth* does not shy away from the difficult issues found in its early modern precursor. Since this narrative is already frequently relocated to realms of organised crime (*Maqbool*, 2003), prison (*Mickey B*, 2007), and other sites (like restaurants), with hierarchical structures that depend as much on determination as on talent, situating *Macbeth* in a police environment rife with drugs, gambling, and violence offers Nesbø a relatively seamless way to move the story to modern times. In this version, Hecate plays a major role, but many Nesbø readers will neither know nor care that Shakespeare is unlikely to have created this character in *Macbeth*. The Hecate included in this *Macbeth* takes a powerful leadership position that none of the witches could fill. It seems clear that we do not have an edition of *Macbeth* that corresponds with the play performed during Shakespeare's lifetime, so borrowing this contemporaneous addition seems to be an innocuous way to transform this story into a believable modern setting. As Stephen Orgel notes in his edition of the drama, no *Macbeth* presented today matches the text written by Shakespeare: "The play, moreover, comes to us not as it would have appeared from Shakespeare's pen in 1606, but in a version that is demonstrably a revision; and the reviser was certainly not Shakespeare."[53]

Nesbø's *Macbeth* works so well because the power dynamics of the play are not specific to the Scottish environment crafted by Shakespeare. This thriller version seems reminiscent of the original series of *Twin Peaks* (1990), with Lady Macbeth transformed into a "Blackie" figure, running a casino with all its attendant side businesses. Transforming Lady Macbeth into a beautiful, canny, and immoral businessperson frees her from the confines of her early modern marriage, but still illustrates societal limits upon her power and ambition. The warrior culture of the original *Macbeth* is so violent that its official status within the legal constructions of that time and place can easily move into similarly fluid zones with crooked cops and unquenchable ambition. Nesbø's powerful prose also ensures that readers will stay with this lengthy novel, even if

112 *Sheila T. Cavanagh*

they are familiar enough with Shakespeare's text to know how it will all end. *Publishers Weekly* suggests, however, that "*Macbeth* is a clever re-engineering of one of Shakespeare's great tragedies, but may disappoint Nesbø's fan base."[54] As a whole, however, this series cannot succeed without interest expressed by those well versed in Shakespeare's canon. Nesbø, like some of the other commissioned authors, demonstrates that the narratives can be gripping and compelling even when the endings are not likely to startle many readers.

Othello in Middle School

Sadly, Tracey Chevalier's *New Boy*, a retelling of *Othello*, makes it apparent that even placing a powerful, classic story in the hands of an accomplished writer does not ensure a successful outcome. This novel is undoubtedly the weakest volume in this series, partially because Chevalier does not create characters with dynamism or credibility. Given that the story is placed in a time and location she experienced herself (the suburbs of Washington, DC in the 1970s), the implausibility of the setting and characters is unexpected. Part of the problem arises because she focuses on a group of children who are too young to correspond well to Shakespeare's narrative. Possibly wishing to avoid comparison with the many 'teen' versions of Shakespeare's plays, Chevalier decides to centre her story on the playground interactions of middle school students, with Othello (here Osei Kokote), presented as the son of an African diplomat recently assigned to Washington. Almost nothing rings true in this narrative, with the possible exception of Osei's sister's pencil case substituting for the infamous strawberry-decked handkerchief. Yes, there were (and are) racist schoolteachers and playground politics, but this novel never overcomes the weakness of its foundational premise. Ian/Iago's manipulative nature and his jealousy of the "New Boy" correspond with familiar situations, but very little else transfers well to this environment. Unlike the other volumes in the series that successfully transition to corporate worlds and shady police officers, this move to middle school never resonates. This devise is so improbable, it even confuses some of the reviewers. Sally Bayley, in the (London) *Times*, for example, mistakenly believes that Chevalier

> transfers the story of Shakespeare's alluring Moor to a 1970s high school in Washington DC. This is *Othello* for young adults, with the presumption that teenage readers cannot cope with poetry, but they can manage yet more of the bitchy culture of high-school politics.[55]

Given the subject matter presented in the book, Bayley understandably thinks that the characters are older than Chevalier makes them, although the review also asserts that "the students seem more juvenile than they need be."[56] Given the differences between British and American school systems, and the problems with *New Boy*, this error says more about the inconsistencies within the novel than about the perspicacity of the reviewer. Chevalier has demonstrated her literary talents elsewhere, but this volume is likely to fade from view quickly. Compressing the actions of the play into one day, fixing the location in one, improbable space, and focusing the emotional weight of the narrative on children make it impossible to create a story that will move and convince its audience. Chevalier provides an anaemic version of a powerful drama that misses most of the elements that render *Othello* as a significant play.

Geographic Displacements

The Hogarth Shakespeare series offers an impressive opportunity to experience Shakespearean issues and characters through modern lenses. Even though they are not equally successful, the invited group has created a valuable new perspective on the ways that Shakespeare's plays can continue to raise pertinent questions. At their best, they also demonstrate that even commissioned reconceptualisations of familiar stories can lead to compelling fiction. As indicated earlier, several of these novels offer such imaginative, thought-provoking explorations of human foibles and possibilities that they make this whole project worthwhile. The weaker volumes offer some value for classroom use, but will probably retreat from view fairly soon. The unevenness of the results is unfortunate, but may well result from the commissioned aspect of this project. All of the prestigious writers involved in this endeavour have busy schedules and some of them may not have had the opportunity to put sufficient time into these compositions to make them as robust and significant as others of them clearly are. The best of these books will add new lustre to the reputations of their authors; the weakest are unlikely to harm the renown associated with all of the writers participating in this undertaking.

The Hogarth series offers a welcome opportunity to think about both the distinctiveness and the malleability associated with the places, motives, and challenges presented through Shakespeare's narratives and legacy. None of these texts, for example, take place in the locations used by Shakespeare. Instead, they are either situated in areas known well by their authors (like Tyler's Baltimore or Atwood's Canada) or moved to modern centres of commerce, such as London. The Mediterranean area, which served as the site for several of the Shakespearean texts reimagined here, largely fades from view, except for the bittersweet glimpses of "the Rialto" provided by Jacobson's "Jessica" figure Beatrice, whose venture there demonstrates Venice's transformation from a place of international business into a space largely known for tourism: "gondoliers singing, waiter shouting, canals rising, church bells ringing, umbrellas going up."[57] Not surprisingly, the comparative ease of twenty-first-century transportation figures prominently in many of these texts, with one of Dunbar's greatest disappointment becoming the loss of personal access to his favourite jumbo jet. His daughter worries, in fact, that he will take issue from flying in a rented Gulfstream: "Florence thought that seeing his old plane and not being allowed onboard would throw her father into a deeper turmoil."[58] The 2016 anniversary of Shakespeare's death offered innumerable opportunities for international celebrations and reconsiderations of this writer's remarkable output. The Hogarth series provides a welcome addition to the resultant new body of work, even if only some of the novels hit what Petruchio might call "the white" (5.2.190)—the centre of the target. Those successes more than compensate for the shortcomings of some of their companion texts.

Notes

1. Jeanette Winterson, *The Gap of Time* (London: Hogarth Press, 2015).
2. Howard Jacobson, *Shylock Is My Name* (London: Hogarth Press, 2016).
3. Anne Tyler, *Vinegar Girl* (London: Hogarth Press, 2016). *The Taming of the Shrew* will be shortened to *Shrew* throughout this chapter. Despite the anonymous extant play published in 1594, *A Pleasant Conceited History, Called the Taming of a Shrew*—with which Shakespeare's play was likely in dialogue—this 'shrew' play's relative obscurity, as well as the context of the chapter, means it is unlikely to cause confusion.
4. Margaret Atwood, *Hag-Seed* (London: Hogarth Press, 2016).
5. Tracey Chevalier, *New Boy: A Novel* (London: Hogarth Press, 2017).
6. Edward St Aubyn, *Dunbar* (London: Hogarth Press, 2017).
7. Jo Nesbø, *Macbeth* (London: Hogarth Press, 2018).
8. Ron Charles, "Margaret Atwood Rewrites Shakespeare. Who Will Do It Next—Gillian Flynn? Yes," *Washington Post*, 3 October 2016, https://washingtonpost.com/entertainment/books/margaret-atwood-rewrites-shakespeare-whos-next--gillian-flynn-yes/2016/10/03/6869e7ba-8389-11e6-a3ef-f35afb41797f_story.html?utm_term=.db65206ad49b.
9. Laurie Osborne, "Narration and Staging in *Hamlet* and Its Afternovels," in *The Cambridge Companion to Shakespeare and Popular Culture*, ed. Robert Shaughnessy (Cambridge: Cambridge University Press, 2007), 114.
10. Douglas M. Lanier, "The Hogarth Shakespeare Series: Redeeming Shakespeare's Literariness," in *Shakespeare and Millennial Fiction*, ed. Andrew James Hartley (Cambridge: Cambridge University Press, 2018), 231.
11. Thomas Leitch, "Introduction," in *The Oxford Handbook of Adaptation Studies*, ed. Thomas Leitch (Oxford: Oxford University Press, 2017), 7.
12. Lanier, "The Hogarth Shakespeare Series," 234.
13. Kamilla Elliott, "Adaptation Theory and Adaptation Scholarship," in *The Oxford Handbook of Adaptation Studies*, ed. Thomas Leitch (Oxford: Oxford University Press, 2016), 682.
14. Elliott, "Adaptation Theory," 682.
15. There have been three 'Shakespeare in Prison' conferences thus far: two at Notre Dame, and one a San Diego's Old Globe Theatre. See: https://shakespeare.nd.edu/spn/.
16. Fiona Tolan, "'I Could Say That, Too': An Interview with Margaret Atwood," *Contemporary Women's Writing* 11, no. 3 (December 2017): 455.
17. Viv Goscop, "Hag-Seed Review – Margaret Atwood Turns the Tempest into a Perfect Storm," *The Guardian*, 16 October 2016, https://theguardian.com/

books/2016/oct/16/hag-seed-review-margaret-atwood-tempest-hogarth-shakespeare.
18 Sofía Muñoz-Valdivieso, "Shakespeare Our Contemporary in 2016: Margaret Atwood's Rewriting of *The Tempest* in *Hag-Seed*," *SEDERI Yearbook* 27 (2017): 106.
19 As Lanier notes, Felix's Festival represents a "thinly disguised version of the Stratford (Ontario) Festival" ("The Hogarth Shakespeare Series," 243).
20 William Shakespeare, *The Tempest*, in *The Complete Works of Shakespeare*, ed. David Bevington (New York: Longman, 1997), 1.2.75–77. All further Shakespeare references will be to this edition, and will be made in-text.
21 Atwood, *Hag-Seed*, 16.
22 Coral Howells, "True Trash: Genre Fiction Revisited in Margaret Atwood's *Stone Mattress*, *The Heart Goes Last*, and *Hag-Seed*," *Contemporary Woman's Fiction* 11, no. 3 (2017): 13.
23 Howells, "True Trash," 13.
24 Atwood, *Hag-Seed*, 62.
25 Atwood, *Hag-Seed*, 62.
26 Muñoz-Valdivieso, "Shakespeare Our Contemporary in 2016," 119.
27 Atwood, *Hag-Seed*. 63.
28 Rob Pensalfini, *Prison Shakespeare: For These Deep Shames and Great Indignities* (New York: Palgrave Macmillan, 2016).
29 Jonathan Shailor, *Performing New Lives: Prison Theatre* (London: Jessica Kingsley Publishers, 2010).
30 *Shakespeare Behind Bars*, dir. Hank Rogerson (Philomath Films, 2005).
31 Class visits at Emory University with Sammie Byron, 12–13 February 2018.
32 Emily St John Mandel, "Margaret Atwood Meets Shakespeare in a Retelling of 'The Tempest,'" *The New York Times*, 28 October 2016, http://nytimes.com/2016/10/30/books/review/hag-seed-tempest-retold-margaret-atwood.html.
33 Charles, "Margaret Atwood Rewrites Shakespeare."
34 Lanier, "The Hogarth Shakespeare Series," 242.
35 Sheila T. Cavanagh, "Whose Play Is It Anyway? Viewing *The Taming of the Shrew* Pedagogically," in *Approaches to Teaching Shakespeare's the Taming of the Shrew*, ed. Margaret Dupuis and Grace Tiffany (New York: Modern Language Association of America, 2013), 181–188.
36 Atwood, *Hag-Seed*, 158.
37 Jane Smiley, "Touch Up Your Shakespeare: Anne Tyler Recasts 'The Taming of the Shrew' for Our Time," *New York Times*, 6 July 2016, http://nytimes.com/2016/07/10/books/review/touch-up-your-shakespeare-anne-tyler-recasts-the-taming-of-the-shrew-for-our-time.html.
38 Lanier, "The Hogarth Shakespeare Series," 241.
39 Joanna Kavenna, "The Gap of Time by Jeanette Winterson, Review: 'Poignant,'" *The Telegraph*, 1 October 2015, http://telegraph.co.uk/books/what-to-read/the-gap-of-time-jeanette-winterson-review/.
40 Paul Joseph Zajac, "'Distant Bedfellow': Shakespearean Struggles of Intimacy in Winterson's *The Gap of Time*," *Critique: Studies in Contemporary Fiction* 59, no. 3 (2018): 10.
41 Winterson, *Gap of Time*, 271.
42 Kavenna, "Gap of Time."
43 Barbara L. Estrin, *Shakespeare and Contemporary Fiction: Theorizing Foundling and Lyric Plots* (Lanham, MD: University of Delaware Press, 2012), 108.
44 Lanier, "The Hogarth Shakespeare Series," 242.
45 James Lasdun, "Shylock Is My Name Review – Howard Jacobson Takes on Shakespeare's Venetian Moneylender," *The Guardian*, 10 February 2016,

http://theguardian.com/books/2016/feb/10/shylock-is-my-name-howard-jacobson-review-retelling-shakespeare-the-merchant-of-venice.
46 Lanier, "Hogarth," 243.
47 Sophie Gilbert, "King Lear Is a Media Mogul in *Dunbar,*" *The Atlantic,* 10 October 2017, http://theatlantic.com/entertainment/archive/2017/10/dunbar-edward-st-aubyn-king-lear-review/542235/.
48 St Aubyn, *Dunbar,* 89.
49 St Aubyn, *Dunbar,* 244.
50 St Aubyn, *Dunbar,* 100.
51 St Aubyn, *Dunbar,* 101.
52 Review of "Macbeth," *Publishers Weekly,* 29 January 2018, http://publishersweekly.com/978-0-553-41905-4.
53 Stephen Orgel, *Shakespeare's Macbeth* (New York: Penguin, 2000), xxix.
54 Review of "Macbeth," *Publishers Weekly.*
55 Sally Bayley, "New Boy: Othello Retold by Tracy Chevalier," *The Times,* 13 May 2017, http://thetimes.co.uk/article/new-boy-othello-retold-by-tracy-chevalier-zd5cdpr8f.
56 Bayley, "New Boy."
57 Jacobson, *Shylock,* 205.
58 St Aubyn, *Dunbar,* 175.

8 Bloody Brothers and Suffering Sisters

The Duchess of Malfi and Harry Potter

Lisa Hopkins

Families

When Harry Potter looks into the Mirror of Erised, he sees his parents. There are other relatives too, including an old man with the same knobbly knees as Harry who is presumably one of his grandfathers.[1] There are, however, no siblings. While this is presumably because the Mirror is showing what has been rather than what might have been, it is remarkable that while Harry often imagines what life might have been like with his parents, he never seems particularly troubled by the lack of siblings: the one brief reference to the idea comes only in the very last book, when he thinks that "He could have invited friends to his house ... he might even have had brothers and sisters."[2] Perhaps he is wise not to dwell on this possibility, however, for in this essay I am going to suggest that siblings in the Harry Potter books are often a source of tension and trouble, and that at least some of the sibling relationships in the book are explicitly and emphatically pathologised in ways which, I propose, are directly informed by John Webster's Jacobean tragedy *The Duchess of Malfi*.

In drawing on the play, Rowling puts what may seem like the distinctively modern cult of celebrity in dialogue with what is thus revealed as its early modern equivalent: Renaissance self-fashioning. Rowling's own growing celebrity, as she shot to fame while still writing the Harry Potter books, is reflected in the books' increasing concern with the nature and effects of publicity, embodied in the character of Rita Skeeter, who enters the series in the fourth book, *Harry Potter and the Goblet of Fire* (2000). It also clearly colours the conception of Cormoran Strike in the detective novels Rowling later published under the pseudonym of Robert Galbraith, for Strike can never escape from the fact that he is the illegitimate and estranged son of a rock star of whom everyone has heard. It is in the nature of adaptation that the source text is likely to be already famous, a fact with which any reworking must contend as best it may, and in the case of *The Duchess of Malfi* that sense of a strong originary identity is confirmed by the heroine's famous declaration that she herself is not subject to change, since whatever may happen to her she is Duchess of Malfi still. Ironically, Rowling herself hamstrung the film adaptations of the Harry Potter books by insisting on a sterile and unproductive fidelity, but her use of *Malfi* is much more subtle than this, for although she is certainly not faithful to it, and indeed does not even hint at its presence, she has taken a number of central concerns and reworked them creatively, intelligently, and productively, in ways which show us how one of the core elements of early-modernism continues to resonate and resurface in contemporary society.[3]

It might initially seem counter-intuitive to suggest an early seventeenth-century tragedy as an influence on a series of late twentieth-century children's books. However, as I shall explore later, the Harry Potter stories are unusually dark for children's books (and indeed in some ways were not conceived as such), and they are in fact not an unlikely place to find echoes from long ago. Structurally, the Potter books are as interested in the past as in the future, and indeed the entire trajectory of Harry's career bears a surprising resemblance to family history. With every step forward in Harry's development and education, he also learns something about the past. This starts early in the first book, when Hagrid first tells him he is a wizard:

> Something very painful was going on in Harry's mind. As Hagrid's story came to a close, he saw again the blinding flash of green light, more clearly than he had ever remembered it before—and he remembered something else, for the first time in his life—a high, cold, cruel laugh.[4]

In *Harry Potter and the Prisoner of Azkaban* (1999), Harry tells Lupin that when the Boggart turned into a Dementor, "I heard my dad... That's the first time I've ever heard him,"[5] but of course it is not literally the first time: the reason Harry is able to hear James now is because the memory of having once done so has been lurking latent in his memory. One of the things magic offers is a link to the past: Ollivanders have been "Makers of Fine Wands since 382 BC,"[6] and the name of St Brutus's Secure Centre for Incurably Criminal Boys, the school which Aunt Marge is told that Harry attends, gestures at the Trojan Brutus, great-grandson of Aeneas, who supposedly gave his name to the then uninhabited land of Britain (this is a story with which Rowling, who studied classics at university, would certainly have been familiar). What Harry learns most about, though, is families: his own, Voldemort's, and those of other people he knows such as Neville Longbottom and Sirius Black—and often that knowledge is painful. Families in the Potter books are rarely a source of unmixed delight. The Weasleys present as an ideal vision of family life and Harry is preserved from danger by his mother's blood, in the shape of Aunt Petunia, but family is a source of vulnerability too: Draco Malfoy's insults typically centre on family; as Hagrid tells Snape, Ron Weasley "was provoked ...

Malfoy was insultin' his family,"[7] and Ron himself says that if Malfoy "makes one more crack about my family, I'm going to get hold of his head and ...."[8] When George tells Percy that "Christmas is a time for family," it comes close to a form of bullying as "They frogmarched Percy from the room, his arms pinned to his side by his jumper."[9] Likewise, Marcus Belby's father and uncle "don't get on very well."[10] Indeed, the whole story becomes in one sense a reverse birth narrative when the cauldron used for Voldemort's resurrection is "a great stone belly large enough for a full-grown man to sit in"; it provides the setting for what he refers to as "my rebirthing party," and Voldemort refers to the Death Eaters as "My *true* family."[11]

Families in general are in fact more often a source of trouble in the books than not, and although it is of course conventional in children's adventure stories to get the parents out of the way as expeditiously as possible, in the Harry Potter books the process is taken to extremes. In one sense, Harry's story is the complete realisation of the family romance, with Aunt Petunia and Uncle Vernon as very bad parents and Dudley as a very bad brother, but actually we come closer to a vision of the family as nightmare. Being a Squib—a non-magical person born to a magical family—is only a source of shame in the context of family, just as the howler sent by Neville's grandmother after he writes down the Gryffindor passwords tells him that he "had brought shame on the whole family."[12] When a witch with a satsuma up her nostril arrives at St Mungo's just after Christmas, the receptionist has no difficulty in identifying the likely cause of the problem: "Family argument, eh? ... You're the third I've seen today."[13] The admission of new members to families is a particular stress point, as witnessed by Mrs Weasley's and Ginny's initial rejection of Bill's fiancée (and later wife), Fleur, but the potential for trouble is always latent. Most disturbingly, it is obvious from fairly early on that the similarities between Harry and Voldemort are likely to indicate a family relationship of some sort, and both do indeed prove to be descended from the Peverells.

The sense of family tension is especially strong in the case of siblings. The Potter books are steeped in references to siblings. Some of these are derived from Jane Austen, identified by J.K. Rowling on many occasions as her favourite author, whose books offer many examples of sibling relationships. The reference to Dumbledore's eyes being "light, bright and sparkling"[14] recalls Jane Austen's own description of *Pride and Prejudice* (1813), one of the most famous stories of sisters ever told.[15] Mrs Norris, after whom Filch's cat is named, owes her prominence in *Mansfield Park* (1814) to the fact of being Lady Bertram's sister. Other sibling relationships work on the level of plot. Harry and Hermione Granger are only children: Hermione was originally intended to have a non-magical younger sister, but she never appears in any of the books.[16] Ron is not, and his many siblings are a source of pressure for him; what Ron sees in the Mirror of Erised is himself alone. When Harry says, "Wish I'd had three wizard brothers, 'Five,' said Ron. For some reason, he was looking gloomy"; shortly afterwards, when Harry asks "What house were your brothers in? 'Gryffindor,' said Ron. Gloom seemed to be settling on him again."[17] Ron has reason to be gloomy, because the House system can work to underline difference as well as similarity: the Patil twins are identical, but Parvati is in Gryffindor and Padma in Ravenclaw, while Sirius becomes the first (and last) Black not to be in Slytherin. It is also suggestive that when Hermione becomes friendly with Krum, Ron's accusation is specifically that she is "fraternising with the enemy,"[18] a term later echoed by Percy when he warns Ron against "continued fraternisation" with Harry:[19] fraternising literally means acting as a brother, the idea being that Harry and Krum are bad and dangerous 'brothers' who will harm their adopted 'siblings.' Indeed, Percy is in general the extreme case of the tribulations of belonging to a family, in ways that give pain both to himself and his relations. In *Harry Potter and the Order of the Phoenix* (2003), Ron recounts how Percy said that "if Mum and Dad were going to become traitors to the Ministry he was going to make sure everyone knew he didn't belong to our family any more."[20] Sirius takes a similar attitude to the Lestranges: "As far as I'm concerned, they're not my family. *She's* [Bellatrix Lestrange] certainly not my family."[21] The possession of siblings proves even more painful, albeit in different ways, for both Dumbledore, whose sister Ariana is killed because of, and possibly even by, him, and Aunt Petunia, who both "pretended she didn't have a sister" and refers to Lily as "my dratted sister."[22] There are even problems for Uncle Vernon, who lives in terror of his sister Marge ever discovering that Harry is a wizard, making Marge's visit to Privet Drive a source of family-based tension for him as well as for Harry. Madame Maxime is ashamed of being half-giant, and Hagrid refuses to leave his house when Rita Skeeter reveals the identity of his mother, prompting Dumbledore to reflect that "My own brother, Aberforth, was prosecuted for practising inappropriate charms on a goat" (though at that stage we still have no idea of the horror of the Dumbledores' family life).[23] Barty Crouch's promising career is cut short by the disgrace of his son, who seeks to replace his father by being to Voldemort "closer than a son,"[24] while Neville has parents who can no longer recognise him.

Some sibling relations are even more profoundly troubled. When Ron is told by Hermione that "Michael Corner and his friends wouldn't have come if he hadn't been going out with Ginny," Ron's response is comic, but also clearly excessive: "'He's WHAT?' spluttered Ron, outraged, his ears now resembling curls of raw beef. 'She's going out with - my sister's going - what d'you mean, Michael Corner?'" This degree of horror is surely unexpected to the reader, but not, it seems, to Ginny, since Hermione explains that "this is exactly why Ginny hasn't told you she's seeing Michael, she knew you'd take it badly." Nor is Ron's objection just

Bloody Brothers and Suffering Sisters 121

to Michael Corner: when Ginny tells him that she is now seeing Dean Thomas, "'WHAT?' shouted Ron, upending the chessboard,"[25] and in *Harry Potter and the Half-Blood Prince* (2005), he complains "I don't want to find my own sister snogging people in public!," leading Harry to worry that if he does ever kiss Ginny he will be confronted by "Ron ripping open the tapestry curtain and drawing his wand on Harry, shouting things like 'betrayal of trust'… 'supposed to be my friend.'"[26] Nor is Ron alone in this: George says of the love potions, "But we're not selling them to our sister… not when she's already got about five boys on the go from what we've-," and Fred joins in with "you're moving through boyfriends a bit fast, aren't you?"[27] It is not surprising that Ron does not seem particularly reassured when Harry tells him that Hermione is "like my sister."[28]

Literary Influences

The Weasley boys' interest in Ginny's love life may possess something of the dependable quality of a running gag, but it also has sinister overtones. Why should Ron regard a relationship between Harry and Ginny as a "betrayal," a word charged with overtones of sexual infidelity? Is it because if Ginny were to be perceived as what Mrs Weasley is pleased to call "a scarlet woman," it would besmirch the family honour, or could there even be overtones of repressed incestuous desire? This may seem far-fetched, but there are other hints in the books of the threat of potential incest. In the first place, we are told that Harry's mother Lily had "long, dark red hair falling over her face,"[29] a description that makes her sound strangely like his love interest, Ginny. In the second, one of the Peverell brothers is called Antioch, and in the context of a story that obviously needs to be read on something more than a purely literal level, it may be pertinent that in Shakespeare's and Wilkins's play *Pericles*, Antioch is where the hero encounters a father and daughter who are in an incestuous relationship (the father is actually named Antiochus).[30] A Shakespearean allusion would be by no means an improbable thing to find in the Harry Potter books:[31] one of the chapters in *Prisoner of Azkaban* is entitled "Cat, Rat and Dog," echoing the scurrilous rhyme about the followers of Richard III, "the Cat, the Rat, and Lovell our Dog / Rule all England under a Hog";[32] the idea of a glance at *Richard III* seems confirmed when we encounter the statue of a humpbacked witch,[33] since Shakespeare dwells on the fact that Richard III was apparently a hunchback, and again when, in *Goblet of Fire*, the ghosts who emerge from Voldemort's wand encourage Harry and impede Voldemort, as the ghosts at Bosworth do to Richmond and Richard. Margaret J. Oakes compares the magic in the books to that of Prospero and Faustus,[34] and Eléonore Cartellier-Veuillen notes Rowling's fondness for Shakespeare (particularly *Macbeth* and *The Winter's Tale*), pointing out that Hermione spends much of *Harry Potter and the Chamber of Secrets* (1998) petrified, echoing her namesake in the play who poses as a statue, and that Ron becomes suddenly jealous of Harry and Hermione in *Harry Potter and the Deathly Hallows* (2007).[35] When we read in *Prisoner of Azkaban* that "still Harry stood frozen there, wand poised,"[36] he recalls the similarly immobile Pyrrhus and Hamlet, as well as foreshadowing Draco standing over Dumbledore, and two names gesture in the direction of the period in general: the Death Eater Rookwood recalls the Bye-Plot conspirator Ambrose Rookwood,[37] and the names of two more Death Eaters bring us strangely close to those of two possible contenders for Elizabeth's crown: "In 1565 Philip II wrote, 'Some claim is put forward by Lord and Lady Lestrange.'"[38] There are also, as I shall explore presently, allusions to the second tetralogy of *Richard II, Henry IV, Part One, Henry IV, Part Two*, and *Henry V*.

Another play of the period, though, seems to have been more directly influential. I want to suggest that one reason for the pathologisation of sibling relationships is that Rowling is influenced by a source which does not seem to have been previously recognised: John Webster's 1613 play, *The Duchess of Malfi*.[39] This might seem far-fetched, but *The Silkworm* (2014), the second of the Cormoran Strike books, written by Rowling under the pseudonym of Robert Galbraith, includes a number of chapter epigraphs from *Malfi*, and Robin's mother is studying it for her Open University course. My hunch would be that Rowling had read it well before that, for there are a number of striking correspondences between Webster's play and the Harry Potter books. Philip Nel points out that for at least one of her critics, "the core of Rowling's 'aesthetic troubles' is her tendency to read books other than fantasy novels";[40] I think *The Duchess of Malfi* is one such text.

As Cartellier-Veuillen notes, the Harry Potter books are in many respects detective novels;[41] there is for instance a direct borrowing from Agatha Christie in that in her 1935 novel *Death in the Clouds* the poison used in the murder comes from the venom of a boomslang.[42] *The Duchess of Malfi* has a long tradition of influencing detective fiction.[43] P.D. James's *Cover Her Face* (1962) takes its title from *Malfi*, Dorothy L. Sayers's *Busman's Honeymoon* (1937) has a chapter epigraph from it,[44] and Patricia Wentworth's *Danger Point* (1942) alludes to perhaps its most famous quotation, "Her eyes dazzled."[45] Most systematically, in Agatha Christie's *Sleeping Murder* (1976), the heroine Gwenda is taken to see a production of the play by Miss Marple's nephew Raymond West and his wife Joan:

> The play drew to a close, came to that supreme moment of horror. The actor's voice came over the footlights filled with the tragedy of a warped and perverted mentality.
> 'Cover her face. Mine eyes dazzle, she died young ...'
> Gwenda screamed.[46]

She has recovered the memory of a murder she witnessed as a small child, which eventually proves to be that of a sister by her brother. She finally realises the truth about the murder when Dr Kennedy looks up the stairs at her and asks, "Is that you, Gwennie? I can't see your face ... My eyes are dazzled –."[47] Miss Marple's reaction to the discovery of Kennedy's guilt is focused on logic: she says,

> I was stupid - very stupid. We were all stupid. We should have seen at once. Those lines from *The Duchess of Malfi* were really the clue to the whole thing. They are said, are they not, by a *brother* who has just contrived his sister's death to avenge her marriage to the man she loved. Yes, we were stupid.[48]

Gwenda's thought is rather different though: "*Cover her face ... Mine eyes dazzle ... she died young ...* that might have been me ... if Miss Marple hadn't been there."[49] Gwenda's primary response is an emotional identification with the Duchess, reminding us that *The Duchess of Malfi* is a text with an affective as well as an intellectual pull.

In the Potter books too, one of the most basic ways in which *The Duchess of Malfi* contributes to meaning is by virtue of being one of the texts that the books are remembering. As Cartellier-Veuillen has shown, there are a great many of these, and their importance is underlined by the fact that memory and remembering play such a prominent part in the books. A Patronus, that vital protector against Dementors (amongst other things, an obvious metaphor for depression and perhaps also other forms of mental illness), can be summoned only by recalling a happy memory. Rowling's magical inventions also include two examples of technologies of memory: the Remembrall, which Neville's grandmother sends him, and the Pensieve, which Dumbledore keeps in his office. The Remembrall in particular seems modelled on the crystal ball, but it is reliable, while indicators of the future in the Harry Potter books are not (the Centaurs' conviction that Harry is doomed is unfounded; the prophecy tells a kind of truth, but ultimately proves only to predict what *might* happen, not what *will*). Moreover, the books' whole structure is predicated on the idea that discovering what *has* happened is as important as discovering what *will* happen: we regress at the same time as we progress, with Harry recovering a little more of his past with every step he takes into the future. In this context, any text that is persistently echoed must also matter, and the echoes of *The Duchess of Malfi* are persistent indeed.

The Duchess of Malfi

The influence of *The Duchess of Malfi* is apparent in a number of ways. For Mrs Weasley, the Boggart in Sirius Black's house takes the shape of

124 Lisa Hopkins

each member of her family in turn, lying dead. The Duchess of Malfi too sees deceptive images of her family apparently dead when her brother Ferdinand arranges for her to be shown wax models of them and told that they are real corpses. Harry spends much of *Prisoner of Azkaban* seeing what is apparently a Grim, "The giant, spectral dog that haunts churchyards… an omen—the worst omen—of *death*!";[50] in *Duchess*, we are assured that the ghost of an old woman is always seen before the death of a member of the House of Aragon.[51] The Cardinal's advice that "Wisdom begins at the end" (I.i) is not dissimilar to the Snitch that opens at the end to reveal a truth, and the Cardinal's fear that he can see something in his fishpond becomes concrete in Harry Potter when the Durmstrang ship surfaces in the lake.

The majority of the parallels, however, centre on the figure of Ferdinand, twin brother of the Duchess. It is he who says, "I have this night digg'd up a mandrake" (II.v.84), foreshadowing the importance of mandrakes in the plot of *Chamber of Secrets*, and he who would wish to see his sister's husband Antonio only "if I could change / Eyes with a basilisk" (III.ii.86–87); it is of course a basilisk that the Chamber of Secrets ultimately proves to contain. Ferdinand also asks

> Can your faith give way
> To think there's pow'r in potions, or in charms,
> To make us love, whether we will or no?
>
> (III.i.66–68)

A love potion proves to have precisely that effect when it makes Ron become suddenly infatuated with Romilda Vane. In the great darkness scene, where Ferdinand visits his sister the Duchess in the prison to which he has condemned her, Ferdinand holds out to her the severed hand of a corpse, which he tells her is his own hand and which she therefore kisses. When lights are brought and the deception is revealed the Duchess asks, "What witchcraft doth he practise that he hath left / A dead man's hand here?" (IV.i.54–55), implying that the hand is not just a cruel trick, but resembles an object considered magical, and in Borgin and Burkes, Draco Malfoy is attracted by a Hand of Glory,[52] which indeed he later buys; traditionally these are made from the hand of a man who has been hanged. Ferdinand tells a story of Reputation, Love, and Death going on separate quests through the world:

> Upon a time, Reputation, Love, and Death
> Would travel o'er the world; and it was concluded
> That they should part, and take three several ways.
> Death told him they should find him in great battles,
> Or cities plagued with plagues. Love gives them counsel

> To inquire for him 'mongst unambitious shepherds,
> Where dowries were not talked of, and sometimes
> 'Mongst quiet kindred that had nothing left
> By their dead parents. 'Stay', quoth Reputation,
> 'Do not forsake me; for it is my nature
> If once I part from any man I meet
> I am never found again.' And so, for you:
> You have shook hands with Reputation,
> And made him invisible.
>
> (III.ii.122–135)

This is not unlike the story of the Three Hallows, and culminates in a reference to being made invisible. Towards the end of the play, Ferdinand starts to imagine himself to be a werewolf (V.ii.6), foreshadowing Lupin, who really is one. Like Morfin Gaunt, Ferdinand tries to kill his brother-in-law, and his appearance in his sister's mirror is a dark foreshadowing of the Mirror of Erised.

More fundamentally, the whole issue of 'Marrying out' is central to both *The Duchess of Malfi* and the Harry Potter books. It seems clear in the play that Ferdinand is incestuously attracted to his sister, while in the Harry Potter books the name of Hermione points to *The Winter's Tale*, where incest is a submerged possibility (it is overtly present in Shakespeare's source). In *Chamber of Secrets*, we hear for the first time a word that is going to loom increasingly large as the books progress when Malfoy calls Hermione "Mudblood." Ron, explaining it, adds, "It's mad. Most wizards these days are half-blood anyway. If we hadn't married Muggles we'd've died out."[53] Sirius concurs: "The pure-blood families are all inter-related ... If you're only going to let your sons and daughters marry pure-bloods your choice is very limited; there are hardly any of us left."[54] Some wizards cling to this madness, though. In *Harry Potter and the Half-Blood Prince* (2005), Dumbledore explains to Harry that

> Marvolo, his son Morfin and his daughter Merope were the last of the Gaunts, a very ancient wizarding family noted for a vein of instability and violence that flourished through the generations due to their habit of marrying their own cousins.[55]

The reason that the Gaunts have done this is to preserve their so-called purity of blood, and this is also an important consideration in *The Duchess of Malfi*, where the Cardinal and Ferdinand are worried about "The royal blood of Aragon and Castile" (II.v.22).

The Harry Potter books also register a growing interest in the concept of royal blood. It is in *Order of the Phoenix* that a concern with royalty first surfaces, when Sirius says that his parents believed "that to be a Black made you practically royal," and after that it never disappears.[56] Looking at Moody's photo of the original Order of the Phoenix, Harry reflects that they "were unaware that their lives ... were drawing to a close,"[57] echoing, in a way unmistakable for anyone familiar with twentieth-century British history, the language of the official announcement of the imminent death of George V, "the king's life is drawing peacefully to a close" (designed, according to legend, to distract attention from the monarch's alleged last words, "Bugger Bognor").[58] Almost immediately afterwards, Harry's response to Hermione's and Ron's receipt of prefects' badges is to dream of them wearing crowns, and a crown is also the symbol chosen by the Slytherin Quidditch supporters for their anti-Ron badge, which bears the words "Weasley is our King."[59] Once back at school, Harry, Ron, and Hermione switch their allegiance from The Three Broomsticks to The Hog's Head, whose sign of "a wild boar's severed head"[60] recalls the tavern frequented by another young Harry with a big destiny, Shakespeare's Prince Hal, who may also be remembered by the title of chapter ten of *Half-Blood Prince*, "The House of Gaunt," since Hal was a grandson of John of Gaunt. Arthur Weasley, bitten by Nagini, finds himself on the "'Dangerous' Dai Llewellyn Ward."[61] According to *Quidditch Through the Ages*, Dai Llewellyn is a famous player of the game, but there was also a real Dai Llewellyn, whose brother Roddy was a lover of Princess Margaret's, and both brothers were much in the papers when Rowling was growing up in the seventies.[62] Finally, at the end of *Order of the Phoenix*, Dumbledore notes his relief that when Harry arrived at Hogwarts, "You were not a pampered little prince."[63]

In the next volume, *Half-Blood Prince*, the idea of royalty provides both the title of the book and a continuing source of metaphor. Dumbledore explains to Harry that Slughorn "has never wanted to occupy the throne himself; he prefers the back seat," while Ron sneers to Hermione that if she goes to the party with McLaggen "Slughorn can make you King and Queen Slug," and calls Harry Slughorn's "little Potions Prince."[64] In *Deathly Hallows*, Scrimgeour tells Harry "You may wear that scar like a crown, Potter, but it is not up to a seventeen-year-old boy to tell me how to do my job!" while Harry says of Marvolo, "as far as he was concerned, having pure blood made you practically royal." Kingsley's pseudonym on *Potterwatch* is Royal, which draws attention to his true name, and gives his eventual elevation to Minister of Magic something of the flavour of a return of the king.[65] We also hear of Ragnuk I, who appears from his regnal number to have been an actual monarch, and Rita Skeeter writes that "The name of Grindelwald is justly famous: in a list of Most Dangerous Dark Wizards of All Time, he would miss out on the top spot only because You-Know-Who arrived, a generation later, to steal his crown."[66]

Royal Families

Perhaps it is not coincidental that the royalty motif should first emerge in *Phoenix*, since that was published in 2003, two years after Rowling met Prince Charles for the first time during her investiture as an Officer of the Order of the British Empire (indeed, the idea of the Order of the Phoenix might perhaps have been suggested in the first place by her receipt of the OBE). Perhaps too there might be a similarity to Rowling's idol Jane Austen, who was informed that the Prince Regent would be gratified if she were to dedicate *Emma* (1815) to him and knew better than to disregard the hint, and there are certainly traces of Georgette Heyer, famous for her Regency novels, to whom Rowling has acknowledged a debt and from whom she borrows several names.[67] In particular, George was the name of the first four Hanoverian kings (including the Regent who is so prominent a presence in Heyer's novels), while Frederick was the name of the lost Hanoverian heir, the eldest son of George II who predeceased his father. However, the focus on royalty is also a manifestation of the books' growing interest in privilege; it is no coincidence that the motif of reference to royalty enters the series at almost exactly the same moment as Kreacher, most abject of House-elves, and that ideas about undue enfranchisement and undue disenfranchisement thereafter run concurrently.

The echoes of *The Duchess of Malfi* also have other consequences. One of the most profound of these affects genre. The Harry Potter books not only chart an excavation of the past, but also darken dramatically in tone. Rowling took the unusual decision of allowing her child characters to grow older relentlessly and realistically. For instance, there is a pointed contrast here with the Narnia books where ageing is rather melodramatically presented as radically incompatible with continued citizenship of the realm of the fantastic. Harry and his friends become teenagers, with concomitant outbreaks of hormones and irritability, and this affects the way the story develops. *Malfi* too can be seen as a story of what happens when three siblings grow into adulthood, developing new desires and new loyalties which threaten the sibling bond and the configuration of the original family. When Ferdinand confronts the Duchess in her bedchamber, he shows her their father's dagger, and thus invokes not just patriarchy in general but her specific, particular status as daughter and sister: he and the Cardinal between them stand for law and the status quo in something of the same way as Percy Weasley does, except that Percy ultimately sees the error of his ways.

A second set of consequences arises from the fact that the Harry Potter books are negotiating English, rather than Italian, identity. However, the two are not so dissimilar as might be supposed. The Italy in which *The Duchess of Malfi* is set was several centuries away from unification, and was still fragmented into city-states and duchies. Moreover, the southern half of it was not Italian at all but was in effect a colony of the House of Aragon, to which the Duchess and her brothers belong, while characters such as Antonio and Delio come from the subjugated Italian population, lending the relationship between Antonio and the Duchess something of the flavour of a *memsahib* in the days of the Raj marrying a native, albeit a promoted one.[68] The Harry Potter books too are interested in the historical and social consequences of colonialism. In the first place, however improbable it may seem, they have, as I have already suggested, a significant interest in the *translatio imperii*. St Brutus' school, the name of Hermione (daughter of Helen and Menelaus, and thus intimately associated with the Trojan War), and the fact that Fluffy (a giant three-headed dog) was given to Hagrid by a Greek all contribute to this, just as the sword in the water and the presence of an enemy named Draco confirm the presence of the Arthur story, a later link in the chain of descent from Brutus; the names Remus and Cassandra, foundational figures in the stories of Rome and Troy respectively, also point in this direction. In the second place, Hermione's campaign to liberate house-elves has obvious echoes of real anti-slavery and equal rights campaigns; Sarah K. Cantrell argues that "the legacies of colonization, servitude, and slavery continue to haunt the wizarding world as much as they do our own."[69] Rowling, herself a former Amnesty International employee, is personally and prominently committed to liberal causes, tweeting strong and sustained support for the Labour party and putting her money—often quite a lot of money—where her mouth is on several high-profile occasions;[70] not for nothing has she declared a self-identification with Hermione. She has also openly declared that Dumbledore is gay, and the books feature a (Muggle) school named after Stonewall.

Rowling did not set out to write for children; famously, the figure of Harry came into her mind unbidden, and because he was a child the books had to be marketed for children. They do of course contain many elements of the traditional school story, but Rowling was, as we have seen, committed from the outset to making the characters progressively older and the storylines progressively darker. To this end, she not only tackled death, killing off several important characters, usually without warning, but also evoked the Second World War, which is clearly referenced in the story of Grindelwald, the Dark Wizard toppled in 1945, the same year as Hitler. In this too she echoes, if not *Malfi*, at least the modern reception of *Malfi*, at least in Rowland Wymer's account:

> It has become commonplace in Marxist and feminist analyses of society and literature to see personal relations and family life as reproducing and enforcing oppressive political structures rather than opposing them or creating a free emotional space ... Yet those tyrannies with genuinely totalitarian ambitions (such as the regimes of

Hitler, Stalin and Mao) have consistently viewed domestic loves and loyalties as threateningly independent of state power and a source of potential resistance. The extensive theorisation of the family as a source of oppression dwindles into insignificance when confronted with the actuality of state violence against the family. The scene on the road near Ancona—the little family group clutching a few possessions and confronted by armed men—awakens memories of a hundred newsreels.[71]

The Harry Potter books thus inevitably touch on one of the major debates of late twentieth-century criticism of early modern English drama, which is whether the plays are conducive to subversion or to containment.[72] This is something on which Potter critics too have been divided. Sarah Cantrell notes that

> If we read Hogwarts through the lens of Michel Foucault's *Discipline and Punish* (1975), we see that despite its otherworldly charms, transfigurations, and enchantments, the school is a site where adults successfully train students to conform to the practices and expectations of the wizarding world,

but she also observes that some critics nevertheless "read Hogwarts as a place that deliberately destabilizes societal norms." She herself proposes that

> Hogwarts functions as a heterotopia, a space at once other and separate but also intimately connected to the world beyond its walls. Still more ambiguous spaces like 12 Grimmauld Place, the tent that Harry, Ron, and Hermione share in volume seven, and most notably, the Room of Requirement—a space within the place of the school proper—occupy positions similar to Deleuzian any-spaces-whatever. Because these spaces exist at the margins of safety and danger, their liminality requires Harry and his friends to be "up to no good": to resist and subvert adult authority, but also to confront the limits of agency. These shifts from order to disorder and from safety to danger suggest that participation and activism—particularly on the part of young adults—can be powerful means of opposing the abuses that permeate the spaces in our own world.[73]

The debate is particularly important because it concerns young readers, and ultimately centres on whether they are to understand themselves as able to change the world they live in or whether they must recognise that they are powerless.

In *The Duchess of Malfi*, the odds are stacked against the Duchess: hers is a world in which men have the power and in which women are too often their victims. Nevertheless, although the Duchess loses everything in worldly terms, she does retain her identity, famously declaring, "I am Duchess of Malfi still" (IV.2.141). This is the final way in which the Harry Potter books echo *Malfi*. Ultimately, all the appealing characters, and even Snape, do choose to resist Voldemort, implicitly subscribing to Dumbledore's view that the prophecy predicts but does not prescribe, and that choice is always possible. Some of those who choose to fight Voldemort die, but none of them forfeits either their identity or their reputation. As Sirius says, some things are worth dying for, but nothing is worth what Voldemort is reduced to when we see all that is left of his personality in the waiting room of a celestial version of King's Cross Station, in marked contrast to the way the castle's ghosts and Harry's parents all retain an essentially conscious identity. Rowling does not promise success to those who fight, but she does very strongly affirm that fighting is both possible and worthwhile.

Rowling's debt to *The Duchess of Malfi*, then, works in a number of different ways. Formally, given the various prominent echoes of *Malfi* in detective fiction, including (albeit later) in one of Rowling's own Cormoran Strike books, it underlines the Harry Potter books' affinity with that genre. In terms of content, the echoes of *The Duchess of Malfi* underline the books' interest in two distinct but related topics, family (particularly siblings) and royalty, while the apparent contrast between the Italian flavour of *Malfi* and the resolute Britishness of the Potter books proves illusory, since both are underpinned by histories of colonialism and oppression. Finally, both *The Duchess of Malfi* and the Potter books can be seen to foreground the question of the potential for and limitations of individual agency. The Harry Potter books are widely and justly credited with boosting literacy and imaginative engagement among children, since they not only sold phenomenally well themselves but sparked the re-publication of authors for whom Rowling in interviews expressed admiration (most notably Diana Wynne-Jones, who published two further Chrestomanci books on the back of Rowling's praise of her). Rowling encourages her young readers to do more than read, though: she also encourages them to believe that they, like Harry, Ron, and Hermione, can make a difference to the world in which they live, and that even if they fail or are killed, they can still have an inviolate identity.

Notes

1 J.K. Rowling, *Harry Potter and the Philosopher's Stone* (London: Bloomsbury, 1997), 153.
2 J.K. Rowling, *Harry Potter and the Deathly Hallows* (London: Bloomsbury, 2007), 263.
3 On the vexed question of fidelity in adaptation, see: Linda Hutcheon, *A Theory of Adaptation* (London: Routledge, 2006); and Robert Stam, "Introduction: The Theory and Practice of Adaptation," in *Literature and Film:*

A *Guide to the Theory and Practice of Adaptation*, ed. Robert Stam and Alessandra Raengo (Oxford: Blackwell, 2005), 1–52.
4 Rowling, *Philosopher's Stone*, 46.
5 J.K. Rowling, *Harry Potter and the Prisoner of Azkaban* (London: Bloomsbury, 1999), 178.
6 Rowling, *Philosopher's Stone*, 63.
7 Rowling, *Philosopher's Stone*, 144.
8 Rowling, *Prisoner of Azkaban*, 64.
9 Rowling, *Philosopher's Stone*, 149.
10 J.K. Rowling, *Harry Potter and the Half-Blood Prince* (London: Bloomsbury, 2005), 138.
11 J.K. Rowling, *Harry Potter and the Goblet of Fire* (London: Bloomsbury, 2000), 555, 565, 561.
12 Rowling, *Prisoner of Azkaban*, 201.
13 J.K. Rowling, *Harry Potter and the Order of the Phoenix* (London: Bloomsbury, 2003), 447.
14 Rowling, *Philosopher's Stone*, 12.
15 "Letter to Cassandra Austen, 4 February 1813," *Letters of Jane Austen*, http://pemberley.com/janeinfo/auslet22.html#letter125.
16 See the transcript of J.K. Rowling's World Book Day chat, 4 March 2004, http://accio-quote.org/articles/2004/0304-wbd.htm. Thanks to Eléonore Cartellier-Veuillen for alerting me to this.
17 Rowling, *Philosopher's Stone*, 75, 80.
18 Rowling, *Goblet of Fire*, 367.
19 Rowling, *Order of the Phoenix*, 266.
20 Rowling, *Order of the Phoenix*, 69.
21 Rowling, *Order of the Phoenix*, 106.
22 Rowling, *Philosopher's Stone*, 7, 44.
23 Rowling, *Goblet*, 394.
24 Rowling, *Goblet*, 589.
25 Rowling, *Phoenix*, 310–311, 763.
26 Rowling, *Half-Blood Prince*, 268, 270.
27 Rowling, *Half-Blood Prince*, 117–118.
28 Rowling, *Deathly Hallows*, 308.
29 Rowling, *Deathly Hallows*, 280.
30 William Shakespeare [and George Wilkins], *Pericles*, ed. Suzanne Gossett (London: Thomson Learning, 2004).
31 Beatrice Groves argues that Rowling is in fact particularly drawn to Shakespeare because his mixing of comedy and tragedy is congenial to her (*Literary Allusion in Harry Potter* [London: Routledge, 2017], 82).
32 William Collingbourne's lampoon is reproduced in Robert Fabyan, *Fabyans Chronicle Newly Printed* (London, 1533), ccxxvii: in July 1484, Collingbourne allegedly pinned the lampoon to the door of St Paul's Cathedral.
33 Rowling, *Prisoner of Azkaban*, 142.
34 Margaret J. Oakes, "Secret Domination or Civic Duty: The Source and Purpose of Magical Power in Harry Potter," in *Reading Harry Potter Again: New Critical Essays*, ed. Giselle Liza Anatol (Santa Barbara, CA: ABC-Clio, 2009), 150.
35 Eléonore Cartellier-Veuillen, "*Harry Potter*: Through the Looking-Glass of Language" (PhD thesis, Université Grenoble Alpes, 2018), 53–54, 178.
36 Rowling, *Prisoner of Azkaban*, 250.
37 Mark Nicholls, "Rookwood, Ambrose, c. 1578–1606," *Oxford Dictionary of National Biography* (Oxford: Oxford University Press, 2008), doi:10.1093/ref:odnb/24066. Rookwood's great-grandson, another Ambrose, was a Jacobite

conspirator: see Paul Hopkins, "Rookwood, Ambrose (1664–1696)," *Oxford Dictionary of National Biography* (Oxford: Oxford University Press, 2008), doi:10.1093/ref:odnb/24067.
38 Mortimer Levine, *The Early Elizabethan Succession Question 1558–1568* (Stanford, CA: Stanford University Press, 1966), 10.
39 There might also be a glance at another of Webster's plays, *The White Devil*, which mentions yew and blackthorn, both trees used for wands.
40 Philip Nel, "Is There a Text in this Advertising Campaign?: Literature, Marketing and Harry Potter," *The Lion and the Unicorn* 29, no. 2 (April 2005): 250.
41 Cartellier-Veuillen, "*Harry Potter*: Through the Looking-Glass of Language," 191.
42 Agatha Christie, *Death in the Clouds* (1935; repr., London: HarperCollins, 2001), 61.
43 Esme Miskimmin observes that "The play that seems to recur most frequently in detective fiction is John Webster's *The Duchess of Malfi*" ("The Act of Murder: Renaissance Tragedy and the Detective Novel," in *Reinventing the Renaissance: Shakespeare and his Contemporaries in Adaptation and Performance*, ed. Sarah Annes Brown, Robert I. Lublin, and Lynsey McCulloch [New York: Palgrave Macmillan, 2013], 295).
44 Dorothy L. Sayers, *Busman's Honeymoon* (1937; repr., London: NEL, 1977), 159.
45 Patricia Wentworth, *Danger Point* (1942; repr., London: Coronet, 1984), 31.
46 Agatha Christie, *Sleeping Murder* (1976; repr., London: HarperCollins, 2002), 34.
47 Christie, *Sleeping Murder*, 288.
48 Christie, *Sleeping Murder*, 297.
49 Christie, *Sleeping Murder*, 303.
50 Rowling, *Prisoner of Azkaban*, 83.
51 John Webster, *The Duchess of Malfi*, ed. John Russell Brown (Manchester: Manchester University Press, 1974), V.ii.90–92. All further quotations from the play will be taken from this edition and reference will be given in the text.
52 J.K. Rowling, *Harry Potter and the Chamber of Secrets* (London: Bloomsbury, 1998), 43.
53 Rowling, *Chamber of Secrets*, 86, 89.
54 Rowling, *Order of the Phoenix*, 105.
55 Rowling, *Half-Blood Prince*, 200–201.
56 Rowling, *Order of the Phoenix*, 104.
57 Rowling, *Order of the Phoenix*, 162.
58 This seems to have been first reported in Kenneth Rose, *Kings, Queens and Courtiers: Intimate Portraits of the Royal House of Windsor from Its Foundations to the Present Day* (London: Weidenfeld and Nicolson, 1985).
59 Rowling, *Order of the Phoenix*, 163, 358.
60 Rowling, *Order of the Phoenix*, 299.
61 Rowling, *Order of the Phoenix*, 430.
62 J.K. Rowling, *Quidditch Through the Ages* (London: Bloomsbury, 2017), 7.
63 Rowling, *Order of the Phoenix*, 737.
64 Rowling, *Half-Blood Prince*, 75, 263, 350.
65 Rowling, *Deathly Hallows*, 110, 348, 356.
66 Rowling, *Deathly Hallows*, 409 and 290.
67 See Cartellier-Veuillen, "*Harry Potter*: Through the Looking-Glass of Language," 186n187.

68 On early modern drama's interest in the political divisions within Italy, see for instance my "'Absolute Milan': Two Types of Colonialism in *The Tempest*," *Journal of Anglo-Italian Studies* 4 (1995): 1–10. On its applicability to *Malfi*, see my "Antonios and Stewards: A Conference about the Succession in *Twelfth Night*, *The Duchess of Malfi* and *The Tempest*," *Journal of Drama Studies* 2, no. 1 (January 2008): 5–15.
69 Sarah K. Cantrell, "'I Solemnly Swear I am Up to No Good': Foucault's Heterotopias and Deleuze's Any-Spaces-Whatever in J. K. Rowling's Harry Potter Series," *Children's Literature* 39 (2011): 199. See also Brycchan Carey, "Hermione and the House-Elves Revisited: J. K. Rowling, Antislavery Campaigning, and the Politics of Potter," in *Reading Harry Potter Again: New Critical Essays*, ed. Giselle Liza Anatol (Santa Barbara, CA: ABC-Clio, 2009), 159–173.
70 See for instance Philip Nel, who argues that Rowling "deserves credit for her attempts to control a marketing apparatus perpetuated by the American legal system" ("Is There a Text in this Advertising Campaign?," 241–243).
71 Rowland Wymer, *Webster and Ford* (London: Macmillan, 1995), 61.
72 The idea that the fundamental cultural work of early modern drama is the containing of potentially subversive ideas dates back to Stephen Greenblatt's *Shakespearean Negotiations* (Oxford: The Clarendon Press, 1988). It has been supported by American New Historicists and contested mainly by British Cultural Materialists. See for instance Chapters 3 and 4 of my *Beginning Shakespeare* (Manchester: Manchester University Press, 2005).
73 Cantrell, "'I Solemnly Swear I am Up to No Good," 195–197.

Section II
Historical Medievalism and Early-Modernism

9 Playing in a Virtual Medieval World
Video Game Adaptations of England through Role-Play

Ben Redder

Empire Earth (2001), a real-time strategy computer game that lets players build and expand civilisations from the prehistoric era to the futuristic robotic age, was my first game experience with medieval England.[1] Unlike other strategy games of that time, *Empire Earth* implemented historical narratives through its campaign structures and game objectives, particularly the English campaign. The English campaign primarily focuses on moments of William the Conqueror, from his early life until the Battle of Hastings (1066) in his conquest of England, and significant military events between England and France during the Hundred Years' War (1337–1453).[2] For its time, *Empire Earth* displayed an extensive representation of medieval England by providing players digital participation in these histories through the game's virtual historical world, dialogue between the characters, rules, and play through global strategy and battles.

Since the release of the game in 2001, however, relatively few game designers have undertaken the task of, or expressed an interest in, adapting the history of medieval England into digital games.[3] Historical games are without a doubt a popular genre for players, as well as being a creative commodity for game designers. Most of them, however, are based on the Second World War (such as the *Call of Duty* series), global-based or macro worlds (such as Sid Meier's *Civilization* series), and histories of East Asia (such as the *Dynasty Warriors* series), or are hybrid sci-fi or fantasy-adventure set in different historical periods (such as the *Assassin's Creed* series).[4] Medieval games have more or less been both a sub-genre of historical games and a genre of video games themselves, but as medieval high-fantasy has a long and popular history in occupying and satisfying the players' niches for fantasy, inhabiting foreign worlds, and adventure, it has either restricted or displaced the historical in many medieval games. This displacement concurrently opened a market demand for game designers to commercialise this trend, with preference for creating and consuming medieval high-fantasy video games, such as *The Elder Scrolls IV: Oblivion* (2006) and *The Witcher 3: Wild Hunt* (2015).[5] The popularity of producing these types of games can be traced to older, and still popular, forms of engagement with medieval culture, role-playing, and fantasy. From the high-fantasy novel series *The Lord of the Rings* by J.R.R. Tolkien to the pre-digital, pen-and-paper table-top game *Dungeons and Dragons*, medieval digital games have more or less followed "remediation," where games "incorporate, contain, reform, and re-establish old media [and literary] forms for a new cultural moment."[6] Nonetheless, the few games that have adapted England in a historical context are interesting in the way they re-use, or renew, both well-known and under-represented histories of medieval England, as well as how they are integrated into the game's structures, narratives, space, and time.

The scarcity of history-based medieval games set in England coincides with the limited study of the relationships and intersections between historical medieval games and medievalism. Tison Pugh and Angela Weisl define medievalism as the "art, literature, scholarship, avocational pastimes, and sundry forms of entertainment and culture that turn to the Middle Ages for their subject matter or inspiration."[7] However, David Matthews argues that even academic medieval studies—ostensibly about the historical Middle Ages—is a form of medievalism, insofar as the scholars' historical representations or reconstructions are post-medieval attempts at re-imagining the Middle Ages.[8] In considering Matthews's point, I argue that historical medieval games are another form of medievalism by co-existing both as histories of the Middle Ages, and as a creative form of entertainment and media culture in renewing these histories through game design for modern audiences.

Oliver M. Traxel provides a provisional framework for thinking about approaches and the limitations of medieval games mediating between the historical and contemporary domains of the Middle Ages.[9] He highlights the fact that when medieval games implement or borrow historical references to, and sources of, the medieval past, aesthetic pleasure, and not historical accuracy, is usually the goal with thin, if any, traces to the "actual" Middle Ages.[10] However, he signifies the compatibility of medievalism with the gamic quality of performance that connects the player's immersion and their activities of play to the entirety of the game's medieval world.[11] Ideas of performance have already been analysed in a number of areas of adaptation studies, particularly those based in Linda Hutcheon and Julie Sander's work. This chapter follows Sander's direction in adaptation studies by working with "re-interpretations of established ... texts in new generic contexts ... [and] as a field engaged with process, ideology, and methodology."[12] Here, she broadly outlines that performance can be seen in itself as an "early adaptive art; we might even argue that each individual performance is an adaptation," using a variety of adaptation elements such as mimesis, improvisation (through player activity), and interpolation.[13] Linda Hutcheon also provides useful insights, particularly with regards to adaptation as a process. As a 'process', adaptation usually appropriates one's story (be it oral, textual, or media based) by filtering it and then creating something new from the adapter's own interests, sensibilities, field of expertise, and objectives, which suggests that adapters are first "interpreters, and then creators."[14] Thus, this element of adaptation can enable performative styles of adaptation that permit "us to think about how adaptations allow people to tell, show, or interact with stories."[15]

Due to the complex nature and application of performance in various works, this chapter examines performance through role-playing, an important concept of medievalism, yet under-studied in its function as a form of adaptation, particularly with historical medieval games.[16] In this chapter, I analyse three medieval games and their approaches in adapting England for a digital game audience through their particular style of combining historical authenticity, game design, and gameplay. These three games are *Medieval II: Total War Kingdoms* (2007), *War of the Roses* (2012–2017), and *Expeditions: Vikings* (2017).[17] By explaining these medieval games' approaches to adapting medieval England, I discuss how their approaches incorporate medievalism and role-playing by using Daniel T. Kline's concept of "participatory medievalism" as an emergent-based theory of adaptation in medieval games.[18] Kline defines participatory medievalism as a "spectrum of active, embodied encounter that carries participants into created medieval worlds with differing degrees of immersion, yielding the sense of participating in, and even inhabiting, a neomedieval fictional world."[19] However, I will diverge from Kline's original use of this concept by arguing that medieval historical games, including those based on England, are another form or activity of participatory medievalism, where medievalism and medieval history intersect. By using this theory of adaptation, I reveal what representation of medieval England is presented to players from these games' adaptation of England.

Medieval II: Total War Kingdoms

The year following the release of *Medieval II: Total War* (2006), game studio Creative Assembly released an expansion game, *Medieval II: Total War Kingdoms*, which provided new game content and gameplay experiences of medieval Europe.[20] Like its predecessor, the expansion game shares many of the original elements and features, including a visually accurate depiction of medieval warfare and armies played out in real-time battles, and the use of diplomacy and marriage in forming alliances and trade.[21] However, this game was the first in the *Total War* series to combine strategy, globalisation, and nation-building with historical narratives and settings from particular periods of medieval history by providing four unique campaigns. For the purposes of this chapter I focus on the Britannia campaign.

The Britannia campaign takes players to the British Isles, starting in 1258 and continuing until the end of the thirteenth century, with the choice to play either medieval Ireland, Wales, Scotland, England, or Norway. The game designers' choice to start the campaign in 1258 is significant, because this year historically marks the series of England's constitutional crises, political insurrections, and external threats during the reigns of Henry III (r. 1216–1272) and his son Edward I (r. 1272–1307), notably the Second Barons' War and the Welsh uprising from English vassalage under the sovereign Prince of Wales, Llywelyn ap Gruffudd (r. 1258–1282).[22]

This specific period serves as a recurring theme, and influences the game design of England in the Britannia campaign. Through various in-game materials, players are given a narrative overview of England under Henry. England is presented as a large kingdom in a fragile state, with a thin supply line and limited forces due to overexpansion, military threats from Ireland and Wales, and discontented nobles within England's provinces.[23] This narrative is more than just a textual background, for it provides players opportunities for historical role-playing experiences by obtaining knowledge about, and how to respond to, these historical events as they occur in the game. While players in this game inhabit the position of an extra-diegetic agent (God's eye view), their level of immersion in their characters is one geared towards perceiving them as virtual constructions of living and perishable entities (they can die from either old age, assassination, or in combat) with their own strengths and weaknesses, as opposed to using them as mechanistic set pieces. This is evident in the player living through their generals and armies on the game's map and real-time battlefields. Here players invest most of their time in choosing what their generals will do next (both on and off the battlefield), and building emerging narrative relationships with them through developing their character's traits (such as loyalty and religious piety) and using them in land battles and sieges. This level of immersion is further enhanced by the player controlling some of England's historical figures of that time, such as King Henry and Prince Edward, giving players the ability to re-tell the lives of these historical figures in their own way, albeit one confined to following the historical context of England. This process of role-playing reflects two components of participatory medievalism: inhabiting the role of the game's character(s), and player awareness and immersion in the details and elements of the game's world. In the latter, the player, as the English faction, can participate in medieval narrative-performances through their responses and interactions with some of the political machinations of thirteenth-century England. These machinations are enacted by the game's implementation of historical events, two of which are the Second Barons' War and the conflicts between England and Wales. These historical events appear as spaces for players to create historical-based performances within the game by existing as visual and spatial modes of gameplay.[24]

The Second Barons' War becomes a mode of gameplay when the player fails to prevent public disorder in England's regions from culminating into a full-scale rebellion.[25] Public disorder occurs through a variety of factors, including bankruptcy, resistance to foreign invaders, ungarrisoned cities and castles, different religions or cultures, and taxes.[26] The severity of this situation is worsened when English

> cities, generals, and characters have a chance of rebelling and joining the Barons' Alliance, creating a united front against the English Monarch ... [as the player] you should work to keep your men loyal, lest they join the alliance against you.[27]

When a rebellion occurs from growing public disorder, the Barons' Alliance is formed as a rival (but unplayable) faction, with their goal being to conquer the rest of England (the player's territories). As long as the Barons' Alliance exists, they provide advantages and obstacles for the other AI (artificial intelligence) or computer-controlled factions, such as distracting English forces from attacking Wales and Ireland.[28] In the context of participatory medievalism, this gameplay mode adapts the Second Barons' War by existing as a challenge or obstacle for players of the English faction, with most experiences of the players' performative activity being an initial attempt to delay, before facing, the rebellion. Unlike the fixed historical narratives that recount the chronological order of this history in written works, here players are given a range of performative options to defeat the Barons' forces. Some of these possibilities are players making preparations with whatever military and economic resources they have available and going on the defensive, eliminating the Barons' faction as swiftly as possible, and creating measures that attempt to avoid their own generals or lords from joining the Barons' faction by increasing their loyalty level. In the player's re-telling of this medieval conflict, their actions and decisions give them a macro perspective into the kinds of experiences and decisions representative of the circumstances and issues that medieval England faced during the Second Barons' War.

In the game, Wales under Llywelyn is presented as a small kingdom with few resources and a limited naval force, but with a growing power base, fervent Welsh support in the provinces, and a relatively large army. As noted in the game's manual, inspired by "the new, self-declared King of Wales, Llywelyn, the inhabitants of the Welsh highlands are eager to rise up and join the rebellion against the English."[29] This historical conflict acts as a game-challenge by functioning as a form of public discontent through cultural difference in England's frontier cities bordering Wales, and Welsh cities recently conquered by England. Cultural difference is an integral game feature in the Britannia campaign, where a region's populace is identified by their ethnic affiliation to the faction.[30]

This game feature, to some degree, historicises the player's role-playing adaptation of England by providing player-narratives that direct the player's English faction to not only conquer enemy regions belonging to Llywelyn, but also to contend with fighting both Llywelyn's forces and Welsh rebels.

The game designers of *Medieval II: Total War Kingdoms* have endeavoured to direct players to create performances that are narrative-driven by using historical and gameplay approaches, based in or pertaining to thirteenth-century England, as a form of medievalism. However, these same game designers implemented other elements of medievalism in popularising their version of medieval England, with one commonly being anachronisms from popular public perceptions and other media and novelistic representations of the Middle Ages.[31] One medieval anachronism featured most prominently in this game's Britannia campaign (and in other *Total War* games) is the emphasis on land battles, while siege battles are relegated to static fights between the attacking and defending force. While real-time land battles are the defining trademark of the game, which is both most enjoyed by players and reinforces public opinion that medieval land battles were a frequent occurrence, historical consensus suggests that siege battles and the plundering or devastation of the countryside and enemy property were not only more common but preferred methods of medieval warfare. As Gregory Fedorenko argues, "[Land] battles carried with them great potential risk—particularly as the surest way for one side to achieve victory was to capture or kill the opposing commander in chief."[32] Moreover, burning and pillaging was effective not only for weakening an enemy's capacity to enact war but also for decreasing the willpower of the enemy's subordinates or vassals to continue to fight, especially if their lands were under imminent threat of devastation.[33]

The appearance of land battles in thirteenth-century England as a popular, romanticised representation of medieval warfare is more obvious when one considers Fedorenko's discussions in his analysis of earlier games *Medieval: Total War* and *Medieval II: Total War*.[34] Examining these from the context of medievalism, his analysis revealed that both games' depictions of warfare, politics, policies, and economy, while appearing to offer or convey authentic representations of medieval Europe on a visual level, were anachronisms from nineteenth-century cultures, practices, and ideologies of these elements.[35] Fedorenko goes further by explaining that the proto-national identities, huge armies, tactics, and 'total warfare' embedded into the game are not reflections or ideas of national identity in medieval Europe, but an ideology resembling that of modern European nation states.[36]

Medieval II: Total War Kingdoms compensates for this issue to some extent through the inclusion of detailed historical narratives from the British Isles in the thirteenth century. Moreover, the game's representations of medieval land battles resonate, surprisingly, with the rare character of the major Battles of Lewes (1264) and Evesham (1265) during the Second Barons' War as military engagements not of "ravaging and attrition, but by manoeuvre and [pitched] battle."[37] Nonetheless, the game does not escape the inevitability of its underlying game structure: winning the game solely by domination of the other factions (or kingdoms) through territorial conquest and successful battles. Essentially, the player controlling the English faction could create an alternate history in the game by forming an earlier, medieval empire comprising of England, Wales, Scotland, and Ireland, but made up of anachronistic, nineteenth-century systems of nation-building.[38]

Medieval II: Total War Kingdoms opens a new direction into adapting medieval England through player-centred performances by re-establishing some of its major historical events and themes during the thirteenth century as both visual and performative forms of historical authenticity, narrative gameplay, and role-play. However, its reliance on combining history with anachronistic or stereotypical representations of the Middle Ages, such as its portrayal of medieval land battles, creates an interesting, yet conflicting, hybridisation of a 'historically' medieval England with popular or contemporary constructions of England, in the attempt to expand or enhance the player's experience of creating their own adaptations of thirteenth-century England through role play.

War of the Roses

Drawing from the popularity of medieval-combat games set in fictional worlds, a multiplayer-online game called *War of the Roses* was developed by game studio Fatshark to give players the opportunity to fight in digital re-enacted historical battles (such as the Battles of Towton [1461] and Bosworth Field [1485]) with other players in two teams (32 players each).[39] The title of the game reveals its setting during the Wars of the Roses (1455–1487), a major historical conflict between two rival households of England's Plantagenet dynasty, the House of York and the House of Lancaster, both of which are recognised by their family emblems: the white rose (York) and the red rose (Lancaster). Historians have contributed a variety of reasons as to the cause of this conflict between these two powerful families, particularly political corruption and inefficient management of the country and its finances under Henry VI (r. 1422–1461, 1470–1471), the loss of territories in France that were gained by his predecessor Henry V (r. 1413–1422), and Henry VI's periods of madness or mental instability in the later years of his life.[40]

The historical rivalry, battles, and settings relating to this turbulent period of English history are the fundamental elements in the design of *War of the Roses*. Moreover, the main forms of participatory medievalism utilised in this game's adaptation are its avatar-generated medieval characters and a digital game style of medieval tournament fighting, a recreational activity inspired by contemporary medieval re-enactment for audiences such as medieval historical battles and professional tournament competitions. Medieval-avatar characters are a type of historical character immersion where the player creates and assumes the role of a medieval historical avatar(s) representative of the game's world, but is simultaneously a digital embodiment of the player. In *War of the Roses*, this is apparent from the player's assuming a pre-configured version of a late-medieval English soldier, and this level of immersion constructs a highly detailed but particular adaptation of the Wars of the Roses in a military context. Therefore, this pseudo-military style adaptation of England's Wars of the Roses through the player's presence as a late-medieval English soldier relies more on visual and combative-performance approaches to renew this history within a multiplayer-online game format.

On a visual level, this form is realised by the game's reconstruction of environments—such as locations where the battles took place—and designing the appearances of medieval English soldiers as either a Yorkist (white colour) or Lancastrian (red colour), which helps to somewhat authenticate the player's performance. The type of clothing, armour, and weaponry that various late-medieval English soldiers wore or carried, in particular, are translated into the game not only as a visual aesthetic, but also as a visual mode of role-play. As players gain experience points (XP) from fighting and defeating opponents in order to level up, this visual mode is evident as they progress through four different pre-made character classes. These classes illustrate the types of units common in the Wars of the Roses: footmen; crossbowmen (later changed to guardsman); archer/longbowman; and foot-knight. Once they have reached foot-knight, players are given the opportunity to create their own version of a medieval English soldier by receiving eight customisable 'slots' to develop and augment their classes with better quality or more visually appealing armour pieces and weaponry. This customised class system, a common game feature in medieval online multiplayer games, conflicts to some extent with the historical reality of the various levels of access English soldiers had to armoury and weaponry due to their social and economic status. Nonetheless, this system provides an aesthetic and strategic enhancement for participatory character role-playing by serving as a playful and interactive tool for players wanting both to improve their character's combat performance, and to have more creative freedom with character appearance. More importantly, this system also avoids players repetitively role-playing the same four classes with pre-configured appearances, statistics, and abilities, let alone choosing the strongest class (that is, foot knight) every time they join a battle.

The game's medieval combat system, however, is by far its most important historical approach in adapting the Wars of the Roses, for this historicises the player's participatory role and performance as a Lancastrian or Yorkist soldier. The combat mechanics in ranged, hand-to-hand, and horseback fighting were influenced by the style and conduct of warfare in England's historical battles between the Houses of York and Lancaster, and provide players some insights into England's transition from medieval to early modern warfare. For instance, in the game's battle matches, players can use double-edged axes, maces, war hammers, and other heavy weapons against opponents wearing plate armour. This aspect of using heavy weapons reflects the historical consensus of knights and footmen during the Wars of the Roses using blunt or crushing weapons to defeat heavily armoured opponents instead of swords, as plate armour was vulnerable to the blunt forces that came from the powerful swings of the weapon.[41]

The combat mechanics in *War of the Roses* further authenticates the player's role-play adaptation of this history of England through medieval fighting by its style of one-on-one duels with another opponent during the game matches. Angle and movement of one's weapons, while predicting the enemy's move, is a key feature in the duel, rather than relying only on brute force and armour protection alone, and it is this mechanism that integrates some of the combat experiences of late-medieval English soldiers into a digital team deathmatch-style arena.[42] Within this team deathmatch setting, where points needed to win the game match are gained by defeating opponents, players are usually killed after incurring one to a few hits with a weapon, depending on where the player hits their opponent, including hits taken on an unprotected head by archers causing an instant kill.[43] As one game reviewer Paul Dean noted, "this is a game of manoeuvring, timing and careful parrying—or, if you find you're bleeding to death, a lot of wild, desperate swinging."[44] These kind of performative experiences of death by combat that players face in their participation of the game's medieval combat arena, as either a Yorkist or Lancastrian soldier, illustrates not only the historical reality of the brutality and quickness of soldiers incapacitated by their opponents, but also the incurring of injuries that were likely to have happened in the real Wars of the Roses. Some of these injuries in the game relate to the archaeological evidence of the soldiers' bones found on the outskirts of Towton, which revealed injuries primarily received to the head in melee, or by arrows.[45]

Analysing the player's combat-style renditions of England's Wars of the Roses, through these two modes of participatory medievalism, reveals medieval experiences through online gaming that concern historicity as well as its validity as a legitimate source of representing aspects of military life on the battlefield. However, as common to online games that use digital tournament-style combat re-enactment, *War of the Roses*' utilisation of role-playing, historical events, combat dramatisation with representations of medieval violence, and player-team network fosters spaces for counterfactual narratives that can play against historical traditions of re-enacting or representing events as they occurred. Digital players in *War of the Roses*, as either Lancastrians or Yorkists, have counterfactual narrative opportunities through teamwork and combat skill to win historical battles contrary to historical outcome, such as players of the Yorkist team winning the Battle of Bosworth Field. These 'what if' scenarios in *War of the Roses* demonstrate the game's use of England's history not as serious attempts to reconstruct the past, but as a stage or spectacle for entertainment and martial prowess in one-on-one fighting.

In addition, the practice or expression of chivalry in *War of the Roses* is a co-existing and contrastive element of role-play with the game's performative constructions of participatory combat violence. Matt Richardson supports this manifestation of chivalry; he found in the one-on-one practice duelling online server that

> players [there] tend to be polite and even, dare I say, 'chivalrous'. Opponents signal their readiness to fight by sketching a salute with a high block, and players are expected to tell each other "gf" or "good fight" after a well-fought bout.[46]

This example demonstrates the unique expression of chivalry in the game as a behavioural act invoked by players from their own moral or personal values, a number of whom showing far more gallantry and honour in their virtual role-playing as a medieval English soldier than their actual historical counterparts in the *real* Wars of the Roses. As a result, the appearance of chivalry as a medievalism, without dismissing the character and motif of England's military history of the Wars of the Roses, creates a sense of friendly rivalry or competition between players within the game's virtual environment. The outcome is one where all players can exercise violence through combat and honour within the safe confines of the digital game and its rules.

War of the Roses illustrates the attempts to integrate the military history of the period for players by developing a digital medieval action game that fosters a game-space for counterfactual game narratives, gladiatorial or tournament-based competitive combat, and players to be chivalrous in their own choosing. Through the analytical lens of participatory medievalism in medieval character-avatar immersion and the systems of digital combat tournament arenas, this game adaptation develops a playful and socially-orientated environment where players can enjoy participating and performing in one of medieval England's military sagas first-hand, but without physically enduring or reliving the bloody, messy, and terrifying ordeals of engaging in the *real* Wars of the Roses.

Expeditions: Vikings

Expeditions: Vikings is a real-time, role-playing (RPG), turn-based strategy computer game that depicts the early years of Viking exploration and involvement with both the northern regions of England and Scotland. The game's premise and overall narrative is similar to Viking historical sagas developed in other media and textual Viking adaptations, such as the ongoing television series *Vikings*.[47] It is 789 AD, and players role-play a Viking warrior (either male or female with a custom name) from a small village called Skjern in Western Denmark, who inherits the position of thane (chieftain) after the death of their father and previous thane of the village.[48] In the early segments of the game, the player endeavours to expand and consolidate their rule of the village, protect it from raids and invasions from neighbouring tribes, and quell rival claimants or challengers to ruling of the village.[49] However, the game is unique in that the player's Viking adventure does not confine to Denmark alone, but also encompasses the regions of northern England (Northumbria) once the player's character has resources to build ships.[50] Thus, the player's role as a Viking leader of his/her party in Northumbria during the second half of the game will be the focus here.

Unlike *Medieval II: Total War Kingdoms* and *War of the Roses*, *Expeditions: Vikings*' approach to role-play adaptations of both early-medieval Denmark and England is derived from a type of medievalism genre common in many medieval RPGs called medieval adventurism. Both a literary sub-genre of medieval fantasy and a digital game sub-genre of fantasy adventure, medieval adventurism can be considered a form of participatory medievalism for it involves "complex characters with a Medieval flavour who go on adventures together and meet a wide variety of obstacles and circumstances."[51] While *Expeditions: Vikings*' use of this genre in constructing Vikings and their society appears to illustrate a pseudo historical-fantasy adventure, the game in fact borrows or embeds these features and characteristics from a fantasy adventure into an historical adventure. Thus, *Expeditions: Vikings* invites players to re-enact or play out some of the Viking experiences, particularly those pertaining to historical interactions and conflicts between the inhabitants of early-medieval England and the Danish Viking raiders.

Evidence of medieval adventurism as a form of participatory medievalism in a historical format can be found in the game's medieval party system, a feature commonly characteristic of older, pre-digital fantasy games such as tabletop game series *Dungeons and Dragons* and the board game *Talisman* (1983), but later adopted by medieval fantasy video games. In a digital game context, the party system will usually comprise of generic classes or archetypes of medieval characters, such as the warrior, mage or wizard, thief, smith, and supernatural or mythical beings including elves and dwarfs. In addition, each of these character archetypes has its own strengths, skills, personalities, and relationships or backstories with the player's character. These elements in a party-based system, however, are more diverse due to the characteristics of the medieval classes encompassing a range of companions that have one or several roles, including close combat, ranged (combat), diplomatic, crafting, medicinal, foraging, and stealth. *Expeditions: Vikings* re-uses this system into a historical context by forming a Danish hirdman (an armed companion of a personal retinue). In this version, both Danish and Anglo-Saxon members in the player's party include doctors, hunters, witches (wise-woman), and Viking warrior classes composing of female and male companions. The use of a fantasy party structure is further transmitted into an historical adventure by the game's mimetic design of realism as game mechanics, gameplay, and player-narratives. To give an example, the battles between the player's party and their enemies, through a turn-based combat structure, comprise close-quarter battles and skirmish-style tactics. In one scenario, fire can be used to attack enemies by laying oil and igniting them by shooting flaming arrows, which engulfs the surrounding enemies in flames and damages their health immensely. This scenario demonstrates performances that are directed towards experiences of early medieval combat in the form of warbands fighting one another, while applying these tactics and combat sequences as a form of action-based entertainment for players.

The non-linearity of events in the game, insofar as there are many possible scenarios or occurrences not entirely known in hindsight by the player, is another primary element of medieval adventurism. While these possible events in a fantasy game are "constrained by rules ... the constraints are much broader than in traditional games; in this way, games are more like life."[52] *Expeditions: Vikings* fosters this element through emergent role-playing narratives, often in the form of the player and his party's series of individual but contingent decisions, actions, and dialogues, and their characters' reputation. These can range from refusing to accept a quest that results in favourable or unfavourable responses, claiming a reward after clearing the village or town from bandits, making deals with other characters but then betraying them afterwards, or engaging in the more serious activities of raiding and devastating villages and towns.[53] These possible scenarios help to centre Vikings and their presence in Northumbria in a historical context, while avoiding one-dimensional, or Hollywood-style, depictions of Vikings and Northumbrians in England. Concurrently, the player's Viking party is spatially positioned initially as outsiders to some of England's regional conflicts, but may decide to participate in this history as part of progressing through the game, and for their story to interweave with the game's historical narratives in Northumbria.

These principal elements of medieval adventurism are enacted as both historical and gamic performances in adapting early medieval northern

England in *Expeditions: Vikings*, and are worth examining. Historical setting and narrative once again play a significant role in embedding these key components, as well as role-playing, into the game. This narrative style in the game invokes a micro, or local, representation of the period by establishing a part of the player's Viking role-playing adventure in Northumbria. When the player's character and hirdman arrive on the shores of Northumbria, their new location culminates into a performative space for historically ethnic, political, and cultural relationships and narratives between the Vikings (mainly through the perspective of the player and his companions) and the inhabitants of northern England (the kingdom of Northumbria) and Scotland to emerge. Despite the player role-playing as a Viking chieftain, the game's historical setting showcases a world where both the Viking clans in Denmark and the kingdom of Northumbria (as well as Scotland) are not wholly united as singular nations, but are both domestically and culturally divided as much as they are in tension with one another.[54] The game designers of *Expeditions: Vikings* achieved these diverse political and social situations by drawing on both fictional narratives and the histories of late eighth-century England, which are explored or uncovered through the player's history-based adventure. For instance, one major event in the game that the player and their hirdman participate in is the first historical Viking raid on England in the island of Lindisfarne. This historical event in the game repeats the typical Viking incursions as marauders plundering and devastating the lands of England, where the player and his/her raiding party re-enact the event by defeating the island's poorly armed civilian defenders, gather their spoils from the island's monastery and village, and then either sail back to Denmark or move inland.[55] The game allows players some control over this event's severity: it is either left as an act of plundering, or can be further worsened by the player's selected dialogue choices and actions in dealing with the island's inhabitants. Some of these actions from dialogue exchanges include allowing one of the player's companions to brutally torture a wounded monk and ordering the killing of young children and old people.[56]

The micro-historical narratives in *Expeditions: Vikings* not only incorporate stand-alone events but also encompass several historical figures, whose stories reflect the social and political climate of northern England at the time. More importantly, the histories of these individuals can be virtually communicated and re-enacted through the player's role-playing activity, where he or she can go on quests that influences or leads to the occurrence of these actual historical events as part of creating their Viking adventure. The historical event of Aethelred I of Northumbria (r. 774–779, 790–796) returning to Northumbria in 790 to reclaim his kingdom and depose Osred II (r. 789–790) is one of the game's major plotlines.[57] In the historical scenario, the player can choose to side with Aethelred in reclaiming his birth right from the current ruler Osred in Northumbria's capital Eoforwic (York), to gain the support of the Bishop of York, Eanbald, who currently serves Osred, thwart attempts for Osred to seek allies in the southern regions of England, and then defeating Osred's army and capture him at the Battle of Yngilswood, whereby he is deposed and goes into self-exile.[58] Eventually, Aethelred offers to help the player and their companions with sending his own warriors to help with defending the village of Skjern from a rival Danish clan.[59]

These micro- and macro-narratives from a combination of history and role-playing activities, such as fights and quests, illustrate the use of Vikings as a spatial, temporal, and dialogue device for participatory role-play that provides insights regarding the local history of late eighth-century Northumbria. Combining the structures and elements of medieval adventurism, as a key activity of participatory medievalism, with historical relationships between Vikings and Northumbrians in England creates an adaptation of England not only as a visual setting, but as a place for the player's role-playing experiences to create narrative opportunities for cultural exchanges and conflicts between the multiple communities in Northumbria. The historical dimensions used in this game present players with the means to create their own adaptation through role play, which may exhibit either a life of turmoil, hardship, and violence in early medieval northern England by Viking intervention, or a peaceful and stable co-existence where Anglo-Saxon, Pictish, and Danish societies can live together in relative harmony.

Space constraints mean I have not discussed the ability of players to choose to play as a female thane or a shield-maiden, and this ability is deserving of its own, further, analysis. Nevertheless, it is worth noting that players who choose to play as women are not simply able to do so because of tokenistic gender equality. The game contains women functioning as they would have in medieval England, including female peasants, nuns, and wise-woman. Significantly, Viking and Pictish women are depicted as warriors leading warbands, or are able to serve alongside their male and/or female counterparts.[60] While this medievalism is certainly ahistorical, the inclusion of female characters in the gameplay is a useful way of changing attitudes about the strict patriarchal and homogenous society that are often presented in modern adaptations.

Conclusion

From major rebellions to tournament-style bouts, each of these medieval games has brought the histories of medieval England outside the confines of academia to a growing, video-game generation. While these games indicate a continuing use of literary and media conventions in representing medieval England, they also illustrate how medieval games borrow a variety of performative forms of medievalism, particularly the practices or modes of role-playing as well. As these games are only a few examples, more studies are needed to examine recent or upcoming digital game adaptations of England, such as *Total War Saga: Thrones of Britannia* (2018), which focuses on England from the ninth until the eleventh century.[61] Despite the uncertainty as to whether digital games using medieval England will be directed to more serious constructions of history or a continued inspiration for medieval fantasy, the recurrent use of England by game designers demonstrates a possibility for a new sub-field dedicated to continuing the study of the growing interconnections between medievalism in England and digital games, with digital role-playing being one of many innovative practices of adapting the histories of medieval England to the digital media world.

Notes

1 Rick Goodman, *Empire Earth* (computer game) (Stainless Steel Studios, 2001).
2 Goodman, *Empire Earth*.
3 I use the terms "digital games," "video games," and "games" interchangeably throughout this chapter to refer to all games in digital or virtual simulated formats, and pre-digital games in referring to non-digital games.
4 Infinity Ward, Treyarch, and Sledgehammer Games, *Call of Duty* (series); MicroPose, Firaxis Games, and Take-Two Interactive, *Sid Meier's Civilization* (series); Omega Force, *Dynasty Warriors* (series); and Ubisoft Montreal, *Assassin's Creed* (series).
5 Todd Howard, *The Elder Scrolls IV: Oblivion* (computer and video console game) (Bethesda Softworks and 2K Games, 2006); Konrad Tomaszkiewicz, Mateusz Kanik, and Sebastian Stępień, *The Witcher 3: Wild Hunt* (computer and video console game) (CD Projekt, 2015).
6 Kevin Flanagan, "Videogame Adaptation," in *The Oxford Handbook of Adaptation Studies*, ed. Thomas Leitch (Oxford: Oxford University Press, 2016), 441. While some of the earliest video games were based in medieval England, their digital adaptations were not of history but of the supernatural and semi-mythical tales of King Arthur, Merlin, and his retinue of knights, with some of the earliest games including *Excalibur* (1983) and *Lancelot* (1988).
7 Tison Pugh and Angela Jane Weisl, *Medievalisms: Making the Past in the Present* (London: Routledge, 2013), 1.
8 David Matthews, *Medievalism: A Critical History* (Cambridge: D.S. Brewer, 2015), 172.
9 Oliver M. Traxel, "Medieval and Pseudo-Medieval Elements in Computer Role-Playing Games: Use and Interactivity," *Studies in Medievalism* XVI (2008): 125–142.
10 Traxel, "Medieval and Pseudo-Medieval Elements," 128–130.
11 Traxel, "Medieval and Pseudo-Medieval Elements," 134–137.
12 Julie Sanders, *Adaptation and Appropriation* (London: Routledge, 2006), 19–20.
13 Sanders, *Adaptation and Appropriation*, 48.
14 Linda Hutcheon, *A Theory of Adaptation*, 2nd ed. (London: Routledge, 2013), 18.
15 Hutcheon, *A Theory of Adaptation*, 22.

16 While the characteristics of role playing as a game genre (RPG) will be used in this chapter, I use the term "role-playing" here as a form or style of performance as expressed in re-enactment activities, table-top games, and live-action role-playing groups.
17 William Davis, *Medieval II: Total War Kingdoms* (computer game) (Creative Assembly, 2007); Mårten Stormdal, *War of the Roses* (computer game) (Fatshark, 2012–2017); Jonas Wæver, *Expeditions: Vikings* (computer game) (Logic Artists, 2017).
18 Daniel T. Kline, "Participatory Medievalism, Role-Playing, and Digital Gaming," in *The Cambridge Companion to Medievalism*, ed. Louise D'Arcens (Cambridge: Cambridge University Press, 2016), 76.
19 Kline, "Participatory Medievalism," 76.
20 Robert T. Smith, *Medieval II: Total War* (computer video game) (Creative Assembly, 2005); Davis, *Medieval II: Total War Kingdoms*.
21 Turn-based strategy is a game style (also common in pre-digital games) where each player has a turn to choose and perform their set of actions, usually on a game map. A common subgenre of this form is real-time strategy, in which players can perform actions and decisions in the game without taking turns, but there are also digital games that contain both these forms.
22 For more on these events, see: Richard Brooks, *Lewes and Evesham: Simon De Montfort and the Second Barons' War* (Oxford: Osprey Publishing, 2015); Matthew Lewis, *Henry III: The Son of Magna Carta* (Stroud: Amberley, 2016); David Walker, *Medieval Wales* (Cambridge: Cambridge University Press, 1990); and Caroline Burt, *Edward I and the Governance of England, 1272–1307* (Cambridge: Cambridge University Press, 2012).
23 *Medieval II: Total War Kingdoms (Instruction Manual)* (SEGA, 2007), 5.
24 Despite the ambiguity of the term, gameplay can be broadly defined as the player's negotiation with and utilisation of the game's rules, objects, environment, characters, and other game mechanics.
25 *Medieval II: Total War Kingdoms.*
26 *Medieval II: Total War Kingdoms.*
27 *Medieval II: Total War Kingdoms (Instruction Manual)*, 8.
28 *Medieval II: Total War Kingdoms.*
29 *Medieval II: Total War Kingdoms (Instruction Manual)*, 8. The game manual's reference to Llywelyn as "King" instead of "Prince" possibly anticipates player familiarity with the title king being the position of authority.
30 *Medieval II: Total War Kingdoms.*
31 For further information on the relationship between medievalism and anachronism, see: Pugh and Weisl, *Medievalisms*, especially Chapter 6, "Movie Medievalisms: Five (or Six) Ways of Looking at an Anachronism," 83–100.
32 Gregory Fedorenko, "The Portrayal of Medieval Warfare in *Medieval: Total War* and *Medieval 2: Total War*," in *Digital Gaming Re-Imagines the Middle Ages*, ed. Daniel T. Kline (London: Routledge, 2013), 55.
33 Fedorenko, "The Portrayal of Medieval Warfare in Medieval," 56.
34 Mike Simpson, *Medieval: Total War* (computer video game) (Creative Assembly, 2002); Smith, *Medieval II: Total War.*
35 Fedorenko, "The Portrayal of Medieval Warfare in Medieval," 61–62.
36 Fedorenko, "The Portrayal of Medieval Warfare in Medieval," 61–62.
37 Richard Brooks, *Lewes and Evesham: Simon De Montfort and the Second Barons' War* (Oxford: Osprey Publishing, 2015), 6.
38 This is also the same end goal for players controlling the other factions (Ireland, Wales, Scotland, and Norway).

39 *War of the Roses* was shut down in 2017 for various reasons, including a decrease in player subscription and the game's lack of a single-player storyline-based campaign.
40 Michael Hicks, *The Wars of the Roses* (London: Bloomsbury, 2010), 4. See also John Ashdown-Hill, *The Wars of the Roses* (Stroud: Amberley, 2015).
41 Andrew W. Boardman, *The Medieval Soldier in the Wars of the Roses* (Stroud: Sutton Publishing, 1998), 120, 76.
42 The term team "deathmatch" is a digital game style that puts players into two teams, where the aim is to kill or defeat as many opponents as possible within a time limit or when certain conditions have been met to win the game.
43 Stormdal, *War of the Roses*.
44 Paul Dean, "War of the Roses Review: Paradox's Medieval Deathmatch Is Bloomin Deadly," *Eurogamer.net*, http://eurogamer.net/articles/2012-10-01-war-of-the-roses-review.
45 Boardman, *The Medieval Soldier in the Wars of the Roses*, 165.
46 Matt Richardson, "War of the Roses - MMO Game Review," *Armchair General*, http://armchairgeneral.com/war-of-the-roses-mmo-game-review.htm.
47 Michael Hirst, *Vikings* (MGM Television, 2013).
48 Wæver, *Expeditions: Vikings*.
49 *Expeditions: Vikings*.
50 Scotland is also another major location in the game, then inhabited by the Picts.
51 Richard Van Eck, *Gaming and Cognition: Theories and Practice from the Learning Sciences* (IGI Global, 2010), 15.
52 Van Eck, *Gaming and Cognition*, 15.
53 *Expeditions: Vikings*.
54 *Expeditions: Vikings*.
55 *Expeditions: Vikings*.
56 *Expeditions: Vikings*.
57 *Expeditions: Vikings* differs slightly from history that it was Osred, and not his first cousin and predecessor Aelfwald I (r. 779–789), who deposed Aethelred when he was a boy.
58 *Expeditions: Vikings*.
59 *Expeditions: Vikings*.
60 Shield maidens were female warriors depicted in many Scandinavian and Germanic sagas and folklore tales. See: Jenny Jochens, *Women in Old Norse Society* (Ithaca, NY: Cornell University Press, 1998); and Judith Jesch, *Women in the Viking Age* (Woodbridge: The Boydell Press, 1991).
61 Jack Lusted, *Total War Saga: Thrones of Britannia* (computer game) (Creative Assembly, 2018).

10 "I can piss on Calais from Dover"

Adaptation and Medievalism in Graphic Novel Depictions of the Hundred Years' War (1337–1453)

Iain A. MacInnes

Of the various periods of history available to modern authors, artists, screenwriters, and directors, it is perhaps medieval history that is most ripe for reconsideration and adaptation in today's media. A relative absence of written sources from the period, and a general lack of popular understanding of 'what happened' allows modern authors fantastic scope to adapt what is known, adapt what is recognised, and create something different.[1] The existence of at least some material from the period being depicted means that authors generally do not work from a completely blank canvas, but the gaps in between what is known allow all manner of creative flights of fancy. Graphic novels are increasingly using historical periods and events as the basis for diverse and fascinating explorations of the medieval period, and through them, the present. As Defne Ersin Tutan and Laurence Raw have argued, authors of such works have a "desire to make sense of the past in terms of the present. They are thus more likely to create imaginative approaches, involving the kind of speculation that might be dismissed as 'inaccurate' by the professional historian."[2] This growth in graphic depictions of the medieval past parallels an apparent upsurge in popular fascination with the medieval period and medieval imagery.[3] This is in part due to the popularisation of medieval and medieval-like tales in other media, in particular in relation to television series such as *Vikings* and *Game of Thrones*.[4]

As a medieval historian, it is important to recognise this developing interest in this period because it brings with it several attendant issues. The rise of the far right across the globe has been accompanied by their increasing use of medieval imagery and arguments based on a mythical medieval past.[5] The perception that medieval Europe was a racially homogenous and "white" world, where the cross-cultural interaction of the present day was absent, is a wholly incorrect one.[6] It is, however, an idea that is repeated by key figures in such groups.[7] The production of medieval graphic novels at this point, then, comes at an important time when historians are actively seeking to influence and (re)shape popular (mis) conceptions about the Middle Ages.[8] The adaptation of medieval narratives in such media has the potential not only to further understanding of the Middle Ages, but also to engender greater misunderstandings of the period. Timothy Corrigan has discussed how adaptation is in part about its reception, through which "readers may understand that different works operate differently for different readers depending on their background."[9] This stance presumes, however, that the reader considers matters beyond their own perspective, and that they possess a frame of reference for what is presented to them. Without such, their perception is surely based on what they 'know' about the period in question, and what is presented to them in the narrative. It is based, therefore, on medievalism. This is the modern perception of a largely imagined past which may be seen either as a dystopic nightmare unlike the present or as a utopian vision of how the world of the present day could return to a now-lost glorious historical era. As Chris Bishop has argued, analysis of medieval graphic novels must focus on the fact that such works "utilise components ascribed to the European Middle Ages by the popular culture that created them" and that "the creators of [these] comics ... believed them to be representations of the Middle Ages, and the intended audiences for these comics believed that too."[10] It is important, therefore, for historians to contribute to the analysis of such texts and for the historian's perspective to be part of the wider consideration of graphic adaptations of the medieval past. This chapter does so through consideration of texts that concentrate on the medieval period, and on the events of the Hundred Years' War in particular. It will focus on the themes of class and national identity, and their representation in these texts. In doing so, it analyses how these themes are portrayed to a modern audience, and what they infer about medieval—as well as modern—society.

The Medieval in Graphic Form

Depictions of the medieval past, or medieval-like worlds, have had a place in comics and graphic novels for a long time. As early as the 1950s and 1960s, comics depicted the medieval world in works such as *The Black Knight*, *Prince Valiant*, and *Robin Hood Tales*.[11] These were increasingly joined by medieval-like outputs of "fantastic neomedievalism," such as *Sword of Sorcery*, *Conan the Barbarian*, and *Red Sonja*, which blended a medieval aesthetic with fantasy literature.[12] Such series have undergone something of a resurgence in recent years, alongside modern works of fantasy medievalism inspired by the likes of *Game of Thrones*.[13] Perhaps as a result of this popularity, graphic novels have increasingly looked to 'real history' as source material. French *bandes dessinées* in particular have considered the French medieval past in some depth.[14] Series such as *Ils ont fait l'histoire*, *Les Reines de Sang*, and

Champs D'Honneur have focused issues on specific medieval individuals and events.[15] *Jour J* has similarly extended its counterfactual history series to encompass 'what-if' stories based in the European Middle Ages, while the series *Je Suis Cathare*, *La Derniere Cathar*, and *Les Aigles Décapitées* focus on specific periods of the French medieval past.[16] This productivity continues apace with the recent production of series such as *Je, François Villon*, *Valois*, and *Ira Dei*.[17]

English-language graphic novels have been a little slower to explore the period, but some have followed the medieval route, with one-shot examples including *Templar* (Jordan Mechner, LeUyen Pham, Alex Puvilland, First Second, 2013), *William, Bastard and Conqueror* (Jean-Francois Miniac, Borja Pena, OREP, 2015), *Debating Truth: The Barcelona Disputation of 1263* (Nina Caputo, Liz Clarke, OUP, 2016), *In the Shadow of the Cross: Imprisonment* (Dmitry Yakhovsky, MadeGlobal, 2016), *Nevsky* (Ben McCool, Mario Guevera, IDW, 2012), and *On Dangerous Ground: Bannockburn 1314* (Fiona Watson, Conor Boyle, National Trust for Scotland, 2014). Some English-language works have, however, also begun to focus on events popular in French-language comics. The Hundred Years' War in particular has increasingly been the focus of graphic novels. As a key point in the development of both English and French national identities, it is a period with popular resonance as national foundation myths revolve around recognisable figures and battles of the conflict.[18] Works that focus on the conflict include *Crécy* (Warren Ellis, Raulo Caceres, Avatar Press, 2010), *Le Trône D'Argile* (Nicolas Jarry, France Richemond, Theo, Lorenzo Pieri, Delcourt, 2006–2015), *Hawkwood: Mercenarie de la Guerre de Cent Ans* (Tommy Ohtsuka, Doki-Doki, 2016–2017), and *Agincourt 1415* (Will Gill, Graeme Howard, Anne Curry, Matador, 2015). This chapter will focus primarily on the two English-language works, as they provide the most focused examination of the English in the Hundred Years' War. *Crécy* and *Agincourt 1415* are two very different novels, both in tone and outlook. Ellis's *Crécy* is both an interesting adaptation of historical sources that discuss the battle and an irreverent, happily offensive consideration of the Middle Ages. Gill's *Agincourt* is more serious in tone, and he worked alongside prominent historians in its development. Still, both works engage with medievalism as they adapt the events of the past for a present audience, and it is this adaptation that will be the focus of my analysis.

The Hundred Years' War was the largest conflict of the medieval period. It began in 1337 as a result of a combination of dynastic and territorial disputes between the French and English monarchies.[19] Kings of England owed homage to their French counterparts for lands they held in France for which French monarchs were feudal superiors. English kings chafed at this perceived slight to their royal dignity, and war periodically broke out between the two kingdoms. Although England lost almost all of its continental possessions at the beginning of the thirteenth century, the memory of holding such territory did not fade.[20] These territorial issues were exacerbated by dynastic considerations in the fourteenth century. When Charles IV of France died in 1328 without issue it broke the line of succession that had rested with the descendants of Hugh Capet since 987. The search for a new king effectively came down to a choice between Philip of Valois and Edward III of England. The French chose to deny the legitimacy of succession through the female line—Edward III's claim coming through his mother—and they elevated Philip of Valois to the throne as Philip VI. After much debate within England, Edward III launched his claim to take what he declared to be his French throne and, as a result, the Hundred Years' War commenced in 1337.[21] It continued through periods of intense warfare and episodes of truce until 1453, drawing in various other kingdoms and territories as proxy wars were fought in the Low Countries, Scotland, and Spain.[22] The conflict also attracted warriors of various nations who sought financial gain and personal glory. The war also witnessed the increasing professionalisation of the medieval soldier as well as new developments, such as the tactical deployment of massed ranks of archers, and the use of artillery weapons.[23] The Hundred Years' War was a crucible in which many Europeans were thrown together in the heat of conflict, and where medieval Europe found itself at something of a crossroads in a changing world. The object here is to consider the extent to which such elements are considered in the graphic novels that depict these events.

Class and Medieval Society

The concept of class as it relates to medieval society is a complex one. It is acknowledged that the idea of class as a construct is a nineteenth-century development, and so its use in relation to the medieval period can be seen as anachronistic.[24] At the same time, however, there is no denying that medieval society was incredibly hierarchical. The majority of people in the Middle Ages 'knew their place,' and that they had little opportunity to elevate their social position.[25] Historians have discussed at length the nature of medieval society and have utilised the terminology of 'class' in numerous works. The fact remains, however, that while there were indeed divisions within medieval society that we might refer to as 'classes,' modern understandings of the term make its use problematic. Historiographical issues aside, the two graphic novels under consideration here make explicit reference to class and to class division throughout their narratives. English-language novels in particular adopt a noticeably 'history from below' approach.[26] They focus on the men of the lower classes—in particular the archers—considered to be the soldiers who turned the tide of battle at both Crécy and Agincourt. Although the English leadership is visible at times, and kings and princes are shown in close-up on occasion, the principal point of view is mainly that of the regular soldier.[27] As a result, it is the perspective of the common man that is heard most often, and through this, the theme of class is considered consistently in narrative dialogue as well as visual depiction.

Agincourt refers to class issues throughout, in particular referencing the French as aloof, above themselves, and looking down on the English. When describing the French forces shadowing Henry V's army on their march to Calais, the narrator notes that "they see an upstart King... An army of few Knights and Noblemen, but many lowly archers and other men of 'no value.'"[28] The French are accused of "arrogance" and "complacency" ahead of the battle, and of perceiving the English to be "impudent."[29] They seek to attack where the greatest concentration of English nobles are gathered, where they "will find opponents they consider 'worthy' of knights," and where they will engage "in 'honourable' combat with enemies of equal high status."[30] As the French cavalry flounders in its attack, French horses "tipped their 'noble' burden right at our feet."[31] Such language emphasises the upper-class nature of the French nobles in comparison to their English enemies. The use of the quotation marks around "noble," "worthy," and "honourable" casts ridicule on French perceptions of their own ability and station, and on their assumptions regarding the enemy. The whole tone of the description of the French revolves around the notion that the French thought themselves better than the English. In large part this is because of the involvement of common soldiers in the English army. Some of this rhetoric aligns with medieval sources. The English chronicler Thomas Walsingham commented that the French "held [the English warriors] cheap" and expected to easily defeat "those tired men who they thought would be captured with no quarter."[32] The context for such comment lies, however, in the different preparations of the two armies, and the fact that the English were weakened by illness and hunger while their French opponents were well fed and rested. Indeed, Walsingham's emphasis on the disparity between the two armies highlights the miraculous nature of the English victory in having overcome adversity to achieve a remarkable success. The graphic novel, however, uses such rhetoric differently and instead focuses on class division as the principal difference between the assembled forces.

The central character of *Crécy*, William of Stonham, adopts this negative view of the French nobility further still. Stonham's comments are replete with disdain and condescension regarding the elite, and can be interpreted as reflecting the opinion of the author himself. Warren Ellis has been described as a writer who utilises his main characters to express his own values, and who adopts the approach of "authorship as role play."[33] That Stonham reflects Ellis's views on class is given credence by comments made in the author's newsletter, where he described himself as "an old English socialist and cultural liberal who is probably way to the woolly left from most of you."[34] Considering Ellis's political leanings, it is clear that the words of Stonham very much reflect the author's viewpoint.

Stonham mixes his class comments with a healthy dose of xenophobia and racism (to which we will return shortly). In an extended discussion, Stonham echoes the *Agincourt* narrative that the French knights perceive fighting against an army of peasant archers as beneath their noble chivalric dignity. As Stonham notes,

> France is run by an internecine aristocracy. War is conducted by people of breeding and the useful scum they hire for pay. In France one does not allow the little people to run around on the field of battle ... [Philip VI has summoned an army, but] obviously he's not going to let the proles take up arms against us. So Philip's bought the use of Genoese mercenaries, the crossbowmen. The Genoese are intended to take out zee [sic] English scum in front, and then knights on horseback, in their mail and plate armour, will ride down the rest of us. For them, it's going to be a day at the hunt, with English villagers taking the place of foxes and pigeons.[35]

This extended monologue is worth considering in some depth. The suggestion that France is dominated by an "internecine aristocracy" is a description that could be applied to most European kingdoms, England included. While warfare was led by those of the chivalric elite, France supplemented its armies through the general levies known as the *ban* and *arrière-ban*.[36] This summoned all men of military age from town and country to serve in the French armies.[37] The suggestion that Philip VI was not going to let the "proles" [e.g. the proletarians] fight appears to be an attempt to insist that the French military effort was purely a noble/elite one.[38] It may also reflect a historical element of French fear of their own peasantry, anticipating events later in the conflict when the rural population rose up in rebellion against those who attacked them and those who failed to protect them. French chronicles describe in horrified tones the violence and barbarity of the *Jacquerie*, as the rebels were known, and the rebellion was violently put down by the French crown.[39] Still, Ellis's use of such wording also ties the monologue into a wider point about "class war." The term "proles" is anachronistic, referring as it does to the proletariat and borrowing from George Orwell's use of it in *1984*.[40] The author attempts to depict matters as a war between the French elite and the English commoner, reinforced later when he describes those in the English army as "English villagers. The common people standing up and saying, no more."[41] This view is reinforced by Stonham's comment that "it's going to be a day at the hunt, with English villagers taking the place of foxes and pigeons."[42] Of course the medieval nobility (French and English) hunted, but this comment can also be read as referencing present-day England, where fox hunting continues to be a contentious issue and one that is often framed as part of a "class war."[43] This extended monologue appears, therefore, to be steeped in modern concepts of class, with the construct of lower class versus elite portrayed playing out on the field of Crécy. While various references are indeed relevant to medieval events and *mores*, this does appear to be an attempt to adapt the historical events of this battle to suit a modern political message.

Both novels emphasise class disparity further when portraying the aftermath of the battle. They depict the English foot soldiers going among the French noble wounded to kill them. Such behaviour aligns with popular perceptions of medieval warfare being exceptionally violent, while at the same time challenging alternative modern assumptions of chivalric conduct in battle. The reality is that medieval chivalry only counted for those of the military elite. Chivalric ideals worked mostly to ensure the protection of knights and nobles and their survival in battle. Treatment of the infantry was very different, and surrender was seldom afforded to such men. This is partially because of latent distrust, hatred, and even fear towards those of the lower classes.[44] Ironically, however, it also ensured that nobles and knights who fell into the hands of lower class soldiers were not often afforded the possibility of surrendering. Although knightly ransoms could make lowly soldiers wealthy, they were often not allowed to keep the whole of any ransom acquired and, in any case, the poor treatment of infantry by knights led to those infantrymen often getting their revenge in first.[45] At the Battle of Courtrai (1302), for example, the elite of the French knightly class were butchered by Flemish foot soldiers who cut off the knights' spurs and took them away as trophies of their victory.[46] Similar behaviour is replicated throughout several scenes in these novels.

In *Crécy*, Stonham kills several stricken French knights and reflects that "peasants aren't supposed to kill knights... Peasants should stand and do as we're told by the likes of him, a man of quality and all that bollocks. But we're not taking prisoners."[47] In *Agincourt*, the first page of the novel depicts a French knight being similarly killed.[48] Later, the *Agincourt* narrator affirms that

> some [French knights] we took prisoner, many we did not. You take yer knife, you finds a gap in that ... fine armour of theirs. Under the arm. Into the groin. You takes yer knife and you finds a gap. Killed 'em quick like. Then the next. And the next. Killed 'em for Henry. For England.[49]

This description mirrors the behaviour of William of Stonham in *Crécy*. The use of language here, with the vernacular "yer" and "you finds," emphasises the English archer's position as a commoner, again stressing

"*I can piss on Calais from Dover*" 161

the class disparity. As indicated elsewhere in *Agincourt*, some knights were in fact taken prisoner and led away to the English rear, but "the injured and the dying are despatched with cruel efficiency."[50] This reflects historical reality with the number of French knightly and lordly fatalities in both battles being particularly high. Where the battles diverge is in relation to those who surrendered. At Agincourt, prisoners were taken throughout the battle and kept under guard at the rear of the English army. An attack on the English rear, coupled with a renewed offensive by French forces against the English line, led Henry V to order the massacre of his prisoners. In *Agincourt*, the men-at-arms mostly refuse such an order and it is left to the lowly archers to carry out the deed, men who are "untroubled by any notions of chivalry."[51] They include "those who've robbed and killed outside of war. Plenty with their blood up this day ready to kill an unarmed man for the ring on his finger or other such prize."[52] This depiction aligns with medieval French sources that emphasise English knights did not wish to lose their valuable ransoms, and it was left to a company of 200 archers to carry out the king's orders.[53] Still, the event and its depiction reinforce the nature of class division, even within the English army itself, with the archers casually murdering Frenchmen of higher status when their fellow Englishmen would not.

William of Stonham's views of the nobility appear to be rather one-sided in nature. He comments that the French knights are "not the cheese-eating surrender monkeys you know. These are the real French, vicious bastards with an inbred sense of entitlement to whatever they see."[54] The use of a modern derogatory phrase regarding twentieth-century French military performance again situates the narrator's commentary in the present while discussing the medieval past.[55] His treatment of the English nobility, although brief, is however less virulently class-related. Stonham speaks of the English nobility little. Indeed, in *Crécy*'s depictions of the battle, English knights and nobles are essentially unseen. This eliding of the English military elite emphasises the main point of the novel: that this was a victory won by the archers, by the common man. Outside of the battle itself, what little depiction there is of the English elite focuses on England's commanders, Edward III, and his son, Edward, the Black Prince. Edward III is "a clever bloke, a born soldier and a bit of a bastard."[56] Prince Edward is "a complete and utter bastard."[57] Considering the irreverent tone of the work as a whole, such comments are meant to be complimentary. When faced with the Black Prince, however, Stonham's irreverence fades. Spoken to directly, Stonham responds politely and averts his eyes from the royal person, a relatively common practice in the Middle Ages.[58] When the Black Prince orders Stonham to dig pits in front of the English line and the archer comments that he is not allowed to look at the prince, Edward retorts "then look at the fucking shovel."[59] Despite the difference in their social status, Ellis draws parallels between the Black Prince and Stonham with comparable mannerisms and use of language. In doing so, Ellis reinforces the difference between the English and French nobility but lessens that between the English nobility and the English commons. As a result, he inserts an 'us and them' dynamic that alters the dichotomy of rich versus poor and makes Stonham's perspective rather more complex. *Agincourt* arguably goes further. Although Edward III and the Black Prince did indeed fight at Crécy, Ellis does not depict them in action. Gill, on the other hand, places Henry V amongst his troops, encouraging them for the fight ahead and fighting on foot alongside his men, just as historical sources suggest. During the *mêlée*, Henry fights to protect the wounded Duke of Gloucester and takes a blow to the head that damages his helm.[60] He is the warrior king and the hero of the victory, perhaps even more so than the archers and infantrymen who are the focus of much of the work. This in part reflects not only the Shakespearean image of Henry V, but also emphasises that the class distinction in both works is not so heavily emphasised when it comes to depicting elite warriors of the "same side."

National Identity/Nationalism and Medieval Europe

There are, then, other factors at work in these narratives beyond a simple class division between elite and common soldiers, and this largely centres upon national identity/nationalism. As already indicated, William of Stonham is particularly vicious when it comes to his description of the French. He is perfectly comfortable with his own bigoted nature and states as early as the third panel of the novel that he is "a complete bloody xenophobe who comes from a time when it was acceptable to treat people in the next village like they were subhumans."[61] Such a view appears to align with modern misconceptions regarding the Middle Ages as an inherently racist period.[62] As with the issue of class, the idea of race meant something very different in the Middle Ages than it does today and "the categories the medieval West used to define other people were far more complicated, and far more flexible, than our own."[63] The use of the term 'race' at all in relation to the Middle Ages is therefore much discussed in wider academia.[64] As such, Stonham's perception and attitude more likely reflects racism and xenophobia in our own day than it does a representation of the past. Still, there is also little doubt that as the Hundred Years' War progressed, there arose an increasingly virulent form of patriotism that emphasised an 'us versus them' dichotomy in the development of an individual and 'national' sense of self. While the term 'nationalism' is also problematic to use here, there was an increasing depiction of the 'enemy,' of 'the other,' as being different and of possessing inherently negative characteristics.[65] English poems from the fourteenth century, for example, provide popular views of the French war from the home front. One poem written about the Battle of Crécy "described the French as effeminate and compared them to the lynx, the viper, and the wolf—cunning, cruel and proud."[66] Such negative associations with the enemy became ever more commonplace as the war progressed; these stereotypes became ingrained in the national consciousness and, to some extent, William of Stonham's words reflect this.

Ellis takes such stereotypes further than their medieval equivalent. The already mentioned reference to the French as "cheese-eating surrender monkeys" is only one such example of a creeping modernism at work in Stonham's xenophobia. At the outset of the novel, Stonham narrates that "this is a story about the English and the French and why the English hate the French."[67] According to him, it is because they are "snail-eating cunts" and because "they eat frogs, they smell bad, and they're twenty five miles away."[68] The combination of culture and proximity is emphasised when he comments that the French "make sausages out of horse's arseholes and have a history of using England as their toilet."[69] Such denigration of French food and French culture echoes British stereotypes of those on the other side of the Channel.[70] Perceived cultural differences between the protagonists are further reinforced in regards to language. In one of the few passages where Stonham says anything remotely positive about the French, he notes that they "speak in music but English only soars when we start being bloody horrible to people."[71] In spite of this inherent criticism of his own language, he also complains that twelfth-century kings of England spoke no English at all.[72] This is a historical point, reflecting the reality that French was the language of the elite and the royal court, while English was the vernacular of the common people. Royal and chancery procedure only adopted English as the language of government in the fifteenth century.[73] And yet, Stonham also argues that England "has a way of making people its own. Angles, Saxons, Danes, even some of the bloody French; they all end up English."[74] This statement ignores the multilingual nature of medieval England, and instead appears to reflect modern considerations. In particular, such comments reflect modern focus on the language of immigrant groups and the perception that migrants to Britain should learn and speak English.[75] In so doing, like their medieval predecessors, they too will presumably "end up English." Stonham therefore provides views on the French, and on English history, that are based in the medieval period, but which also tap into modern considerations of both the past and the present. In doing so he presents a view that is recognisable to a modern audience, but one that also needs to be challenged by the reader in terms of its medieval relevance and modern resonance.

William of Stonham is not just virulent in his xenophobia towards the French. Others also bear the brunt of his views. For example, he states that Scotland "is of no use to us. Limited amount of land. Limited amount of people. I mean, it's not like there are any bloody humans living there, is it?"[76] This continued denial of empathy towards any of those who are not "English" is a further sign of Stonham's racist nature, and something that also extends to members of his own army. There are Welsh troops on campaign who are described as "Sheep Shaggers," a modern term for the Welsh used primarily in sports fan culture.[77] A friend of Stonham's shouts at a Welshman, "fuck off you Welsh cunt. I hate you and I hate fucking France."[78] In the English camp ahead of the battle, Stonham notes that the Welsh brought their families with them on campaign. He calls them "a poisonous fucking people and no mistake."[79] He suggests that the Welsh hate their Welsh neighbours more than they do the English, and that such attitudes led to their conquest. He considers shooting some of the Welsh children to "teach these wankers a lesson," and he confronts a Welshman who remonstrates with him by yelling "you're not fucking human" and emphasising the point by threatening to "turn your bollocks into a pocket and sell your wife to the butcher!"[80] Interestingly, the Welsh are rarely depicted directly although they are heard, albeit briefly.[81] The use of language here again denotes difference. The Welsh refer to their English comrades by the diminutive "boy bach" ("little boy"). Whether the English understand the meaning of the phrase or not, the use of Welsh language undercuts Stonham's statement that all of those who come into the English sphere "become English." This point is reinforced by the involvement of Cornish troops who "don't talk to anyone," a potential reference to language and to separate dialects used in specific parts of England.[82] This again strikes at the homogeneity that Stonham suggests in regards to the English army and reflects the medieval reality of English armies with troops summoned from all parts of the extended English realm. It also undermines the point he makes that he is amongst a large group of "mates" campaigning in the service of Edward III and that this is an army of common English looking to stop the French invading England. Fundamentally, it challenges the idea that it is a class/national war of English commons versus French elites; and this is perhaps the point. Stonham's racism and xenophobia stand out to counter his portrayal of himself and his fellow warriors as the oppressed, the "underdogs." He is, in effect, no different in his opinions or his actions than those he fights against. Stonham can be read as a critique of xenophobic/racist views. He is ridiculous in his racist outbursts, inviting the reader to interrogate their interpretation of his actions and implicit alignment with him. Stonham emphasises that the differences between people are ones that we create ourselves. In fashioning a picture of homogeneity around national identity, all we do is make an image that is reflective of our own prejudices and that elides those who are there, but who do not fit our view of ourselves.

Conclusion

Both *Crécy* and *Agincourt* provide a fascinating depiction of war in the medieval period, and of these two battles in particular. They take much that has been written, both in primary source evidence from the time and in modern interpretations of that evidence, and adapt it to suit the visual medium. Their stories are quite different in approach, in tone, and in what is presented, but they both deal with elements of medievalism that reflect a good deal about what people of the present day think about the medieval past. Although steeped in the historical events of Crécy and Agincourt, the analysis provided here has demonstrated the extent to which the medieval past has been adapted to consider themes that have a modern relevance. The issues of class and nationalism come with a sizeable amount of post-medieval meaning that affects interpretation of such themes, especially when dealt with in a medieval context. Yes, there were different social groups within medieval society, and yes there were the beginnings of some form of national consciousness during this conflict. Such developments were, however, very different to how readers today would consider the themes of class and national identity. In focusing on these elements, the novels utilise the events of the Hundred Years' War and place them within an understandable modern context, utilising themes that a modern reader can comprehend even if they know nothing about the conflict itself. This is not to undermine the historical reality of what is depicted, and indeed both works provide portrayals of these battles that are based on good quality research and contemporary sources. The novels do, however, adapt the medieval world and re-contextualise it within a modern framework that could be said to reinforce stereotypes of the period. As a result, it is important that historians do not overlook works such as these, and that they engage with graphic novels that depict historical events. Adding to the contributions of comics and literary scholars, historians can provide analysis of the medievalisms utilised in such works to emphasise both their historical and modern relevance. Graphic novel readers could quite easily reflect that what is presented is the Middle Ages 'as it was.' By engaging with novels such as these, historians can instead aid the reader in understanding which depictions are medieval, and which are a product of medievalism.

Notes

1 See, for example: Kevin J. Harty, *The Reel Middle Ages: American, Western and Eastern European, Middle Eastern and Asian Films About Medieval Europe* (Jefferson, NC: McFarland, 1999); Tison Pugh and Angela Jane Weisl, *Medievalisms: Making the Past in the Present* (London: Routledge, 2013); Andrew B.R. Elliott, *Remaking the Middle Ages: The Methods of Cinema and History in Portraying the Medieval*

World (Jefferson, NC: McFarland, 2011); and Meriem Pagès and Karolyn Kinane, eds., *The Middle Ages on Television: Critical Essays* (Jefferson, NC: McFarland, 2015).
2 Defne Ersin Tutan and Laurence Raw, "Introduction: What Does 'Adapting' History Involve?," in *The Adaptation of History: Essays on Ways of Telling the Past*, ed. Laurence Raw and Defne Ersin Tutan (Jefferson, NC: McFarland & Company, 2013), 9.
3 Mónica A.W. Vadillo, "Comic Books Featuring the Middle Ages," *Itinéraires* 2010–3 (2010): 153–163. For a growing online list of graphic publications dealing with medieval history and medieval-like worlds, see: *Medieval Comics: How to be Human in the Middle Ages*, https://medievalcomicsblog.wordpress.com/modern-comics/.
4 Michael Livingston, "Getting Medieval on Game of Thrones," https://tor.com/2017/03/10/getting-medieval-on-game-of-thrones/; "Viking TV shows boost Denmark tourist attractions," *BBC News*, 18 May 2016, http://bbc.co.uk/news/blogs-news-from-elsewhere-36323270.
5 "The far right's new fascination with the Middle Ages," *The Economist*, 2 January 2017, https://economist.com/blogs/democracyinamerica/2017/01/medieval-memes; David M. Perry, "What to Do When Nazis Are Obsessed with Your Field," *Pacific Standard*, 6 September 2017, https://psmag.com/education/nazis-love-taylor-swift-and-also-the-crusades. Marina Gerzic also draws attention to the far right's appropriation of faux-medieval culture and imagery in her chapter "From *Cabaret* to *Gladiator*: Refiguring masculinity in Julie Taymor's *Titus*" in this volume.
6 Josephine Livingston, "Racism, Medievalism, and the White Supremacists of Charlottesville," *New Republic*, 15 August 2017, https://newrepublic.com/article/144320/racism-medievalism-white-supremacists-charlottesville; Paul B. Sturtevant, "Race, Racism, and the Middle Ages: Tearing Down the 'Whites Only' Medieval World," *The Public Medievalist*, 7 February 2017, https://publicmedievalist.com/race-racism-middle-ages-tearing-whites-medieval-world/.
7 Helen Young, "Where Do the 'White Middle Ages' Come from?," *The Public Medievalist*, 21 March 2017, https://publicmedievalist.com/white-middle-ages-come/; Helen Young, "White Supremacists love the Middle Ages," *In the Middle*, 16 August 2017, http://inthemedievalmiddle.com/2017/08/white-supremacists-love-middle-ages.html.
8 Dorothy Kim, "Teaching Medieval Studies in a Time of White Supremacy," *In the Middle*, 28 August 2017, http://inthemedievalmiddle.com/2017/08/teaching-medieval-studies-in-time-of.html; David M. Perry, "How Can We Untangle White Supremacy from Medieval Studies?," *Pacific Standard*, 9 October 2017, https://psmag.com/education/untangling-white-supremacy-from-medieval-studies.
9 Timothy Corrigan, "Defining Adaptation," in *The Oxford Handbook of Adaptation Studies*, ed. Thomas Leitch (Oxford: Oxford University Press, 2017), 23.
10 Chris Bishop, *Medievalist Comics and the American Century* (Jackson: University of Mississippi Press, 2016), 14.
11 *The Black Knight* (Atlas Comics, 1955–1956); *Prince Valiant* (1937–present); *Robin Hood Tales* (Quality Comics/DC Comics, 1956–1958); Vadillo, "Comic Books Featuring the Middle Ages," 153–163; Bishop, *Medievalist Comics and the American Century*, 27–48.
12 *Sword of Sorcery* (DC Comics, 1973); *Conan the Barbarian* (Marvel Comics, 1970–1993); *Red Sonja* (Marvel Comics, 1973–1986); Kim Selling, "'Fantastic Neomedievalism': The Image of the Middle Ages in Popular Fantasy," in *Flashes of the Fantastic: Selected Essays from the "War of the*

Worlds" Centennial, Nineteenth International Conference on the Fantastic in the Arts, ed. David Ketterer (Westport, CT: Kraeger, 2004), 211; Bishop, Medievalist Comics and the American Century, 97–120, 121–144.

13 See, for example: George R.R. Martin, Ben Avery, Mike S. Miller, *The Hedge Knight* (Jet City Comics, 2013); George R.R. Martin, Ben Avery, Mike S. Miller, *The Sworn Sword* (Jet City Comics, 2014); George R.R. Martin, Ben Avery, Mike S. Miller, *The Mystery Knight* (HarperVoyager, 2017); and Michael A. Torregrossa, "Camelot 3000 and Beyond: An Annotated Listing of Arthurian Comic Books Published in the United States c. 1980–1998 (Revised Edition, May 2000)," *The Camelot Project*, http://d.lib.rochester.edu/camelot/text/torregrossa-camelot-3000-and-beyond-an-annotated-listing.

14 For the French comic depiction of medieval French history, see the various essays contained in *Le Moyen Âge en Bande Dessinée*, ed. Tristan Martine (Paris: Karthala, 2016).

15 *Ils ont fait l'histoire* (Glénat, 2014–2016) includes volumes on Charlemagne, Genghis Khan, Joan of Arc, Philip IV, Louis IX, and Saladin: http://glenatbd.com/bd/collections/ils-ont-fait-l-histoire.htm. *Les Reines de Sang* (Delcourt, 2012–2016) includes issues on Eleanor of Aquitaine and Isabella of France: http://editions-delcourt.fr/bd/nos-collections-bd/histoire-amp-histoires.html. The *Champs D'Honneur* series (Delcourt, 2016) focused on the Battle of Castillon (1453) in one of its recent issues (Thierry Gloris, Gariele Parma, Dimitri Fogolin, *Castillon – Juillet 1453* [Delcourt, 2016]).

16 Fred Duval and Jean-Pierre Pécau, *Jour J* (2010–present); Makyo, Alessandro Calore, Claudia Chec, *Je Suis Cathare* (Delcourt, 2008–2017); Arnaud Delalande, Eric Lambert, Bruno Pradelle, *La Derniere Cathar* (Glenat, 2016); Patrice Pellerin, Jean-Charles Kraehn, Jean-Jacques Chagnaud, *et al*, *Les Aigles Décapitées* (Glenat, 1986–2017).

17 Luigi Critone, *et al*, *Je, François Villon* (Delcourt, 2011–2016); Thierry Gloris, Jaime Calderon, Felideus, *Valois* (Delcourt, 2018–); Vincent Brugeas, Ronan Toulhoat, *Ira Dei* (Dargaud, 2018–).

18 See, for example: Ardis Butterfield, *The Familiar Enemy: Chaucer, Language and Nation in the Hundred Years' War* (Oxford: Oxford University Press, 2009); Denise N. Baker, ed., *Inscribing the Hundred Years' War in French and English Cultures* (Albany: State University of New York Press, 2000); David Green, "National Identities and the Hundred Years' War," in *Fourteenth Century England VI*, ed. Chris Given-Wilson (Woodbridge: Boydell and Brewer, 2010), 115–130.

19 For general histories of the Hundred Years' War, see, for example: Edouard Perroy, *The Hundred Years War* (New York: Capricorn Books, 1965); and Christopher Allmand, *The Hundred Years War: England and France at War, c.1300–c.1450* (Cambridge: Cambridge University Press, 2008).

20 For the longer-term nature of Anglo-French antagonism, see, for example: M.G.A. Vale, *The Origins of the Hundred Years War: The Angevin Legacy, 1250–1340* (Oxford: Clarendon Press, 1996).

21 For the dynastic causes of the Hundred Years' War, see: C. Taylor, "The Salic Law and the Valois Succession to the French Throne," *French History* 15, no. 4 (2001): 358–377; R.E. Giesey, "The Juristic Basis of Dynastic Right to the French Throne," *Transactions of the American Philosophical Society* 51, no. 5 (1961): 3–47; and G. Templeman, "Edward III and the Beginnings of the Hundred Years' War," *Transactions of the Royal Historical Society* 2 (1952): 69–88.

22 Kelly DeVries, "The Hundred Years' War: Not One But Many," in *The Hundred Years' War, Part II: Different Vistas*, ed. L.J. Andrew Villalon and Donald J. Kagay (Leiden: Brill, 2008), 3–36.

23 Brian G.H. Ditcham, "The employment of foreign mercenary troops in the French royal armies 1415–1470" (PhD thesis, University of Edinburgh, 1978); John France, ed., *Mercenaries and Paid Men: The Mercenary Identity in the Middle Ages. Proceedings of a Conference held at University of Wales, Swansea, 7th–9th July 2005* (Leiden: Brill, 2008); Clifford J. Rogers, "The Military Revolutions of the Hundred Years' War," *Journal of Military History* 57, no. 2 (1993): 241–278.
24 See, for example: David Crouch, *The Birth of Nobility: Constructing Aristocracy in England and France, 900–1300* (London: Routledge, 2014), Chapters 7 and 8.
25 See, for example: Georges Duby, *The Three Orders: Feudal Society Imagined*, trans. Arthur Goldhammer (Chicago, IL: University of Chicago Press, 1980); and Susan Reynolds, *Fiefs and Vassals: The Medieval Evidence Reinterpreted* (Oxford: Clarendon Press, 1994).
26 Interestingly, French-language works appear to take a different approach. For example, *Le Trone d'Argile* portrays its history from a "top-down" perspective. It is the history of kings and queens, of nobles and warriors, and takes a "kings and battles" approach to its history. The peasantry are only depicted to show the poor people of France suffering from war. The only difference to this picture comes, unsurprisingly, in the depiction of Joan of Arc who is mostly shown in largely idyllic depictions of rural life devoid of the mud and blood that is seen in relation to others of that class. See Damien Boone and Frédéric Zalewski, "En bande dessinée aussi, Lorànt Deutsch écrit sa propre histoire," *ActuaBD*, http://actuabd.com/DAMIEN-BOONE-et-FREDERIC-ZALEWSKI.
27 *Agincourt*'s narrator is not named, and the point of view changes throughout the narrative. At various points, however, it does provide the soldier's-eye-view of matters. *Crécy* provides a consistently soldierly view of proceedings through its sole narrator, William of Stonham.
28 Gill, *Agincourt*. The quote "men of no value" is also used in *Crécy* and appears to have been taken from a fourteenth-century French chronicle (*Grandes Chroniques de France*, ed. P. Paris [Paris, 1836] 1:1377–1378). It does not appear to have been used in relation to Agincourt, and so this would appear to be a deliberate borrowing of the quote to suit the purposes of this novel. See Anne Curry, *The Battle of Agincourt: Sources and Interpretations* (Woodbridge: Boydell Press, 2009).
29 Gill, *Agincourt*.
30 Gill, *Agincourt*.
31 Gill, *Agincourt*.
32 Curry, *Battle of Agincourt*, 63–64.
33 Jochen Ecke, "Warren Ellis: Performing the Transnational Author in the American Comics Mainstream," in *Transnational Perspectives on Graphic Narratives: Comics at the Crossroads*, ed. D. Stein, S. Denson, and C. Meyer (London: Bloomsbury, 2013), 166.
34 *Orbital Operations: The Warren Ellis Newsletter* (http://orbitaloperations.com/), cited in Rich Johnson, "Warren Ellis, On Whether Nazis Should Be Punched in the Face, Or Not," *Bleeding Cool*, 22 January 2017, https://bleedingcool.com/2017/01/22/warren-ellis-whether-nazis-punched-face-not/.
35 Ellis, *Crécy*.
36 Bertrand Schnerb, "De l'armée féodale à l'armée permanente," in *Le miracle capétien*, ed. Stéphane Rials (Paris: Perrin, 1987), 123–132; Philipe Contamine, *Guerre, état et société à la fin du Moyen Age. Études sur les armées des rois de France, 1337–1494* (Paris: Mouton, 1972), 26–55.
37 Betrand Schnerb, "Vassals, Allies and Mercenaries: The French Army before and after 1346," in *The Battle of Crécy, 1346*, ed. Andrew Ayton and Philip Preston (Woodbridge: Boydell Press, 2005), 265–272.

38 Ellis, *Crécy*.
39 David M. Bessen, "The Jacquerie: Class War or Co-opted Rebellion?," *Journal of Medieval History* 11, no. 1 (1985): 43–59; Justine Firnhaber–Baker, "Soldiers, Villagers, and Politics: The Role of Mercenaries in the Jacquerie of 1358," in *Routiers et mercenaires pendant la guerre de Cent ans*, ed. Guilhem Pépin, Françoise Laine, and Frédéric Boutoulle (Ausonius: Bordeaux, 2016), 101–114.
40 Jean-Jacques Courtine and Laura Willett, "A Brave New Language: Orwell's Invention of *Newspeak* in *1984*," *SubStance* 15, no. 2 (1986): 69–74.
41 Ellis, *Crécy*.
42 Ellis, *Crécy*.
43 Allyson N. May, *The Fox-Hunting Controversy, 1781–2004: Class and Cruelty* (London: Routledge, 2016), 51–84.
44 Matthew Strickland, *War and Chivalry: The Conduct and Perception of War in England and Normandy, 1066–1217* (Cambridge: Cambridge University Press, 1996), 176–181.
45 Denys Hay, "The Division of the Spoils of War in Fourteenth-Century England," *Transactions of the Royal Historical Society* 4 (1954): 91–109; Rémy Ambühl, *Prisoners of War in the Hundred Years' War: Ransom Culture in the Late Middle Ages* (Cambridge: Cambridge University Press, 2013); Strickland, *War and Chivalry*, 176–181.
46 J.F. Verbruggen, *The Battle of the Golden Spurs (Courtrai, 11 July 1302): A Contribution to the History of Flanders' War of Liberation, 1297–1305* (Cambridge: Boydell and Brewer, 2002), 242–245.
47 Ellis, *Crécy*.
48 Gill, *Agincourt*.
49 Gill, *Agincourt*.
50 Gill, *Agincourt*.
51 Gill, *Agincourt*.
52 Gill, *Agincourt*.
53 Curry, *Battle of Agincourt*, 167–168.
54 Ellis, *Crécy*.
55 The phrase "cheese-eating surrender monkeys" appears to have made its debut in a 1995 episode of *The Simpsons*. It was then taken up in later years, such as in a Jonah Goldberg article for the *National Review*, and around 2003 when the French refused to join the military effort in Iraq (Gervase Phillips, "'Cheese-eating surrender monkeys'? It's time to give the French Army the credit it deserves," *The Conversation*, 1 August 2017, https://theconversation.com/cheese-eating-surrender-monkeys-its-time-to-give-the-french-army-the-credit-it-deserves-81853).
56 Ellis, *Crécy*.
57 Ellis, *Crécy*.
58 Sergio Bertelli, *The King's Body: Sacred Rituals of Power in Medieval and Early Modern Europe*, trans. R. Burr Litchfield (University Park: The Pennsylvania State University Press, 2001), 29.
59 Ellis, *Crécy*.
60 Gill, *Agincourt*. The depiction of Henry V as a man who is involved in military endeavours is reinforced by an earlier close-up of his face with a prominent scar on his right cheek. This reflects historical reality and was obtained at the Battle of Shrewsbury, when he was struck in the face with an arrow at the age of only sixteen. See Michael Livingston, "'The Depth of Six Inches': Prince Hal's Head-Wound at the Battle of Shrewsbury," in *Wounds and Wound Repair in Medieval Culture*, ed. Larissa Tracy and Kelly DeVries (Leiden: Brill, 2015), 215–231.

61 Ellis, *Crécy*.
62 Paul B. Sturtevant, "Were Medieval People Racist?," *The Public Medievalist*, https://publicmedievalist.com/medieval-people-racist/.
63 Sturtevant, "Were Medieval People Racist?"
64 Lisa Lampert-Weissig, *Medieval Literature and Postcolonial Studies* (Edinburgh: Edinburgh University Press, 2010), 31–107.
65 For such negative stereotyping in relation to the Anglo-Scottish conflict of this period, see Michael A. Penman, "*Anglici caudati*: abuse of the English in Fourteenth-Century Scottish Chronicles, Literature and Records," in *England and Scotland in the Fourteenth Century: New Perspectives*, ed. Andy King and Michael A. Penman (Woodbridge: Boydell Press, 2007), 216–235.
66 Green, "National Identities and the Hundred Years' War," 116; A.G. Grigg, "Propaganda of the Hundred Years' War: Poems on the Battle of Crécy and Durham (1346): A Critical Edition," *Traditio* 54 (1999): 169–211.
67 Ellis, *Crécy*.
68 Ellis, *Crécy*.
69 Ellis, *Crécy*.
70 Pierre Larrivée and Julien Longhi, "The Foundations of Discourse: The Case of British Stereotypes of the French," *Corela: Cognition, représentation, langage* 10, no. 1 (2012): http://09.edel.univ-poitiers.fr/corela/index.php?id=2676.
71 Ellis, *Crécy*.
72 Ellis, *Crécy*.
73 Gwilym Dodd, "The Rise of English, the Decline of French: Supplications to the English Crown, c. 1420–1450," *Speculum* 86, no. 1 (2011): 117–150.
74 Ellis, *Crécy*.
75 "Migrants should have to learn English, say MPs and peers," *BBC News*, 5 January 2017, http://bbc.co.uk/news/uk-politics-38510628.
76 Ellis, *Crécy*.
77 Martin Johnes, "We Hate England! We Hate England? National Identity and Anti-Englishness in Welsh Soccer Fan Culture," *Soccer Review 2008*, ed. Gavin Mellor and Patrick Murphy (Leicester: Professional Footballers Association, 2009), 7–13.
78 Ellis, *Crécy*.
79 Ellis, *Crécy*.
80 Ellis, *Crécy*.
81 Ellis, *Crécy*.
82 Ellis, *Crécy*.

11 Beyond "tits and dragons"
Medievalism, Medieval History, and Perceptions in *Game of Thrones*

Hilary Jane Locke

While doing the media rounds to promote his upcoming appearance on season six of the television series HBO's *Game of Thrones* (2011–present), Ian McShane dismissed the series as nothing more than "tits and dragons."[1] Sparking outrage from dedicated fans, McShane was described as going rouge in interviews, dropping spoilers for the show's highly guarded plot, and upsetting fans by telling them all to get a life.[2] The response to McShane's comments—which arguably describe a surface-level reading of the show—demonstrates just how dedicated the millions of invested fans are. Moreover, if the show is just "tits and dragons"—as the actor jokingly stated—was the outrage warranted? For a television series, it certainly relies heavily on those factors: frequent female nudity, high sexualisation, and a stunning use of visual effect elements like dragons. *Game of Thrones* is connected, however, to what people perceive to be a deep and engaging depiction of time and place. McShane's comments and, most importantly, the reaction, show the particular trends in the discussions and representations of *Game of Thrones* in the public: a depiction that remains true to the historical-inspired setting, which clearly has merits beyond "tits and dragons."

Game of Thrones was released in 2011 to much acclaim, quickly becoming a phenomenon around the globe. Based on the series of fantasy novels *A Song of Ice and Fire* by George R.R. Martin, it is set in a medieval, historically inspired world of Westeros, and the similarly classical Mediterranean-inspired Essos. The setting of *Thrones* is familiar in its adaptation of history for a fantasy setting with countless books, video games, television series, and films on the market that use the framework of the medieval as a fantasy setting for their content. In *Thrones* case, this works in its favour. The show features themes we have seen depicted in popular culture frequently: magical abilities and mystical religions, warfare, and court style rivalries. However, *Thrones* is also situated in a slightly different popular culture climate, in part due to the huge fan base and following, but also due to the way it uses historical setting and events to fuel the show's narrative. As a consequence, the representation of the historical-inspired setting, which often depicts the grimier aspects, such as poverty and violence, conveys to the audience a reality that is often mistaken for truth and, ultimately, better historical accuracy than traditional history mediums.

Medieval history is a useful setting for those writing fantasy series, and Martin's choice was no different. As David Matthews notes, "the ghosts of the Middle Ages are unquiet."[3] *Game of Thrones* fits neatly into the literary canon of high fantasy, a subgenre of fantasy that uses epic storytelling and world building—often over several novels—to tell complex stories set in alternative realities. The novels of *A Song of Ice and Fire* sits alongside popular fantasy series such as *The Lord of the Rings* by J.R.R. Tolkien, *The Wheel of Time* series by Robert Jordan (and Brandon Sanderson), *The Realm of the Elderliness* by Robin Hobb, and *Riftwar Cycle* by Raymond E. Feist, all of which rely on the trope of medieval-inspired settings for their worlds. It is easy to see why. With the existing folk tales, myths, imagery, and romanticised ideals, the medieval world is perfect for creating a world by adapting an existing era into imagined stories. The medieval has "fed into the early modern fairy tale ... and enter[ed] directly into modern fantasy, for which it provides stories and tropes."[4] The adaptation of the medieval period for a fantasy setting is typically no more than using the look of costume, behaviours (chivalric principals, for example), and inspirations for some events. As a consequence, medievalism, or content that uses or is an adaptation of medieval culture to some extent, has a substantial cultural position in popular imagination, particularly with the blended representations of the medieval period in our public spheres.

However, the forms of medievalism that fantasy creators engage with (in various degrees) result in conflicting depictions of medieval historical settings. This can muddle public perceptions of the historical setting. Matthews's summary of the degrees of medievalism in popular culture provides a clear framework for how medievalism is frequently used, particularly relevant to the fantasy genre. Broken down into three simple categories, the medieval period is represented either: (1) as it was, (2) as it might have been, or (3) as it never was.[5] *Game of Thrones* fits into all three of these categories. The series uses history selectively to create detailed representations of events and aspects of life, as will be explored later. It relies heavily on the image of the romanticised past, such as the Pre-Raphaelite influenced, post-medieval idealisation of what might have been occurring throughout history.[6] And finally, it shows an imagined medieval period, one that relies on the hybridisation of varying historical periods, cultural and geographical differences, to make a society that somehow reflects something that is medieval, but also completely imaginary.

This chapter looks beyond the basic critique from Ian McShane to argue that as a consequence of using the medieval period, *Game of Thrones* has shaped how audiences and fans have engaged with, and perceived, the history it is loosely based on. This is also extended to other pop culture and public forms of historical content, such as internet content, historical televisions series, and popular history texts. By first examining the *Game of Thrones* in context, the chapter explores the varying ways *Thrones* is presented in relation to history to the public audience. Unlike previous fantasy and popular culture, *Thrones* has made its own clear space in the public consciousness, and as a result, the discussion within the public sphere is hugely focused on comparing, selling, and promoting the show alongside its historically adapted setting. This chapter thus explores how (and why) audiences desire to know historical 'truth,' and the lengths they will go to in order to uncover this 'truth.' By viewing internet commentary and discussions on platforms such as Reddit, it becomes clear that audiences have an on-going need to understand the 'accuracy' behind *Thrones*' depiction of historical content. This, in turn, is effected by the on-going public discussions of historians, which will also be discussed, and the ways that their input shifts public discourse of historical studies and the relationship between *Game of Thrones* overall.

The 'Realness' Behind the Iron Throne: Medieval History, Adaptation, and Fantasy in Popular Culture

What follows is a very brief outline of the main plot and characters of the series.[7] From the beginning of the series, the main focus has been House Stark, based in Winterfell in the North of Westeros. This house focuses on the Lord of Winterfell's family, headed by Eddard (Ned) Stark, his wife Catelyn Stark (née Tully), and their children Robb, Sansa, Arya, Bran, and Rickon, and Ned's bastard son Jon Snow. Similar to this, most of the main characters belong to family groups, structured around land, titles, allegiances, and personal wealth, each with their own sigil. The other crucial families in the story are the Baratheons, headed by Robert, who in season one is King of the Five Kingdoms of Westeros and sits on the Iron Throne at King's Landing, the capital city of Westeros, as well as his brothers Stannis and Renly; the Lannisters, headed by Tywin, with his children, twins Ser Jamie of the King's Guard and Queen Cersei—married to Robert and mother to his heirs Joffrey, Myrcella, and Tommen—and Tyrion; and the Targeryeon family, the previous royal family until Robert's army overthrew 'The Mad King' Aerys Targeryeon in events before the series begins, headed by the Mad King's daughter Daenerys Targeryeon, who, for the most part, resides in Essos, attempting to rally support to take back the Iron Throne. Other families of note include the Tullys, Greyjoys, Tarlys, Mormonts, Tyrells, Freys, Boltons, and Martells.

Geographically, Winterfell is situated in The North of Westeros, just south of The Wall. The Wall is a giant structure of ice, stretching across the continent to guard the rest of Westeros from what lies "beyond the wall." This includes Wildlings, the term used for the "uncivilised" folk who live simply in the forests and mountains, the unexplored landscapes, magical creatures such as giants and the Children of the Forest (elf-like magical beings), and ice zombie creatures called Whitewalkers, who, as the series progresses, become the main source conflict in Westeros. The Wall itself is manned by The Night's Watch, which at the time of the first series is a group made up of misfits, ex-criminals, and strays, but was once an honourable and chivalric guard. Furthermore, each family is usually located in their stronghold of land within Westeros. For example, the Tullys hold the Riverlands, the large section of land between King's Landing and Winterfell, and the Lannister's home is Casterly Rock in the Westerlands. Furthermore, the capital of King's Landing on the southeast coast has a Mediterranean climate that contrasts with the cold climate of The North. The seasons, however, do not follow traditional patterns, with winters and summers lasting for years at a time; House Stark's motto "winter is coming" is a constant reminder in the show of how desperate winters are for Westeros. Indeed, by the end of series seven, snow beings to fall in King's Landing, a reminder that winter has set upon the continent, a foreboding omen of the coming times.

While this summary is in no way comprehensive, it shows how ingrained medieval structures of society are to Westerosi culture and society. The feudal nature of lords and landed gentry, the use of alliances and bannermen (or men-at-arms) for support, and political networks based on family connections and marriages are all grounded in a medieval historical setting. Culturally, men follow the rules of chivalric conduct, with honour-bound codes. The aesthetic and cinematography of the show also reflects upon the medieval: costumes have most women wearing long gowns, somewhat Asian inspired, with the romanticised tight waisted, long sleeves and long braided hair, and the men dressed equally as predictably in assortments of garb and armour throughout. Likewise, Early Middle Ages castles—gritty and made of rough stone—feature heavily as settings.

The source of the series' look is of course the creator of the books, George R.R. Martin. Martin's own relationship with historical content gives some insight into the philosophy behind the books and the adapted television series. In an interview with *Rolling Stone* in 2014, he reflected on his own process of writing, and his affection for historical fiction as a genre. For his own stories, though, he wanted something deeper: "I thought these books could have the gritty feel of historical fiction as well as some of the magic and awe of epic fantasy."[8] Martin also stated, "the problem with straight historical fiction is you know what's going to happen," going on to say, "if you know anything about the Wars of the Roses, you know that the princes in the tower aren't going to escape.

I wanted to make it more unexpected, bring in some more twists and turns."[9] While Martin clearly relies on the adaptation of history, the complex theoretical problems of historical fiction become no longer his issue.

Furthermore, Martin discussed the shallowness within Tolkien's fantasy world, reflecting on his desire to create 'realness' in his stories, and the genre legacy he works within:

> *Lord of the Rings* had a very medieval philosophy: that if the king was a good man, the land would prosper. We look at real history and it's not that simple. Tolkien can say that Aragorn became king and reigned for a hundred years, and he was wise and good. But Tolkien doesn't ask the question: What was Aragorn's tax policy? ... My [characters] are trying to rule [but they] don't have an easy time of it. Just having good intentions doesn't make you a wise king.[10]

In this vein, money is a conversation for those in political spheres in Westeros. Martin has considered the various layers of society, and how the economy functioned, and the effects of these on its citizens. Essos, for instance, functions through a slave economy, which the main character Daenerys Targaryen attempts to break down as she liberates slavery strongholds throughout Essos. Alternatively, in King's Landing, the outright poverty on the streets can be seen to reflect medieval London, where just streets away from the grand palace of The Red Keep, people (smallfolk) live in squalor and starve; they are, however, accepting of their positions in society, as can be seen through their whole-hearted worship of the kings Robert and, although more tentatively, Joffrey in the first three seasons of the show.

Game of Thrones also features characters who rise through society's ranks to echo the 'new men' of the early modern courts in rags-to-riches stories. Flea Bottom, the poorest community of King's Landing, is the origin of such characters as Ser Davos Seaworth, who rises to be the chief advisor to Stannis Baratheon (a contender for the Iron Throne from series two to five). Flea Bottom blacksmith Gendry, who is revealed to be Robert Baratheon's bastard son, also rises to be connected with the story through his relationship with many of the characters, including Ser Davos and Arya Stark. The exchange of money; the displays of wealth and grandeur, or the lack thereof; and the effect this has on those left behind echo Martin's comments and his need to give the stories an added quality of solidity. This has an effect on the perceptions of how the series depicts an accurate historical setting, which will be explored later. Tolkien also gives his works a hyper-reality, which is echoed in Peter Jackson's film adaptations of *The Lord of the Rings*, released between 2001 and 2003, and *The Hobbit,* released between 2012 and 2014, through the use of highly airbrushed visual effects and the stylised production. The world of Westeros allows viewers to accept the realness of the society depicted before them, since, as Martin points out, the lack of indication of how Middle Earth functions in Tolkien's world immerses the viewer completely into the imagined world.

Alternatively, comparing these texts to *Monty Python and The Holy Grail* (1975), as an example, there is little glamour and glitz, despite the main character being the king. 'Dark Ages' Britain is grey, populated by plague-riddled citizens and "filth"-gathering peasants.[11] This cleverly undermines the existing dynamics of a highly romanticized historical narrative and setting to convey a version of medieval Britain that was difficult and grimy. Furthermore, the satirical presentation of medieval Britain as grubby runs contrary to the often highly glamourised setting within pop culture. Viewing *The Holy Grail* alongside film and television series that have depicted the medieval period in more recent years, such as *The Pillars of the Earth* (2010) and its sequel *World Without End* (2012), *Vikings* (2013–present), *Camelot* (2011), *The Other Boleyn Girl* (2008), *The White Queen* (2013), *The Tudors* (2007–2010), and *The Last Kingdom* (2015–present), proves that the airbrushed, and frequently mystical, qualities of television and film are hard to lose when depicting medieval settings. Some of these examples try to present violence, but due to their glazing over the grubby nature of living and the harsh realities of those within medieval society, the shows are often criticised for blurring the lines between historical accuracy and stylistic vision.

This is perhaps why *Game of Thrones* is such an interesting case to explore. The adaptation of medieval Europe for setting and inspiration leaves the two concepts, fantasy and history, in a conflicting position in the public's mind. The consequence, explored here with *Game of Thrones*, is revealed through the on-going public dialogue and presentation of *Game of Thrones* as history, accurate or not, being inspired by historical events. As Philippa Byrne states, in her criticism of the series' usefulness in historical public discourse, at the very least, "talking about *Game of Thrones* is one way in which medieval historians have attempted to engage with the public."[12] The following section will explore how this is done and the prolonged effect this is having on the perceptions of medieval history in the public eye.

The *Game of Thrones* Effect and Public Discussions of Medieval History

If you search for *Game of Thrones* on any search engine, you will quickly come across a selection of articles linking the series imaginary world and a medieval setting. The most popular are from general outlets such as *Buzzfeed*, *The Independent*, and *History Extra*, and are list articles (or listicles) describing commonalities between historical events and the series' narrative. *History Extra* compiled an article, "Game of Thrones: medieval inspiration," which lists characters and cultural practices from history that have played out in the series.[13] *Buzzfeed's* "9 Times Actual History Was More Fucked Up Than *Game Of Thrones*" highlights the frequently cited inspirations such as The Wars of the Roses, Hadrian's Wall, and The Black Dinner in Scotland of 1440, which inspired, in great detail, the events of the Red Wedding in season three.

However, it is also clear that audiences of *Game of Thrones* are seeking answers, beyond what they can get from the abundance of listicles. *LiveScience* published an article before season three aired, interviewing medieval historian Kelly DeVries and PhD candidate Carl Pyrdum III, to find out "How Real Is the *Game of Thrones* Medieval World?" The conclusion was that history was more boring and devalued, as Martin suggested, in various ways in the series, especially pertaining to the complexities of religion, violence, and armour.[14] A more recent article, "Getting Medieval on Game of Thrones," published on *Tor*, went into more detail, explaining that the general consensus of what people consider to be medieval belongs in the second category of Matthews's definition of medievalism: the highly romanticised and imagined world.[15] Ultimately, "because it is what we want to see, what we want to imagine—is in a sense more 'medieval' than the real thing. That isn't good history. It's better than history."[16] While it is a highly contentious statement, the theoretical idea behind it—that viewers need to look beyond the historical groundings to see the show as a cherry-picked creation of a historically savvy author—situates audiences in a productive place for watching *Game of Thrones* in the context of medievalism.

Audiences turn to forums, such as the sub-Reddit "Ask Historians," to ask the deeper questions about the accuracy of the series. These platforms provide a survey of the online community, who clearly seek answers about the historical background of *Game of Thrones* and to find out how accurately it reflects medieval life and society. In general, the questions posed are as simple as "Is Game of Thrones an accurate depiction of medieval times?" which appears time and time again. Follow on questions desire general surveys, such as wanting to know if the Middle Ages were really like how the show depicts. Fans also wish to know specific details of the series, including battle arrangements and combat strategies, economics, character treatment (for example, illegitimate children), medieval culture, and gender. "Ask Historians" is moderated carefully and aims to provide a higher standard of responses to questions beyond general speculation.[17] However, the frequency of questions asked, particularly throughout the airing periods, points towards an audience who is willing to confront the medievalism and hybridised historical content on screen.

Many people, however, want to probe deeper. The level of detail within *Game of Thrones* draws the public's curiosity to the representation of overt depictions within the show and the correlation with medieval society. Perhaps the most frequently asked question is regarding the depictions of violence in comparison to historical periods; indeed violence in the series is even growing tiresome to some viewers, one *Vox* commentator saying, "hammering that home [the] grotesqueries no longer feels purposeful. The 'medieval times suck' horse has been well and truly beaten."[18] One survey by Leeds Trinity University's Kate Lister and Paul Smith found that an unfortunate "90% of teenagers [surveyed] believe that scenes of sexual violence ... are realistic, true to life and an accurate representation of medieval history."[19] Despite believing the violence to be accurate, viewers clearly wish to know more. One Reddit user asked, "To what degree is the depiction of casual violence an accurate portrayal of life in feudal society?" with another asking, "Were the Middle Ages anywhere near as violent as the TV Show *Game of Thrones*?"[20] When the series producers comment in behind-the-scenes featurettes about large-scale, violent, battle scenes, it is easy to see why people need to seek answers. When recounting the production of "The Battle of the Bastards," which took place in season six, David Benioff and D.B. Weiss explained that they took their inspiration from medieval battles by "reading accounts both medieval [but also] the [American] Civil War," where "bodies were piled so thick it became an obstruction on the battlefield."[21] In detailing their inspiration, it gives audiences direct access to the ways in which the creative adaptation of history occurs in the show. However, it also indicates how easy the blurring of historical accuracy and the events that inspired them.

Public commentary and content on the internet is the easiest place to assess the conversation regarding these perceptions of the medieval relationship to *Game of Thrones*. Not only do listicles, and the internet more broadly, help to perpetuate the public's knowledge of the historical grounding of the series—these platforms also facilitate space for misgivings to develop and for public areas of discussions to be accessed. As Jerome de Groot, in his work exploring historical fiction, argues, "these texts allow a culture to think in new ways about what historical engagement, and writing of the past, might actually be, and to rethinking the terms of historical understanding."[22] *Game of Thrones* is a clearly 'hot topic' when it comes to popular culture and the pervasive nature is having a dynamic effect on how history is discussed, particularly in the public sphere.

Game of Thrones is marketed differently, compared to any previous television or film phenomena. A basic example of this is headlines like "This Live-Tweeted Medieval Irish War Is The Real *Game Of Thrones*" from *Buzzfeed* in 2014.[23] Considerably, history is no longer sold to the public for its own interest, but it is sold as the inspiration for the *Game* of *Thrones* series. In most bookstores, history texts are sold with tag lines like 'Based on the Events Behind Game of Thrones.' An even more overt example is Martin J. Dougherty's 2015 book, which is called *The Wars of the Roses: The Conflict that Inspired Game of Thrones*. Reporting of large archaeological discoveries are also marred by *Game of Thrones*: "England's first civil war raged for almost 20 years—and outdid Game of Thrones for violence and treachery" is how *The Guardian's* Robin McKie introduced an article about the archaeological research of England's medieval battles, and interviews with Professor Oliver Ceighton and Duncan Wright, both of the University of Exeter.[24]

Even other historical fiction series are continually being compared, incorrectly, to the historical aspects within the series. For instance, the 2017 BBC adaptation of Guy Fawkes's life and the attempted assassination of James I, *Gunpowder*, is unable to escape comparison with *Game of Thrones* for its depiction of bloody violence and gruesome executions scenes.[25] Similarly, *The Last Kingdom*, the BBC and Netflix series, based on the novels by Bernard Cornwell and set in Anglo-Saxon Britain, has been described by *GQ* as "*Game of Thrones* Without Dragons." The article goes on to say, while "there aren't any dragons or evil ice elves, but let's be real: you love *Game of Thrones [sic] for the political intrigue and the violence. And in this Middle Ages BBC drama, there is plenty of both."[26] Both of these series have little to do with the content of *Game of Thrones*, yet they prove it is seemingly impossible for commentators to ignore when commenting on other forms of historical popular culture, simply because of the number of people who watch the show and the effect this has had on the television landscape in recent years.[27]

Furthermore, recent texts, such as the edited collection *Game of Thrones verses History: Written in Blood*, are an example of such a clear need for public consumption and relationship between the perception of *Thrones* as medieval history.[28] This work pulls together contributors of different academic and historical backgrounds to review almost all aspects of history in the series, and marketed as a popular, non-academic text, making it more desirable for the show's wider audiences. Other texts important to note include *The Real Game of Thrones: The Power Crazed Medieval Kings, Popes and Emperors of France* by Andrew Rawson; *You Win or You Die: The Ancient World of Game of Thrones* by Ayelet Haimson Lushkov; *Mastering the Game of Thrones: Essays on George R. R. Martin's A Song of Ice and Fire*, edited by Jes Battis and Susan Johnston; and *Game of Thrones and the Medieval Art of War* by Ken Mondscein.[29]

The publication of these works indicates how historians (attempt to) get involved in this discussion. With the emergence of these texts, commentary is now available to those wanting to explore *Thrones* beyond that surface-level analysis. Moreover, the feedback given to the public through the association with historical setting and *Thrones* communicates that the show holds some foundations in history worth exploring. As a consequence, the public's understanding that there *is* a link between historical setting and the show's setting becomes further cemented with each publication.

Academics and public historians have also offered commentary on the varying positive and negative effects of the series on public perceptions of history in the show. Dan Jones, public historian and author, offers readers a brief look at the medieval inspiration, asserting slightly more strongly the medieval origins of the series: "bloody and deliberately 'medieval' cruelty punctuates the story: heads and hands are lopped off, throats slashed, torsos porcupined with arrows and crossbow bolts, guts spilt and heads fried with molten gold."[30] His occasional on-screen colleague, historian Suzannah Lipscomb, argued in *The Guardian* that "Game of Thrones has Hacked our History."[31] Rather than taking a negative view, as the title suggests, Lipscomb states, "no matter how dark and fascinating GoT gets, the history books can keep throwing up real-life stories that are just as gory, just as beguiling, and even more convoluted."[32] She further states, in some shameless cross promotion, "in the desperate wait between episodes, you could do far worse than dusting down a history book–try Dan Jones's *The Hollow Crown*–and immersing yourself in the stories that inspired GoT's creator." Dan Jones stated similarly in his article, Martin's "grossest fantasies seldom out-gruesome the history they imitate."[33] In other words, *Game of Thrones* is a way for historians to get the public to engage with medieval history unlike any platform they have had before. As Marta Cobb, Senior Congress Officer at the International Medieval Congress at the University of Leeds, states, "if I tell someone I'm a medievalist, the first thing they ask about is *Game of Thrones*, but at least that gives me a way to engage."[34]

Academics have also attempted to appeal to audiences by capitalising on the *Thrones* interest. Shiloh Carroll's *Medievalism in "A Song of Fire and Ice" and "Game of Thrones"* was published in 2018, and analyses the underlying medievalism within Martin's own writings and the impacts this has on the series.[35] Similarly, Carolyne Larrington published *Winter Is Coming: The Medieval World of Game of Thrones*.[36] The book relies on Larrington's extensive background in medieval literature. It outlines the historical foundations, however, with more context and detail than any *Buzzfeed* article, appealing to those who would want to directly know exactly what history and events lie behind the series. For example, Larrington highlights the historical legacy of legitimacy and how that affects the characters in the show: "Jon Snow's illegitimate birth shapes his fate entirely ... [and] the implications of Joffrey and Tommen's illegitimacy exclude them from rightfully occupying the Iron Throne."[37] Larrington further states that while the many bastards that [King] Robert sired among the lower classes of King's Landing do not present much of a threat to the thrones, Joffrey, like King Herod, or indeed King Arthur in Sir Thomas Malory's fifteenth-century account of his life, the *Morte D'Arthur*, decides it is safest to eliminate all potential rivals.[38]

Referring to the opening events of season two, when the new King Joffrey orders a slaughtering spree against *all* children who are potentially Robert's offspring, Larrington is able to find a connection with biblical and medieval literary depictions of certain events. Furthermore, Larrington is able to link the incestuous roots of Joffrey's parentage—he is the child of twins Jamie and Cersei's on-going sexual relationship, discovered by Ned Stark in season one—to Malory's version of the Arthurian legend: "Merlin prophesies that Arthur's incest-begotten, May-born son, will cause the downfall of the kingdom."[39] In a similar style, the security of the Iron Throne begins to crumble once Joffrey takes the throne. The book similarly outlines historical legacies between the series' narrative, although it offers little further analysis. The text, however, was produced to appeal to the viewing audience, and to inform them of the complex, historical, and literary backgrounds the series uses.

Also of note is the 2016 edited collection *Women of Ice and Fire: Gender, Game of Thrones and Multimedia Engagements*.[40] The collection as a whole reflects the gradual academic acceptance of *Game of Thrones*' popularity. This work engages far more in-depth with series' continuing, often problematic, description of female characters in relation to strength, sexuality, and gender. For instance, the chapter "Women Warriors from Chivalry to Vengeance" describes the female warrior character Brienne of Tarth in the context of both historical setting and genre conventions: "Brienne's ritualistic denials of the titles 'lady' and 'knight' ... restates with enduring archetypes of the medieval-inflected fantasy genre: the exceptional warrior woman—she who resists and subverts patriarchal structures of the medieval world."[41] This section's analysis focuses considerably on the medievalism that public commentators misrepresent: the links between *Game of Thrones* and historical content are not as simple as adaptation, accuracy, and the confines of fantasy genre. As such, the chapter shows that Brienne's character, like many others, can utilise the idea of medievalism to push the boundaries in adapting historical cases of warrior women, such as Joan of Arc, Margaret of Anjou, and Isabella of Castile. Unlike Larrington's work, *Women of Ice and Fire* consistently analyses, to engage more so with the featured medievalism, rather than the limitations or historical fiction and the medieval history apparent.

Furthermore, while the book is for a specific academic readership, published by Bloomsbury Academic, it is accessible on public platforms. Another example of this accessibility is the first *Game of Thrones* academic conference, held in 2017 at Hertfordshire University, which made headlines around the world.[42] This is a result of the increasing professionalisation of the study of *Game of Thrones*, which reflects the validity of such commentary and discussions of its relationships to various aspects of society and scholarly pursuits. The conference was open to the public, with the organiser Kim Akass stating, "I want to really get to grips with the phenomenon, to get people talking about fans and viewing practices, and asking what makes the show so huge and popular."[43] That this event received attention in public discussions and the media, unlike many other academic conferences, evidently proves that *Game of Thrones* is clearly shifting how the public views academic spaces and practices. The conference also launched the Martin Studies International Network, which was designed to unite scholars in their studies of all work related to Martin's *A Song of Ice and Fire* and *Game of Thrones*; the Martin Studies group have announced on their Twitter they will have an International Conference in 2018.[44] Additionally, various media outlets reported that several courses would be offered at universities, including Harvard, Northern Illinois University, and University of New Hampshire, which will study the relationships between history, literature, and media.[45]

However, it is also a difficult area for academics to discuss, particular when it invades the general perception of the medieval period. For instance, Benjamin Breen argues that it is "the non medieval features of the series that help explain its enormous popularity," stating that essentially what *Game of Thrones* depicts is not medieval, but a mishmash of historical periods into one world.[46] Breen further states that "Martin has created a fantasy world that chimes perfectly with the destabilized and increasingly non-Western planetary order today. And seemingly unwittingly, he's brought a fairly obscure sub-discipline of academic history—the early modern world—to the masses."[47] His frustration lies in the hybridisation of history has been dominated with discussion of the medieval adaptations:

> So why, outside of dorky pedantry, does any of this matter? Because fantasy worlds are never just fantasy. They appeal to us because they refract our own histories and speak to contemporary interests. George R. R. Martin's fantasy has grown to enormous popularity in part because of its modernity, not its 'medieviality'.[48]

So, while the effect on historical knowledge is an important development of *Game of Thrones* in the public conversation, it has been detrimental to overall periodisation and the public's knowledge of what Martin got from where. As it stands, the existing tensions seem to only push people to explore web-related content, or the more serious academic approaches, in relation to *Thrones*.

There are others, in particular Philippa Byrne, who have a harsh view on *Game of Thrones* and its relationship to public discussions of history. The problems she raises come, also, from the periodisation and the 'mishmash' of content. She states that the show "being set in every period and no period, chronology is … a problem: it implies that all 'pre-modern' history can be mashed together, without any sense of change or development."[49] Byrne further states that the reason this is problematic is that "we risk setting up medieval history as something 'ornamental', relegating it to the status of fantasy, as alien to the modern world as Whitewalkers and Wargs [people with the ability to enter the mind of another creature or human]."[50] Arguably, the medieval period has already reached the status of the ornamental because of historical appropriation from the early modern period to the more recently nineteenth-century Romanticism.[51] As Andray Domise states, "the appeal to 'historical accuracy' leans on a flimsy and self-defeating presumption: that the point of fantastic storytelling is to affirm the past through the lens of the present."[52] However, despite the resistance of some, the continual comparison between medieval history and the series is here to stay. As this section has shown, the utilisation of this by academics for public discussions progresses the public's understanding and desire to know more about the adaptation of real events from medieval history in *Game of Thrones*.

Conclusion

The traditions of High Fantasy that *Game of Thrones* relies on have served thousands of stories. Yet, *Game of Thrones* is different. When interviewed by *TIME* in 2017, Martin stated, "I think I have that obligation to the *world* and my readers" regarding the completion of *A Song of Fire and Ice*.[53] In this statement, Martin communicates that the fantasy setting of *Game of Thrones* is a created and imagined setting, designed by an individual, and therefore not historically accurate. However, this chapter has demonstrated that through the series' engagement with medievalism, the audience's, and public's, perception of medieval history is thoroughly shaped by the television series, which is a complex and difficult issue. Essentially, this television series goes beyond "tits and dragons" and captures the public's want to know more historical content. While *Game of Thrones* continues to draw the public's attention to the mixing of history and fantasy, the conversations will continue regarding the effective ways in which historical practices can use, or reject, the highly discussed adaptation used in the series. Consequently, as this chapter has argued, the 'realness' in the Martin's novels, and the television series by HBO, creates a dynamic between the audiences and commentators, which pushes for answers on public platforms such as the internet. *Game of Thrones,* wholly fantasy and imagined, relies on world building for its appearance. The series, however, does not shy away from using the intimate details, which, in turn, has a large effect on the public's perceptions of, and desire to understand, the medieval period of history.

As we have seen, medievalist and academic commentators feel this has some negative effects, shifting the real focus of historical studies away from serious discussion and conservation efforts. As Philippa Byrne states in her article,

> Instead of looking to Westeros, medievalists should look to northeast England. Bede's World is a museum in Jarrow, Northumbria, commemorating the life and writings of the early medieval monk Bede (d. 735), and highlighting the importance of the great medieval Kingdom of Northumbria (653–954). It combines museum exhibits with archaeological reconstructions of Anglo-Saxon buildings. It powerfully challenges the idea that this was a "dark" time in English history. But Bede's World closed in February due to lack of funds, although the local community is fighting to reopen it.[54]

However, contrary to this harsh commentary, if the curiosity of the millions of fans for the show results in some pursuing medieval studies, then, in turn, Byrne's desired effect might happen. As Olivia B. Waxman says, if

> undergrads—or any fan inclined to look up whether something that happened on the show could have ever happened in real life—may come to medieval studies [and] they stick around ... to learn that the real past is even more fascinating and nuanced than what HBO can bring to life.[55]

Furthermore, with forums such as "Ask Historians" and university courses designed to have audiences engaging in-depth with the source material and themes of adaptation, they can gain knowledge of the medievalism traditions that *Game of Thrones* evokes.

As we have seen, there is an increasing demand not only for cultural commentary to situate any medieval contexts of the show in accurate ways, but also for answers to direct questions about the accuracy and the medievalism on display. That the public and viewers of the series can see the correlation between the historical periods, but also want to know what is 'fact' and what is 'fiction,' is a positive aspect to perceptions of history. Ultimately, the presence of the show has changed people's discussions regarding the medieval period and history in general. Clearly, for a television series dismissed by Ian McShane for being nothing but a raunchy romp through a landscape of dragons and galloping knights, the show is much more in terms of the public's relationship to historical discussions, and the continual desires to know, and to ask, more.

Notes

1. "Game of Thrones spoilers: how much damage can Ian McShane do?," *The Guardian*, last modified 20 December 2017, https://theguardian.com/tv-and-radio/shortcuts/2016/mar/15/ian-mcshane-game-of-thrones-season-six-tits-and-dragons.
2. "Game of Thrones spoilers," *The Guardian*.
3. David Matthews, *Medievalism: A Critical History* (Cambridge: D.S. Brewer, 2015), 1.
4. Edward James and Farah Mendlesohn, "Unending Romance: Science Fiction and Fantasy in the Twentieth Century," in *The Cambridge History of the Novel*, ed. Robert L. Caserio and Clement Hawes (Cambridge: Cambridge University Press, 2012), 874.
5. Matthews, *Medievalism*, 37–38.
6. Matthews, *Medievalism*, 38.
7. It is crucial to state that this chapter will contain spoilers for the series to season seven, and that this chapter will focus more on the television series than the novels. This chapter will also consider George R.R. Martin, the creator of the series and characters.
8. Mikal Gilmore, "George R.R. Martin: The Rolling Stone Interview," *The Rolling Stone*, 23 April 2014, https://rollingstone.com/tv/news/george-r-r-martin-the-rolling-stone-interview-20140423.
9. Gilmore, "George R.R. Martin."
10. Gilmore, "George R.R. Martin."
11. *Monty Python and the Holy Grail*, dir. Terry Gilliam and Terry Jones (EMI Films, 1975).
12. Philippa Byrne, "Why Medievalists Should Stop Talking about *Game of Thrones*," *The Conversation*, 15 June 2016, https://theconversation.com/why-medievalists-should-stop-talking-about-game-of-thrones-61044.
13. "Game of Thrones: Medieval Inspiration," *BBC History Extra*, 24 March 2016, http://historyextra.com/period/medieval/game-of-thrones-medieval-inspiration/.
14. Stephanie Pappas, "How Real is the 'Game of Thrones' Medieval World?," *LiveScience*, 3 April 2014, https://livescience.com/44599-medieval-reality-game-of-thrones.html.
15. Michael Livingston, "Getting Medieval on *Game of Thrones*," *Tor*, 10 March 2017, https://tor.com/2017/03/10/getting-medieval-on-game-of-thrones/.
16. Livingston, "Getting Medieval."
17. See: Reddit User Georgy_K_Zhukov, "Answers," modified 19 January 2018, https://reddit.com/r/AskHistorians/wiki/rules#wiki_moderation.
18. Zack Beauchamp, "Game of Thrones' Violence Used to Make Sense. Now It's Just Gratuitous," *Vox*, 5 May 2016, https://vox.com/2016/5/5/11595982/game-of-thrones-convo-ultraviolence.
19. "9 Out of 10 Believe Sexual Violence in Game of Thrones Is Historically Accurate," *Leeds Trinity University*, 25 August 2017, http://leedstrinity.ac.uk/news/teenagers-game-of-thrones-sexual-violence-historically-accurate.
20. Reddit User t-slothrop, https://reddit.com/r/AskHistorians/comments/23w6z6/to_what_degree_is_the_depiction_of_casual/; Reddit User Ding_A_Ling, https://reddit.com/r/AskHistorians/comments/22izmf/were_the_middle_ages_anywhere_near_as_violent_as/.
21. "Game of Thrones Season 6: An Anatomy of a Scene: The Battle of Winterfell (HBO)," *Youtube*, 19 June 2016, http://youtube.com/watch?v=B93k4uhpf7g.
22. Jerome de Groot, *Remaking History: The Past in Contemporary Historical Fiction* (London: Routledge, 2016), 2.

186 Hilary Jane Locke

23 Luke Bailey, "This Live-Tweeted Medieval Irish War Is The Real *Game Of Thrones*," *Buzzfeed*, 17 April 2014, https://buzzfeed.com/lukebailey/this-live-tweeted-medieval-irish-war-is-the-real-game-of-thr?utm_term=.ekAGaAkwg#.piXZbN2K3.
24 Robin McKie, "Family Feuds, War and Bloodshed – England's Medieval *Game of Thrones*," *The Observer*, 5 February 2017, https://theguardian.com/culture/2017/feb/05/scars-of-englands-medieval-game-of-thrones-unearthed-anarchy.
25 Sam Wollaston, "*Gunpowder* Review – It's *Game of Thrones* Minus Dragons Plus History," *The Guardian*, 23 October 2017, https://theguardian.com/tv-and-radio/2017/oct/23/last-nights-tv-review-gunpowder.
26 Lincoln Michel, "*The Last Kingdom* is *Game of Thrones* Without Dragons," *GQ*, 28 May 2017, https://gq.com/story/the-last-kingdom-is-game-of-thrones-without-dragons.
27 Another pertinent example of *Game of Thrones* and its popularised medievalism being a point of reference in the marketing of a television series set in medieval times, is *The Hollow Crown*. For more on this, see Marina Gerzic's chapter "Re-fashioning Richard III: Intertextuality, fandom, and the (mobile) body in *The Hollow Crown: The Wars of the Roses*" in this volume.
28 Brian A. Pavlac, "*Game of Thrones*" *verses History: Written in Blood* (Hoboken, NJ: John Wiley & Sons, 2017).
29 Andrew Rawson, *The Real Game of Thrones: A Clash of Thrones, The Power-Crazed Medieval Kings, Popes and Emperors of France* (Stroud: The History Press, 2015); Ayelet Haimson Lushkov, *You Win or You Die: The Ancient World of Game of Thrones* (London: I.B. Tauris, 2017); Jes Battis and Susan Johnston, *Mastering the Game of Thrones: Essays on George R. R. Martin's A Song of Ice and Fire* (Jefferson, NC: McFarland and Company, 2015); Ken Mondscein, *Game of Thrones and the Medieval Art of War* (Jefferson, NC: McFarland and Company, 2017).
30 Dan Jones, "*Game of Thrones*: The Bloody Historical Truth Behind the Truth," *The Telegraph*, 3 April 2014, http://telegraph.co.uk/culture/tvandradio/game-of-thrones/10693448/Game-of-Thrones-the-bloody-historical-truth-behind-the-show.html.
31 Suzannah Lipscomb, "*Game of Thrones* has Hacked Our History," *The Guardian*, 26 April 2016, https://theguardian.com/commentisfree/2016/apr/23/game-of-thrones-hacked-history-britains-bloody-past.
32 Lipscomb, "*Game of Thrones* has Hacked Our History."
33 Jones, "*Game of Thrones*."
34 Olivia B. Waxman, "*Game of Thrones* is Even Changing How Scholars Study the Real Middle Ages," *TIME*, 14 July 2017, http://time.com/4837351/game-of-thrones-real-medieval-history/.
35 Shiloh Carroll, *Medievalism in a "Song of Ice and Fire" and "Game of Thrones"* (Woodbridge: D.S. Brewer, 2018).
36 Carolyne Larrington, *Winter Is Coming: The Medieval World of Game of Thrones* (London: I.B. Taurus, 2016).
37 Larrington, *Winter Is Coming*, 16.
38 Larrington, *Winter Is Coming*, 16.
39 Larrington, *Winter Is Coming*, 16.
40 Anne Gjelsvik and Rikke Schubard, *Women of Ice and Fire: Gender, Game of Thrones and Multiple Media Engagement* (London: Bloomsbury Academic, 2016).
41 Yvonne Tasker and Lindsay Steenberg, "Women Warriors from Chivalry to Vengeance," in *Women of Ice and Fire: Gender, Game of Thrones*

and Multiple Media Engagement, ed. Anne Gjelsvik and Rikke Schubard (London: Bloomsbury Academic, 2016), 176.
42 Adam Lusher, "World's First Academic Game of Thrones Conference to Discuss Fan Theories, Medieval Parallels and 'Exetential Explosive Plasticity,'" *The Independent*, 6 September 2017, http://independent.co.uk/arts-entertainment/tv/game-of-thrones-worlds-first-academic-conference-fan-theories-season-7-season-8-existential-a7921476.html.
43 Lusher, "World's First Academic Game of Thrones Conference."
44 Martin Studies Network (@MartinStudies), "The @MartinStudies will hold an International Conference next year! More details coming soon! #ASOIAF #gameofthones @GRRMspeaking," *Twitter*, 14 September 2017, 12:22 p.m., https://twitter.com/MartinStudies/status/908289789560016897.
45 Lauren Reamy, "7 Colleges Where You Can Take a Class on Game of Thrones," *Fresh U*, 13 May 2017, https://freshu.io/lauren-reamy/7-colleges-where-you-can-take-a-class-on-game-of-thrones.
46 Benjamin Breen, "Why 'Game of Thrones' Isn't Medieval—And Why That Matters," *Pacific Standard*, 12 June 2014, https://psmag.com/social-justice/game-thrones-isnt-medieval-matters-83288.
47 Breen, "Game of Thrones."
48 Breen, "Game of Thrones."
49 Breen, "Game of Thrones."
50 Byrne, "Why Medievalist Should Stop."
51 See: Stephanie Trigg, *Shame and Honor: A Vulgar History of the Order of the Garter* (Philadelphia: University of Pennsylvania Press, 2012).
52 Andray Domise, "'Game of Thrones'—and the fantasy genre—has a diversity problem," *Maclean's*, 4 August 2017, http://macleans.ca/culture/television/game-of-thrones-and-the-fantasy-genre-has-a-diversity-problem/.
53 Daniel D'Addrio, "George R. R. Martin on One *Game of Thrones* Change he 'Argued Against,'" *TIME*, 13 July 2017, http://time.com/4791258/game-of-thrones-george-r-r-martin-interview/.
54 Byrne, "Why Medievalist Should Stop."
55 Waxman, "Changing How Scholars Study."

12 Re-fashioning Richard III

Intertextuality, Fandom, and the (Mobile) Body in *The Hollow Crown: The Wars of the Roses*

Marina Gerzic[1]

Just as the twisted shape of Richard III looms large over Shakespeare's first tetralogy of English history plays, so too Benedict Cumberbatch's performance as Richard casts a shadow over the second series of the BBC television adaptation of Shakespeare's history cycle, *The Hollow Crown: The Wars of the Roses* (2016). This chapter examines how Cumberbatch's Richard is a creation of patchwork intertextual references; *House of Cards* (2013–present) and *Game of Thrones* (2011–present) are cited in filming, editing, and costume choices, and along with Cumberbatch's celebrity status and intertextuality from his previous roles such as Smaug the Terrible, Sherlock Holmes, and Doctor Frankenstein/ The Monster are used to shape Richard's disability and character for the screen. This chapter shows that the resulting reception of Cumberbatch's performance is the creation of a 'new Richard' that exists outside the adaptation in the realm of fandom. Zoe Fraade-Blanar and Aaron M. Glazer define fandom as "a minimum required number of people who have enough of a positive emotional response to a fan object and access to a communications platform on which to express it."[2] This chapter is not an in-depth analysis of the concepts of fandom or fan practices, though I reject the idea that fan practices supersede or even erase the source material and instead argue that they heighten an emotional reaction to the source material. Furthermore, this chapter is not an analysis of why celebrity fandoms have especially gravitated to these online spaces, or how these particular spaces influence the production and consumption of fan practices. For more on this, see in particular Mark Duffet's work on fandom.[3] Duffet builds upon Henry Jenkins's work on fan networks[4] in his assertion that online fan communities "allow isolated people to participate in an imagined community."[5] My use of fandom in this chapter therefore describes the community of fans of the actor Benedict Cumberbatch, in particular those who actively engage in fan practices online, on various microblogging and social networking websites. Paul Booth loosely describes fans as "emotionally involved over something";[6] what I am interested in is the emotional reaction and reception of Benedict Cumberbatch's performance as Richard III by his fandom.

Re-fashioning Richard III 189

In her discussion of Shakespearean 'fangirls' and their playful promotions of Shakespeare's cultural value, Jennifer Holl argues that "a significant portion of fangirl identity is invested in the active promulgation of her devotions amongst others."[7] Citing Christine Schoenwald's 2015 article for the online zine *Bustle* on "Dating a Shakespeare Freak," Holl notes that this Shakespearean fandom engages in practices such as "fangirling" over Tom Hiddleston and Benedict Cumberbatch, "not only for their portrayals of Shakespearean characters but for their ability to 'add a Shakespearean element to non-Shakespearean roles.'"[8]

Schoenwald's comment shows the crossover between Shakespearean fandom and Cumberbatch's fandom.[9] This crossover is something that is acknowledged by Holl, who states that inter-fandom crossover opens "reciprocal paths of access and mutually promotes values."[10] Holl concludes that such work "not only opens up new paths of access to Shakespearean texts but opens Shakespeare up to new modes of intermedial and intertextual exploration that allow him to continue to resonate with diverse audiences through rapidly evolving media landscapes."[11] This chapter examines some examples of this promulgation by Cumberbatch's fandom of their devotion, predominantly posts on social media platforms such as Twitter and Tumblr. Their reception of, and engagement with, his portrayal as Richard III through playful fan practices demonstrates the inter-fandom crossover Holl speaks about, and opens up news paths into understanding Shakespeare's Richard. In an example of early-modernism, this recalls Richard Burbage's apparent prowess and popularity in the role of Richard III; this 'new Richard,' dubbed by the media as "sexy Richard" and by some of his fandom as "RichardBatch," sees Cumberbatch's actor's body become an adaptive site, where Shakespeare's Richard, as played by Benedict Cumberbatch, and 'Benedict Cumberbatch' the 'celebrity,' conflate. This leads to a fascinating defence and glamorising of Richard's evil twisted body, character, and actions by some parts of Cumberbatch's fandom, who transfer their devotion of Cumberbatch to a new devotion to this hybrid identity 'RichardBatch.'

The Hollow Crown is a series of British television adaptations of Shakespeare's history plays. The first cycle of *The Hollow Crown* series screened in 2012 and is an adaptation of Shakespeare's second historical tetralogy, the Henriad: *Richard II, Henry IV, Parts I* and *II* and *Henry V*; it stars Ben Whishaw, Jeremy Irons, and Tom Hiddleston. The BBC aired the concluding cycle in 2016 under the title *The Hollow Crown: The Wars of the Roses*, a reference to the historical events of the same name. Directed by the former artistic director of the Royal Court Theatre, Dominic Cooke, and adapted by playwright Ben Power, this second series of *The Hollow Crown* was produced by the same team who made the first series of films and is based on Shakespeare's first historical tetralogy—*Henry VI, Parts 1, 2,* and *3,* and *Richard III*. The adaptation *The Hollow Crown: The Wars of the Roses* presents *Henry*

VI in two film parts (running time: 112 minutes and 123 minutes, respectively) along with *Richard III* (running time: 130 minutes)—and stars Benedict Cumberbatch, Judi Dench, and Sophie Okonedo.[12] Cooke asserts that *The Hollow Crown: The Wars of the Roses* tells "the story of two men, an overly empathetic man called Henry VI and an overly villainous Richard III";[13] both the marketing and editing of the trilogy, however, suggest that the story is firmly focused on Cumberbatch's Richard.

In *The Hollow Crown: The Wars of the Roses* the character of Richard III first appears on-screen in the final moments of *Henry VI, Part 1*. In an instance that is entirely the creation of director Cooke and screenwriter Power, Richard of York returns home and calls out to his four sons; each is counted off as they are shown on screen, first Edward; then George; then young Edmund; and finally Richard, who appears as a shadowy hunchback figure, shuffling along like Marty Feldman's Igor in *Young Frankenstein* (1974) as he enters the frame from the right. Richard here bears a resemblance to the vampire figure in *Nosferatu* (1922), an example of the several tropes and imagery drawn from the horror/slasher genres that appear in *The Hollow Crown*.[14] From his first moments on screen in *Henry VI, Part 2*, Benedict Cumberbatch completely owns the screen as the hunchbacked Richard III; he uses the camera as Richard's unseen confessor, delivering his chilling monologues and asides directly to the audience by breaking the fourth wall (see Figure 12.1). This direct reference to the camera is a theatrical technique rarely used in television and film, and immediately draws parallels with the character of Frank Underwood in the American political drama *House of Cards*,[15] something that has been picked up by scholars, as well as both media and fans in their reviews and analysis of *The Hollow Crown*.[16] Neal Justin, writing in the *Star Tribune*, notes that Cumberbatch, as Richard, charms the audience by talking directly to the camera, just like Spacey does in *House of Cards*.[17] Twitter user @ChampCelluloid also highlights how similar the characters Richard and Frank are (to the point of interchangeability) by substituting Richard's name for Frank's, in their (obviously sarcastic) tweet that states they are "Catching up with Benedict's Cumberbatch's performance as Frank Underwood in The Hollow Crown: Richard III."[18]

House of Cards, itself inspired by both Shakespeare's *Richard III* and *Macbeth*, is the story of Francis (Frank) J. Underwood (played by Kevin Spacey), a power-hungry congressman, and his rise to the office of the President of the United States of America. Spacey has a history of playing suave and charismatic villains; his performance as Frank is arguably influenced by his previous role as Richard III in The Bridge Project's 2012 stage production of *Richard III* (directed by Sam Mendes, who coincidentally also produced *The Hollow Crown*). In turn, Spacey's conception of Richard III is itself coloured by one of his previous, and

Figure 12.1 Benedict Cumberbatch as Richard III addresses the camera in *The Hollow Crown: The Wars of the Roses*. Image courtesy of the British Broadcasting Corporation.

most iconic roles, as Roger "Verbal" Kint, a con artist with a limp and a palsied arm, in *The Usual Suspects* (1995) as much as it is by previous notable stage and screen Richards, such as Ian McKellen and Laurence Olivier.[19]

The Hollow Crown and *House of Cards* both deal with storylines of political machinations and intrigue, and feature a seductive scheming villain. The breaking of the fourth wall by both Richard and Frank serves a similar purpose, making characters that are, essentially, villains, much more likeable to the audience. They create a rapport with the audience by drawing them into their schemes, but at the slightest provocation are likely to stab them, or push them off a subway platform in front of a moving train. Both Richard and Frank are "villain-like characters who feel passed over in the distribution of power."[20] Mario Klarer summarises the similarity between the two men:

> Francis Underwood, who had been promised a nomination for secretary of state, has to accept that the position goes to a different candidate, but swears to take revenge through usurping power in a long-winded ploy. ... Being ridiculed and marginalized for his physical defect, Richard employs vicious cunning in order to get rid of his competitors for the Crown of England, including his own brother whom he ultimately deprives of his kingship.[21]

The parallels between *The Hollow Crown* and *House of Cards* are further solidified by shared imagery, notably the tapping of fingers and the playing of chess. Frank's ability and practice of playing chess suggest that he truly is the mastermind, and everyone else is his pawn. Both Frank and Richard also constantly tap their ring-clad fingers. Frank describes the action as something his father taught him to harden his knuckles so he doesn't break them in a fight, with the "added benefit of knocking on wood."[22] For Frank (and his father) success is a mixture of preparation and luck, and "tapping the table kills both birds with one stone";[23] thus the tapping symbolises toughness, ambition, and success. At the end of Season 2 of *House of Cards*, when Frank has finally clawed his way into the Oval Office, he double-taps the President's desk in victory. Like Frank's tapping, Richard's tapping also symbolises ambition and success. The dominant image of Cumberbatch's Richard is of his index finger tapping a chessboard as he works out how to remove the pieces that stand between him and the crown (Figure 12.2). Chess becomes a visual metaphor for Richard as he makes his manoeuvres to secure the throne for himself. However, his tapping eventually becomes a nervous tick that indicates Richard's emerging paranoia. On the night before the Battle of Bosworth, the tapping then becomes like a stopwatch counting down the time until Richard's eventual downfall.

Along with *House of Cards*, the other major reference drawn on in *The Hollow Crown* is that of fantasy drama series *Game of Thrones*. In describing the aesthetic of *Game of Thrones*, television critic Dan Jones notes that "[b]loody and deliberately 'medieval' cruelty punctuates the story: heads and hands are lopped off, [and] throats [are] slashed."[24] Stevens adds that the fictional Westeros is "a place of continual fear and

Figure 12.2 Benedict Cumberbatch as Richard III plays chess in *The Hollow Crown: The Wars of the Roses*. Image courtesy of the British Broadcasting Corporation.

Re-fashioning Richard III   193

danger of violent death" that is supposed to loosely suggest England during the Wars of the Roses.[25] George R.R. Martin, the author of the *A Song of Ice and Fire* fantasy fiction series—the basis for the *Game of Thrones* television series—has been very candid about his plundering of historical events for use in his own work in numerous interviews. Martin channels mockumentary *This Is Spinal Tap* (1984) in his brash assertion that "I take it [i.e. history] and I file off the serial numbers and I turn it up to 11."[26] In a 2014 interview with *Rolling Stone* magazine, Martin happily acknowledges that the events of the Wars of the Roses are the principal inspiration for *Game of Thrones*, stating:

> You look at Shakespeare, who borrowed all of his plots. In *A Song of Ice and Fire*, I take stuff from the Wars of the Roses and other fantasy things, and all these things work around in my head and somehow they jell into what I hope is uniquely my own.[27]

In candidly revealing the sources for *Game of Thrones*, Martin deliberately draws parallels with Shakespeare, who himself drew inspiration from various medieval and early modern historical accounts of the Wars of the Roses and adapted them to suit his creative and political purpose.[28] However, unlike Martin, Shakespeare arguably does not wear his sources so self-assuredly on his sleeve.

The events of the Wars of the Roses are undeniably a point of reference for Martin's *Game of Thrones*, and I would be remiss to not mention Carolyne Larrington's work on *Game of Thrones*, in particular, *Winter Is Coming: The Medieval World of Game of Thrones* (2016), which links Martin's novels and his real-life influences, including the Wars of the Roses as well as the French medieval history featured by Maurice Druon in his *Les Rois maudits* (*The Accursed Kings*) series of historical novels (1955–1977) (about the French monarchy in the fourteenth century).[29] Martin has publicly stated his great admiration for Druon and his work, calling him France's best historical author since Alexandre Dumas in an article for *The Guardian*.[30] Significantly, in this article, Martin also refers to *The Accursed Kings* series as "the original *Game of Thrones*."[31] While Martin may see himself as Druon's unofficial successor, Shiloh Carroll highlights the problematic nature of viewing Martin as a pseudo-medieval historian: namely, Martin's tendency to generalise about the period—a specific time or place becomes a "marker for the entirety of the era," focusing primarily on the "juicy stuff," such as "big historical movements like ... the Wars of the Roses," and "heightening history to make it more interesting" while creating a neomedieval fantasy world that is largely not multiracial.[32] To Carroll's insights here, I add that Martin's narrative often focuses on white characters, a narrative that is usually told from their perspective, and he portrays characters of colour in very problematic ways.[33] The result, Carroll laments, is that Martin's fans believe that "his neomedieval world is authentically medieval and use that believe to shape their idea of history."[34] Citing Helen Young's work on fantasy fandoms,[35] particularly the idea that "readers [or I argue audiences] are exposed to a medievalist version of the Middle Ages through fantasy," Carroll further argues that people come to believe this "medievalist version is an 'accurate' portrayal of the Middle Ages," and then "insist on this version of the Middle Ages in future" texts because "it is 'accurate.'"[36]

It is no wonder then that *Game of Thrones* and its neomedieval world have now become shorthand for medieval political treachery and intrigue that is punctuated by explicit and extreme violence. The immense popularity of *Game of Thrones* among audiences and critics alike has led to gripping narratives, synonymous with the Middle Ages, such as kings clashing for a throne, the rise and fall of epic dynasties, and passionate romances set against a backdrop of gruesome violence and betrayal becoming a mainstay of prime-time television. More recently, the BBC television miniseries *Gunpowder* (2017), which chronicles the notorious Gunpowder Plot of 1605, has incited media to again turn to *Game of Thrones* as a point of reference for 'medievalesque' or, more correctly, given the events depicted, 'early-modernesque' harsh and graphic imagery and on-screen violence.[37] Thus, it is no surprise that *Game of Thrones* has become a point of reference for the media when they report on *The Hollow Crown*. When *The Hollow Crown* premiered in 2012, critic David Hinckley wrote that "Pound for pound, the drama in *The Hollow Crown* matches almost everything in *Game of Thrones*."[38] In relation to *The Hollow Crown: The Wars of the Roses*, numerous critics (as well as fans) again turned to *Game of Thrones* to describe the graphic horror and violence, political manoeuvring and intrigue, and adrenalin-fuelled action and bloody battles that dominate this Shakespearean adaptation.[39] James Rampton goes so far to frame Cumberbatch's Richard in reference to *Game of Thrones*, describing his political scheming and brutal actions as "[making] *Game of Thrones* look like *Play School*."[40] Actor Adrian Dunbar, who plays Richard of York, also turns to *Game of Thrones* in his description of the allure of *The Hollow Crown*, saying, "It's got everything—battles, power being wrested from people, witchcraft—it's the proper game of thrones."[41] While I acknowledge that the use of the word "proper" is problematic in this instance, Dunbar's imagery is meant to evoke an idea of the popularised medieval that audiences associate with *Game of Thrones*. *The Hollow Crown* shares not only the penchant for graphic violence, epic bloody battle scenes, and political machinations that dominate *Game of Thrones*, but also what I term its 'medievalesque' aesthetic. Fans have also picked up on the shared aesthetic between the two television shows. Twitter user @drmarbles jokingly declares in a tweet that he doesn't "recognise any of the

Lannisters in this episode of Game of Thrones," ending his Tweet with the hashtag #hollowcrown, indicating that the characters, plot, setting and aesthetics of *The Hollow Crown* recall (to him) those in *Game of Thrones*.[42] Production designer for *The Hollow Crown* John Stevenson argues that this aesthetic offers "a general brushstroke"[43] of the medieval period; the mood is dreary, it's dirty and muddy, the imagery is often dark and shadowy, and the palette, textures, and fabrics of the costumes help in defining characters as brutal and grim. Cumberbatch's costume even evokes those of characters such as Robb Stark and Jon Snow in *Game of Thrones*. The use of fur connects Robb and Jon to the direwolf sigil of the House of Stark, as well as to their own direwolf companions. In *The Hollow Crown*, the use of fur functions in a similar fashion, connecting Richard to an animal, in his instance a wild boar: the personal badge of Richard III. Cumberbatch's costume combines with the animalistic physicality of his performance that is marked by a hunched stance and unusual running style. This recalls Shakespeare's use of animal imagery in various characters' insults directed at Richard: he is a "hedgehog" (I.ii.104); a "dog" (I.iii.216); a "rooting hog" (I.iii.228); a "bottled spider" (I.iii.242; IV.iv.81); a "bunch-backed toad" (I.iii.246; IV.iv.81); a "hell-hound" (IV.iv.48); and a "wretched, bloody and usurping boar" (V.ii.7).[44] When Richard charges into battle with his back bent forward and his paralysed arm leading the way, his movements are animal-like and monstrous, his appearance matching his brutal character.[45]

Along with references to both *House of Cards* and *Game of Thrones*, the impact of Benedict Cumberbatch's own intertext is influential to the construction of his version of Richard III in *The Hollow Crown*. Anna Blackwell notes the bulk of Cumberbatch's filmography consists of adaptations, both period and modern, and these roles "perpetuate Cumberbatch's persona as upper middle class, sophisticated, and intellectual," traits that are further "reinforced in his casting as typically 'Shakespearean' villains in international film franchises,"[46] such as Smaug in *The Hobbit* trilogy. Cumberbatch not only provides the voice for the dragon Smaug, but his facial expressions and movements were also tracked with motion capture and strongly inform his performance. Director Peter Jackson notes of Cumberbatch's performance that he "was interested in exactly the same ideas" as Jackson, which was "to make Smaug a psychopath," adding that Smaug's personality in the films is unpredictable, charming, and scary.[47] These are all traits that can also be ascribed to Cumberbatch's performance as Richard III, with critic Rafi Yahya Syed arguing Cumberbatch's Richard usurps "his tyrannical mastery as Smaug,"[48] while Chase Branch suggests that as Richard, Cumberbatch is "at his Smaug-iest, chewing Shakespeare's dialogue with villainous glee."[49] When Richard sneers and snarls at the camera in anger and frustration, or threatens characters in his low timbre voice, one cannot help but recall Smaug. Tumblr user @professorfangirl aptly illustrates the connection between the character and physicality of both roles as well as emphasising the monstrous and animalistic side of Richard's body and mind, by subtitling her fan art, "Benedict Cumberbatch as Smaug the Dragon as Richard III."[50]

Along with Smaug, the two most influential roles that colour Benedict Cumberbatch's performance as Richard III are Sherlock Holmes in the television series *Sherlock* (2010–present), and his joint lead role, with Jonny Lee Miller, as Doctor Frankenstein/The Monster in Danny Boyle's staging of Nick Dear's adaptation of *Frankenstein* at the Royal National Theatre (2011). Cumberbatch has a history of playing highly intelligent outsiders: asexual sociopaths, anti-heroes, extreme intellectuals, artists, and spies. Ben Power cites Cumberbatch's performance in *Frankenstein*, playing both Doctor and Monster, as evidence of his brilliant ability to play outsiders.[51] In stage productions of *Richard III*, Richard's body has often been something to hide, while in the opening scenes of *Richard III*, Richard's body is revealed for all to see as Cumberbatch hunches topless over a chessboard before turning around to deliver his opening soliloquy. Rather than an exaggerated hunchback look, Cumberbatch's body has been fitted with realistic-looking prosthetics; the curvature of his spine matches the recently discovered remains of Richard III (see Figure 12.3). While attempting to be anatomically and "historically" accurate, this scene also works against normalising Richard's disability; Cumberbatch's appearance is reminiscent of the look of his character The Monster in *Frankenstein*, and thus comparisons between his disability and disfigurement with monstrous birth are hard to avoid.

Figure 12.3 Benedict Cumberbatch as Richard III in *The Hollow Crown: The Wars of the Roses*. Image courtesy of the British Broadcasting Corporation.

As well as parallels to *Frankenstein*, Cumberbatch's Richard III also recalls his most well-known performance as Sherlock Holmes in the television series *Sherlock*. Both Richard III and Sherlock share an intellectual sophistication, antisocial behaviour, and a disdain for emotional empathy, and seem to live by Sherlock's ethos that "sentiment is a chemical defect found on the losing side."[52] Sherlock also describes himself as a "high-functioning sociopath."[53] This characterisation—although inaccurate[54]—is one of the hallmarks of Cumberbatch's performance both as Sherlock and Richard, resulting in both critics and fans to connect the two in their discussion of *The Hollow Crown*. Instagram user @Cumber_romaniac declares that "Richard III your Sherlock is showing," and the front page of *RadioTimes* magazine crowns Cumberbatch "King Sherlock."[55] The parallels between the characters are aptly illustrated by Tumblr user @moriartysskull, who describes them both as "bored sexy sociopaths, desperate for murder,"[56] suggesting that Richard will commit the murder, and then Sherlock will solve the crime. The use of the adjective "sexy" in this fanart leads me to its use by both media and Cumberbatch's fandom in their characterisation of Richard III.

Benedict Cumberbatch's performance as Richard III has captivated fans, scholars, and the media. Neela Debnath calls Cumberbatch "sexy and compelling" as Richard, and Lauren Humphries-Brooks describes his performance as "Sexy Richard," while Shannon Vestal Robson draws attention to the "historical hotness" of Cumberbatch as Richard.[57] Sam Mendes, whose company produced *The Hollow Crown*, concedes that Cumberbatch's appeal led to him being cast as Richard, noting that he has "a strange sex appeal." Mendes describes Cumberbatch as "not obviously sexy ... yet he is," adding that "I think you can say the same about Richard III. In fact, it's necessary that he's sexy—the play asks him to seduce not one but two women."[58] Benji Wilson draws attention to the allure of Cumberbatch's celebrity and its influence on his casting in *The Hollow Crown*:

> [H]e is Benedict Cumberbatch, the guy from *Sherlock* who appears on *Graham Norton*; the guy adored by Cumberbitches; the guy people compare to an otter in never-ending internet memes. The hope is that Cumberbatch might be enough of a lure to get a younger audience to watch Shakespeare.[59]

Wilson argues that Cumberbatch wasn't just cast as Richard due to his acting prowess, but also due to his celebrity and fan appeal, particularly amongst young people, in order to draw a younger demographic towards an appreciation of Shakespeare and his works. How then has Cumberbatch's fandom responded to his casting as Richard III in *The Hollow Crown*?

This idea of 'sexy Richard' has also been embraced by Cumberbatch's passionate fandom, referred to by the self-ascribed terms 'Cumberbitches,' 'Cumberbabes,' and 'CumberCollective,' who discuss and respond to his performance through fan practices, such as the creation of fanart and engagement on social media. While some of the media refer to Cumberbatch as "sexy Richard," Cumberbatch's fans largely congregate online under several social media hashtags such as #HollowCrown, and #RichardIII. The most interesting of these is that of "#RichardBatch." Literally a conflation of the names 'Richard' and 'Cumberbatch', the term "RichardBatch" comes to signify the fandom's response to Cumberbatch's performance, where their idea of Shakespeare's Richard, as played by Benedict Cumberbatch, and 'Benedict Cumberbatch' the 'celebrity' merge. This new hybrid fan entity of 'RichardBatch' is seen in numerous social media posts, fanart, and memes. For example, Twitter user @Doga_ comments that after watching *The Hollow Crown*, they not only think Shakespeare wrote *Richard III* with Benedict Cumberbatch in mind but now believe that Richard wasn't as bad as Shakespeare portrayed.[60] Twitter user @elfinholly argues that Anne being seduced by Shakespeare's Richard III is wrong, but Anne being seduced by Cumberbatch's Richard is totally fine, presumably because he's a 'sexy Richard.'[61] Finally, Twitter user @AlanHardy78 cleverly uses a variation of the popular internet meme "Otters Who Look Like Benedict Cumberbatch"[62] to react humorously to Cumberbatch's performance.[63] BBC's marketing team has also picked up on the idea of "RichardBatch," using it to market *The Hollow Crown* to Cumberbatch's fandom,[64] who, in turn, have picked up the media's use of "RichardBatch" and used it generate further fan practices.[65]

The influence that Cumberbatch's intertext and celebrity have on his conception of Richard III and the resulting conflation between his celebrity and the role he plays recall actor Richard Burbage's apparent prowess and popularity in the role of Richard III, and are themselves an example of early-modernism. I acknowledge the popularity of actor David Garrick's revolutionary performance of Richard III (immortalised in two paintings: one by William Hogarth, c. 1745; the other by Nathaniel Dance-Holland, 1771); however, an in-depth analysis of Garrick's popularity and celebrity is beyond my scope in this chapter.[66] Jack R. Crawford argues that the popularity of *Richard III* in early modern England "appears to have been great, judging from the number of contemporary references and the frequent parodies of the line 'A horse! A horse! My Kingdom for a horse!'"[67] Julie Hankey adds that "the number of quarto editions of … [*Richard III*] printed before the first folio collection in 1623 exceeded all the other Shakespeare plays except *Henry IV, Part 1*," and that "horse, a horse, my kingdom for a horse" became "a byword, turning up with variations in plays throughout the period."[68] Burbage did not simply originate the role of Richard, but as Hugh

M. Richmond suggests, the role was "specifically created with his talents in mind," a point echoed by Martin Holmes who states the "part was cut, accordingly, to ... [Burbage's] measure."[69] Hankey further adds that "Richard was one of Burbage's most famous parts, and the historical figure was virtually synonymous with the actor."[70] One account that recalls Burbage's great fame is that by Bishop Corbet from his work *Iter Boreale* (1647).[71] Corbet tells of a visit he made to the scene of the Battle of Bosworth. Corbet's guide shows him over the site and names Burbage, by a slip of the tongue, instead of Richard in his description of events:

> He mistooke a Player for a King,
> For when he would have said, King Richard dy'd,
> And call'd a Horse, a Horse, he Burbage cry'd.[72]

Burbage's mastery of the role is also acknowledged in the play *Return from Parnassus* (1601), where Burbage is portrayed as examining a Cambridge student in the art of acting by making him recite the opening soliloquy of *Richard III*.[73] Perhaps the most brilliant anecdote that testifies to the power of Burbage's popularity, fame, and sex appeal as Richard comes from John Manningham's *Diary* from 1602. Manningham records the amusing story of Burbage being propositioned by a woman, who asks him to visit her under the name Richard III:

> Upon a time when Burbage played Richard 3, there was a Citizen grew so far in liking with him, that before she went from the play she appointed him to come that night unto her by the name of Richard the 3rd. Shakespeare, overhearing their conclusion, went before, was entertained, and at his game ere Burbage came. Then message being brought that Richard the 3rd was at the door, Shakespeare caused return to be made that William the Conqueror was before Richard the 3rd. Shakespeare's name William.[74]

While Burbage's "power of impersonation was so great that he became his characters,"[75] no woman in this way was wooed or won while Shakespeare was around.

Benedict Cumberbatch as Richard III is no less appealing to his twenty-first-century fandom than Richard Burbage was to his seventeenth-century one. While no fan has, to my knowledge, propositioned Cumberbatch and asked him to visit them as 'sexy Richard,' social media responses to his performance by some of his fandom show a fascinating defence and glamorising of Richard's evil twisted body and character. Twitter users @weareonenamaste and @deetzzz, and Instagram user @enerjaxart all glamorise the hybrid identity of RichardBatch.[76] For @weareonenamaste, "RichardBatch is damn fine!"; @deetzzz proclaims that "Even with King Richard III's hump, I'd still do Benedict Cumberbatch";

finally, @enerjaxart modifies an official promotional image from *The Hollow Crown* (a photograph by Robert Viglasky) of Cumberbatch (as Richard) astride a horse in full armour. The new fan art has a cartoon Cumberbatch, astride a unicorn with an embellished rainbow in the background smirking at the viewer: perhaps a reaction to the caption, which reads "My Kingdom for a Cumberbatch xD." The comments of Twitter users @erin_shore, @AFarray, and @cabbage_babble demonstrate that their opinions of Richard III are strongly influenced and framed by Cumberbatch's performance and celebrity, and are also an example of inter-fandom crossover.[77] @erin_shore acknowledges Cumberbatch's performance has provided her new insight and sympathy with Richard: "I know I really shouldn't but I do feel sorry for Richard III. I blame Benedict's acting"; @AFarray exclaims that "Benedict Cumberbatch has me lusting after Richard III" (a twenty-first-century version of Burbage's admirer, perhaps); and finally, @cabbage_babble posted an animated image (a GIF) of Buster Bluth from the television comedy series *Arrested Development* (2003–present) fainting (from Season 1, Episode 5, "Charity Drive"),[78] captioning the image "Benedict Cumberbatch as Richard III in @The_hollowcrown on @PBS has me liking his evil self like." Despite, or in some cases because of, the evil and morally bankrupt character of Richard, they find him sexy and worthy of pity and/or adulation. This conflation between celebrity and character, and the creation of "RichardBatch" is not that different from the media's recent preoccupation with the fact that Cumberbatch is a distant relative of Richard III and was asked to speak at the King's reburial ceremony.[79] Richard Burbage was unable to shake the shadow of Richard III from his identity as performer, and it appears Benedict Cumberbatch may possibly be destined for the same fate.

Notes

1 I thank Aidan Norrie and Robin Macdonald for their assistance during the preparation of this chapter. Earlier versions of this chapter were presented at both the 2017 ANZAMEMS Conference and the Association of Adaptation Studies Conference (at De Montfort University in 2017), and I thank the participants at both these events for their helpful feedback.
2 Zoe Fraade-Blanar and Aaron M. Glazer, *Super Fandom: How Our Obsessions Are Changing What We Buy and Who We Are* (London: Profile Books, 2017), 61.
3 Mark Duffett, *Understanding Fandom: An Introduction to the Study of Media Fan Culture* (London: Bloomsbury, 2013). Duffet argues that generally fans have supported online mediums as it has made them more visible, digital archiving has greatly increased fan access to information, and the cost of online services to engage in practices is relatively marginal (and often free) and therefore an attractive option (236–237).
4 For Jenkins, fan networks are communities that offer people a sense of belonging, and allow active communality with those who share their interests.

Henry Jenkins, *Textual Poachers: Television Fans and Participatory Culture*, Twentieth Anniversary ed. (London: Routledge, 2013), 22–23; 40–41.
5 Duffett, *Understanding Fandom*, 243.
6 Paul Booth, *Digital Fandom: New Media Studies* (New York: Lang, 2010), 17.
7 Jennifer Holl, "Shakespeare Fanboys and Fangirls and the Work of Play," in *The Shakespearean User: Critical and Creative Appropriations in Networked Culture*, ed. Valarie Fazel and Louise Geddes (New York: Palgrave Macmillan, 2017), 122.
8 Christine Schoenwald, quoted in Holl, "Shakespeare Fanboys and Fangirls," 122.
9 The crossover is also acknowledged and utilised by the media, for example, the post on the *Metro News* blog, "Why Sherlock Fans Should Watch Benedict Cumberbatch in BBC's Shakespeare Adaptation The Hollow Crown: The Wars of the Roses," *Metro News*, 28 April 2016, http://metro.co.uk/2016/04/28/why-sherlock-fans-should-watch-benedict-cumberbatch-in-bbcs-shakespeare-adaptation-the-hollow-crown-the-wars-of-the-roses-5844279.
10 Holl, "Shakespeare Fanboys and Fangirls," 123.
11 Holl, "Shakespeare Fanboys and Fangirls," 122.
12 Combining Shakespeare's minor tetralogy into a production titled *The Wars of the Roses* has been done before on both stage and television. Peter Hall and John Barton staged the tetralogy in their 1963 Stratford production of *The Wars of the Roses*, and more locally (to Australia) and recently, the Bell Shakespeare Company staged *The Wars of the Roses* in 2005, and Sydney Theatre Company staged it in 2009. In 1960, the BBC produced the television series *An Age of Kings*, which, over thirteen hour-long episodes, covers precisely the same sequence as *The Hollow Crown*, spanning from *Richard II* to *Richard III*. From 1978 to 1985, the BBC Shakespeare Collection project filmed every surviving Shakespeare play and linked the historical tetralogies together.
13 Dominic Cooke, quoted in BBC Media Centre, *The Hollow Crown: The Full Media Pack*, 3 May 2016, http://downloads.bbc.co.uk/mediacentre/hollow-crown-RIII.pdf.
14 Other examples include: Richard emerging silently out of the dark shadowy woods before his sojourn with Anne Neville at her former husband's gravesite, which is reminiscent of teen slashers, such as the *Scream* film series (1996–2011); and Margaret of Anjou's haggard appearance and "haunting" of Richard III by "emerging" from the reflection of a handheld mirror, which draws on imagery from the Japanese horror film *Ringu* [The Ring] (1998).
15 An adaptation based on the trilogy of novels in the "House of Cards" series written by Michael Dobbs (*House of Cards*, London: Collins, 1989; *To Play the King*, London: HarperCollins, 1992; *The Final Cut*, London: HarperCollins, 1995), and the three UK television miniseries (BBC: 1990, 1993, 1995), which also adapted Dobbs's novels.
16 For a more in-depth analysis of Frank Underwood's direct-to-audience delivery in *House of Cards* and how it is influenced by Shakespeare's *Richard III*, see Mario Klarer, "Putting Television 'Aside': Novel Narration in *House of Cards*," *New Review of Film and Television Studies* 12, no. 2 (2014): 205–206.
17 Neal Justin, "Benedict Cumberbatch and Gael García Bernal Add Sizzle to the Classics in TV Roles," *StarTribune*, 9 December 2016, http://startribune.com/benedict-cumberbatch-and-gael-garcia-bernal-add-sizzle-to-the-classics-in-tv-roles/405520276.

18 Dallas King (@ChampCelluloid), *Twitter*, June 13, 2016, 5:19 AM, https://twitter.com/ChampCelluloid/status/742103953710718976.
19 In the film's major twist, "Verbal" suddenly loses his limp and regains use of his seemingly paralysed arm and is revealed to be Keyser Söze, the mythical crime lord who is the main antagonist of the film. Thus, both Richard and Verbal use their disability in order to manipulate those around them.
20 Klarer, "Putting Television 'Aside,'" 205.
21 Klarer, "Putting Television 'Aside,'" 206.
22 *House of Cards*, "Chapter 12" (Season 1, Episode 12, 2013). Transcriptions from this episode are my own.
23 *House of Cards*, "Chapter 12."
24 Dan Jones, "Game of Thrones: The Bloody Historical Truth behind the Show," *The Telegraph*, 3 April 2014, http://telegraph.co.uk/culture/tvandradio/game-of-thrones/10693448/Game-of-Thrones-the-bloody-historical-truth-behind-the-show.html.
25 Jones, "Game of Thrones."
26 Suzannah Lipscomb, "Game of Thrones Has Hacked Our History," *The Guardian*, 23 April 2016, https:// theguardian.com/commentisfree/2016/apr/23/game-of-thrones-hacked-history-britains-bloody-past. In this article, historian Suzannah Lipscomb herself states that "chief among the historical stories that Martin has turned up to 11 are, of course, the 15th-century Wars of the Roses."
27 Mikal Gilmore, "George R.R. Martin: The Rolling Stone Interview," *Rolling Stone*, 23 April 2014, http:// rollingstone.com/tv/news/george-r-r-martin-the-rolling-stone-interview-20140423#ixzz3EdpzY4KT.
28 For more on *Game of Thrones*' self-referential citation of its literary predecessors, particularly Shakespeare's history plays, see Amy Rodgers, "History as Echo: Entertainment: Historiography from Shakespeare to HBO's *Game of Thrones*," in *Shakespearean Echoes*, ed. Adam Hansen and Kevin J. Wetmore, Jr. (New York: Palgrave Macmillan, 2015), 142–154.
29 Carolyne Larrington, *Winter Is Coming: The Medieval World of Game of Thrones* (London: I.B. Tauris, 2016). Ben Milne also examines the connection between *The Accursed Kings* and *Game of Thrones* in his article, "Game of Thrones: The Cult French Novel That Inspired George RR Martin," *BBC News Magazine*, 4 April 2014, http://bbc.com/news/magazine-26824993.
30 George R.R. Martin, "My Hero: Maurice Druon by George R.R. Martin," *The Guardian*, 6 April 2013, https://theguardian.com/books/2013/apr/05/maurice-druon-george-rr-martin.
31 Martin also provides the foreword to the recent English translations of "The Accursed Kings" series, where he states: "*A Game of Thrones* and its sequels were also influenced by the works of great historical novelists like … Maurice Druon, the amazing French writer who gave us the *The Accursed Kings*, seven splendid novels that chronicle the downfall of the Capetian kings and the beginnings of the Hundred Years' War." Maurice Druon, *The Iron King*, trans. Humphrey Hare (London: HarperCollins, 2013), vii.
32 Shiloh Carroll, "Race in A Song of Ice and Fire: Medievalism Posing as Authenticity," *The Public Medievalist*, 28 November 2017, https://publicmedievalist.com/race-in-asoif.
33 My thanks to Robin McDonald for bringing this to my attention. For more on this see, for example: Saladin Ahmed, "Is 'Game of Thrones' Too White?," *Salon*, 1 April 2012, http://salon.com/2012/04/01/is_game_of_thrones_too_white; and Helen Young, "Game of Thrones' Racism Problem," *The Public Medievalist*, 21 July 2017, https://publicmedievalist.com/game-thrones-racism-problem.

34 Carroll, "Race in A Song of Ice and Fire."
35 Helen Young, *Race and Popular Fantasy Literature: Habits of Whiteness* (London: Routledge, 2015), especially 63–87; and Helen Young, "'It's the Middle Ages, Yo!': Race, Neo/medievalisms, and the World of Dragon Age," *The Year's Work in Medievalism* 27 (2012), https://sites.google.com/site/theyearsworkinmedievalism/cabinet/27%20Youngx.pdf.
36 Carroll, "Race in A Song of Ice and Fire." For more on medievalisms in *Game of Thrones*, see Shiloh Carroll, *Medievalism in "A Song of Ice and Fire" and "Game of Thrones"* (Cambridge: D.S. Brewer, 2018). For more on how *Game of Thrones* has influenced discussions regarding the depiction of the medieval period and history in general on screen, see Hilary Jane Locke's chapter in this volume.
37 For example, Sam Wollaston's review of *Gunpowder* in *The Guardian* called it "Game of Thrones minus dragons plus history," and Lily Waddell's article for *The Daily Mail* highlights the show's "graphic Game of Thrones-style torture scene," and subsequent viewer outrage at the graphic violence depicted on-screen. Sam Wollaston, "Gunpowder review – It's Game of Thrones minus Dragons plus History," *The Guardian*, 23 October 2017, https://theguardian.com/tv-and-radio/2017/oct/23/last-nights-tv-review-gunpowder; Lily Waddell, "Fury at the BBC as Gunpowder's graphic Game of Thrones-style torture scene of a priest being hung, drawn and quartered leaves shocked viewers THROWING UP," *The Daily Mail Online*, 22 October 2017, http://dailymail.co.uk/tvshowbiz/article-5004773/Gunpowder-viewers-horrified-BBC-GOT-violence.html#ixzz4xAROGMjA. The casting of Kit Harington (who plays Jon Snow in *Game of Thrones*, and who also produced *Gunpowder*), as Robert Catesby, the mastermind behind the Gunpowder Plot, further cements the connection between these television series.
38 David Hinkley, "'The Hollow Crown': TV review," *Daily News*, 20 September 2013, http://nydailynews.com/entertainment/hollow-crown-tv-review-article-1.1461321.
39 See, for example, Benji Wilson, "King of all he surveys," *The Sunday Times*, 8 May 2016, 4; and Tim Auld, "The Henrys meet Game of Thrones - The Hollow Crown: Henry VI part one, review," *The Telegraph*, 9 May 2016, http://telegraph.co.uk/tv/2016/05/07/the-henrys-meet-game-of-thrones---the-hollow-crown-henry-vi-part.
40 James Rampton, "Benedict Cumberbatch Interview: *The Hollow Crown* actor on his ties to Richard III and Shakespeare's legacy," *Independent*, 12 May 2016, http://independent.co.uk/arts-entertainment/tv/features/benedict-cumberbatch-interview-the-hollow-crown-actor-on-his-ties-to-richard-iii-and-shakespeares-a7025591.html.
41 Adrian Dunbar, quoted in "Benedict Cumberbatch on The Hollow Crown, bloody warfare and discovering he's Richard III's cousin," *RadioTimes*, 14 May 2016, http://radiotimes.com/news/2016-05-14/benedict-cumberbatch-on-the-hollow-crown-bloody-warfare-and-discovering-hes-richard-iiis-cousin.
42 Andrew Tracey (@drmarbles), *Twitter*, 8 May 2016, 4:32 AM, https://twitter.com/drmarbles/status/729046149726928896.
43 John Stevenson, quoted in BBC Media Centre, *The Hollow Crown: The Full Media Pack*, 3 May 2016, http://downloads.bbc.co.uk/mediacentre/hollow-crown-RIII.pdf.
44 All quotations taken from Shakespeare's *Richard III* come from William Shakespeare, *King Richard III*, ed. Antony Hammond (London: Methuen, 1981). Further references will be given in-text.
45 Compare this with Richard's animal-themed syllogism used to win Anne over: ANNE: Villain, thou know'st not law of God nor man. / No beast so

fierce but knows some touch of pity. RICHARD: But I know none, and therefore am no beast" (I.ii.70–73).
46 Anna Blackwell, "Shakespearean Actors, Memes, Social Media and the Circulation of Shakespearean 'Value,'" in *Shakespeare's Cultural Capital: His Economic Impact from the Sixteenth to the Twenty-first Century*, ed. Dominic Shellard and Siobhan Kennan (New York: Palgrave Macmillan, 2016), 89.
47 Peter Jackson, quoted in "Summoning Smaug: The Last of the Fire-drakes," in Peter Jackson, dir. *The Hobbit: The Desolation of Smaug*, extended ed. (Warner Brothers, 2014). For more on the techniques and technology used to translate Smaug from page to film, see David Falconer, *Smaug: Unleashing the Dragon* (London: HarperCollins, 2014), 61–71.
48 Rafi Yahya Syed. "A Praise of Benedict Cumberbatch's 'The Hollow Crown: Richard III,'" *The Web Graffiti*, 2 July 2016, https://web.archive.org/web/20161122093936/http://www.thewebgraffiti.com/a-praise-of-benedict-cumberbatchs-the-hollow-crown-richard-iii.
49 Chase Branch, "'The Hollow Crown: The War of the Roses' Gives Shakespeare A Modern Twist," *The Fellowship of the Screen*, 11 December 2016, http://screenfellows.com/2016/12/the-hollow-crown-the-war-of-the-roses-gives-shakespeare-a-modern-twist.
50 @Professorfangirl, *Tumblr*, 3 September 2016, http://professorfangirl.tumblr.com/post/149901458544/benedict-cumberbatch-as-smaug-the-dragon-as. The fan art consists of three images, stacked vertically. The top image is a screen capture of the dragon Smaug the Terrible from Peter Jackson's *Hobbit* series of films; the middle an animated image (GIF) of Benedict Cumberbatch recording motion capture for Peter Jackson's *Hobbit* series of films; the final image is of Cumberbatch as Richard III in the beginning *Richard III* episode of *The Hollow Crown: The Wars of the Roses*: Richard is topless and hunched over, and gazes directly at the viewer. The caption below all three images reads, "Benedict Cumberbatch as Smaug the Dragon as Richard III. Yep."
51 Ben Power, quoted in BBC Media Centre, *The Hollow Crown: The Full Media Pack*, 3 May 2016, http://downloads.bbc.co.uk/mediacentre/hollow-crown-RIII.pdf.
52 "A Scandal in Belgravia," dir. Paul McGuigan, *Sherlock* (BBC, 2012).
53 "A Study in Pink," dir. Paul McGuigan, *Sherlock* (BBC, 2010).
54 An incorrect diagnosis, as a psychopath/sociopath wouldn't admit they are one. Sherlock does not lack emotions or empathy; he has merely trained himself to not let emotions cloud his judgement.
55 @cumber_romaniac, *Instagram*, 1 June 2016, https://instagram.com/p/BGHK4Lky0C; *RadioTimes*, 14–20 May 2016.
56 @Moriarty's Skull, *Tumblr*, 2016, http://moriartysskull.tumblr.com/post/144828067932/bored-sexy-sociopaths-desperate-for-murder.
57 Neela Debnath, "Benedict Cumberbatch is 'sexy and compelling' as Richard III in *The Hollow Crown*," *Express*, 6 May 2016, http://express.co.uk/showbiz/tv-radio/661073/Benedict-Cumberbatch-sexy-Richard-III-The-Hollow-Crown-Dominic-Cooke; Lauren Humphries-Brooks, "Benedict Cumberbatch Is A Sexy Richard III In The Hollow Crown," *We Got This Covered*, 2015, http://wegotthiscovered.com/tv/benedict-cumberbatch-sexy-richard-iii-hollow-crown; Shannon Vestal Robson, "Here's the First Look at Benedict Cumberbatch as King Richard III," *PopSugar*, 1 October 2014, http://popsugar.com/entertainment/Benedict-Cumberbatch-Hollow-Crown-Picture-35849462.
58 Sam Mendes, quoted in Wilson, "King of all he surveys," 5.

Re-fashioning Richard III 205

59 Wilson, "King of all he surveys," 6.
60 Doğa İstanbulluoğlu (@Doga_), *Twitter*, 13 June 2016, 3:18 AM, https://twitter.com/Doga_/status/742073676036747264; and Doğa İstanbulluoğlu (@Doga_), *Twitter*, 13 June 2016, 3:23 AM, https://twitter.com/Doga_/status/742074821253697536.
61 Holly Dean (@Elfinholly), *Twitter*, 22 May 2016, 4:16 AM, https://twitter.com/Elfinholly/status/734115743147667456.
62 For more on the "Otters Who Look Like Benedict Cumberbatch" meme, see "Benedict Cumberbatch," *Know Your Meme*, 2015, http://knowyourmeme.com/memes/people/benedict-cumberbatch.
63 twitting by hardy (@Alanhardy78), *Twitter*, 27 June 2016, 7:22 AM, https://twitter.com/Alanhardy78/status/747208349138116608; and twitting by hardy (@Alanhardy78), *Twitter*, 27 June 2016, 7:23 AM, https://twitter.com/Alanhardy78/status/747208646816194560.
64 @BBC Store, *Twitter*, 23 June 2016, 8:45 PM, https://twitter.com/bbcstore/status/745960938528968704; and @The Hollow Crown Fans, *Twitter*, 18 June 2017, 4:00 PM, https://twitter.com/hollowcrownfans/status/876348759109718016.
65 Cumbermuffin (@vereentjoeng), *Twitter*, 24 June 2016, 2:13 AM, https://twitter.com/vereentjoeng/status/746043477448765440; Paula™ (@Paula_Dorepa), *Twitter*, 11 April 2017, 6:39 PM, https://twitter.com/Paula_Dorepa/status/851746445627707392; and @enerJax, *Tumblr*, 2016, http://enerjax.tumblr.com/post/144302909927/benedict-cumberbatch-as-richard-iii-aka-arcade.
66 For more on Garrick's celebrity, and popularity in the role of Richard III, and its subsequent cultural currency, see: Janine Barchas and Kristina Straub, "Repetition Is celebrity: Shakespeare and Austen," *Shakespeare & Beyond*, 23 September 2016, https://folger.edu/exhibitions/will-and-jane?_ga=2.267483726.179344808.1511247185-1948669365.1500605257; and Sylvia Morris, "Great Shakespeare Performances: David Garrick's Richard III," *The Shakespeare Blog*, 18 June 2014, http://theshakespeareblog.com/2014/06/great-shakespeare-performances-david-garricks-richard-iii.
67 Jack R. Crawford, "Appendix B: The History of the Play," in William Shakespeare, *The Tragedy of Richard III*, ed. Jack R. Crawford (New Haven: Yale University Press, 1927), 178. Crawford lists the following works: "Peele, *The Battle of Alcazar* (1594); Martson, *Scourge of Villanie* (1598); Heywood, *Edward the Fourth* (pub. 1600); Chapman, *Eastward Hoe* (1605); Marston, *Parasitaster, or Fawne* (1606), [and] *What You Will* (1607); Heywood, *Iron Age* (1611); Brathwaite, *Strappado for the Divell* (1615); Fletcher and Massinger, *Little French Lawyer* (c. 1620)" (178n1).
68 Julie Hankey, "Introduction," in *Plays in Performance: Richard III by William Shakespeare*, ed. Julie Hankey, 2nd ed. (Bristol: Bristol Classic Press, 1988), 8.
69 Hugh M. Richmond, *King Richard III* (Manchester: Manchester University Press, 1989), 33; Martin Holmes, *Shakespeare and Burbage* (London: Phillimore & Co. Ltd, 1978), 55.
70 Hankey, "Introduction," 8.
71 *Iter Boreale* was first published in Richard Corbet, *Certain elegant poems, written by Dr. Corbet, Bishop of Norvvich* (London, 1647), 1–17.
72 Corbet, *Certain elegant poems*, 12. For more on Corbet's anecdote about Burbage, see: Crawford, "Appendix B," 178; Hankey, "Introduction," 8; and Judith Cook, *Shakespeare's Players* (London: Harrap, 1983), 36–37.
73 *Return From Parnassus* (1601), Part 2.iv.iii, quoted in Corbet, *Certain elegant poems*, 178. The *Parnassus Plays* were written and performed anonymously at Christmas by students from St John's College at Cambridge

University. For more on the *Parnassus Plays*, see: Andrew Muir, *Shakespeare in Cambridge: A Celebration of the Shakespeare Festival* (Stroud: Amberley Publishing Limited, 2015); and Sylvia Morris, "The Parnassus Plays: Our Fellow Shakespeare," *The Shakespeare Blog*, 23 September 2011, http://the shakespeareblog.com/2011/09/the-parnassus-plays-our-fellow-shakespeare.

74 John Manningham, *The Diary resumed, May 1602, with many Abstracts from Sermons; also Verses, and miscellaneous remarks, extracts from poems, &c.*, entry dated 13 March 1602 (British Library Harleian MS 5353, fol. 29v), quoted in *Shakespeare Documented*, 18 August 2016, http://shakespearedocumented.org/file/harleian-ms-5353-folio-29-verso.

75 C.C. Stopes, *Burbage and Shakespeare's Stage* (London: Alexander Moring, 1913), 116.

76 A Midnight Song (@weareonenamaste), *Twitter*, 17 September 2016, 5:47 PM, https://twitter.com/weareonenamaste/status/777081540257787904; Rory McDonald (@deetzzz), *Twitter*, 16 June 2016, 5:33 AM, https://twitter.com/deetzzz/status/743194818541723648; and @enerjaxart, *Instagram*, 25 August 2016, https://instagram.com/p/BJiRiiKj7RN.

77 Janine (@erin_shore), *Twitter*, 22 May 2016, 7:05 PM, https://twitter.com/erin_shore/status/734339290000416768; Bodak Red (@AFarray), *Twitter*, 26 December 2016, 12:05 PM, https://twitter.com/AFarray/status/813234213134667776; and Rachel (@Cabbage_Babble), *Twitter*, 4 January 2017, 12:51 AM, https://twitter.com/Cabbage_Babble/status/816326060568670208.

78 The GIF is of the scene where Buster faints after bidding $10,000 on the wrong Lucille at the Save the Wetlands Bachelorette Auction: he was supposed to bid on his mother Lucille Bluth (in a prearranged transaction) but ends up bidding on Lucille Austero, a rival of his mother.

79 See, for example: Jenny Awford, "Genealogist claims Benedict Cumberbatch is as closely related to Richard III as the QUEEN as actor prepares to play 15th century monarch in new BBC series," *Daily Mail*, 6 January 2015, http://dailymail.co.uk/news/article-2897477/Benedict-Cumberbatch-closely-related-Richard-III-QUEEN-actor-prepares-play-15th-century-monarch-new-BBC-series.html; Maev Kennedy, "Benedict Cumberbatch is related to Richard III, scientists say," *The Guardian*, 26 March 2015, https://theguardian.com/uk-news/2015/mar/25/benedict-cumberbatch-is-related-to-richard-iii-scientists-say; Press Association, "Benedict Cumberbatch: being dressed as Richard III when told they are related was 'extraordinary bit of serendipity,'" *The Telegraph*, 10 May 2016, http://telegraph.co.uk/tv/2016/05/10/benedict-cumberbatch-extraordinary-bit-of-serendipity-to-be-dres.

13 The Many Afterlives of Elizabeth Barton

Annie Blachly

In the winter of 1534, Henry VIII and Thomas Cromwell faced opposition to their plans to pass the *Act of Supremacy* from an unusual source. This opposition was spearheaded by Elizabeth Barton, a young woman who had become a vocal opponent of Henry's divorce and subsequent marriage to Anne Boleyn. Barton had risen from the lowly position of maid to the status of 'Holy Nun,' and in doing so, she had harnessed the power of political prophecy to oppose the King's will. By 1534, she stood as a crucial and singular threat, who both Henry and Cromwell sought to eradicate. In a series of calculated attacks, Barton's credibility and reputation of sanctity were destroyed, culminating in her public execution. Her death, however, was not enough to diminish the influence of her prophecies, and here Henry and Cromwell took a remarkable step. In the first instance of what was to become a popular Tudor weapon, Cromwell composed an Act of Attainder, which both condemned Barton to death and warned against using political prophecy against the King. Most notable was the inclusion of complete censorship of all written records of Barton's words.[1] With this move, however, Cromwell and Henry achieved the opposite: in attempting to eradicate Barton's writings, they established her notoriety. They left the figure of Elizabeth Barton open to interpretations and re-inventions. By erasing contemporary accounts, Cromwell and Henry's actions gave Barton an afterlife that was to become repeatedly adaptable in a consistently changing world.

Elizabeth Barton existed in a key moment in the history of Catholicism: a tenuous period of Catholic and Protestant co-existence in early modern England. She was both a political prophet and a spiritual casualty of the English Reformation. Barton's intrinsic connection to political and spiritual dissent ascribed her a position of deviance within her own society, as Catholicism became a marginalised position. Her twofold exclusion from the Tudor social norm has made her a useful avatar of the nature of the deviant or marginal in successive ages, reflecting shifting attitudes to the spiritual in particular.

This chapter explores how Barton was re-interpreted over time, and uses the development of her image(s) to examine the afterlives of early modern Catholicism, and women's mystical experiences, from the

Reformation to today. Considering the intersection of history and adaptation studies, this chapter asserts that alternate representations of Barton established over time tell us far more about the contemporary concerns of each adaptation than they do about Barton herself.[2] As I demonstrate, Barton's association with (marginalised) Catholicism was used by early Protestants, who adapted her tale to present a deceptive enemy, standing against the values of Elizabethan Protestantism. During the Enlightenment, and the growth of literal and sceptical readings of ecstatic religious experience, she became sexualised and deemed a fraudulent impostor. By the late nineteenth century, a growing scientific ethos meant Barton's prophetic experiences were retrospectively diagnosed as madness, associated with the gendered physiological weakness of hysteria. Contemporary fictionalised representations of Barton have reflected modern values, where the rise of feminism has sought to afford Barton an agency previously unseen in her adaptations. Furthermore, the popularity of magic as a discursive space for exploring the meaning of deviance and belonging in young adult fiction has enabled yet another adaptation of Barton to emerge, in which her 'powers' of prognostication have been re-labelled as supernatural. Ultimately, Barton's many afterlives tell us more about the changing face of the Anglophone world's troubled relationship with female spiritual and political authority than they do about the story of a particular Catholic woman at the dawn of the English Reformation. Yet, the nature of her successive adaptations has also been driven by the divisions generated by that upheaval. Attempts to reconcile what Barton represented in the past offer insight into attempts to grapple with contemporary concerns, where Barton's afterlives represent an early-modernism particular to her original Tudor context.

Early Protestant Interpretations

The interpretation of Catholic figures from the late medieval and early Tudor period was a contested element of political discourse in sixteenth-century England. Barton was no exception. Following Mary I's reinstating of Roman Catholicism during her reign (1553–1558), her successor Elizabeth I's early reign saw moderate treatment of Catholics, as the English Mass and Protestant Bible were reinstated. Pope Pius V declared Elizabeth a heretic and excommunicated her in the 1570 papal bull, *Regnans in Excelsis*, which also released Catholics from their loyalty to Elizabeth as queen. Pius's actions forced the English government to take far more repressive and aggressive actions against Catholics and Catholic clergy.[3] Within this climate, William Lambarde's *A Perambulation of Kent, conteining the description, hystorie, and customes of that shire; written in the yeere 1570* was published.[4] This first extant representation of Barton and her prophecies was mediated through highly critical Protestant eyes, emerging during heightened concerns around

Catholic plots to overthrow the Queen. Viewing her as representative of inappropriate Catholic interference in the politics of the English nation, Lambarde linked Barton intrinsically to contemporary concerns around the risks posed to the English body politic by Catholic enemies fomenting politico-religious rebellion.

Lambarde established a pattern for Barton's Elizabethan afterlives, marked by critiques of her "pretended revelations" from a Protestant position of denunciation.[5] Characterised as the "good and honest Lambarde"[6] by Elizabeth, Lambarde was a significant political figure of the sixteenth century: a politically aware participant, commentator, and critic.[7] Lambarde's *A Perambulation of Kent*, the first English county history, examined "the description, hystorie, and customes of that shire."[8] Anxious to establish the historical credentials of his portrayal, Lambarde placed the origins of his knowledge of Barton in a "little Pamphlet" he "chanced" to see whilst collecting writings of the area.[9] The "little pamphlet" was supposedly *A marveilous woorke of late done at Court of Streete in Kent*, written by Edward Thwaits and Edward Bocking, the priest who was said to have coached her in prophecy, both of whom would go on to be condemned to death alongside Barton. If it indeed existed, no copy of this pamphlet now survives, perhaps due to the censorship that followed the executions.[10]

Lambarde's *Perambulation* has become an enduring and influential historical portrayal, establishing three key components of subsequent depictions of Barton: that her visions were untrue, that her spirituality was deviant, and that she was a threat to the interests of the proper body politic.[11] Lambarde begins Barton's tale in the Easter of 1525, when she was in service as a maid in the house of Thomas Cobb. Lambarde describes Barton's confinement to bed due to severe illness, when after seven months she received her first prophetic experience. Describing a conversation between Barton and the attendant, Lambarde claims that Barton asked if Cobb's child, who was also ill, was still alive. When the attendant replied that the child was, Barton replied, "it should be anone," and with that the child died.[12] The experience was declared one of "divination and foretelling," and as her visions continued they were reportedly received in a similar manner.[13]

Lambarde's account of Barton's growing spiritual authority served to situate her as representative of deviant Catholic practice. He described how Barton's legitimacy in the eyes of the people was bolstered as many of her earlier visions occurred in or around the local church of St Martin's, and the church at Court-at-Street, Kent, creating intrinsic links between her visions and local religious sites. In particular, Barton is said to have claimed that she would be "restored to health by miracle," declaring that "Our blessed Lady will shew mo[re] miracles [at Court-at-Street] shortly" if she were to attend the church to pray, thus linking her visions with the Virgin Mary.[14] Lambarde explicitly critiques Barton's Marian devotion, a feature of Catholicism frequently linked to idolatry by Protestant authors, claiming "the holy Virgine [had been] mishonoured" by her, casting her devotion as excessive and inappropriate.[15] Lambarde's criticisms seem to suggest the danger of a Catholic figure's ability to manipulate the faithful, his details serving as accusations of Barton's corruption of faith and a disordered kind of Christianity.

According to Lambarde, Barton's prophecies quickly gained the attention of key figures, and in 1526 the parish priest, Richard Master, reported Barton's prophecies to the Archbishop of Canterbury, who, in turn, sent an ecclesiastical commission to investigate her. Headed by Edward Bocking, the commission found Barton to be genuine, with Thomas Cranmer deeming her visions as proof of "great miracle."[16] Thus, her visions had been deemed as sent from heaven by powerful figures of the Church, making Barton a legitimate figure of attention. Barton gained a key position at the Benedictine priory of St Sepulchre's, Canterbury, and Archbishop Warham appointed Bocking as Barton's confessor for her postulation.

Lambarde's description of these developments makes Barton's acceptance by, and advancement through, the Catholic hierarchy an example the corruption of the faith in sixteenth-century Protestant eyes:

> Thus Elizabeth Barton was advaunced from the condition of a base servaunt, to the estate of a glorious Nonne: The Heremite of Court of Strete was enriched by daily offring; S. Sepulcres got the possession of a Holy Mayden; God was blasphemed; the holy Virgine his mother mishonoured; the silly people were miserably mocked; The Bishops, Priestes, and Monkes, in the mean time with closed eyes winking, and the Devill and his lymmes, with open mouthe laughing at it.[17]

With this, Lambarde's vitriolic condemnation is clearly situated in a religious realm. Furthermore, Lambarde details Barton's prophecies against Henry, where his descriptions are laced with denunciation, calling her a hypocrite and clearly representing her prophecies as feigned.[18] The turning point for Barton, an "openly seditious Eucharistic vision," was not recorded by Lambarde, but is extant in the Act of Attainder.[19] With this vision, Barton aligned herself definitively with Rome; wherein she condemned heresy, spoke in defence of the existence of purgatory, and supported the authority of the Pope.[20] As her audacity grew, Barton's correspondence and influence extended to Henry himself, when Barton was brazen enough to declare that if the King proceeded with the divorce, "he shoulde not bee King of this Realme one moneth after."[21] Importantly, this prophecy occurred just as Anne Boleyn discovered herself pregnant.

Lambarde's descriptions of Barton's final years are brief, merely detailing that she was executed "worthely," wherein the "Devill [her] Maister was quite and clean confounded."[22] In linking her to the devil, Lambarde implicitly connected Barton to the biblical idea that false prophecy represented "official corruption" and was deserving of "imminent divine retribution."[23] Here, the four distinctions between true and false prophecy, as established by French theologian and cardinal of the Catholic Church, Pierre d'Ailly, were evoked: in particular, the 'final cause.' Claiming Barton was hypocritical conformed to d'Ailly's beliefs that false prophets seek temporal gain as well as his 'material cause': that Barton's "feigned" prophecies demonstrated her ability to speak falsehoods.[24]

Lambarde's scathing view of Elizabeth Barton is reflective of his Protestant, post-Reformation stance on Barton's deviance. Lambarde's representation of Barton presents Catholicism as deviant in its idolatry, its superstitious and credulous belief in the divine and miraculous, and its dominance by clerical authority figures. Through rhetoric and symbolism, Lambarde marks Barton as a hypocrite and an impostor, where her loyalty to "Popish Creede" establishes her as a threat to the Protestant body politic.[25] Lambarde's depiction becomes the origin of Barton's subsequent, and often critical, afterlives, where later authors and artists re-frame elements of Barton's deviance as presented by Lambarde, and situate them according to their own context.

The 'Imposture'

In England, the Enlightenment saw a discourse of rationality emerge. Religion and morality became subjected to critical examinations, whereby thinking became more methodical, establishing a 'critical consciousness' that is seen as a foundation of modern thinking.[26] Within England, the *Toleration Act of 1689* had allowed the possibility of opposition to the Church of England, changing the way England dealt with religious heterodoxy, and discrimination and persecution of dissenters.[27] In this climate, Barton's Enlightenment afterlives treated her with a rationalised social contextualisation and a developed Protestant criticism of unchecked spiritual devotion.

Within David Hume's *The History of England* (1754–1761), Henry Tresham's engraving of Elizabeth Barton reflects late eighteenth-century views of the nun (Figure 13.1). The image accompanies Hume's discussion of Barton's tale, which closely follows Lambarde's narrative. There is, however, one key difference between Hume and Lambarde's depictions. The way that Hume describes Barton's physical ecstasy as "unusual convulsions," producing "equal disorder in her mind," links to the concerns of Catholicism as representative of excessive, unreasoned, passionate spiritual practices. Furthermore, Hume calls her followers "silly," and names Barton's actions as "knavery," clearly "counterfeit" and "pretended."[28] Hume's comment of "silly," and by extension, its relation to weakness, vulnerability, or simplicity of character, is a charge against both her easily influenced followers and the power of Catholic corruption. The image accompanying Hume's words demonstrates the development of Barton's afterlives in the 'Age of Reason.'[29] Entitled *The Imposture of the Holy Maid of Kent*, it shows Barton bare breasted, her eyes aloft to the sky, as rosary beads hang limply from her outstretched hands.[30]

Figure 13.1 A. [Henry] Tresham, *The Imposture of the Holy Maid of Kent*. c.1830. Print, 202 × 158 mm. The British Museum, London.

The title of the etching declares Barton's actions as deceptive, and draws upon the familiar figure of the impostor in early modern England. The "impostor phenomenon," where "an impostor mocks and surmounts social control mechanisms and displays their weaknesses," often served to break social taboos, while a religious impostor bore resemblance to, or was labelled, a heretic.[31] The dichotomy of Protestantism and Catholicism, in particular, spurred the increasing use of the label of 'impostor' for those who diverged from Protestant orthodoxy, so much so that in 1559 Protestant reformers claimed Catholic prophets were not merely frauds but were a "mark of the church of the Antichrist," representing the spiritual corruption of the Catholic Church itself.[32] The label and language of 'religious imposture' became a significant rhetorical tool, one that reflected an early modern view and continued to develop into the seventeenth and eighteenth centuries. The condemnation of the 'impostor' highlighted the belief in the corruption of Christianity, reflecting the struggle of the opposing denominations, and carried with it implications of deception and duplicity.

Within the etching, the inclusion of the rosary beads and the statue of the Madonna and Child, fading into shadows in the background, connect Barton iconographically to Catholic culture and identity. In the context of early modern England and the loss of public places of worship, the rosary became "miniature shrines" for English Catholics, which stood as private, secret, and potent connections to the figure of Mary.[33] The Marian connection to the rosary, also called "Our Lady's Psalter," is an important symbol in the hands of Barton. The repetitive presence of Mary in the etching serves as a reminder of Barton's connection with the Virgin. Barton's Mariolatry, with its identification of idolatry with the veneration of Mary, reinforced the idea of Catholicism as corrupt.

Barton's bare-breasted appearance in the etching echoes the accusations of sexual behaviour levelled by Henry and Cromwell, reframed for an age concerned with restrained and rational spirituality. In the eighteenth century, the acceptance of erotic subject matter within artwork meant that the female form could appear without needing an allegorical justification, such as being symbolic of Vanity.[34] Images of women exposing one breast, as seen in representations of Greek Amazons and the Christian Virgin Mary, were linked with heroism, devotion, and sacrifice,[35] while the trend of neoclassical imagery was to represent women in distress or ecstasy, as though exposing themselves in the throes of passion.[36] Two bare breasts, however, may have had a slightly different symbolic meaning. The presence of nudity could allude to the main consequences of sin: the degeneracy of spiritual values and morals depicted in the loss of worldly possession or, quite literally, their clothing.[37] In particular, in the eighteenth century, the concept of the Rake associated implications between sex and social class, and saw the idea of "sartorial dishevelment" charged with sexuality and expressions of submission.[38]

Barton's sexualised representation in the etching drew upon elements of her story established by Cromwell prior to, and directly after, her execution. Accusations of a sexual relationship between her and Bocking, her confessor, were circulated to discredit her through a repeated public sermon and printed proclamations. Preached first in London in November 1533, the sermon was repeated in Canterbury in December, with both locations strategically chosen due to their centrality to Barton's influence.[39] The repetition of the sermon not only served to disseminate the accusations, but it has been asserted that Cromwell—rather than either John Capon, who preached the sermon in London, or Nicholas Heath, who did so in Canterbury—had been the author.[40] The Attainder, which sent Barton and her co-accused to their deaths, mirrored the accusations in the sermon and was released as a proclamation that was sent out to all towns and cities.[41]

The sermon had focused on three clear themes: Barton was used and manipulated by rebellious churchmen; she was disingenuous in her religious practice; and she was licentious and, therefore, not 'holy' but rather human, female, and corrupted. The sermon asserted that Bocking attempted to induce and craft Barton's 'visions,' coaching her words and taunting her if she failed to perform. The sermon emphasised that Barton had been controlled and manipulated by the King's enemies, reinforcing the idea that her prophecies had merely been propaganda and shameless criticism of the king by disgruntled men.[42]

To further her public shaming, Barton's weakness of character was demonstrated through examples of her apparent corruption through hypocrisy, where she was charged with the cardinal sin of 'vainglory,' or narcissistic vanity. Demonstrating Barton's degenerate character through this hypocrisy, which is so prevailing that Lambarde references this within his *Perambulation*,[43] the sermon accuses her of living in a luxury above her means, allowing her to become "fat and ruddy" whilst making her followers perform penance and fast so that the "sharpness of their bones had almost worn through their skin."[44] Insinuations of sexual immorality suggest that Barton often spent the night with Bocking, so not only were her words impure, but also her actions. Her manipulations were said to be so perverse that Barton "feign[ed] that she was so often troubled and vexed with the devil to the intent her sisters should be afraid to stir in the night,"[45] as to give her the freedom to sneak out of her cell "twice or thrice a week" to visit Bocking.[46] By utilising familiar themes of traditional sermons, Cromwell drew upon the concepts of sin, contrition, and penance to charge Barton with committing cardinal sins. For those who attended the sermons or read the Attainder, this presented Barton as the antithesis of a 'Holy woman.' Stripped of religious authority, Barton's prophecies were 'proven' false through an association with moral weakness.

This received image of moral weakness finds an Enlightenment expression in the etching, in which her licentiousness, sexuality, and potential to deceive are embodied in signs of her unreasoned and immoderate spirituality. Not only is Barton caught in a moment of swooning ecstasy, but her loose clothing has exposed her, both her breasts, and her shoulder for the layman, the scribing priest, and the viewer themselves to observe. This is an image charged with sexuality: it suggests she is not a chaste nun, but rather sexually motivated, lying in the lap of the priest, his hand on her exposed wrist. Hints of skin, including her shoulder, naked neck, and bare foot, show no sign of the 'Holy Maid' Barton was claiming to be. The sexual tones further reinforce her 'imposture,' and the duplicitous nature of Barton's visions and positioning as a nun are critiqued through an 'Enlightened' Protestant gaze.

In the iconoclastic fervour of the Reformation, Barton's political prophecy was a threat, and while Henry and Cromwell may have been able to silence her words, their extreme treatment also served somewhat to turn her into a legendary figure. By the time of the publication of Hume's *History of England*, Lambarde's view of Barton as represented in Hume's dismissal of Barton as "silly" and "pretend" was reiterated. Hume's comments build upon the post-Reformation equation between Catholicism, irrationality, and gullibility. The sexual lilt, however, as represented in the etching and the deeming of Barton as an 'impostor'—both in Hume's words and in the title of the image—deem Barton a deviant both spiritually and politically within a successive age. Ultimately, the sexual accusations that were already present in Barton's Tudor context were offered new and historically contingent significance, representing the possible corruption that Catholicism could produce, and offered a developing step in Barton's adaptation.

The Mad Maid of Kent

As the nineteenth century progressed, readings of spiritual excess became increasingly linked not to the lack of reason as a choice or perversion, but to a medicalised incapacity to reason, associated with madness. The interpretation of many female medieval mystics was directly influenced by this shift, and Barton was no exception. With the emergence of psychiatry in the nineteenth century, what had once been deemed a religious experience was removed from its context, and pathologised within the constructs and classifications of mental illness.

In England, the eighteenth and nineteenth centuries saw changes to both legal and social views, and treatment of madness. The 1774 *Lunacy Act* saw the beginning of regulations for madhouses and their inmates.[47] In addition, George III's bouts of mental illness, and the assassination attempt against him (which spurred the *Criminal Lunacy Act* of 1800), raised social, cultural, and legal concerns about madness.[48] The *Asylums*

Act of 1845, and its companion, the 1845 *Lunatics Act*—touted as a "watershed" in the emergence of psychology in England—provided the institutional basis for a new "professional elite."[49] The psychiatric care that developed during this period came to be known as "moral treatment," seeing the fusion of moral values and science into a model of insanity.[50] It was both this increase in professionals and a moral viewpoint that saw substantial religious influences within psychiatry. In turn, this led to psychiatric analysis of historical religious figures and widespread re-interpretation of religious experience as mental illness.

Barton's afterlives in the age of psychiatry were characterised by this shift from mysticism to madness. A notable example is Horace Francis Lester's 1887, *Ben D'ymion, and Other Parodies*. Lester presented a satirised account of Barton's prophecies, where the King is "incensed about the mad Maid of Kent."[51] This incidental application of a diagnosis of madness suggested a revised view of Barton, demonstrating the increasing interest in psychology and retrospective diagnosis. Depictions of Barton's madness likely derived from descriptions of Barton's prophetic experiences, such as Hume's, in which she was "subject to hysterical fits, which threw her body into unusual convulsions; and having produced an equal disorder in her mind, made her utter strange sayings."[52] Now, however, these were understood as symptoms of physiological and neurological derangement, rather than a swoon of excess spiritual passion. The connection between this interpretation, moving from Lambarde's belief in Barton suffering from the "falling Evill"[53] (otherwise known as the 'falling sickness') to Hume's description of "disorder in her mind,"[54] is clear, yet it was expressed in distinctly nineteenth-century terms.

Jean-Martin Charcot (1825–1893), who was the first to systemise the pathology of the supernatural, established retrospective diagnosis as a respectable scientific method.[55] Charcot, who served as a neurologist at the women's hospital of Salpêtrière (at the time the world's largest psychiatric hospital), first drew explicit connections between the supernatural and current psychology in *Les démoniaques dans l'art*, in 1887.[56] Charcot saw parallels between the visual representations of the ecstasy of saints with the positions and poses he witnessed of his own patients. As such, pathology emerged from iconography, and with it, the beginnings of retrospective diagnosis.[57] Charcot's attempts to diagnose mystical figures, such as Beatrice of Nazareth, Francis of Assisi, and Catherine of Siena, were extended in *La foi qui guérit* (*Faith Healing*) in 1892, equating the mystical and the hysterical, and converging ideas of contemporary understanding and historical mystics.[58] Situated in what has been deemed "the golden age of hysteria" (1870–1914), Charcot's work reflected the shift from hysteria as a medical term, to an aesthetic, and even a cultural, category.[59] Charcot attributed miracles of mystics to hysterical origins, diagnosing both Francis of Assisi and Teresa of Avila as "undeniable hysterics," and, by the end of his life, focused much attention on the uncomfortable relationship between religion and medicine.[60]

Charcot's influence was especially prominent in the early twentieth-century studies of female mystics. While the nineteenth century saw attempts to dismiss women's experiences as inauthentic, these dismissals and claims of affected piety led, rather, to psychological evaluation. Modern scholarship tends to be critical of the trend of retrospective diagnosis, yet the incidence of these diagnoses reflects both the emergence of medical and psychological understandings, and a desire to understand and explain the behaviours of mysterious figures of the past.[61]

The trend for retrospective diagnosis served to further marginalise mystical and prophetic women of the early modern and medieval past, explaining away their visions with scientific reasoning. By removing their political or spiritual deviance from the interior realms of choice to the exterior causation of disease, retrospective diagnosis both excused women from the sin of their deeds, and turned them into objects of pity, rather than fear. Charles Singer's 1913, *Studies in the History and Method of Science*, saw Hildegard of Bingen diagnosed as a migraine sufferer, a fundamental step in the history of retrospective diagnoses of mystic and female visionaries.[62] Singer's diagnoses reflected the new dominant understanding of migraines that had developed within the nineteenth century, emphasising the associations between migraines and auras, vision, and science.[63] Following Singer's study of Hildegard, others studies, such as Robert Thouless's examination of Julian of Norwich in 1922[64] and David Knowles's pathologising of Margery Kempe's visions in 1927, illustrate the increasing attempts to ascribe psychiatric diagnoses to the experiences of mystical figures, especially women.[65] By these means the significance of their historical voices was reduced along with the threat they posed to political or religious order.

The pathologising of Barton mirrors the timeline of the emergence of retrospective diagnosis as a legitimate scientific study. Thomas Edward Bridgett's reference to Barton as "seemingly hysterical" in 1888 serves to reflect the rising view of her as suffering psychologically, increasingly connected with the feminine weakness of hysteria.[66] The flippancy of Bridgett's diagnosis demonstrates the pervasive view of hysteria by the end of the nineteenth century, where hysteria was being recognised and referenced by medical professionals, historians, and popular writers alike.[67] By 1911, Barton's entry in the *Encyclopædia Britannica* described her as "a neurotic girl, subject to epilepsy, and an illness in her nineteenth year [that] resulted in hysteria and religious mania."[68] Her prophetic identity had become subsumed by her diagnosis, and Barton emerged as a woman who unequivocally suffered both physically and mentally: her visions products of mental illness, disassociated from religious experience.

When popular historian Philip Sergeant referred to Barton as "the Mad Nun of Kent" in 1923, it reflected not a view of madness that stemmed from Barton's own time, but a reflection of early twentieth-century concerns.[69] His characterisation of Barton as a "crazy woman" may have seemed like a logical conclusion within Sergeant's context; however, this diagnosis not only shifts the view of Barton but has also had the most profound impact on modern depictions of the Maid.[70] Barton's "Holy Maid" moniker is now so often replaced by "Mad Maid," which has become synonymous with her identity and her visions.

Agency in Fiction

In the contemporary Western world, the inherited models of the Reformation, Enlightenment, and the age of psychiatry have been enhanced by the increasing secularisation of public discourse and private practice. Barton the religious prophet, having given way to Barton the mad woman, is benefiting from contemporary discourse, and in particular modern literature has allowed her history to be infused with contemporary values. What was previously considered deviant is now profiting from an inclusiveness that aims to rehabilitate those who were demonised in the past. For Barton, once seen as a dangerous woman labelled as mad, new literary representations of her character and prophecies have emerged. Fuelled by twentieth-century feminist moments and current attempts to find space for neuro-atypical people in mainstream society, adaptations of Barton have taken on a particular modern lilt. Barton's contemporary characterisation can be found most notably in Hilary Mantel's Man Booker Prize-winning novel *Wolf Hall*[71] and K.C. Held's young adult fiction novel *Holding Court*.[72] While dissimilar in many ways, the two novels demonstrate a significant similarity: female agency through the use of prophecy. Mantel's adaptation offers multilayered perspectives of historical views of Barton, where despite claims of madness and witchcraft, Barton's central role is one of agency. Conversely, Held's young adult fiction novel offers a discourse in diversity for her teenage audience, reflecting current regard for the supernatural as a virtuous metaphor for understanding diversity and reintegrating deviance.

Written in the context of third wave feminism, Mantel's depiction of Barton serves as a meeting point between previous historical adaptations and contemporary concerns around the agency of women. Arguably the most faithful adaptation of what is known of Barton's life, Mantel's presentation reinforces sixteenth-century views of deviance, while simultaneously challenging these views. In presenting Barton through the eyes of Thomas Cromwell and those of the Tudor court, Mantel reveals concerns that Barton is mad, and perhaps that she is even a witch. These concerns mirror those presented in both the sermon and the Attainder, and conform to those perspectives established in the past. While Mantel is a scrupulous researcher who relies on historical fact, she acknowledges the difficulty in ascertaining historical accuracy, stating "the problem occurs when there are gaps in the story ... I will apply my imagination and see how, psychologically, this might all fit together."[73] By engaging in early-modernism, Mantel is able to 'fill' gaps in the historical record with the contemporary, extending what many modern scholars ascertain: that early modern women had more agency than previously believed, and that this agency was especially potent in the hands of religious women.[74]

Mantel establishes a contradiction in her characterisation of Barton, which allows her to situate Barton as complementary to both Tudor and contemporary values. By using the perspective of multiple characters, Barton conforms to notions of historical deviance, and it becomes almost possible to view all previous adaptations of Barton through their various comments. Mantel's characterisation, however, presents a woman in control of both her body and mind. While Barton is depicted as audacious and condescending—with hints of hypocrisy in her piety—she also contradicts the licentious nun of Cromwell's sermon. Outwardly, Barton is the picture of chastity and purity, and yet, Mantel's choice of language reflects a power that is tied to her sexuality. Undermining his masculinity, and playing upon Henry's inability to produce a male heir, Mantel utilises charged sexual language throughout her depictions of Barton. When meeting Barton, the King is described as having "a ready, priapic body,"[75] of which the phallic implications cannot be ignored. Furthermore, when Cromwell connects both Anne Boleyn and Barton through their powerful virginity, Mantel emphasises the use of sexuality as a means of manipulation and control. This view of Barton seems to draw from the accusations of an improper sexual relationship with Bocking, while also mirroring the iconography within the etching. Mantel, however, suggests Barton's use of sexuality is not a deviant trait but rather a strength. Through this reading of Barton's prophecies, her urging can be seen as not just a political statement; by demanding that Henry relinquish his divorce attempts, Barton is literally refusing him the opportunity to leave his wife for a new sexual partner. Unlike the accusations Barton received in her lifetime, Mantel's depiction, placed within a feminist discourse, can present Barton's use of sexuality as a strength and not as a perversion.

Mantel's Barton can be seen as attempting to separate Henry from those sexual urges of the body, where Barton's revelations are shown as an attempt to deprive Henry of title, name, and the dignity of a legitimate king. In Mantel's world, Barton is still viewed by her contemporaries as possibly mad and increasingly hysterical; however, to the modern audience, she is also a woman with a clear and active agency. Mantel's Barton demonstrates a female rebellion that places her use of political prophecy within a heightened gender context, and one that extrapolates upon previously established readings of Barton.[76]

While Mantel's adaptation of Barton is distinct, she is not alone in giving Barton a role that is reflective of female empowerment. K.C. Held's *Holding Court* is the first novel to appropriate Barton for a young adult audience. Held's novel affords her protagonist individual agency, where prophetic gifts are removed from the voice of God and shifted from the religious sphere of a 'Holy Woman' into the supernatural, a more palatable realm for the modern audience. For Barton's most recent contemporary iteration, her previously demonised and diagnosed prognostications can be once again interpreted as a 'gift' or, in the case of *Holding Court*, the tool to solve a murder mystery.

The place of mysticism and miracles, which was once largely explained through religious mythology, has been filled increasingly over the twentieth century by popular literature, relegating what was once considered religious to a supernatural realm. In a time when young adult fiction is one of the fastest-growing categories of literature, the genre has simultaneously established a developing and separate identity, increasingly utilising elements of fantasy, romance, Gothic, and historical fiction. Monsters and the magical have played crucial roles in contemporary young adult fiction, offering meaningful representations and discussions around difference, inclusion, and facing one's fears. The prevalence of the representation of supernatural elements that were once considered deviant is particularly striking. These deviants, or those who possess deviant attributes, are now very often depicted as the hero, heroine, or love interest, and as positive inclusions and qualities within young adult fiction.

Within *Holding Court*, sixteen-year-old protagonist, Jules Verity suffers from what her best friend refers to as "Psychic Tourette's Syndrome," an uncontrollable ability to blurt out often indecipherable visions of the future. At her summer job at the theatre restaurant, Tudor Times, Jules is given the role of Elizabeth Barton, the "Mad Maid of Kent," who is described as "raving like a lunatic" and "batshit crazy."[77] The crux of Held's novel is Jules's struggles with her own form of difference: her supernatural abilities that place her apart from her peers. Jules sees herself the monster of the story, the freak with supernatural abilities common in both horror and young adult fiction. These monsters, while traditionally frightening, dangerous, and evil, can very often be presented within young adult fiction as "sexy, attractive, alluring and tempting," and it is no surprise that Jules becomes the figure at the centre of a love triangle.[78]

While Jules's journey of self-discovery conforms to a recognizable trope of young adult fiction, the use of Barton as a tool to do so is important both to the novel itself and in the wider context of Barton's evolving afterlives. Naming Jules's 'gifts' first as "Psychic Tourette's Syndrome" draws parallels to Barton's own retrospective diagnoses, where Jules's visions are explained through reference to a neurological disorder.[79] Contrastingly, Jules's grandmother repeatedly refers the Jules's powers as "gifts," a far more favourable view of mystics than Barton's prior iterations. As supernatural phenomena, these powers are presented not as 'gifts' from God but rather a genetic quirk shared by the women in the family. There is a secularised logic to Jules prophecies: a genetic ability seems far more palatable to the understandings of a modern audience. In giving Jules the role of the "Mad Maid of Kent," Jules's outbursts are explained away to visitors of the castle as part of the act, using Barton as a means for Jules to hide her 'gifts.' Eventually, through the realisation that Jules's 'gifts' can be used to solve the murder and save herself from danger, the power of prophecy is relegated from deviance to heroics. Jules's powers become used for good, and she is ultimately able to play the starring role in the primary love triangle. She gets the boy, while finding self-acceptance and fulfilling her own Hero's Journey. For Barton, her narrative may not have been rehabilitated by this use of her story, but her prophetic 'gifts' are nevertheless returned to the realm of 'true' prophecies under the guise of pop-culture supernatural elements.

Herd's depiction of a prophetic woman encapsulates the continual re-interpretations of Barton's identity. In a time where young adult fiction and supernatural 'gifts' often go hand in hand, it is unsurprising that Barton is used as a prop for a young girl to discover herself through the use of psychic abilities. While Barton's spiritual experiences may be incompatible with the views of a contemporary young adult audience, this supernatural reinterpretation affords her an afterlife where she can belong within modern understandings and perhaps become an autonomous heroine. For Mantel, Barton's characterisation reflects modern arguments, not only in that it may be necessary to re-evaluate the agency of women in the early modern period but in that it may also be possible to present Barton as a woman who reflects more contemporary views on the use and power of sexuality. Whilst Mantel's attempts to retain a historical truth see her place female agency as operating through sexuality, Herd normalises the deviant in the world of young adult fiction, using the supernatural as a metaphor for acceptance and placing her protagonist as an empowered heroine. These modern conceptions offer further credence to using adaptation theory to examine the evolution of Barton, and to argue that each adaptation serves far more as a mirror to its contemporary world than to offer a truthful account of Barton's life.

Conclusion

The varying representations of Elizabeth Barton offer an elucidating case study for the development of early-modernism. The Tudor era, and the sagas of Henry VIII's court, have caught the attention and imaginations of subsequent authors, artists, and historians, just as the medieval world has. As such, Barton is emblematic of a Tudor figure that is representative not only of the views and values of the beginnings of the early modern period, but also of the continually developing understandings of the use of political prophecy and the specific forms of deviance ascribed to Catholic opponents of the Reformation and the Tudor dynasty. The aim of this chapter is not to rehabilitate Barton, nor to end at a conclusive view of her and her actions, but rather to examine how and why she has been variously represented over time.

The trajectory of the reinterpretations of Barton and her prophecies mark how particular elements of the past have been represented, re-examined, and reused over time. For her contemporary world, Barton was not only a dangerous individual, but was also representative of a wider threat in the guise of prophetic challenges. Instead, Barton's use of prophecy, once removed from the context of a Catholic realm, created difficulties for contemporary audiences: how could her prophetic gifts be explained in social and cultural settings where prophecy no longer belonged? Following her execution and the censorship of her works, her Catholic allegiance placed her in a position of sociopolitical opposition to subsequent eras, where history has condemned and subverted Barton's position as a 'Holy Woman.' When Barton's prognostications were shifted from a Holy sphere and medicalised, the rationalisation of religious experience led to the classification of mental illness; however, Barton's most final iteration gives her modern autonomy, as a means of understanding and explaining the mysteries of her Catholic mysticism.

Ultimately, the truth of Barton's identity was written out of history. The censorship that aimed to eradicate her instead left a story and a figure that has tempted following generations to fill in the gaps. Barton encapsulates the appeal of a notorious figure, while also posing difficult questions for a changing and evolving world. Barton's continuously evolving afterlives highlight the interest that those of the early modern world continue to produce, and the possibility of figures to be adapted time and time again to represent the concerns of multiple societies and eras.

Notes

1 "Elizabeth Barton," in *Letters and Papers, Foreign and Domestic, Henry VIII: Volume 7, 1534,* ed. James Gairdner (London: 1883), 28–30.
2 Defne Ersin Tutan, "Adaptation and History," in *The Oxford Handbook of Adaptation Studies,* ed. Thomas Leich (Oxford: Oxford University Press, 2017), 577.
3 Thomas Barlow, *Brutum Fulmen: Or, The Bull of Pope Pius V Concerning the Damnation, Excommunication, and Deposition of Q. Elizabeth*

(London, 1681). For further discussion, see: Lisa McClain, *Lest We Be Damned: Practical Innovation and Lived Experience among Catholics in Protestant England, 1559–1642* (London: Routledge, 2004); and Aislinn Muller, "Transmitting and Translating the Excommunication of Elizabeth I," *Studies in Church History* 53 (2017): 210–222.
4 William Lambarde, *A Perambulation of Kent: Conteining the Description, Hystorie, and Customes of That Shire* (London, 1826).
5 David Hume, *The History of England, from the Invasion of Julius Caesar to the Revolution in 1688* (London, 1825), 7:103.
6 J.D. Alsop and W.M. Stevens, "William Lambarde and Elizabethan Polity," *Studies in Medieval and Renaissance History* 8 (1987): 240.
7 Wilfrid Prest, "William Lambarde, Elizabethan Law Reform, and Early Stuart Politics," *Journal of British Studies* 34 (1995): 465.
8 Lambarde, *Perambulation*, 1.
9 Lambarde, *Perambulation*, 170.
10 For a study of the way that Barton's story and her prophecies were disseminated, with a focus on her (immediate) posthumous legacy, see: Ethan H. Shagan, "Print, Orality and Communications in the Maid of Kent Affair," *Journal of Ecclesiastical History* 52, no. 1 (January 2001): 21–33.
11 Lambarde, *Perambulation*, 170.
12 Lambarde, *Perambulation*, 171.
13 Lambarde, *Perambulation*, 171.
14 Lambarde, *Perambulation*, 173.
15 Lambarde, *Perambulation*, 174.
16 Henry Jenkins, *The Remains of Thomas Cranmer, D.D., Archbishop of Canterbury* (Oxford, 1833), 1:79–84 (Letter 84).
17 Lambarde, *Perambulation*, 174–175.
18 Lambarde, *Perambulation*, 174–175.
19 Diane Watt, *Secretaries of God: Women Prophets in Late Medieval and Early Modern England* (Cambridge: D.S. Brewer, 1997), 69.
20 Diane Watt, "Reconstructing the Word: The Political Prophecies of Elizabeth Barton (1506–1534)," *Renaissance Quarterly* 50, no. 1 (1997): 148.
21 Lambarde, *Perambulation*, 175.
22 Lambarde, *Perambulation*, 175.
23 Wendy Love Anderson, *The Discernment of Spirits: Assessing Visions and Visionaries in the Late Middle Ages* (Tübingen: Mohr Siebeck, 2011), 18.
24 Anderson, *The Discernment of Spirits*, 164.
25 Lambarde, *Perambulation*, 175.
26 Louis Dupré, *The Enlightenment and the Intellectual Foundations of Modern Culture* (New Haven, CT: Yale University Press, 2008), xiii.
27 Lionel Laborie, *Enlightening Enthusiasm: Prophecy and Religious Experience in Early Eighteenth-Century England* (Oxford: Oxford University Press, 2015), 166.
28 Hume, *The History of England*, 7:103.
29 Hume, *The History of England*, 7:105.
30 "The Imposture of the Holy Maid of Kent," *The British Museum*, accessed 4 December 2017, http://britishmuseum.org/research/collection_online/collection_object_details.aspx?assetId=329704001&objectId=3035899&partId=1.
31 Tobias B. Hug, *Impostures in Early Modern England: Representations and Perceptions of Fraudulent Identities* (Oxford: Oxford University Press, 2013), 2.
32 Daniel Pickering Walker, *Unclean Spirits: Possession and Exorcism in France and England in the Late Sixteenth and Early Seventeenth Centuries* (Philadelphia: University of Pennsylvania Press, 1981), 67.

33 Nathan D. Mitchell, *The Mystery of the Rosary: Marian Devotion and the Reinvention of Catholicism* (New York: New York University Press, 2009), 154.
34 Anne Hollander, *Seeing Through Clothes* (Berkley: University of California Press, 1993), 199.
35 Margaret Miles, "The Virgin's One Bare Breast," in *The Female Body in Western Culture: Contemporary Perspectives*, ed. Susan Rubin Suleiman (Cambridge, MA: Harvard University Press, 1986), 202.
36 Hollander, *Seeing Through Clothes*, 199.
37 Matilde Battistini, *Symbols and Allegories in Art* (Los Angeles, CA: Getty Publications, 2005), 280.
38 Hollander, *Seeing Through Clothes*, 210.
39 Leonard Elliott Whatmore, "The Sermon against the Holy Maid of Kent and Her Adherents, Delivered at Paul's Cross, November the 23rd, 1533, and at Canterbury, December the 7th," *English Historical Review* 58, no. 232 (1943): 463–475.
40 Cecilia Hatt, ed., *English Works of John Fisher, Bishop of Rochester: Sermons and Other Writings 1520 to 1535* (Oxford: Oxford University Press, 2002), 46.
41 E.J. Devereux, "Elizabeth Barton and Tudor Censorship," *Bulletin of the John Rylands Library* 49, no. 1 (1966): 106.
42 Whatmore, *Sermon against the Holy Maid of Kent*, 467.
43 Lambarde, *Perambulation*, 171.
44 Whatmore, *Sermon against the Holy Maid of Kent*, 469.
45 Whatmore, *Sermon against the Holy Maid of Kent*, 469.
46 Whatmore, *Sermon against the Holy Maid of Kent*, 470.
47 William Parry-Jones, *The Trade in Lunacy: A Study of Private Madhouses in England in the Eighteenth and Nineteenth Centuries* (London: Routledge, 2013), 9.
48 Parry-Jones, *The Trade in Lunacy*, 64.
49 David Wright, "The Certification of Insanity in Nineteenth-Century England and Wales," *History of Psychiatry* 9, no. 35 (1998): 267.
50 Heidi Rimke and Alan Hunt, "From Sinners to Degenerates: The Medicalization of Morality in the 19th Century," *History of the Human Sciences* 15, no. 1 (2002): 61–62.
51 Horace Francis Lester, *Ben D'ymion, and Other Parodies* (London, 1887), 159.
52 Hume, *The History of England*, 7:103.
53 Lambarde, *Perambulation*, 173.
54 Hume, *The History of England*, 7:103
55 Cristina Mazzoni, *Saint Hysteria: Neurosis, Mysticism, and Gender in European Culture* (Ithaca, NY: Cornell University Press, 1996), 28.
56 Jean Martin Charcot and Paul Marie Louis Pierre Richer, *Les démoniaques dans l'art* (Paris, 1887).
57 Mazzoni, *Saint Hysteria*, 21.
58 Jean-Martin Charcot, "La foi qui guérit," *La Revue hebdomadaire* 7 (1892): 112–132.
59 William Portier and C.J.T. Talar, "The Mystical Element of the Modernist Crisis," in *Modernists and Mystics*, ed. C.J.T. Talar (Washington, DC: Catholic University of America Press, 2009), 10.
60 Charcot, "La foi qui guérit," 114.
61 For a critique on "interdisciplinary borrowing," see Constantina Papoulias and Felicity Callard, "Biology's Gift: Interrogating the Turn to Affect," *Body & Society* 16, no. 1 (2010): 29–56.

62 Charles Joseph Singer, *Studies in the History and Method of Science* (Oxford: Clarendon Press, 1917).
63 Katherine Foxhall, "Making Modern Migraine Medieval: Men of Science, Hildegard of Bingen and the Life of a Retrospective Diagnosis," *Medical History* 58, no. 3 (2014): 355.
64 Robert Henry Thouless, *The Lady Julian: A Psychological Study* (London: Society for Promoting Christian Knowledge, 1924).
65 David Knowles, *The English Mystics* (London: Burns, Oates & Washbourne, 1927).
66 Thomas Edward Bridgett, *Life of Blessed John Fisher: Bishop of Rochester, Cardinal of the Holy Roman Church and Martyr Under Henry VIII* (London, 1888), 234.
67 See: Ford Madox, *The Half Moon: A Romance of the Old World and the New* (New York: Doubleday, Page and Company, 1909); and Horace Francis Lester, *Ben D'Ymion, and Other Parodies* (London, 1887).
68 Hugh Chisholm, ed., *The Encyclopædia Britannica* (Cambridge: Cambridge University Press, 1911), 29:452.
69 Philip Walsingham Sergeant, *The Life of Anne Boleyn* (London: Hutchinson and Co., 1923), 201.
70 Sergeant, *The Life of Anne Boleyn*, 201.
71 Hilary Mantel, *Wolf Hall* (London: Fourth Estate, 2009).
72 K.C. Held, *Holding Court* (Fort Collins, CO: Entangled Publishing, 2016).
73 Bryan Appleyard, "A Novelist Goes on Working Where a Biographer Has to Stop," *Sunday Times*, 11 October 2009.
74 See Polito's detailed discussion of shifting views in the historiography of female agency in early modernity: Mary Polito, *Governmental Arts in Early Tudor England* (Farnham: Ashgate, 2005), esp. Chapter 4, "Elizabeth Barton, Tempered Tongues and Tudor Treason," 109–130.
75 Mantel, *Wolf Hall*, 325.
76 See: Watt, *Secretaries of God*; and Sharon L. Jansen, *Dangerous Talk and Strange Behavior: Women and Popular Resistance to the Reforms of Henry VIII* (New York: St Martin's Press, 1996).
77 Held, *Holding Court*.
78 Joni Richards Bodart, *They Suck, They Bite, They Eat, They Kill: The Psychological Meaning of Supernatural Monsters in Young Adult Fiction* (Lanham, MD: Scarecrow Press, 2012), xxiv.
79 Held, *Holding Court*, 9.

14 The Queen, the Bishop, the Virgin, and the Cross
Catholicism versus Protestantism in *Elizabeth*

Aidan Norrie[1]

The way that historical films depict conflict often says much more about the contemporary religious and political climate than it does about the period portrayed on the screen. Shekhar Kapur's first film about Elizabeth I of England—*Elizabeth* (1998)—clearly reflects, and adapts, contemporary religious tensions. While a film about Elizabethan England can hardly avoid engaging with religious politics, it is clear that Kapur took contemporary religious debates, and re-purposed them for his films. This re-purposing is visible in the contrasting depictions of Catholics and Protestants: the Catholics are presented as evil and scheming—a metaphor, perhaps, for modern religious fundamentalism; whereas the Protestants, embodied by Elizabeth, are portrayed as being moderate and rational—people who wish to rise above religious divides, and rule for the common good. By focusing on the religious conflict that pervades *Elizabeth*, this chapter argues that the early-modernism Kapur is engaging in is both a product of decades of Elizabethan scholarship—much of it overtly Whiggish and triumphantly Protestant—and a retrospective application of modern, Western values in a setting where they do not apply. As this chapter demonstrates, the depiction of Elizabeth, and indeed Elizabethan England, on the silver screen acts as "a barometer that measures our own value and place in the world."[2]

I am by no means the first person to comment on the barely concealed religious undertone of Kapur's film. Thomas Betteridge did not shy away from observing that *Elizabeth*—relatively unashamedly—gives a "cinematic expression to a Protestant view of the past."[3] Likewise, Susanne Wofford highlights how "the film presents scenarios that endorse not only the Protestant interpretation of Tudor History, but [also] a Protestant mythology of Elizabeth."[4] Wofford also observes that the film engages in a "Protestant and nationalistic understanding of the meaning and importance of Elizabeth's reign."[5] Finally, Andrew Higson notes that with *Elizabeth*, Kapur aimed to "dramatise the emergence of England ... as a modern powerful and Protestant nation."[6] These three comments underpin the importance of analysing the early-modernism in *Elizabeth* because, as Defne Ersin Tutan eloquently argues, "all historical representations are radically adaptive, and ... the ways in which these alternative representations are conceived and perceived tell us more about the present than about the past they refer to."[7]

The early-modernism Kapur is engaging in is overt. In an interview shortly after the film's release, Kapur explained, "I've made a contemporary film out of a 16th-century life. History is interpretation. And this is ours."[8] In responding to Kapur's vision, Jack Mathews declared, "Period movies inevitably reflect more on the period in which they're made than on the period of their subject, and rarely has that fact been more evident, or more distracting, than it is with ... *Elizabeth*."[9] Such early-modernism, then, seeks to adapt the past and demonstrate its applicability in the present. The intersection between early-modernism and adaptation is therefore central to *Elizabeth*. As Tutan argues, "It is through the present that the past and the future remain in constant dialogue, demonstrating the inescapably contemporaneous character of history."[10] Thus, this chapter focuses on the depiction of Protestantism and Roman Catholicism in *Elizabeth* in order to ascertain what Kapur is doing in re-purposing the past for his own purposes or, in other words, to analyse the early-modernism he is engaging in.

Kapur's early-modernism leads me to argue the following points. First, that Kapur had a very specific image in mind in depicting the two queens: Mary's unflattering portrayal means that she stands proxy for all Catholics; and likewise, Elizabeth's overly flattering depiction exemplifies all of the rational and peaceable Protestants. Second, two specific scenes—the burning of three Protestant martyrs at the opening of *Elizabeth*, and the film's depiction of the passing of the *Act of Uniformity* (1558)—demonstrate not only that Kapur was re-purposing the past to comment on contemporary religious conflict, but also that in imposing modern understandings of religion, and indeed of the past, Kapur inconsistently twists the historical reality to ensure that audiences (reductively) believe that the Protestant Elizabeth is 'good,' and that the Catholic Mary is 'bad.' I conclude the chapter by discussing some of the criticisms of anti-Catholicism directed at the film, which, when combined with Kapur's own response to the criticisms, demonstrate that the early-modernism Kapur is engaging in serves mainly to perpetuate his own, postcolonial view of history, and is informed by his desire to comment on contemporary religious sectarianism, particularly in Northern Ireland during The Troubles.

This chapter focuses only on *Elizabeth*, primarily because the film has a clear religio-political context that it is drawing on, as confirmed by Kapur himself. Certainly, religious conflict plays a key part in Kapur's sequel to *Elizabeth*, *Elizabeth: The Golden Age* (2007), as well as in *Mary, Queen of Scots* (1971, dir. Charles Jarrott). Similarly, the two miniseries *Elizabeth R* (1971, dir. Claude Whatham) and *The Virgin Queen* (2005, dir. Coky Giedroyc) devote considerable time to the issue of Elizabeth's religion under Mary, and the move to a Protestant Church of England under Elizabeth. I am, however, most interested in the continued use of Elizabeth and Elizabethan England as a means to comment on contemporary issues, and exploring the context of *Elizabeth* allows a much stronger analysis to be made.

Background

Elizabeth premiered at the Venice Film Festival on 8 September 1998. Much of the film's writing and principal photography took place against the backdrop of The Troubles—a very contemporary parallel of Kapur's subject matter. Indeed, the Good Friday Agreement was signed on 10 April 1998, and both Ireland and Northern Ireland held referenda on 22 May 1998 to approve the agreements.[11] Likewise, I do not think it a coincidence that the film was: directed by an Indian man known for him staunch anti-colonialist campaigns—which has led to accusations of him being "anti-British" in English tabloids; edited by the Australian Jill Bilcock—whose most famous works are arguably Baz Lurhmann's *Romeo + Juliet* (1996) and *Moulin Rouge!* (2001); and starred two Australians—Geoffrey Rush as Sir Francis Walsingham and Cate Blanchett as Elizabeth—the first time an English film featured a non-English actor portraying Elizabeth. These two points—that the film was produced against the background of The Troubles, and that the film's technical team and cast were drawn from outside 'normal' English talent—highlight the importance of reading *Elizabeth* not as a 'standard' historical film. Rather than being focused on elaborate costuming and imagined historical scheming, the film engages in early-modernism to offer a commentary on Britain's religious sectarianism. It demonstrates the increasing intolerance of, and discrimination towards, other religions around the world, as well as the impact of colonialism around the world—colonialism that had much of its roots in, and took its legitimisation from, religion.

Depicting the Queens

The writers of *Elizabeth*—primarily Kapur and Michael Hirst, who is perhaps best known as the creator of the Showtime television series *The Tudors* (2007–2010)—were very obvious in what picture of the two queens they wanted to portray, and the way that religion was used as the reason for their conflict. Kapur made it clear that he wished to convey to his audience that the queens, while being half-sisters, were polar opposites, and the religious conflict they both inflicted upon England is the epitome of this opposition.

The scenes that feature Mary are dark and sinister. In her first on-screen appearance, Mary (Kathy Burke) wears black, as do the people around her (Figure 14.1). To ensure that this point cannot be missed, all

Figure 14.1 The audience's first glimpse of Mary I (Kathy Burke) in *Elizabeth*. Image courtesy of PolyGram and Working Title Films.

the scenes are filmed in Gothic-style rooms—architecture that predates Mary's reign by several centuries.[12] This scene is all the more interesting, as it is where Mary's first pregnancy is announced to her courtiers. Viewers are aware, however, that Mary cannot be pregnant. An angry Duke of Norfolk (Christopher Eccleston) thunders through the palace, angry that the bells are ringing to announce Mary's pregnancy.[13] However, he meets with one of Mary's maids in a darkened side chamber, demanding to know, "Is it true?" The maid responds first by saying, "there are symptoms. She has ceased to bleed, her breasts have produced some milk, and her stomach is swollen." Norfolk does not buy it, and asks again more forcefully, "Is it true?" The reluctant maid then admits that Mary's husband, Philip II of Spain, "has not shared her bed for many months. He has a repugnance for it."[14] It is thus impossible that Mary is pregnant—at least by Philip, anyway. Norfolk then walks to greet the king and queen, who appear to be about to hold a Privy Council meeting in a bedchamber. Mary clutches her stomach as he approaches and greets him by saying, "Norfolk." Norfolk then says, "Your Majesties, this is most wondrous news," to which Mary replies, "Indeed. We do thank God for this, our most happy condition." She takes her husband's hand as she replies, but Philip (George Yiasoumi) tries to pull away and looks visibly uncomfortable—possibly even disgusted.[15] Norfolk then turns and addresses Philip, "We must also thank His Majesty for this blessed event, which is nothing short of a miracle." Philip squirms uneasily, and the Spanish Ambassador looks away awkwardly. They all know it is not true. The historical reality of Mary's two phantom pregnancies is well known, but it is clear this was not what Kapur and Hirst were aiming to depict.[16] Everyone else knows Mary cannot be pregnant, but Mary is convinced that she is, and the religious significance of a 'Mary' immaculately conceiving is unlikely to have been lost on the film's audience. Mary's faith is the reason she is so convinced—against all sense—that she is pregnant, which serves to equate Catholicism with irrationality.

The scene also plays with the ideas of pregnancy, gender, and motherhood. While I am confident that Kapur was aiming to depict Mary as the stereotypically 'hysterical' woman known to both film history and the historiography,[17] Philip's reaction to Mary's attempt to take his hand invites us to consider a more sixteenth-century view of Mary's "most happy condition." Mary's phantom pregnancies were fairly widely known across all levels of society;[18] various stories circulated when no royal child was announced that she had delivered a "shapeless mass," or, more outrageously, that the foetus "was a lapdog or a marmot."[19] Monstrous births—where a child was born with what today would be considered congenital anomalies—were a common anxiety around childbirth: especially so when the mother was a queen.[20] The reason I discuss this is that Burke's depiction of Mary—a grotesque woman who repels her husband—combined with the ominous way that Mary's reign is depicted, encourages viewers to pass judgement on Mary, her gender, and her authority. As Jo Eldridge Carney observes, "it was commonly believed that the monstrous birth was not merely an unfortunate natural occurrence, but a revelation of divine punishment for the mother's sins."[21] It thus seems that Kapur is insinuating that Mary's sins—both against the Protestants, and against England—mean her pregnancy is doomed from its very announcement.

After this rather awkward exchange between Norfolk and the monarchs, the conversation then moves on to discuss the Wyatt Rebellion, and the threat that Elizabeth is to Mary by being a Protestant rallying point. There is, however, something wholly unsettling about the scene: Mary is convinced that she is pregnant and that she soon will bring new life into the world, but she then goes on to confirm that the leaders of the Rebellion have been executed, and the scene ends with her instructing Norfolk to find proof of Elizabeth's treachery against her, implicitly with the goal of having her executed. These various interactions, exchanges, and outbursts in Mary's first on-screen appearance in *Elizabeth* all serve to leave the audience with the implicit impression that Mary has brought a darkness over England, and that her reign will only bring about despair.

The Queen, the Bishop, the Virgin, and the Cross 231

These scenes depicting Mary are in stark contrast to those of Elizabeth. They are all light and bright. In fact, the film employs three distinct white washout transitions for Elizabeth, but nothing similar for Mary.[22] Even the people around Elizabeth wear colourful clothing. Elizabeth's first on-screen appearance has her outdoors, in the afternoon sunshine, dancing, surrounded by a group of colourfully dressed, pretty, and very giggly, young ladies-in-waiting (Figure 14.2). To cap off the scene, an object of sexual desire in the form of Robert Dudley (Joseph Fiennes) appears. He is riding his horse, and has evidently just taken one of Elizabeth's giggling ladies for a ride. He dismounts his horse and moves—with unmistakable attraction in his eyes—towards Elizabeth. Elizabeth, for her part, pointedly ignores Dudley and continues to pay concerted attention to her dance routine. As he moves closer, Dudley asks Elizabeth, "May I join you, my lady?" The sexual tension is palpable. Elizabeth pointedly carries out a few more steps of her dance before replying, "If it please you, Sir." The mutual flirtation is clear, and its unfulfilled nature means it will certainly re-appear later in the film.

The contrast between the two queens could not be greater. Elizabeth is light and life, is healthy and youthful, and brings hope for the future; Mary is darkness and death, is haggard and overweight, and allows her judgement to be impaired by her irrational and dogged adherence to her faith.[23] The historical accuracy of these polarising depictions is of course questionable, at best, but it is indicative of the stereotypes that exist in films of Elizabethan England. While the unflattering depiction of Mary is often commented on, the ridiculous depiction of Elizabeth is often overlooked and is worth considering.[24] While Mary looks

Figure 14.2 The first appearance of Elizabeth I (Cate Blanchett) in *Elizabeth*. Image courtesy of PolyGram and Working Title Films.

menacing and malign, she at least looks the part of a ruler. Elizabeth, on the other hand, is outdoors, dancing, giggling, and flirting: these are hardly admirable characteristics for a queen. The ridiculous depiction of the two queens allows Kapur to tie religion and personality. Elizabeth's immaturity allows her to experience 'growth' as the film continues. This growth, however, is tied to religion: virtually everything Elizabeth does in *Elizabeth* comes back to, or is entwined with, religion. She is forced to grow up as a ruler when arguing for the passing of the *Act of Uniformity*, and the Ridolfi Plot, which attempted to replace Elizabeth with a Catholic monarch, is what causes her to put aside her flirtations and focus on being married to England. Elizabeth is thus allowed to grow and make mistakes, whereas Mary, who is only seventeen years older than Elizabeth, is lambasted for her mistakes and held up to a different standard. Kapur has meddled with the historical timeline in the film to enhance his early-modernism, as the Wyatt Rebellion, which was actually intended to dissuade Mary from marrying Philip II of Spain, is depicted as being an attempt to overthrow Mary and Philip because of their Catholicism, and place the Protestant Elizabeth on the throne.[25] The role religion plays in deciding the standard by which people are judged is thus made painfully clear.

"Let them burn for all eternity in the flames of hell"

The stark contrast between the Catholic Mary and the Protestant Elizabeth is made abundantly clear in *Elizabeth*'s opening scene, in which three Protestant heretics are burned at the stake. This opening dispels any doubts as to the point Kapur wanted to make about religion in his film. However, before the action of the film begins, viewers are faced with opening titles intended to set the scene. These titles are not part of a 'neutral' foreword; instead, "in combinations of red and black, shadowed crosses and superimposed portraits of the historical players float across the screen, titles fade in and out, all while ominous choral music resonates."[26] The titles are characterised by short sentences in jarring, capitalised text. Reading them, combined with the ominous music—terrifying Latin chanting that increases in volume, accompanied by penetrating drumming—and intense font and colours, almost immediately forces the viewers to take the side of Elizabeth:

> England 1554. Henry VIII is dead. The country is divided. Catholic against Protestant. Henry's eldest daughter Mary, a fervent Catholic, is Queen. She is childless. The Catholics' greatest fear is the succession of Mary's Protestant half-sister. Elizabeth.

In addition to completely ignoring the reign of Edward VI (Mary and Elizabeth's half-brother), and choosing to ignore the fact that Mary ascended the throne in July 1553—perhaps because the Heresy Laws that precipitated the burnings were only enacted in November 1554, with the first burnings being carried out in February 1555—these titles conjure up images that only would have been found in Bishop Gardiner's worst nightmares.[27] While the accession of the 36-year-old (and unmarried) Mary was a cause for great concern to those Catholics who wished to see the succession settled by the birth of a Catholic child, Elizabeth was by no means a hated figure—indeed, she rode with Mary at her entry into London. By leaving his viewers in no doubt as to his feelings on the matter, Kapur has highlighted two points. First, it is obvious that the state of religion in Marian and Elizabethan England is an early-modernism, designed to comment on the sectarian violence perpetuated by the Protestants and the Catholics in The Troubles. Indeed, Kapur's adaptation seems to be making the issue essentially all about religion, even though The Troubles was primarily fought between unionist and nationalist groups who had different views concerning Northern Ireland's constitutional relationship with the United Kingdom and the Republic of Ireland.[28] Second, by placing the succession issue front and centre, Kapur was both drastically exaggerating the issue of Mary's childlessness—a 36-year-old royal woman in sixteenth-century England could easily expect to live to her late fifties and beyond—and portraying Elizabeth as some kind of Machiavellian mastermind, ready to take the throne at a moment's notice. The primary purpose of these titles was thus to frame the succession issue as a religious issue, which highlights Kapur's focus on religious conflict as a way to discuss contemporary issues.

These titles then fade out to show a piece of parchment, upon which sits an oozing blob of blood-red wax. A royal seal is stamped into the wax, and it is clear that the seal is being affixed to an execution warrant. Three people, a woman and two men—presumably those affected by the execution warrant—then appear on screen. The camera focuses on the woman, who is clad only in a dirty, white shift-dress. She is having her head brutally shaved with a knife—the guard performing the shaving takes chunks of her scalp off with the clumps of hair, and soon the bowl of water used to wash off the knife is red with blood. One of the men has already been shaved, and the other is shaved alongside the woman. The three pray continually—only briefly stopping to sob in pain. The only hint that the three condemned are Protestants comes from their English prayers.

The film cuts to the three being herded into a yard, where numerous soldiers hold back a loud and rowdy crowd. We watch as a black-clad man carries a gold crucifix onto the pyre. Then, Stephen Gardiner, Bishop of Winchester (Terence Rigby), intones, "By order of their gracious majesties, Queen Mary and King Philip, we are come to witness the burning of these Protestant heretics, who have denied the authority of the one true Catholic church, and of His Holiness the Pope. Let them burn for all eternity in the flames of hell." There can be no doubt now that the three are Protestants, and Mary's direct role in the burnings is made clear. It is interesting that none of the three are given the chance to recant, which was often part of the proceedings.

The three Protestants continue praying, but as the flames are lit, the woman's prayers become increasingly high-pitched and shrill. The smoke begins rising, and the three Protestants begin choking. A man in the crowd then cries out, "God bless you, Master Ridley." This means that one of the heretics is Nicholas Ridley, the former Bishop of London, and one of King Edward VI's most prominent Protestant reformers. Bishop Ridley was executed with Hugh Latimer, the former Bishop of Worcester, in 1555.[29] Thus, it is safe to assume that he is the other male heretic. The woman in the group, however, is fictitious: she is simply present for added dramatic effect. As Bethany Latham observes of the scene, "a ruler who would burn a woman alive is obviously a monster."[30] The scene ends with guards on horses chasing away the assembled crowd because of their attempts to interfere with the pyre, which leaves no doubt in the audience's mind that this monstrous act is disastrous for society and is wholly caused by religious conflict (see Figure 14.3).

It is also significant to note that this is the only burning at the stake in the film. By beginning the film in this way, the viewers gravitate towards Elizabeth, who throughout the course of the film shows tolerance and mercy to religious victims. This is not reflective of the historical reality. While Mary certainly burnt more heretics than any other English monarch, several non-conformists were executed in this way during Elizabeth's reign, including the Unitarian Matthew Hamont, and the Arianist Francis Kett.[31] This is, of course, to say nothing of the more than 180 Catholics who were executed at Elizabeth's order—including those killed by being hung, drawn, and quartered.[32]

This burning scene also includes what some have regarded as the film's most sickening moment. As the heretics burn, they cry out for more wood to be thrown on the fire because "it burns too slowly." By throwing more wood on the fire, the crowds are actually showing mercy to the heretics: but it is a sick perversion of mercy. As the monarch was considered the fountain of clemency, it is clear that Mary has failed her solemn duty, because the crowd had to intervene on the heretics' behalf.[33] This moment, while painting Mary and the Marian regime in a terrible light, may refer to Ridley's actual execution. While the flames quickly smothered Latimer, Ridley burned very slowly, and was in such great pain that his brother-in-law threw more wood onto the fire in an attempt to hasten Ridley's death (although the extra wood only caused his lower parts to burn more fiercely).[34]

Thus, in opening the film with this scene, Kapur has perpetuated a number of stereotypes that exist in films of Elizabeth. The violence and conflict caused by religion cannot be ignored. The crowd gathered to watch the execution are clearly Protestants, or at least Protestant-sympathisers: not only do they watch in morose fascination as the Protestants burn, the amount of wood thrown on the fire so quickly and immediately after Ridley's pleas invites the thought that the crowd came prepared to help

Figure 14.3 The burning at the stake *Elizabeth* opens with. From top to bottom: the Protestants are led into the yard; the Catholic bishops look on without emotion; the guards have to hold the crowd back. Images courtesy of PolyGram and Working Title Films.

the martyrs, which is a deeply unsettling thought. Likewise, while the crowd has to be chased away by mounted soldiers, the three Catholic clerics—Gardiner and two other unidentified men—watch on from a small raised platform, and they betray no sign of emotion at the request for more wood, or when the crowd has to be dispersed.

The stark contrast between the Roman Catholics, as exemplified by Mary, and the Protestants, as embodied in Elizabeth, is thus central to the film's narrative. This oversimplified, black and white, 'good guys versus bad guys' motif is of course reductive and unhelpful, considering one has only to contemplate the number of people executed for their faith under successive Tudor and Stuart monarchs. Kapur is thus trying to simplify the past to justify his engagement with early-modernism, and as a comment on modern religious conflict. These attitudes are foisted on the audience before either Mary or Elizabeth even appears on screen. As William Robison has observed, this scene positions viewers to see Mary as a violent, intolerant, religious fanatic, whereas "the film presents Elizabeth as the defender of very modern sounding concepts of liberty and toleration."[35]

"I have no desire to make windows into men's souls"

The contrast and conflict between Catholics and Protestants is further expanded on in the film's depiction of the passing of the *Act of Uniformity*, which was one of Elizabeth's first acts as Queen. The law re-established the Church of England as a Protestant church, with Elizabeth as its Supreme Governor. It also required all church services to be conducted using the English Book of Common Prayer, and mandated that all Bible readings be delivered in English.[36] The *Act of Uniformity*'s partner piece of legislation, the *Act of Supremacy* (1558), required all English clergy to swear the Oath of Supremacy: any clergy who did not swear this oath were removed from their position.[37] Despite being distinct pieces of legislation, the film conflates the debates of the *Act of Uniformity* and the *Act of Supremacy* into the same scene.

Viewers are quickly made aware of the importance of the laws. The first hint comes from the Duke of Norfolk. While he is getting dressed to sit in the House, his mistress—the same maid who told him about Mary's pregnancy symptoms—whines, "must you leave?" to which Norfolk replies, "I would not miss this for the world. Today I shall watch the fall of that heretic girl." Norfolk, entirely clad in black, alerts the viewers both to the severity of what he is discussing, and to the fact that the conflict is, once again, about religion. The scene then cuts to Elizabeth rehearsing her speech. She tries various rhetorical approaches—"I am your Queen, and like my father I mean to rule"; "There is one God. We have a common… There is one God"; and, finally, "My Lords, your votes are nothing without my consent"—before the scene fades to her walking into the House.

The Queen, the Bishop, the Virgin, and the Cross 237

The Lords are loud, shouting over the top of each other. Elizabeth struggles to make herself heard, and she stumbles over her words:

> If there is no uniformity of religious belief here, then there can only be fragmentation, disputes, and quarrels. Surely, my Lords, it is better to have a single Church of England. A single Church of England! With a common prayer book. And... and a... And... a common purpose. I ask you to pass this Act of Uniformity. Not... not for myself, but for my people, who are my only care.

During the response to the Queen's speech, the viewers are taken to the dark chambers below the House, where a group of bishops, including Gardiner, are locked up. A bishop bangs on the door, demanding it be opened. Gardiner then looms out of the shadows: "This is Walsingham's doing. It is the devil's work. It will not serve her in any case. The Bishops will pass no measure which severs us from Rome." The camera returns to the debate in the chamber, where Elizabeth brings everything together, highlighting her role as some kind of early modern peace envoy: "Each of you must vote according to your conscience. But remember this. In your hands, upon this moment, lies the future happiness of my people, and the peace of this realm. Let that be upon your conscience also."

William Cecil, later Lord Burghley (Richard Attenborough), then announces that the House will divide to vote. We do not get to see the outcome of the vote; instead, we see Walsingham come to release the imprisoned bishops. Gardiner is livid: "I am sure this infernal work has not saved your bastard Queen." Walsingham, who is one of the few Protestants in *Elizabeth* to be morally ambiguous, replies with barely concealed glee: "Her Majesty has won the argument." Gardiner demands to know the count. "By five, Your Grace. Five," replies Walsingham, staring down at the seven bishops he is about to release. As Walsingham walks away, Gardiner unleashes: "You will be damned for this! And I pray God your wretched soul will burn in hell!" Somehow, even though Walsingham is in the wrong for (illegally) locking up the bishops, the scene ends with the viewers entirely on the side of Elizabeth and the Protestants.

What is perhaps most interesting about this scene is that in terms of historical accuracy, the film is actually less dramatic than the real event. The film simplifies the debate by pitting the Catholics against the law, and the Protestants for it. However, Elizabeth and Cecil had trouble convincing some of the radical Protestants, who thought that the law was not prescriptive enough, to support the Bill. Also, Walsingham announces to the imprisoned bishops that the law passed with a majority of five votes. In reality, the Act only passed the House of Lords by three votes—all bishops present voted against it, as well as seven other nobles—and this majority had only been secured by excluding two bishops and an abbot from voting.[38] Thus, the drama of this adaptation does not come from the closeness with which the Act passed, but from Walsingham imprisoning a fairly large number of bishops in a cell under Westminster. Is religious uniformity a worthy goal if God's anointed bishops have to be locked in a cellar under parliament to secure its passage?

In opposing the Bill, one of the bishops—probably the Archbishop of York, Nicholas Heath, whose surviving speech against the Bill uses similar wording—claims that the law will force Roman Catholics to relinquish allegiance to the Pope.[39] This was legally true—the *Act of Supremacy* required any person taking public or church office in England to swear allegiance to the monarch as Supreme Governor of the Church of England.[40] All but one of the bishops lost their sees for not swearing the Oath.[41] However, in response to the archbishop's claim, Elizabeth replies, rather seductively, "How can I force you, Your Grace? I am a woman." There are two key points to take from this. First, it accurately highlights Elizabeth's (original) goal in enacting the *Act of Uniformity*—as long as her people outwardly conformed to the state religion, she would leave them in peace to privately act on their religious conscience.[42] One of the bishops describes this as heresy, to which Elizabeth counters with, "No, Your Grace, it is common sense, which is a most English virtue." The contrast between the religion of Mary and the religion of Elizabeth could not be greater. While Mary burned people at the stake, Elizabeth simply wishes for the "peace of this realm." This is of course historical manipulation: the increasing Catholic threat caused Elizabeth and her supporters to introduce increasingly punitive punishments against non-conformists (radical Protestant and Catholic alike). These included the *Treasons Act* (1571), which declared anyone who would "affirm, that the Queen ought not to enjoy the crown, but some other person [should]; or to publish, that the Queen is a heretic, schismatic, tyrant, infidel or usurper of the crown" guilty of high treason, and the 1585 *Act against Jesuits, seminary priests, and other such disobedient persons*, which expelled any Jesuit and Catholic clergy from England (giving them 40 days to leave the country), and made it a capital crime for any Catholic ministers to set foot on English soil or for any English subject to harbour a Catholic minister.[43] Second, this response from the archbishop serves to emphasise the gender issues that require grappling with when Elizabeth is depicted on film. While a discussion of the cinematic depictions of Elizabeth's gender is beyond the scope of this chapter, it is interesting, and indeed important, to think about the role of religion in perpetuating gender inequality, and the way that Kapur might be making a pointed reference to the absence of women in positions of authority in the Catholic Church.[44]

Films, Religion, and the Media

Various studies of *Elizabeth* have noted the negative way that Catholics are depicted. This view appears more overtly in the critical responses to the films. In their review of *Elizabeth*, the Catholic League for Religious and Civil Rights accused the filmmakers of anti-Catholicism, stating that the film gives the "impression that the religious strife was all the doing of the Catholic Church."[45] The League also emphasised the concurring points made in other reviews. The reviewer in *The New York Times* considered the film "resolutely anti-Catholic," complete with a "scheming pope."[46] Likewise, Mary Kunz, in her review in the *Buffalo News*, pointed out that "every single Catholic in the film is dark, cruel and devious" and that the "Anglicans [sic], on the other hand, are rational and humorous, glowing with faith and common sense."[47] The validity of these various observations is of course debateable, but is extraneous to my point. Instead, these reviews reinforce how *Elizabeth* is a product of a long history of depicting the last Tudor monarch on film. Films of Elizabeth all seem to perpetuate a very Whiggish view of Elizabeth's reign: that the reign of the Catholic Mary had plunged England into darkness—both spiritually and economically—and that the accession of the young, Protestant Elizabeth restored England to its former glory, and her reign heralded in a new era of peace and prosperity.[48] This image has been dismissed in the recent and more revisionist historiography;[49] but the hold this view has in the popular imagination is such that films cannot help but perpetuate it—it is a familiar (anachronistic) trope that audiences have come to expect, much like Elizabeth's elaborate costumes, Sir Walter Raleigh's 'swashbucklingness,' or Shakespeare's close personal acquaintance with the Queen.

As the various scenes analysed here demonstrate, Kapur was deliberately engaging in early-modernism to convey his point. In addition to the interview already discussed—where he claimed to have "made a contemporary film out of a 16th-century life"—Kapur also spoke about his focus in making the film: "The central focus in *Elizabeth* was Power. The … conflict was between Elizabeth and her Catholic detractors, in their struggle for Power."[50] In dramatising the conflict between the Protestant Elizabeth and her Catholic opponents, Kapur chose to put the focus on Elizabeth's "struggle." Elizabeth "struggled" for a variety of reasons—not least of which was her gender—but Kapur engaged in early-modernism by focusing on one particular element, and adapted it as a commentary on the present.

This commentary, as Andrew Higson points out, was no accident: it was precisely what the producers were intending to engage in. Indeed, the film's marketing material highlighted how *Elizabeth* was "a 'modern' film about a historical character" that was "less concerned with establishing historical accuracy in the unfolding of the narrative than with imaginatively interpreting that history for contemporary audiences."[51] This marketing material, combined with the two interviews discussed, demonstrates that Kapur was indeed re-purposing the past to tell a 'relevant' story, and that he was engaging in early-modernism by perpetuating a highly idealised version of Elizabeth.

Elizabeth's overt early-modernism—which combines the contemporary backdrop of The Troubles with a visibly Protestant view of the reign of Elizabeth I—underscores the way that the past is adapted for the present. As previously noted, the *Act of Uniformity* had introduced a kind of religious tolerance into England, as long as one outwardly conformed to the Church of England. However, as Elizabeth's reign progressed, England began to crack down on Catholics and non-conformists with increasing severity.[52] Modern concepts, such as religious liberty and toleration, should not—and cannot—be retroactively imposed on sixteenth-century Europe, which seems to be what Kapur was attempting to do.[53]

Kapur's Early-Modernism

Kapur's comments concerning the film's engagement in early-modernism sum up rather well the point I am making here. While seemingly about depicting and adapting the past, historical films are intrinsically about commenting on the present. Using the past to comment on the events of the present is, on the one hand, a rather safe option. There is no need to specifically point out what it is you are commenting on: The Troubles, while certainly important contextually, were not the film's *raison d'être*. Indeed, the only reference to Ireland in the whole film is at Elizabeth's coronation, when the bishop crowns her "Queen of England, Ireland, and France." Film tropes—especially those based on the years of intertextuality and intervisuality concerning the depiction of the reign of Elizabeth I—are ubiquitous enough that audiences can draw connections between the content and what is being commented on. But, on the other hand, using the past in this way can have a dangerous impact on the continued (usually negative) stereotyping of different groups, cultures, religions, and customs. Reinforcing the difference between Catholics and Protestants, as Kapur does, will not help to heal past wounds or encourage toleration. This is the great import of studying these cinematic adaptations of the past:

> while watching a historical film, … we cannot avoid the sense of personal engagement, not only looking at the ways in which the author or authors re/construct historical material, but also making comparisons between the representation and our own experiences.[54]

Krista Kesselring's keen observation in her discussion of the depiction of violence in the Showtime television series *The Tudors* (which was

The Queen, the Bishop, the Virgin, and the Cross 241

written by *Elizabeth*'s co-writer, Michael Hirst) also has great relevance here. If the engagement in early-modernism through adapted and repurposed depictions of

> crime, punishment, and violence prompt reflection on such issues today, then perhaps a bit of ahistoricism is not all a bad thing ... [these] depictions of violence, crime, and punishment might well prompt us to rethink the histories we write, and those which we create.[55]

Demonstrating that films perpetuate religious-based violence and conflict allows us to point out when the past is being used to perpetuate current antagonism—in whatever form it takes—and to ask ourselves what we are learning from these past mistakes, and what these continued adaptations say about our shared values and beliefs.

Notes

1 I thank Lawrence Clarkson, Marina Gerzic, Robert Norrie, and Jo Oranje for their assistance in the writing of this chapter.
2 Elizabeth A. Ford and Deborah C. Mitchell, *Royal Portraits in Hollywood: Filming the Lives of Queens* (Lexington: The University Press of Kentucky, 2009), 294.
3 Thomas Betteridge, "A Queen for All Seasons: Elizabeth I on Film," in *The Myth of Elizabeth*, ed. Susan Doran and Thomas S. Freeman (New York: Palgrave Macmillan, 2003), 256.
4 Susanne L. Wofford, "'Is There Any Harme in That?': Foxe, Heywood, and Shekhar Kapur's *Elizabeth*," in *Resurrecting Elizabeth I in Seventeenth-Century England*, ed. Elizabeth H. Hageman and Katherine Conway (Madison, WI: Farleigh Dickinson University Press, 2007), 261.
5 Wofford, "'Is There Any Harme in That?,'" 261.
6 Andrew Higson, *Film England: Culturally English Filmmaking since the 1990s* (London: I.B. Tauris, 2011), 240.
7 Defne Ersin Tutan, "Adaptation and History," in *The Oxford Handbook of Adaptation Studies*, ed. Thomas Leitch (Oxford: Oxford University Press, 2017), 577.
8 Shekhar Kapur, quoted in Andrew Higson, *English Heritage, English Cinema: Costume Drama Since 1980* (Oxford: Oxford University Press, 2003), 244.
9 Jack Mathews, "A Prideful Queen Cuts to the Chaste," *Newsday Online*, quoted in Higson, *English Heritage, English Cinema*, 245–246.
10 Tutan, "Adaptation and History," 577.
11 Paul Arthur, "The Long War and Its Aftermath, 1969–2007," in *The Oxford Handbook of Modern Irish History*, ed. Alvin Jackson (Oxford: Oxford University Press, 2014), 755.
12 Bethany Latham, *Elizabeth I in Film and Television: A Study of the Major Portrayals* (Jefferson, NC: McFarland & Company, 2011), 150.
13 For more on bell-ringing's place in commemorating the various life stages—particularly the lives of royals—see: Christopher Marsh, *Music and Society in Early Modern England* (Cambridge: Cambridge University Press, 2010), esp. 454; and Dolly MacKinnon, "'The Ceremony of Tolling the Bell at the Time of Death': Bell-ringing and Mourning in England c.1500–c.1700," in

    Music and Mourning, ed. Jane W. Davidson and Sandra Garrido (London: Routledge, 2016), 31–39.
14. All transcriptions from the film are my own. *Elizabeth*, dir. Shekhar Kapur (Universal Studios, 1998).
15. Latham, *Elizabeth I in Film and Television*, 150.
16. Judith M. Richards, *Mary Tudor* (London: Routledge, 2008), 176–178.
17. See, for example: Thomas S. Freeman, "Inventing Bloody Mary: Perceptions of Mary Tudor from the Restoration to the Twentieth Century," in *Mary Tudor: Old and New Perspectives*, ed. Susan Doran and Thomas S. Freeman (New York: Palgrave Macmillan, 2011), 78–100.
18. For a discussion of Mary's false pregnancies within the early modern English context, see: Carole Levin, "Pregnancy, False Pregnancy, and Questionable Heirs: Mary I and Her Echoes," in *The Birth of a Queen: Essays on the Quincentenary of Mary I*, ed. Sarah Duncan and Valerie Schutte (New York: Palgrave Macmillan, 2016), 179–193.
19. Jo Eldridge Carney, *Fairy Tale Queens: Representations of Early Modern Queenship* (New York: Palgrave Macmillan, 2012), 39.
20. For more on monstrous birth in the early modern period, see: Julie Crawford, *Marvelous Protestantism: Monstrous Births in Post-Reformation England* (Baltimore, MD: The Johns Hopkins University Press, 2005); and Ross Hagen, "A Warning to England: Monstrous Births, Teratology and Feminine Power in Elizabethan Broadside Ballads," *Horror Studies* 4, no. 1 (2013): 21–41.
21. Carney, *Fairy Tale Queens*, 40.
22. Latham, *Elizabeth I in Film and Television*, 150.
23. Latham, *Elizabeth I in Film and Television*, 150.
24. See, for example: Christopher Haigh, "Kapur's *Elizabeth*," in *Tudors and Stuarts on Film: Historical Perspectives*, ed. Susan Doran and Thomas S. Freeman (New York: Palgrave Macmillan, 2009), esp. 132–134.
25. Ford and Mitchell, *Royal Portraits in Hollywood*, 280.
26. Latham, *Elizabeth I in Film and Television*, 149.
27. Richards, *Mary Tudor*, 194.
28. Claire Mitchell, *Religion, Identity, and Politics in Northern Ireland: Boundaries of Belonging and Belief* (Aldershot: Ashgate, 2006), 1–5.
29. Betteridge, "A Queen for All Seasons," 255.
30. Latham, *Elizabeth I in Film and Television*, 149.
31. Dewey D. Wallace, "From Eschatology to Arian Heresy: The Case of Francis Kett (d. 1589)," *Harvard Theological Review* 67 (1974): 460–465.
32. Anne Dillon, *The Construction of Martyrdom in the English Catholic Community, 1535–1603* (Aldershot: Ashgate, 2002), 3–4, 3n9.
33. See: Mary Villeponteaux, *The Queen's Mercy: Gender and Judgments in Representations of Elizabeth I* (New York: Palgrave Macmillan, 2014).
34. Susan Wabuda, "Nicholas Ridley (*c*. 1502–1555)," in *Oxford Dictionary of National Biography* (Oxford: Oxford University Press, 2004), doi:10.1093/ref:odnb/23631.
35. William B. Robison, "Stripped of Their Altars: Film, Faith, and Tudor Royal Women from the Silent Era to the Twenty-First Century, 1895–2014," in *Women During the English Reformations: Renegotiating Gender and Religious Identity*, ed. Julie A. Chappell and Kaley A. Kramer (New York: Palgrave Macmillan, 2014), 166.
36. Brett Usher, "New Wine into Old Bottles: The Doctrine and Structure of the Elizabethan Church," in *The Elizabethan World*, ed. Susan Doran and Norman Jones (London: Routledge, 2011), 207.
37. Usher, "New Wine into Old Bottles," 207.

38 William J. Sheils, "The Catholic Community," in *The Elizabethan World*, ed. Susan Doran and Norman Jones (London: Routledge, 2011), 254.
39 J.E. Neale, *Elizabeth I and Her Parliaments, 1559–1581* (London: Jonathan Cape, 1958), 65.
40 Susan Doran, *Elizabeth I and Religion: 1558–1603* (London: Routledge, 1994), 51–52.
41 Usher, "New Wine into Old Bottles," 213.
42 Louise Montrose, *The Subject of Elizabeth: Authority, Gender, and Representation* (Chicago, IL: University of Chicago Press, 2006), 188–189. Montrose notes, however, "the limits of royal toleration depended upon where the distinction between private conscience and public agency was to be drawn" (188).
43 Danby Pickering, ed., *The Statutes at Large, from the Fifth Year of Queen Mary to the Thirty-Fifth Year of Queen Elizabeth, Inclusive* (Cambridge, 1763), 6:257; 6:349. I have modernised the text of the 1571 Treason Act.
44 For detailed discussion of Elizabeth's gender in the Kapur films, see: Aidan Norrie, "A Man? A Woman? A Lesbian? A Whore?: Queen Elizabeth I and the Cinematic Subversion of Gender," in *Premodern Rulers and Postmodern Viewers: Gender, Sex, and Power in Popular Culture*, ed. Janice North, Karl C. Alvestad, and Elena Woodacre (New York: Palgrave Macmillan, 2018), 319–340.
45 "'Elizabeth' Is 'Resolutely Anti-Catholic,'" *Catholic League for Religious and Civil Rights*, 27 January 1999, http://catholicleague.org/elizabeth-is-resolutely-anti-catholic.
46 Janet Maslin, "Film Review; Amour and High Dudgeon in a Castle of One's Own," *The New York Times*, 6 November 1998, http://nytimes.com/movie/review?res=9C0DE7D6173EF935A35752C1A96E958260.
47 Mary Kunz, quoted in "'Elizabeth' is 'Resolutely Anti-Catholic.'"
48 This 'view' is explained and contextualised in Judith M. Richards, "Reassessing Mary Tudor: Some Concluding Points," in *Mary Tudor: Old and New Perspectives*, ed. Susan Doran and Thomas S. Freeman (New York: Palgrave Macmillan, 2011), 206–224.
49 See, for example: Julia M. Walker, ed., *Dissing Elizabeth: The Negative Representations of Gloriana* (Durham, NC: Duke University Press, 1998); and John Edwards, *Mary I: The Daughter of Time* (London: Allen Lane, 2016).
50 Shekhar Kapur, "Film Design and Narrative: *Elizabeth*," http://shekharkapur.com/blog/2009/07/fim-design-and-narrative-elizabeth.
51 Higson, *Film England*, 233.
52 Susan Doran, "Elizabeth I's Religion: The Evidence of Her Letters," *The Journal of Ecclesiastical History* 51, no. 4 (October 2000): 699–720.
53 Maddalena Pennacchia, "Culturally British Bio(e)pics: From *Elizabeth* to *The King's Speech*," in *Adaptation, Intermediality and the British Celebrity Biopic*, ed. Márta Minier and Maddalena Pennacchia (Farnham: Ashgate, 2014), 36–39. Indeed, Pennacchia notes that the concept of "common sense" only emerged in English in the eighteenth century (38).
54 Tutan, "Adaptation and History," 579.
55 Krista J. Kesselring, "Crime, Punishment, and Violence in *The Tudors*," in *History, Fiction, and "The Tudors": Sex, Politics, Power, and Artistic License in the Showtime Television Series*, ed. William B. Robison (New York: Palgrave Macmillan, 2016), 244.

15 "Unseen but very evident"
Ghosts, Hauntings, and the Civil War Past

Michael Durrant

Hauntings have played an important part in fictional and non-fictional uses of the English Civil War. This chapter traces the visible engagements in early-modernism in both the adaptations of, and the historiography concerning, the English Civil Wars in order to interrogate different aspects of the War's haunting returns. It begins with a discussion of Peter Young's 1967 military history, *Edgehill 1642: The Campaign and the Battle*, which marshals the stuff of the archive to depict in "vivid" detail the first major military encounter of the English Civil War, a chaotic and inconclusive battle fought on a flat-topped ridge near the village of Kineton, Warwickshire, between King Charles I's royalist forces and the opposing forces of England's parliamentarian troops, led by Robert Devereux, 3rd Earl of Essex.[1] It then moves on to discuss Ben Wheatley's art-house costume drama, *A Field in England* (2013), which follows a group of English Civil War soldiers who, having fled an unnamed battlefield in 1648, are taken hostage by a conjurer, an Irishman named O'Neil, and forced to help him search for buried treasure. On the face of it, these texts—separated by over four decades, and appealing to different audiences and very different expectations—may seem like unlikely companions, and indeed neither text can be said to be a ghost story, at least in any straightforward way. However, they are representative of, and are both haunted by, ghosts: the ghosts of the Civil War, and more broadly by the ghosts of historical loss and erasure. Indeed, while both texts seek to bring back and re-enact the past, and were together praised as highly realistic engagements with England's revolution, bringing their consumers closer to the action of the 1640s through documentary evidence, or realistic dialogue and costume, they at the same time introduce questions regarding the limits of historical recovery and return, and it is through metaphors and tropes associated with the ghost and the haunting that these questions emerge.

The Haunting of Romney-Woollard

Published to symbolically align with the 325th anniversary of the Civil War skirmish that the text sought to re-represent and memorialise,

Edgehill 1642 has been described as a textual expression of Peter Young's "fascination with the minutiae of military life in the seventeen century"—an interest that was no doubt enlivened by Young's real-life experiences as a military commander during the Second World War.[2] Young draws on and (re)deploys official government correspondences, news reports, diary and journal entries, as well as documents related to the battle's organisation, and to the clothing and equipment worn by soldiers on both sides of the conflict's ideological divide. The cumulative effect of Young's reading and research is, to quote Veronica Wedgwood, one of historical embodiment, in that its readers get to experience "the physical conflict in close-up," and one of painstaking "assemblage," which brings readers as close as possible to the "action as it probably happened."[3] This is, in other words, history writing at its most forensically authentic and intimate, and in her introduction to the work, Wedgwood is keen to emphasise *Edgehill 1642*'s lack of "picaresque flourishes or ... excursions," noting instead the "straightforward" nature of Young's "documentation."[4] For the most part this is true, but Young was innovative enough to have built-in narratives that suggest an unseen, odd, and even an ongoing history of the Edgehill battle that has previously been "concealed" from the cultural memory.[5] Indeed, on my first encounter with *Edgehill 1642*, what interested me most was the way in which Civil War "ghosts" emerge as a part of the text's historiographical apparatus, signalling to the reader Young's concomitant interest in the Civil War's "influence on succeeding generations."[6]

In a chapter entitled "Of Apparitions," for example, Young introduces quotations from two seventeenth-century ghost (or "wonder") pamphlets, *A Great Wonder in Heaven* and *The New Yeares Wonder*, printed in January 1643.[7] They recount the story of a supernatural battle re-enactment that is said to have taken place shortly after the Edgehill skirmish, in which survivors living near the battlefield claimed to have heard the ghostly "noyse of Drumes and Trumpets," and "visibly saw" maimed and wounded spectral forces "performing the same actions of hostilitie and bloud-shed."[8] Together, these texts represent what is perhaps the most well-known haunting of the seventeenth century, and in recent years the Edgehill ghosts have been subject to media interest,[9] as well as academic scrutiny, particularly for the way in which the story signalled "the nation's trauma," bringing back aspects of the war that were "repressed and silenced in traditional, sanctioned, authoritative accounts."[10] Although Young transcribes long passages from both texts, he provides no comparable commentary on the contents of either *A Great Wonder in Heaven* or *The New Yeares Wonder*. Instead, the Edgehill haunting of the 1640s is situated as a precedent for later supernatural encounters in the area. Drawing on effectively oral histories preserved in his private collection, Young briefly quotes one "Miss B. M. Seaton, formerly a matron of Uppingham School [in Rutland],"

246 *Michael Durrant*

who affirmed that her "very old uncle, born just after the Crimean War," had visited the Edgehill site in the 1860s with a group of local newspaper reporters. The group apparently encountered a spectral battle "being fought again" and heard the "clash of weapons," which left the group "shaking & frightened."[11] Young then segues into another first-person testimony, this one from "more recent times," delivered to him in November 1966 by an "international concert pianist" named Michael Howard Romney-Woollard.[12]

Romney-Woollard's account, which Young quotes at length, begins as a narrative of battlefield tourism, but soon descends into something much darker. The story goes that on a June day in 1960, Romney-Woollard drove the 85 miles from London up to the Edgehill battlefield with two close friends. Not far from their destination, the trio lost their way. Romney-Woollard, a Suffolk native who had "never visited this part of the country before," asked his friends to pull the car to the side of the road so that he could try and get his bearings. "Getting out of the car" to look around, he was immediately struck by what he describes as a "strange instinct, which seemed to come from the past" that allowed him to successfully guide the vehicle some two miles to the correct location. As he approached the site of the Edgehill battlefield on foot, he again "became conscious of the fact that all the scenery was familiar." This sensation of uncanny familiarity was compounded by the realisation that the area around this historical site was still being exploited by the military, housing both a former Second World War transit camp for Polish and Czechoslovakian troops and R.A.F Gaydon, a bomber base.[13]

When Romney-Woollard finally reached the part of the battlefield where it is said royalist and parliamentarian soldiers are buried together in mass graves, he became

> very disturbed, for I was aware that hundreds of unseen men were watching me. My agitation must have been quickly noted by my two friends who asked me why I looked so unwell and frightened, but all that I remember saying was that I wished to return home immediately.[14]

On his return to London that evening, Romney-Woollard became aware "of the most terrifying fact": he had "brought back" with him "one of the dead of the battlefield." This "unseen but very evident visitor" haunted Romney-Woollard "for about a month," following him "everywhere [he] went in [his] house." Although it never visually manifested itself to him, he was sure that it was "a Roundhead"—a Parliamentarian—"for he wore armour, and had a small moustache, with deep piercing eyes, and carried a sword." This "presence" caused "such alarm"—"being as I was, alone"—that he soon became "highly nervous and unwell." The ghost's presence caused the home itself, a place that should be safe and reliable, to become a space of the unknown, the strange, and the horrible. At night, Romney-Woollard claims to have "left lights burning" in all his rooms "until morning came, when [he] felt less uneasy with the coming of daylight." This ghostly "man, whoever he was," vanished from Romney-Woollard's home "as suddenly as he had appeared," leaving in its absence a "highly nervous disposition" in the property's living occupier.[15] Some six years after the haunting, Romney-Woollard would describe the episode as having been one of "the most terrifying experience of my life, and will be remembered by me to the end of my days."[16]

(Re)Interpreting Romney-Woollard's Haunting

At first, Romney-Woollard's encounter with a Roundhead ghost describes a quintessentially uncanny experience, in which the unfamiliar (a ghost) is unexpectedly located within the familiar (the home), in a way that unsettles Romney-Woollard's identity. The present, in his account, is deprived of agency, with Romney-Woollard describing himself as having been "forced" to revisit this, or perhaps even his own, past. It is also history as both "familiar"—he "recognised the countryside and the site," even though he had never been there before—and history as alien, unsettling, or, in Romney-Woollard's terms, "unseen but very evident," a phrase that captures a "double sense of ghosts of their own and in current time."[17] The armoured apparition is said to have come "from the past," an active agent that appears and disappears from his home according to its own logic. Its meanings appear altogether mysterious, but the "unseen" ghost nonetheless requires interpretation. To this end, Romney-Woollard imagines it "clad in the period," its "armour," "small moustache," and "sword" appearing to historicise and authenticate the ghost's very *pastness*—to make it not a figure of the 1960s but one of the 1640s—but those same accoutrements are what make it domesticated, simplifying the complexities of history into the flattened image of a "Roundhead."

Revisionist historical criticism has shown that there was, visually, "little distinction in dress between sides" during the Civil War and that the binary configurations of the Roundhead and the Cavalier should be understood as a historical back-projection.[18] The Roundhead/Cavalier (and, by extension, the Charles/Cromwell) binary sits amongst a number of "convenient stereotypes" in popular culture: Civil War stereotypes that, perhaps paradoxically, exist "despite the lack of popular cultural representation of [the] period."[19] While simplistic, the Roundhead/Cavalier view of England's revolutionary past has "permeated" the cultural imaginary, and in Romney-Woollard's experience, these configurations offer a means by which the otherness of an unfamiliar past can be stabilised, fixed, and made nameable in the present.[20] It does not explain, however, why the ghost has returned.

This ambiguity leads Romney-Woollard to posit a number of questions: was the ghost "a memory transmitted through my family generation by generation until it transplanted itself so firmly in my mind that I was forced to revisit an ancestor's battlefield?" Or, as he tentatively suggests, "is there such a thing as reincarnation?"[21] It has been claimed that reincarnation "offers hope that death is not the end," and in its structural pattern of historical re-embodiment, reincarnation satisfies human desires to "recapture, re-experience, [and] relive" the past.[22] Such beliefs "increased substantially" in Britain in the early 1960s, widely "linked with the therapeutic search for the self" in a post-Freudian age that was becoming increasingly anxious about the "fragmentation of modern society."[23] While beliefs in reincarnation have "been entertained by human beings throughout history," it had culturally specific meanings in twentieth-century Britain, "linked to a self-identity that is individualistic, coherent and reflexive."[24] Although Romney-Woollard is keen to point out that he is "not an adherent of spiritualism," the reincarnation hypothesis shifts the boundaries and nature of how he reads the haunting, since as a theme, the notion of past lives introduces paradigms of interpersonal and historical continuity rather than psychic disruption, overwriting the experience as one not simply defined by fear and horror, but also with potentially therapeutic paradigms associated with "family," "memory," and Romney-Woollard's individuated relationship to his "ancestor's battlefield."[25]

This Civil War ghost therefore becomes a lens through which Romney-Woollard can reconsider and reinterpret his relationship to the historical conflict that the ghost's apparel signifies. That the Roundhead ghost might in fact be a family "memory," one that has been "transplanted" into Romney-Woollard's mind means that the Civil War past is itself a part of his everyday life, imprinted in the body: it is where he comes from, and he unwittingly has become a part of that past's survival. At the same time, it is a past that is subject to variation and adaptation in the present, since what begins as a terrifying encounter ultimately offers him new perspectives on an aspect of English history of which he had formally little knowledge. The presence of haunting (re)activates in Romney-Woollard remembrance and mourning, a "longing" to return to the Edgehill site to discover who is buried there.[26]

For Jacques Derrida, history writing is a comparable act of mourning, one that "consists always in attempting to ontologize remains, to make them present, in the first place by identifying the bodily remains and by localizing the dead."[27] This process of ontologising remains is indicative of Romney-Woollard's testimony, which gestures towards the presence of "hundreds" of "unseen men" who lie buried at the Edgehill site. When reading across and between its chapters and paratexts, Romney-Woollard's account, in which he was followed home by a Roundhead ghost in 1960, haunted for a while, and left with the impression that he

"Unseen but very evident" 249

may be a reincarnated soldier from the time, might even stand in for the kind of ontologising experience that *Edgehill 1642* promises to deliver.

Like the Edgehill site, which functions as a mass grave, Young's historiography is similarly posited as a site of resurrection, and it is possible that the text's inclusion of ghostly elements reinforces, rather than undermines, its ideology of realist historical rendering. Indeed, the book is portrayed by Wedgwood as a being akin to a resurrection narrative: "in these pages," she writes, "we ... meet our ancestors face to face in action and hear in their own words what they had to say about it."[28] Wedgwood's representation of Young's historiography is, like the haunting, therefore characterised by the "sense of opening oneself up to the inhabitation by the [historical] other."[29] In allowing us to "meet our ancestors" and to "hear" them, the book conjures a historical fantasy of presence, a felt remembrance, or something akin to a séance.[30] The alleged haunting actually reads like an allegory in miniature for the experience one might have reading Young's military history, which, through Wedgwood's introduction, advertises itself as a less terrifying, but nonetheless still powerfully authentic, form of historical interaction. When Young himself claims that "Englishmen have not greatly changed over the last 300 years" or that it "demands no great imaginative powers to see one's friends and neighbours as Cavaliers and Roundheads," it is difficult not to find echoes of the intimate interplay between past and present as manifest Romney-Woollard's testimony.[31] And when he maps out a brief genealogical history for the Woollard family, who, Young claims, can "trace their ancestry back to the 11th century" and are therefore imbued with "a sense of history natural to a family long established in one place," there is the concomitant suggestion that history is embedded not only in people but in landscapes, which at once contains and helps to construct a romance of historical continuity.[32]

However, while the present may be rooted in the past, it is in ways that may be complex and questionable; the past may have important lessons to teach the present, but those lessons are sometimes hard to read. As the introduction to *Edgehill 1642* attests, there are "doubts and difficulties" over the limits of the historian's "imaginative reconstruction."[33] Those who fought at Edgehill "did not have watches" or "maps"; "black powder smoke" would have "obscured the scene" for many participants, and eye-witness testimony tended to change over time, incorporating "personal observations" with "hearsay picked up afterwards around the camp fire." As Young goes on to suggest, history writing is also hampered by gaps and silences in the archive: many regiments at Edgehill, "whose doing were of real importance," have had "no chronicler."[34] To put it another way, then, history is complex, its truths are difficult to obtain, and different sources can give completely different interpretations of the same historical facts or even describe the facts differently. Young continues to articulate these problems when he says that the "rights and wrongs of the struggle are still capable of rousing passions," and for this reason, "impartiality" is difficult to attain even with historical distance, and a historian's reconstruction of the period can be easily (re)shaped by their own personal "bias."[35]

How, then, can we recreate the experiences of that passionate and divisive history without reproducing the prejudices that drove it? How do we see through or past the "black powder smoke," restructuring an experience of a battle that was difficult to know even to those who participated? Romney-Woollard's experience might provide answers, at least within the contexts of *Edgehill 1642*. By including quotations from a range of first-person testimonials, which together evidence "the strange psychic aura of Edgehill," Young posits alternative historical perspectives that seem to breach the remits of mainstream history.[36] Encrypted within his testimony is a version of historical interaction that bypasses the tribulations of archival study. While Young himself notes that he had visited the Edgehill site "many times since the late [19]30s," although, unlike Romney-Woollard, he had done so "without encountering a single spectre," his inclusion of strange tales related to the site might be seen to posit the ghost story as a form of sense-making when the historiographical record is seen to fail us.[37]

Re-enactment, Digging, and Dirt

In *Edgehill 1642*, then, the presence of ghosts speaks towards the possibilities of acknowledgement: the acknowledgement of non-linear realities, as exemplified by the story's nod towards "reincarnation," and, by extension, an acknowledgement of history as an embodied epistemology, as a personalised form rather than a text to be read. This seemed to me to be a striking set of interconnections threaded through Young's historiography, pointing towards articulations of the Civil War past manifested in ghostly yet subjective dispositions. It would not, though, be altogether unusual to suggest that Young was interested in themes and issues related to historical embodiment. Young was, after all, one of the founding members of The Sealed Knot Society, the UK's biggest historical re-enactment society, and he is said to have co-founded the group at the launch party for *Edgehill 1642* in 1968. The book itself is an important part of the mythology of the Sealed Knot's foundation, since during that launch party, in which participants dressed up in home-made seventeenth-century military uniforms, the idea of forming an English Civil War re-enactment society was apparently first born.[38]

Key to re-enactment is the "immersion of the actors in their roles," and through the performative adoption of authentic attire, props, and bodily gestures, historical re-enactment is driven towards collapsing "the gap between past and present."[39] Like Young's history book, which draws together early modern archival sources with contemporary ghost

"*Unseen but very evident*"   251

stories, re-enactment does not neatly polarise present experience from past experience. Rather, re-enactors aim towards a "felt historical connection (what civil war re-enactors call 'wargasm')," moments "when they feel like they really were in the past," becoming the "persona they perform."[40] Echoing Romney-Woollard's experience, and Wedgwood's description of Young's book, re-enactment posits that history can be felt and experienced in the now, a practice that has been read as a form of "reincarnation."[41]

However, re-enactment can also be understood as an adaptive process, a form of historical rendering that works towards the reworking of the past through its restaging. As Rebecca Schneider argues, in "the syncopated time of re-enactment, where *then* and *now* punctuate each other," a gap opens up through re-enactment in which the past is "re-composed."[42] For instance, while historical re-enactment might be seen as a way of preserving cultural memory through repetition and re-performance—The Sealed Knot's official website states that their aim is to "honour those that died" and to "educate the public about [the Civil War]"—forgetting and rewriting is constantly in play, too.[43] Re-enactment therefore orders and contains the vagaries of history, with the Sealed Knot offering participants the opportunity to engage in the re-performance of historical Civil War battles, but in such a way that no one dies or gets injured, and accompanying this is a concomitant concern with burying the politico-religious motivations that instigated the conflict. As the Sealed Knot website goes on to insist, the "name of the Society derives from a group, which, during the Protectorate, plotted for the restoration of the monarchy," but the "present society is NON POLITICAL AND HAS NO POLITICAL AFFILIATIONS OR AMBITIONS."[44] As such, in returning to, and re-staging, battles from the Civil War past, the multiple and overlapping politico-religious fault lines that motivated the conflict are reinterpreted and therefore adapted into depoliticised theatrical forms.

This dialectic, of forgetting and/through remembering, is at the heart of Wheatley's film *A Field in England*, which was visually inspired by his "experience of shooting a film about the Sealed Knot Civil War re-enactment society."[45] *A Field* is characterised by what one reviewer describes as an "absolute authenticity," and Wheatley has been quoted as saying that he intended for the film to generate the feeling "that you're actually there."[46] This is partly achieved through the use of costume, archaic dialogue, folk music, and visual tableaux that resemble the flattened perspectives of seventeenth-century woodcuts and the deployment of black-and-white photography, which aesthetically links Wheatley's 2013 film to Peter Watkins's 1964 *Culloden*, an experimental docudrama based on the 1745 Jacobite Rebellion. Jump cuts, handheld camera work, and sudden, jolting edits also help capture a sense of urgency and historical presence. However, although *A Field*'s advertising picked up on a sense of the film's commitment to historical specificity—its trailer, for example, invites us to "take a trip into the past," while the film's website includes an "A-Z" guide that historicises and therefore authenticates key terms and concepts used in the film, including its heavy use of the word "fuck"—the film's historical staging supplants narrative coherence with a jarring indecisiveness, ultimately highlighting disjunctures between the past and/in the present.[47] Its characters experience drug-induced trips after having consumed magic mushrooms, and they see visions of celestial prodigies and encounter demonic forces that could be either real or imagined. Added to this, characters repeatedly refer to themselves as "forgotten" figures, gesturing to a past that has been denied, and allusions to hell and purgatory conjure the impression that viewers are watching, in Jerome de Groot's words, "a kind of embodied haunting."[48]

Central to De Groot's understanding of the film is that its haunting techniques offer consumers a challenging redefinition of empirical traditions underlying Western historiographical practices, highlighting the constructedness of historical narratives, and the more general role of storying in the creation of more linear modes of history writing.[49] *A Field* offers, in other words, a form of historical rendering that establishes and then negates the Civil War's presence, drawing together the tropes of realism associated with costume drama and historical re-enactment only to collapse them into a ghost story. Central to this effect is the film's concern with the English Civil Wars as a recurring history, one that unsettles ideals of linearity, but also as a suppressed or buried past, issues that draw *A Field* into thematic parallel with earlier British cinematic renderings of the Civil War, particularly *Witchfinder General* (dir. Michael Reeves, 1968) and *The Blood on Satan's Claw* (dir. Piers Haggard, 1971). *A Field*'s plot, for example, plays out in a haunting loop, its narrative ending doubling back to replay its beginnings, suggesting a history that is destined to replay and repeat. Another notable feature of *A Field* is that it is set almost entirely on the edge of a battlefield, and the film plays with what is on the periphery of the viewer's perception. It begins and ends, for example, with the half-obscured sights and sounds of an unspecified Civil War battle, a historical event that is taking place just off-screen and therefore on the edge of what can be seen and known; the violence and turmoil are situated behind a hedge through which four deserting protagonists emerge, birth-like, in the film's opening frames.

These figures include an alchemist's servant, Whitehead, on a mission to capture an as yet unseen Irishman, O'Neil, who, we are told, has stolen important examples of his unseen master's mystical books and papers. Whitehead is first seen scrambling to escape Trower, a mounted soldier who attempts to stop him from escaping the battlefield. Trower is almost immediately impaled by an unseen pikeman and then shot by Cutler, a mercenary fighter who appears to have followed Whitehead through the hedge. Trower's death is highly stylised, his corpse coming to rest amongst the leaves and branches of the hedge, his arm outstretched with one finger pointing towards the empty field in which Whitehead stands. Turning to look in the direction of the pointing finger, which in its framing takes on the quality of a manicule (or "little hand"), Whitehead's gaze is directed towards the sight of two figures, described by Whitehead as "only shadows," loitering in the residual smoke of cannon fire. This represents the film's first visual cue that themes of repetition and doubling will frame the action: the shadow figures bear the uncanny resemblance of Whitehead and Culter themselves.

Whitehead soon encounters two other figures who have escaped the battlefield: these include a foul-mouthed soldier, Jacob, and the poor, illiterate, Fool-like Friend. For the most part, Friend's dialogue provides the film with much of its humour, although his language often alludes to his status as an embodiment of a return. Commenting on the prospect of returning to the battle from which he has escaped, Friend points out that to "go back and suffer" is what he "does best." The line exemplifies Friend's overall demeanour: accepting of his unequal status amongst his fellow escapees, and dejectedly aware that his relationship to God is one defined only by punishment and inescapable providence. But the idea that Friend will "go back," that he will (or already has) come back, is mirrored in terms of his character's trajectory throughout the film. We first encounter Friend lying lifeless on the ground, and Whitehead, Cutler, and Jacob all assume that he is dead. Friend soon reanimates, however, which presages his death later in the film, when he is shot and killed by Cutler and afterwards buried only to unexpectedly return to life again, after which he is killed for a second, or perhaps a third, time, turning the "living" Friend into a ghostly absent presence.

A Field's deserting soldiers are frequently seen burrowing into the earth, constructing, entering, and dying in sodden pits at the behest of O'Neil, who has enslaved them in his sinister quest to find buried treasure. Locating Wheatley's film within a nexus of other art forms that have taken the English landscape as a site of inexplicable strangeness and buried trauma (including works by M.R. James and songs by the band These New Puritans), Robert Macfarlane argues that *A Field*'s aesthetic topography—its depiction of an English landscape that is punctuated by open holes—is both a visual sign of "suppressed" English pasts and a potential source of contemporary "political rethinking." "Digging down to reveal the hidden content of the under-earth," he writes, becomes *A Field*'s way of exposing a previously buried dissenting and radical English past, one that, in the contexts of post-2012 Tory austerity politics, and the cultural decline of "the rural to *Bake Off* tents in flower meadows," was ripe for exhumation.[50] Yet, if the film seeks to restage the radicalisms of the 1640s as a contemporary brand of leftist dissenting politics, it does so in very subtle ways.

A Field shares with The Sealed Knot a desire to strip away the politics that motivated the events it depicts. Indeed, one of the most striking aspects of the film is that it removes narrative cues that might help its audience decipher the complex history being visually re-staged. For instance, the script reduces discussion of the events of the Civil War conflict and its religious and political contexts to a minimum; well-known historical figures like Cromwell and Charles are briefly mentioned but never seen. The film's characters allude to events and places, which, although familiar to them as they move about within the world of the film, might be decidedly unfamiliar, or out of joint, for contemporary audiences. Signposting techniques—the inclusion, for example, of a character whose sole purpose is to fulfil the role of historical exposition, explaining events, concepts, and the significance and/or role of historical personalities for the audience—have been entirely expunged. The film's dialogue—including Cutler's "There are no sides here"—might even emphasise a deep sense of disappointment with, or even a casual dismissal of, the politico-religious partisanship embedded in the Royalist versus Parliamentarian binary.

The cumulative effect of all this is that the audience is kept at a distance from the history in which the film's characters are confined. In the process, *A Field* renders the English Civil War as an unknowable, rather than a recognisable, past, one that slips out of focus even as it is summoned.[51] This paradigm is made manifest by the film's climax, when Jacob and Friend find not treasure but bones in the pit they have been busy digging. "These bones," to quote Ryan Arwood,

> conjure the digression of the characters' ultimate demise. These ... characters come from this grave they dig themselves. They will return and they will act out their fiendish plights again and again for our hungry bewitched eyes from the bottom of this pit.[52]

Here, tropes associated with the ghost and the haunting are deployed as a mournful reminder that the past's return is also part of its disappearance. The sight of the pit in *A Field*, and the discovery of deathly disappearance therein, functions as a provocative metaphor for the adaptive nature of looking back. Mournfully shadowing *A Field's* own invitation to "take a trip into the past" is the visual telos of a dank pit, and with it comes a self-conscious awareness that to revisit (to "dig" into) that past is to always to encounter that past's vanishing or restructuring in the present, a characteristic that Derrida playfully defines as "a hauntology."[53]

Conclusion

Derrida's conceptualisation of the ghost—a "repetition *and* first time"[54]—and the hauntological have been highly influential in academic circles, coming to encompass the ways in which "uncomfortable elements of the past," elements thought to be "suppressed," can "return," but not always in the ways in which we might expect, since "historical events or memories … may give rise to vastly different hauntings."[55] Derrida's ghost is representative of history as cycle, as repetition, as something weirdly disjointed; the present is uncomfortably inhabited by the past, yet the ghost/history returns again and again, always within different contexts. This means that, while the figure of the ghost and the metaphor of the haunting can represent an uninhibited return of the past in the present, the meanings that might be attached to the ghost and to the haunting are historically contingent and subject to variation. Here at this chapter's end, I want to link these competing ghostly claims to a propensity within and without academic scholarship to describe the English Civil Wars as a "haunted" history and as a "ghost in the machine" of the contemporary.[56]

This is particularly true in Restoration historiography, where we can find frequent descriptions of post-1660 English society and culture as having been haunted, by memories of the English Civil War conflict of the 1640s, its dead and wounded, and by the threat of that past's unbidden continuation or re-emergence. Metaphors associated with "ghosts," "hauntings," and "spectres," as well as "afterlives," have in fact been fruitfully utilised to capture the ongoing, and sometimes harrowing, presence of the Civil War past, and to think about the ways in which the events of the 1640s and 1650s continued to shape later cultural and political configurations, well into the nineteenth century and beyond.[57] In these readings, post-1660 England is itself a kind of haunted house, always pulled back to traumatic visions of regicide and rebellion, and like a "trauma patient," it is unable to fully escape the fractures of identity that its last intrastate conflict brought about.[58]

However, running alongside these metaphors, which associate the Civil War past with the haunting, the ghost, and the afterlife, and that together suggest that past's ongoing presence in later periods, are claims relating to the period's "suppression" from official narratives of English history.[59] While the 1640s has been conceptualised as a deeply "transformative" moment in English national history, having a "profound effect" on subsequent understandings of relationships between monarchy and state, the same period has been identified by Christian Kerslake as a "gaping hole or wound," and he suggests that images from the period, including the spectacle of regicide, occupy "an anomalous place in British iconography."[60] Perry Anderson similarly suggests that the Civil War "occupies a strange niche in contemporary memory," a historical "blackout" and even something of "a historical freak."[61] This position has been echoed by Nigel Hunt, who argues that the Civil War is "dead to memory," a provocative phrase and maybe even an accurate one given the period's underrepresentation in film, television, and other forms of popular media.[62]

Vacillating, then, between the claim that English culture has "an anxiety to revisit and re-evaluate" the Civil War past, to broader suggestions that England has suffered, and continues to suffer from, what has been described as a kind of "cultural amnesia," there seems to be either too much memory about the Civil War or not enough.[63] It is of course possible that these are not mutually exclusive issues but rather interrelated. Indeed, what stands out about post-1660 cultural attitudes to England's revolutionary past is this kind of dividedness, with the culture straddling a permeable hinterland between the remembering and forgetting of "the collective memory of the dead."[64] Forgetting was central to England's national foundations, as demonstrated by the *Act of Free and General Pardon, Indemnity and Oblivion* (1660), which made it an "offence" to remember certain "aspects of the [recent] past," prescribing instead a programme of obligatory "forgetting" as a salve for the nation's former phase of revolutionary madness.[65] Other stylised acts of expurgation, designed to enforce "a comprehensive rewriting of the history and literature of the preceding decades," included having Charles II's reign backdated to the day after his father's death in 1649, which in effect collapsed the historical distance between regicide and return.[66] Some eight months into the Restoration, and three months before Charles II was officially crowned at Westminster Abbey, Cromwell's body was disinterred from the same site, and, together with the bodies of John Bradshaw and Henry Ireton, posthumously executed.[67] At the same time, there was an overdetermined drive towards constructing cultural and political meanings out of the traumas of the 1640s: to commemorate Charles I as a royalist hero in sermons, verse, prose, and other art forms; to pattern the Civil War and republican period as having been part of a God-given design, in which ideological radicalism, regicide, and royalist defeat had been miraculously traded for triumph; and to evoke the myth of England's Civil War as a historical interruption.[68]

As Anne Hermanson has argued, the uneasy ebb and flow between oblivial and commemorative enactments meant that the "English psyche was not allowed to come to terms with its trauma," which left the culture vulnerable "to both nostalgia ... and nightmares."[69] Those nightmares often centred on a "profound fear of the [Civil War] happening again," and this "tendency to repetition" has been described as a key motif in the Restoration literary scene, with themes of "return and reenactment" imbuing not only the culture's political polemic and satire, but also sparking a sharpened appetite for narratives involving ghosts and hauntings.[70] In this context, the Civil War past comes back to haunt not only metaphorically but literally, and those ghosts return not in spite of, but *because* of, official attempts to have the period disremembered.

Ghosts and hauntings are therefore bound up with, and perhaps a product of, the "divided and divisive cultural legacy of the English Revolution," giving expression to that which has been "repressed or blocked from view" and now serving as useful metaphoric devices for historians seeking to navigate the English Civil War past and its legacies.[71] This chapter has continued some of this work. It has considered the kinds of insights tropes involving ghosts and haunting can offer into English Civil War's subsequent manifestations in sites of cultural memory. By reading two disparate texts into each other, it has shown that the issue of the Civil War past as a haunting presence is an early-modernism that manifests in diverse forms, at different levels (from individuals up to the social imaginary), and with different implications for those who are haunted (for some it is a good thing, for others it is a problem). Young's history book understands the Civil War past as a haunting but one that can be used to cast new light on familial frameworks and legacies, and the text hints towards a Civil War past that can be, and has been, passed down through generations, forging memories in people who never actually lived through it. Conversely, *A Field in England* offers a far less assured vision of the Civil War past as ghost, positing that the haunting is not a transformational experience of recognition, as Young's book does. Instead, imagery and themes associated with repetition and re-enactment; historic cycles rather than linear lines; and surrealist images, including the sight of characters' doubles or walking ghosts together symbolise the transgression of temporal frontiers, opening a space of resistance to modes of historical discourse that emphasise continuity. Through tropes associated with the ghost and the haunting, *A Field in England* gestures towards an understanding of the Civil War past as something that is transformed and adapted through interpretation, a traumatic point that disappears through acts of remembering and re-representation.

Notes

1 Peter Young, *Edgehill 1642: The Campaign and the Battle* (Kineton: The Roundwood Press, 1967), xv; John Wroughton, *The Routledge Companion to the Stuart Age, 1603–1714* (London: Routledge, 2006), 261.
2 Alison Michelli, *Commando to Captain-Generall: The Life of Brigadier Peter Young* (Barnsley: Pen and Sword, 2007), 223.
3 Young, *Edgehill*, xv–xvi.
4 Young, *Edgehill*, xv–xvi.
5 Young, *Edgehill*, xviii.
6 Young, *Edgehill*, 164.
7 For the sake of clarity, I give years as if they started 1 January.
8 Anon, *The New Yeares Wonder* (London, 1642/43), 7; Anon, *A Great Wonder in Heaven* (London, 1642/43), 7.
9 "Echoes of War Still Surround Edgehill," *BBC*, last modified 18 April 2008, http://bbc.co.uk/coventry/content/articles/2006/05/24/weird_edgehill_ghosts_feature.shtml.

10 Erin Murphy, "'I remain, an airy phantasm': Lucy Hutchinson's Civil War Ghost Writing," *English Literary History* 82 (2015): 97; Diane Purkiss, *Literature, Gender and Politics during the English Civil War* (Cambridge: Cambridge University Press, 2005), 34.
11 Young, *Edgehill*, 164.
12 Young, *Edgehill*, 164.
13 Young, *Edgehill*, 164.
14 Young, *Edgehill*, 165.
15 Young, *Edgehill*, 165.
16 Young, *Edgehill*, 166.
17 Young, *Edgehill*, 166; Caron Lipman, *Co-Habiting with Ghosts: Knowledge, Experience, Belief and the Domestic Uncanny* (London: Routledge, 2014), 75.
18 Thomas Corns, *Uncloistered Virtue: English Political Literature, 1640–1660* (Oxford: Clarendon Press, 1992), 5.
19 Jerome de Groot, "'Welcome to Babylon': Performing and Screening the English Revolution," in *Filming and Performing Renaissance History*, ed. Mark Thornton Burnett and Adrian Streete (New York: Palgrave Macmillan, 2011), 71–72.
20 De Groot, 'Welcome to Babylon,' 71–72.
21 Young, *Edgehill*, 166.
22 David Lowenthal, *The Past Is a Foreign Country Revisited* (Cambridge: Cambridge University, 2015), 59, 55.
23 Tony Walter, "Reincarnation, Modernity and Identity," *Sociology* 35 (2001): 21, 24.
24 Walter, "Reincarnation," 36.
25 Young, *Edgehill*, 165.
26 Young, *Edgehill*, 164.
27 Jacques Derrida, *Specters of Marx: The State of the Debt, the Work of Mourning and the New International*, trans. Peggy Kamuf (1994; repr., London: Routledge, 2006), 9.
28 Young, *Edgehill*, xvi.
29 Young, *Edgehill*, xv; Carla Freccero, *Queer/Early/Modern* (Durham, NC: Duke University Press, 2006), 91.
30 Young, *Edgehill*, xvi.
31 Young, *Edgehill*, xviii.
32 Young, *Edgehill*, 164.
33 Young, *Edgehill*, xv.
34 Young, *Edgehill*, xv.
35 Young, *Edgehill*, xviii.
36 Young, *Edgehill*, xviii.
37 Young, *Edgehill*, 166.
38 See: "About Us," *The Sealed Knot*, http://thesealedknot.org.uk/about-us.
39 Warwick Frost and Jennifer Laing, *Commemorative Events: Memory, Identities, Conflict* (London: Routledge, 2013), 93; Iain McCalman and Paul A. Pickering, "From Realism to the Affective Turn: An Agenda," in *Historical Reenactment: From Realism to the Affective Turn*, ed. Iain McCalman and Paul A. Pickering (New York: Palgrave Macmillan, 2010), 1.
40 Katherine M. Johnson, "Rethinking (re)doing: Historical Re-enactment and/as History," *Rethinking History* 19 (2015): 202.
41 Raphael Samuel, *Theatres of Memory, Volume 1: Past and Present in Contemporary Culture* (London: Verso, 1994), 180.
42 Rebecca Schneider, *Performing Remains: Art and War in Times of Theatrical Reenactment* (London: Routledge, 2011), 2, 11.

43 "About Us," *The Sealed Knot*, http://thesealedknot.org.uk/about-us.
44 "About Us," *The Sealed Knot*. Capitalisation found in the original text.
45 Jerome de Groot, *Remaking History: The Past in Contemporary Historical Fictions* (London: Routledge, 2016), 122.
46 Chloe Hodge, "Ben Wheatley," *Aesthetica Magazine*, last modified 5 July 2013, http://aestheticamagazine.com/ben-wheatley/.
47 "An A-Z of the World of *A Field in England*," last modified 2014, http://afieldinengland.com/masterclass/historical-terms/.
48 De Groot, *Remaking*, 121.
49 See also Jerome de Groot, "Fugitives, Fields, Pubs and Trees," *The Seventeenth Century* 32 (2018): 493–512.
50 Robert Macfarlane, "The Eeriness of the English Countryside," 10 April 2015, https://theguardian.com/books/2015/apr/10/eeriness-english-countryside-robert-macfarlane.
51 My reading of *A Field in England* has been influenced by Robert A. Rosenstone's *Visions of the Past: The Challenge of Film to Our Idea of History* (Cambridge, MA: Harvard University Press, 1995), and Rosenstone's edited collection, *Revisioning History: Film and the Construction of a New Past* (Princeton, NJ: Princeton University Press, 1995). These books offer a valuable platform to consider historical cinema not as a simplification of history, but as a radically self-conscious source of alternative historical rendering, or, in Rosenstone's words, "revisioning."
52 Ryan Arwood, "The Haunted Voice and Spherical Narrative of Ben Wheatley's *A Field in England*," *The Luminary* 4 (2014), https://lancaster.ac.uk/luminary/issue4/issue4article10.htm.
53 Derrida, *Specters*, 10.
54 Derrida, *Specters*, 10.
55 Simon R. Doubleday, "The Re-Experience of Medieval Power: Tormented Voices in the Haunted House of Empiricism," in *The Experience of Power in Medieval Europe: 950–1350*, ed. Robert F. Berkhofer (Aldershot: Ashgate, 2005), 278; Maria del Pilar Blanco and Esther Peeren, *The Spectralities Reader: Ghosts and Haunting in Contemporary Cultural Theory* (New York: Bloomsbury Academic, 2013), 15.
56 Mark Stoyle, "'Memories of the Maimed': The Testimony of Charles I's Former Soldiers, 1660–1730," *The Journal of the Historical Association* 88 (2003): 225; Simon Phillips-Hughes, "Star Wars is just a Folk Memory of the English Civil War," *The Huffington Post*, last modified 21 December 2016, https://huffingtonpost.co.uk/simon-phillipshughes/star-wars-is-just-a-folk-memory_b_8851340.html.
57 For the use of "hauntings" and "ghosts" as a metaphor for post-Restoration legacies of the Civil War, see: Jonathan Scott, *Algernon Sidney and the Restoration Crisis, 1677–1683* (Cambridge: Cambridge University Press, 1991), 9; Michael Cordner, "Sleeping with the Enemy: Aphra Behn's *The Roundheads* and the Political Comedy of Adultery," in *Players, Playwrights, Playhouses: Investigating Performance, 1660–1800*, ed. Michael Cordner and Peter Holland (New York: Palgrave Macmillan, 2007), 71; John Seed, *Dissenting Histories: Religious Division and the Politics of Memory in Eighteenth-Century England* (Edinburgh: Edinburgh University Press, 2008), 88; and Murphy, "'I remain," 97. On "afterlives," see: Mark Stoyle, "Remembering the English Civil War," in *The Memory of Catastrophe*, ed. Peter Gray and Kendrick Oliver (Manchester: Manchester University Press, 2004), 20; Laura Lunger Knoppers, "Cultural Legacies: The English Revolution in Nineteenth-Century British and French Literature," in *The Oxford Handbook of the English Revolution*, ed. Michael J. Braddick. (Oxford:

260 Michael Durrant

Oxford University Press, 2015), 535–554; and De Groot, "Fugitives, Fields, Pubs and Trees."
58 Scott, *Algernon*, 9.
59 Peter Middleton and Tim Woods, *Literatures of Memory: History, Time, and Space in Postwar Writing* (Manchester: Manchester University Press, 2000), 174.
60 Steve Pincus, *1688: The First Modern Revolution* (New Haven, CT: Yale University Press, 2009), 482; Stoyle, "Remembering," 19; Christian Kerslake, "Repetition and Revolution: Primal Historicization in Deleuze, Regnault and Harrington," *SubStance* 39 (2010): 56.
61 Perry Anderson, *Spectrum: From the Right to the Left in the World of Ideas* (London: Verso, 2005), 232.
62 Nigel C. Hunt, *Memory, War and Trauma* (Cambridge: Cambridge University Press, 2010), 174. For a discussion of the Civil War's underrepresentation in contemporary popular culture, see De Groot, "'Welcome,'" 65–82.
63 Rachel Willie, *Staging the Revolution: Drama, Reinvention and History, 1647–72* (Manchester: Manchester University Press, 2015), 75, 206; Kevin Sharpe, *Reading Authority and Representing Rule in Early Modern England* (London: Bloomsbury, 2013), 195.
64 Elizabeth Hodgson, *Grief and Women Writers in the English Renaissance* (Cambridge: Cambridge University Press, 2015), 100. For a similar argument, see: Matthew Neufeld and Rachel Hatcher, "Civil-War Stories in Lands of Commanded Forgetting: Restoration England and Late Twentieth Century El Salvador," in *Civil War and Narrative: Testimony, Historiography, Memory*, ed. Karine Deslandes, Fabrice Mourlon, and Bruno Tribout (New York: Palgrave Macmillan, 2017), 191, 196.
65 Erin Peters, *Commemoration and Oblivion in Royalist Print Culture, 1658–1667* (New York: Palgrave Macmillan, 2017), 51.
66 Joad Raymond, *Pamphlets and Pamphleteering in Early Modern Britain* (Cambridge: Cambridge University Press, 2006), 247.
67 See: Jonathan Fitzgibbons, *Cromwell's Head* (London: Bloomsbury Academic, 2008).
68 For a similar argument, see: Matthew Neufeld, *The Civil Wars After 1660: Public Remembering in Late Stuart England* (Woodbridge: The Boydell Press, 2013), esp. 84–85; and Kyle Pivetti, *Of Memory and Literary Form: Making the Early Modern English Nation* (Lanham, MD: University of Delaware Press, 2015), esp. 116.
69 Anne Hermanson, *The Horror Plays of the English Restoration* (London: Routledge, 2014), 128; Scott, *Algernon*, 9.
70 Tim Harris, "Understanding Popular Politics in Restoration Britain," in *A Nation Transformed: England After the Restoration*, ed. Alan Houston and Steven Pincus (Cambridge: Cambridge University Press, 2001), 129; Purkiss, *Literature*, 133; Thomas Healy and Jonathan Sawday, "Introduction," in *Literature and the English Civil War*, ed. Thomas Healy and Jonathan Sawday (Cambridge: Cambridge University Press, 1990), 11. For a further discussion of the increased circulation of narratives of hauntings in the Restoration period, see: Peter Marshall, *Mother Leakey and the Bishop: A Ghost Story* (Oxford: Oxford University Press, 2007), esp. 217.
71 Dolly MacKinnon, Alexandra Walsham, and Amanda Whiting, "Religion, Memory and Civil War in the British Isles," *Parergon* 32, no. 3 (2015): 4; Avery F. Gordon, *Ghostly Matters: Haunting and the Sociological Imagination* (Minneapolis: New University of Minnesota Press, 1997), xvi.

Index

28 Days Later (2002), *see* Boyle, Danny

A Field in England (2013) 13, 244, 251, 252, 253, 254, 257
A Great Wonder in Heaven (1643) 13, 245
A Knight's Tale (2001) 9, 52, 54, 55, 57, 64
A Song of Ice and Fire series, *see* Martin, George R.R.
Aaron (character) 90, 91, 94
academia 150, 162, 179, 180–1, 182, 184
accuracy 5–6, 7, 16n24, 139, 142, 143, 245, 250, 251; historical accuracy 11, 16n24, 172, 176, 177, 178, 184
Act of Attainder 207, 210, 214, 219
Act of Supremacy (1558) 207, 236, 238
Act of Uniformity (1558) 12, 227, 232, 236, 237, 238, 240
adaptation 1, 3–7, 8, 9, 10, 11, 12, 15n16, 21, 37, 38, 39, 40, 41, 46, 47, 49, 49n3, 52, 54, 57, 58, 59, 64, 68, 82, 84, 85, 94, 95n12, 96n15, 97n37, 99, 100, 101, 117, 118, 130n3, 138–9, 142, 143, 144, 145, 150–1, 151n6, 154, 155, 156, 171, 172, 175, 176, 178, 179, 181, 182, 183, 184, 188, 189, 194, 195, 196, 201n15, 208, 215, 218, 219, 220, 221, 227, 233, 238, 240, 241, 244, 248, 251, 257; adaptation studies 3–7, 38, 208, 221
adventurism 147, 148, 150
Agincourt 1415 (2015) 11, 156, 158, 159, 160, 161, 162, 165
Agincourt, Battle of (1415) 89, 157, 161, 165, 168n28

Alexander 23, 25, 28
Amazon women 21, 24, 25, 26, 27–8, 32, 213
animal (imagery) 69, 72, 195–6
Apotropaics 68, 77, 78, 79
archers 145, 157, 158, 159, 160, 161, 162
Arthur (character) 23, 25, 41, 42, 43, 45, 46, 47–8
Arthur, (legendary) king 36, 37, 38, 39, 40, 42, 44, 46, 48, 50n16, 151n6, 181
Arthurian (genre) 36, 37, 38, 39, 40, 41, 42, 43, 44, 45, 46, 47, 48, 49, 49n3, 49n5, 50n8, 50n13, 51n21, 181
Arthurian legend 8–9, 36, 37, 38, 43, 44, 48, 49, 50n10, 151n6
Atwood, Margaret 10, 99, 100, 101, 102, 103, 104, 113; *Hag-Seed* (2016) 10, 99, 100, 101–4, 106, 107, 108
Austen, Jane 119, 127; *Pride and Prejudice* 119; *Mansfield Park* 119; *Emma* 127; *Emma* (1996) 83
authenticity *see* accuracy

Bannon, Stephen K. 84–5, 95n12, 95n13, 96n15
Barton, Elizabeth 5, 12, 207–11, *212*, 213–5, 215–7, 217–8, 219–21, 222
Beowulf 7, 17n43
Beowulf (2017) 50
Bettany, Paul 55
bisexuality, *see* sexuality
Black, Sirius (*Harry Potter* character) 118, 120, 123, 125–6, 130
Boccaccio, Giovanni 1, 24; *Il Filostrato* 1; *De Claris Mulieribus* 24
Bocking, Edward 209, 210, 214, 219

262 Index

Boleyn, Anne 207, 210, 219
Boyle, Danny 196; *28 Days Later* (2002) 70, 71, 72, 75, 76, 77; *Frankenstein* (2010) 196–7
Braveheart (1995) 44, 93
Britannia campaign 11, 139–40, 141, 142
British Civil Wars *see* English Civil War
Burbage, Richard 12, 189, 198–200, 205n72
Burke, Kathy 228, 229, 230
Buzzfeed 176, 177, 178, 180
Byland Collection 71, 73

Cabaret (1972) 87; Joel Grey 87
Cabaret (1998) *see* Mendes, Sam
Cameron, James 21, 26, 29–30, 31–2, 33, 35n30, 35n41
Cardinal, The (*Duchess of Malfi* character) 124, 125, 127
Catholic and Catholicism 12, 41, 207, 208, 209, 210, 211, 212, 213, 215, 222, 226, 227, 230, 232, 233, 236, 237, 238, 239–40
Caxton, William 53, 54, 59; "Proheme to the Second Edition of *The Canterbury Tales*" (1484) 53, 54, 59
Cecil, William, later Lord Burghley 237
celebrity 12, 109, 117, 188, 189, 197, 198, 200, 205n66
Charles I, king of England, Scotland, and Ireland 244, 247, 254, 256
Chaucer, Geoffrey 1, 4, 8, 9, 22, 23, 24, 27, 33n1, 33n8, 52, 53, 54, 55, 56, 57, 58, 59, 60, 61, 62, 63, 64, 65n17; *The Book of The Duchess* 55; *The Canterbury Tales* 9, 52, 53, 54, 57, 58, 59, 62; *The Cook's Tale* 59, 60–1; *The Friar's Tale* 59, 60; *The Knight's Tale* 27, 56; *Legend of Good Women* 22, 24, 27; *The Man of Law's Tale* 63–4; *The Pardoner's Tale* 60; *Troilus and Criseyde* 1
chess (imagery) 192, *192*, 196
Chevalier, Tracy 10, 99, 106, 112, 113; *New Boy* (2017) 10, 99, 106, 112, 113
chivalry 7, 23, 36, 39, 146, 159, 160, 161, 172, 174
Chrétien de Troyes, 38, 40, 43
Christie, Agatha 122; *Death in the Clouds* 122; *Sleeping Murder* 122

class 9, 11, 22, 28, 44, 45, 46, 47, 49, 64, 144, 147, 148, 155, 157, 158, 159, 160, 161, 162, 164, 165, 213; class war 159, 160
Clement, Jennifer 4, 6
comic books 3, 5, 31, 38, 67
Connor, Sarah (*Terminator* character) 29, 30, 31–2, 35n30, 35n41
Cooke, Dominic 189, 190
Coriolanus (character) 94, 98n51
costume design 12, 39, 44, 83–4, 87–8, 91–2, 172, 174, 188, 195, 239, 244, 251
courtly love literature 22, 23, 24; mechanics of 23, 24, 56, 57
Crécy (2010) 11, 156, 158, 160, 161, 165
Crécy, Battle of (1346) 157, 160, 162, 163, 165
Cromwell, Oliver 247, 254; posthumous execution 256
Cromwell, Thomas 207, 213, 214, 215, 218, 219
Cumberbatch, Benedict 11, 12, 188, 189, 190, *191*, 192, *192*, 194, 195, 196, *196*, 197, 198, 199, 200, 204n50, 205n62
Cumming, Alan 82, 83, 84, *84*, 85, 86, 87, 88, 96n27

D'Arcens, Louise 2
Dawn of the Dead (1978) 70, 72, 73, 75, 76, 77
Dawn of the Dead (2004) 72, 77, 78
Day of the Dead (1985) 74
DC Comics 22, 31
de Sainte-Maure, Benoît 1; *Le Roman de Troie* 1, 14n5
death 9, 53, 57, 63, 64, 67, 69, 70, 71, 72, 77, 79, 88, 89, 99, 107, 110, 111, 114, 123, 124, 126, 128, 145, 147, 193, 207, 209, 214, 231, 234, 248, 253, 254, 256
Deipyle 24, 25, 26, 28
Derrida, Jacques 248, 254, 255; *hauntology* 254; and mourning 248
Deschamps, Eustace 22, 23, 24, 53; *Ballade to Chaucer* 53
detective fiction 117, 122, 130, 132n43
digital games 137, 138, 139, 144, 146, 147, 151
disability 3, 12, 32, 188, 196, 202n19
diversity 8, 41, 44, 46, 49, 218

Druon, Maurice 193, 202n31; *Les Rois maudits* (*The Accursed Kings*) 193, 202n29, 202n31
Duchess of Malfi (*Duchess of Malfi* character) 118, 123, 124, 127, 128, 129–30
Dumbledore, Albus (*Harry Potter* character) 119, 120, 122, 123, 125, 126, 128, 130

early modern 1, 2, 3, 4, 5, 7, 10, 12, 13, 15n12, 27, 36, 46, 47, 53, 68, 86, 88, 89, 91, 92, 99, 108, 111, 117, 129, 145, 172, 175, 182, 183, 193, 198, 207, 213, 217, 219, 221, 222, 237, 250
early-modernism 4, 5, 7, 10, 13, 85, 86, 88, 89, 92, 106, 118, 189, 198, 208, 219, 221, 226, 227, 228, 232, 233, 236, 239, 240, 241, 244, 257; definition of 3
Edgehill 1642: The Campaign and the Battle (1967) 13, 244, 245, 249, 250
Edgehill, Battle of (1642) 245, 246, 248, 249, 250
Edward III, king of England 157, 161, 162, 164
Edward of Woodstock, the Black Prince 161, 162
Edward VI, king of England 232, 234
Elizabeth (1998) see Kapur, Shekhar
Elizabeth I, queen of England 4, 12, 122, 208, 209, 226, 227, 228, 230, 231, 231–2, 233, 234, 236–8, 239–40
Elizabeth: The Golden Age (2007) see Kapur, Shekhar
Ellis, Warren 11, 156, 158, 159, 162, 163
Emcee (character) 83, 87, 97n29
emotions 32, 85, 88, 107, 109, 113, 123, 188, 197, 204n54, 235, 236
England 3, 7, 12, 63, 99, 121, 156, 157, 159, 160, 161, 163, 164, 193, 198, 207, 208, 211, 213, 215–6, 226, 228, 230, 231, 232, 233, 238, 239, 240, 244, 247, 255, 256; medieval England 11, 40, 53, 59, 71, 137, 138, 139, 140, 141, 142, 143, 144, 145, 146, 147, 148, 149, 150, 151, 179
English Civil War 2, 13, 244, 245, 247, 248, 250, 251, 252, 254, 255, 256, 257

English Reformation 2, 9, 64, 94, 207, 208, 211, 215, 218, 222
epic 11, 37, 39, 82, 83, 92, 172, 174, 194
Excalibur 36, 37, 45, 46, 48
Expeditions: Vikings (2017) 11, 139, 147–9

families 46, 63, 64, 89, 101, 105, 117, 118, 119, 120, 121, 124, 125, 127, 128–9, 130, 143, 164, 173, 174, 221, 248, 249, 257
fandom 12, 188, 189, 194, 197, 198, 199, 200, 200n3
fantasy (genre) 4, 10, 11, 37, 137, 138, 147, 148, 171–3, 174, 175, 176, 181, 182, 183, 192, 193, 194, 220, 249; high fantasy 10, 137, 138, 172, 183; medieval fantasy 44, 46, 138, 147, 151, 155, 181
Fascism 9, 52, 60, 65n22, 82, 83, 84, 85, 86, 87, 92, 94, 95n11, 98n55, 98n65; Gestapo 84, 87; Nazi, imagery 85, 87
female gaze 21, 34n13
female warrior 27, 28, 33, 147, 148, 153n60, 181; women warriors 8, 21, 23, 24, 25, 27, 28, 150, 181; warrior-queen 25, 42
femininity 26, 28, 31, 83, 86, 87, 94, 98n50, 217
feminist 8, 21, 23, 29–30, 32, 35n30, 218, 219; anti-feminist 52
Ferdinand, Duke of Calabria (*Duchess of Malfi* character) 124–5, 127
fidelity 4, 5–7, 99, 101, 118, 130n3
fingers (imagery) 191, 192
Fletcher, John 102, 106; *The Tamer Tamed* 106
France 37, 56, 137, 143, 156, 157, 159, 164, 168n26, 193, 240
Frankenstein (2010) see Boyle, Danny
Frankenstein, Dr (*Frankenstein* character) 188, 196
Fuqua, Antoine 37, 39, 40, 41, 42, 43, 46, 48, 51n19; *King Arthur* (2004) 8, 36, 39–44, 51n19

Galbraith, Robert (pseud. of J.K. Rowling) 117, 122; Cormoran Strike series 10, 117, 122, 130; *Cuckoo's Nest, The* 59; *The Silkworm* 122

Index

game design 137, 138, 139, 140, 142, 149, 151
Game of Thrones (2011–) 9, 11, 44, 45, 47, 154, 155, 171–84, 186n27, 188, 192–5, 202n28, 202n29, 202n31, 203n36, 203n37
Gardiner, Stephen, Bishop of Winchester 233, 236, 237
Garrick, David 198, 205n66
gender 3, 7, 9, 10, 27, 31, 42, 44, 45, 46, 49n3, 51n24, 82, 83, 85, 86, 88, 91, 92, 98n50, 150, 177, 181, 208, 220, 230, 238, 239, 243n44; *see also* masculinity, femininity, genderqueer
genderqueer 9, 83, 86
Geoffrey of Burton 68, 70, 71, 73, 74, 75, 77, 80n10
Gerzic, Marina 9–10, 11–2, 17n47, 65n22, 95n3, 166n5, 186n27
Gestapo *see* Fascism
ghosts 12–3, 67, 121, 124, 130, 172, 244, 245, 246–50, 254, 255–7, 259n57
gladiator (imagery) 9, 83, 92, 93, 94, 146
Granger, Hermione (*Harry Potter* character) 119, 120, 121, 122, 125, 126, 128, 129, 130
graphic novels 1, 3, 6, 11, 154, 155, 156, 157, 158, 165
Guenevere (character) 36, 40, 41, 42, 43, 46
Gunpowder (2017) 179, 194, 203n37

Hagrid, Rubeus (*Harry Potter* character) 118, 120, 128
Harry Potter (book series); *see* Rowling, J.K.
haunting 12–3, 72, 201n14, 244, 245, 247, 248, 249, 252, 254, 255–7
Hector 23, 25, 28
Held, K.C. 218, 220; *Holding Court* (2016) 218, 220
Henry V, king of England 89, 143, 158, 160, 161, 162, 169n60
Henry VIII, king of England 12, 207, 210, 213, 215, 219, 222, 232
Hippolyta 24, 25, 26, 27, 28, 34n15
Hirst, Michael 228, 230, 241
historical fiction 172, 174, 175, 178, 179, 181, 183, 220
historiography 225n74, 230, 239, 244, 249, 250, 255

history 1, 3, 5, 7, 8, 11, 13, 21, 36, 44, 53, 67, 82, 83, 94, 99, 106, 118, 126, 137, 139, 141, 143, 144, 145, 146, 150, 151, 153n57, 154, 155, 156, 157, 163, 168n26, 171, 172, 173, 175, 176, 177, 178, 179, 180, 182, 183, 184, 188, 189, 190, 193, 194, 196, 202n28, 203n36, 207, 208, 209, 217, 218, 222, 226, 227, 230, 239, 240, 244, 245, 247, 248, 249, 250, 251, 252, 254, 255, 256, 257; medieval history 11, 137, 138, 139, 154, 166n3, 167n14, 172, 173, 176, 178, 179, 180, 181, 183, 193
Hitler, Adolf 83, 84, 128, 129
Hogarth Press *see* Hogarth Shakespeare
Hogarth Shakespeare 10, 13, 99–114
Hogwarts *see* Rowling, J.K.
Hollow Crown, The (2012) 186n27, 189, 194
Hollow Crown: The Wars of the Roses, The (2016) 11, 188, 189, 190, *191*, *192*, 194, 195, *196*, 197, 198, 200
Hollywood 21, 36, 39, 42, 50n13, 51n20, 148
Holy Grail 36, 41, 49n1
Holy Maid 5, 12, 210, *212*, 215, 218
Holy Woman 214, 220, 222
honour 26, 46, 53, 86, 89, 92, 94, 102, 121, 146, 158, 174, 251
House of Cards (2013) 188, 190, 191, 192, 195, 201n15, 201n16; Frank Underwood (*House of Cards* character) 190, 191, 192, 201n16
Hull, Lady Eleanor 1, 13; *Meditations Upon the Seven Days of the Week* 1
Hume, David 211, 212, 215, 216; *The History of England* (1762) 211, 215
Hundred Years' War 2, 11, 137, 155, 156, 157, 162, 165, 167n19
Hunnam, Charlie 45, 46, 48
Hutcheon, Linda 4, 5, 6, 7, 15n16, 130n3, 138
hysteria and hysterics 13, 17n47, 85, 88, 208, 216, 217, 219, 230

impostor 208, 211, 212, 213, 215; impostor phenomenon 213
incest 121, 125, 181
Instagram 197, 199
internet forums 177, 184
Ireland 140, 141, 143, 228, 233, 240
Iter Boreale (1647) 199, 205n71

Jackson, Peter 175, 195, 204n50; *The Hobbit* (2012–2014 film trilogy) 175, 195, 204n50; *The Lord of the Rings* (2001–2003 film trilogy) 175
Jacobson, Howard 10, 99, 108, 109, 110, 113; *Shylock is My Name* 10, 99, 106, 108–9, 113
Jenkins, Patty 21, 29, 33, 34n15; *Wonder Woman* (2017) 8, 21, 26, 29, 33, 34n13, 34n15

Kapur, Shekhar 12, 226–7, 228, 230, 232, 233, 234, 236, 238, 239, 240; *Elizabeth* (1998) 12, 226, 227, 228, 230, 232, 237, 239–40, 241; *Elizabeth: The Golden Age* (2007) 227
Kempe, Margery 52, 217
King Arthur (2004), *see* Fuqua, Antoine
King Arthur: Legend of the Sword (2017) *see* Ritchie, Guy
knights 36, 37, 38, 39, 40, 41, 44, 46, 49, 51n21, 56, 57, 145, 158, 159, 160, 161, 184

Lambarde, William 208, 209–11, 214, 215, 216; *A Perambulation of Kent* (1576) 208, 209, 214
Lampedo 24, 25, 28
Lancelot (character) 36, 40, 41, 42, 44, 46
Lanier, Douglas 99, 100, 103, 106, 108, 109, 115n19
Les Rois maudits (*The Accursed Kings*) *see* Druon, Maurice
Life and Miracles of St Modwenna 68, 78, 80n10
listicles 177, 178
Longbottom, Neville (*Harry Potter* character) 118, 119, 120, 123
Lucan (*Pharsalia*) 67, 81n42
Lucius (character) 9, 82, 83, 86, 88–94, *91*, 97n46, 98n51

MacFayden, Angus 83, 89, 91, *91*, 93
Mad Maid of Kent 5, 12, 215, 216, 218, 220, 221
madness 125, 143, 208, 215, 216, 218, 219, 256
Maggie (2015) 77, 81n26
male gaze 21, 31, 33, 34n13
Malfoy, Draco (*Harry Potter* character) 119, 122, 124, 125, 128

Mantel, Hilary 218, 219, 220, 221; *Wolf Hall* (2009) 218
Map, Walter 69, 73, 77, 80n12
Marian devotion 210, 213
Marpesia 24, 25, 28
Marston, William Moulton 21, 31
Martin, George R.R. 171, 172, 174–5, 176, 177, 180, 182, 183, 193–4, 202n26, 202n31; *A Song of Ice and Fire* series 171, 172, 182, 183, 193
Mary I, queen of England 12, 208, 227, 228–36, 229, 238, 239, 242n18
masculinity 9, 10, 82, 83, 85, 86, 89, 91, 92, 94, 95n3, 98n50, 219
medieval 1, 2, 3, 4, 5, 7, 8, 9, 10, 11, 12, 13, 13n3, 15n12, 22, 25, 28, 29, 30, 36, 37, 38, 39, 40, 42, 43, 44, 45, 46, 47, 48, 49, 50n13, 52, 53, 54, 59, 60, 62, 67, 68, 69, 70, 71, 72, 73, 74, 75, 76, 77–9, 85, 96n14, 137, 138, 139, 140, 141, 142, 143, 144, 145, 146, 147–8, 150, 151, 154–8, 160–5, 171–2, 174, 175, 176, 177, 178, 179, 180, 181, 182, 183–4, 192, 193, 194, 195, 208, 215, 217, 222
Medieval Historical Avatar 144, 146
Medieval II: Total War Kingdoms (2017) 139–42, 143, 147
Medieval Party system 147–9
Medieval Tournament Fighting 38, 55, 57, 144, 145, 146, 150
medievalism 1–3, 4, 5, 7, 8, 9, 10, 11, 13, 14n7, 37, 40, 45, 48, 52, 54, 59, 67, 68, 79, 92, 138, 139, 142, 146, 147, 150, 151, 155, 156, 165, 172, 177, 180, 181, 183, 184; participatory medievalism 139, 140, 141, 143, 145, 146, 147, 150
meme 197, 198, 205n62
Menalippe 24, 25, 26, 28
Mendes, Sam 83, 87, 190, 197; *Cabaret* (1998) 83, 86–7; *Richard III* (2012) 190
Merlin (character) 36, 41, 46, 48, 151n6, 181
Middle Ages 1, 2, 3, 4, 7, 14n7, 15n12, 36, 38, 40, 67, 70, 71, 155, 156, 157, 161, 162, 165, 172, 174, 177, 178, 179, 194
Monster, The (*Frankenstein* character) 188, 196

Monty Python 37, 50n13, 87
Monty Python and the Holy Grail (1975) 50n13, 176
Mussolini, Benito 83, 84

narrative 9, 10, 11, 13, 32, 36, 37, 38, 40, 44, 45, 49, 55, 59, 60, 61, 62, 63, 67, 68, 70, 71, 72, 73, 74, 75, 76, 77, 78, 79, 100, 101, 102, 103, 104, 106, 107, 108, 109, 111, 112, 113, 119, 137, 138, 139–40, 142, 143, 144, 147, 148, 149, 150, 155, 157–9, 162, 171, 176, 177, 193, 194, 221, 239, 245, 249, 252, 255, 256
national identity 7, 9, 11, 53, 64, 142, 155, 162, 164, 165
nationalism 48, 162, 165
Nazi (imagery) *see* Fascism
Nesbø, Jo 10, 99, 106, 111, 112; *Macbeth* (2018) 10, 99, 106, 111, 112
Night of the Living Dead (1968) 76, 77
Night of the Living Dead (1990) 76, 77, 78
nine female worthies 23, 28, 31
Nine Ladies Worthy 8, 21, 22, 23, 24, 25, 26, 28, 29, 30, 31, 33, 33n1
nine male worthies 23, 25, 28, 29
Norfolk, Duke of 229–30, 236
Norrie, Aidan 12, 16n24, 243n44
Northern Ireland 227, 228, 233
Northumbria 147, 148, 149, 150, 184
nostalgia 36, 49n1, 256

Pasolini, Pier Paolo 9, 52, 59, 60, 61, 64; *I Racconti di Canterbury* (1972) 9, 52, 59, 60, 64
peasants 50n13, 68, 69, 71, 73, 74, 75, 76, 77, 78, 150, 159, 160, 168n26, 176
Penthesilea 24, 25, 26, 28
performance 11, 58, 83, 84, 85, 86, 87, 99, 138, 139, 140, 142, 143, 144, 145, 148, 149, 188, 190, 195, 196, 197, 198, 199, 200
Philip II, king of Spain 122, 229–30, 232, 233
Philip VI (Philip of Valois), king of France 157, 159
postmodern 8, 36, 37, 40, 43, 44, 45, 47
Potter, Harry (*Harry Potter* character) 117, 118, 119, 120, 121, 122, 123, 124, 125, 126, 127, 128, 129, 130

Power, Ben 189, 190, 196
prophecy 123, 130, 207, 208, 209, 210, 213, 216, 218, 220–1, 222, 223n10; political 207, 211, 214, 215
Protestant and Protestantism 2, 12, 64, 207–9, 210, 211, 213, 215, 220, 226–8, 230, 232–4, 235, 236–8, 239–40
public perception 11, 142, 154, 155, 160, 163, 171, 172, 173, 176, 178, 179, 180, 182, 183, 184

race 3, 9, 40, 162, 193
re-enactment 5, 13, 42, 58, 143, 144, 145, 146, 147, 149, 152n16, 244, 245, 250, 251, 252, 256, 257
reddit 173, 177, 178
Reformation 2, 9, 64, 94, 207, 208, 211, 215, 218, 222
Refugee Tales (2016) 9, 52, 61–2, 64; Todorovic, Dragan, "The Migrant's Tale" 63
reincarnation 36, 248, 249, 250, 251
Renaissance 2, 3, 7, 15n14, 36, 85, 92, 96n14, 117
Resident Evil (2002) 71, 72, 73, 75, 76, 77, 78, 81n25
Restoration 9, 251, 255, 256, 259n57, 260n70
retrospective diagnosis 208, 216–7, 218, 220
Return From Parnassus (1601) 199, 205n73
revenge 47, 57, 88, 89, 90, 94, 97n34, 103, 104, 160, 191
'RichardBatch' 189, 198, 199
Richard III (character) 11, 12, 121, 188–200, *191*, *192*, *196*, 201n14, 203n45, 204n50, 205n66
Richard III, king of England 37, 121, 195, 196, 198, 200
Ridley, Nicholas, Bishop of London 234
Ritchie, Guy 41, 43, 44, 45, 46, 47, 48; *King Arthur: Legend of the Sword* (2017) 36, 44, 45, 47, 48, 49; *Lock, Stock, and Two Smoking Barrels* (1998) 47; *Revolver* (2005) 47; *RocknRolla* (2008) 47; *Sherlock Holmes* (2009) 47; *Sherlock Holmes: Game of Shadows* (2011) 47; *Snatch* (2000) 47
Robin Hood 37, 46, 50n13

role-playing 138, 139, 140, 142, 143, 144, 145, 146, 147, 148, 149, 150, 151; role-playing game (RPG) 147, 152n16
romance 27, 37, 38, 39, 43, 47, 48, 49, 56, 107, 108, 194, 220, 249
Rome 9, 40, 41, 43, 44, 83, 84, 85, 86, 87, 88, 89, 90, 92, 93, 94, 97n34, 98n51, 128, 210; Roman 8, 10, 36, 39, 40–1, 42, 43–4
Romero, George A. 67, 68, 78
Romney-Woollard, Michael Howard 244, 246–50, 251
Round Table 36, 37, 39, 41, 46, 51n21
Roundhead 246, 247, 248, 249
Rowling, J.K. 4, 10, 37, 117, 118, 119, 121, 122, 123, 126, 127, 128, 130, 131n31, 133n70; *Harry Potter* (book series) 4, 10, 37, 117, 118; *Harry Potter and the Chamber of Secrets* 121, 124, 125; *Harry Potter and the Prisoner of Azkaban* 118, 121, 122, 124; *Harry Potter and the Goblet of Fire* 117, 121; *Harry Potter and the Order of the Phoenix* 120, 125, 126, 127; *Harry Potter and the Half-blood Prince* 121, 125, 126; *Harry Potter and the Deathly Hallows* 122, 126; Hogwarts 126, 129; *Quidditch Through the Ages* 126

Saturninus (character) 9, 82, 83–92, 94
scars (imagery) 92, 98n51
Scotland 71, 140, 143, 147, 149, 157, 164, 177
Scott, Ridley 43; *Kingdom of Heaven* (2005) 43; *Gladiator* (2000) 92, 98n55
Sealed Knot Society, The 250, 251, 254
Semiramis 24, 25, 26, 28, 34n20
sermon 214, 218–9, 256
sexuality 87, 96n22, 96n27, 96n28, 181, 214, 215, 219, 221; bisexuality 87, 96n27, 96n28; queer 13, 87
'sexy Richard' 189, 197, 198, 199
Shakespeare Behind Bars 102, 103
Shakespeare in Prison 100, 101, 102, 104, 114n15
Shakespeare, William 1, 3, 4, 5, 9, 10, 11, 12, 13, 52, 82, 83, 86, 88, 90, 92, 93, 94, 98n50, 99, 100, 101, 102, 104, 105, 106, 107, 108, 109, 110, 111, 112, 113, 114, 114n3, 121, 125, 126, 131n31, 162, 188, 189, 190, 193, 194, 195, 197, 198, 199, 201n12, 201n16, 202n28, 239; *Coriolanus* 85, 94; *Hamlet* 99, 111; *Henry IV, Part I* 122, 189, 198; *Henry IV, Part II* 122, 189; *Henry V* 122, 189; *Henry VI, Part I* 189; *Henry VI, Part II* 189; *Henry VI, Part III* 189; *King Lear* 10, 109, 110; *Macbeth* 99, 111, 121, 190; *The Merchant of Venice* 99, 108, 109, 110; *Othello* 99, 106, 112–3; *Pericles* 121; *Richard II* 122, 189, 201n12; *Richard III* 121, 189, 190, 196, 198, 199, 201n12, 201n16; *The Taming of the Shrew* 10, 99, 104, 105, 106, 114n3; *The Tempest* 84, 99, 100, 101–4; *Titus Andronicus* 9, 82, 85, 91, 92, 93, 94, 95n12, 97n37; *Troilus and Cressida* 1; *The Winter's Tale* 99, 106, 107, 108, 121, 125
Sherlock (2010 TV series) 196, 197
Sherlock Holmes (character) 47, 188, 196, 197
sin 9, 51n21, 60, 69, 71, 72, 73, 75, 77, 79, 98n51, 213, 214, 217, 230
Sinope 24, 25, 26, 28
Smaug the Terrible (*The Hobbit* character) 188, 195–6, 204n47, 204n50
Snape, Severus (*Harry Potter* character) 118, 130
St Aubyn, Edward 10, 99, 109–10; *Dunbar* (2017) 10, 99, 106, 109, 110, 111, 114
St Kenelm 71, 75
St Modwenna 68, 75, 76
Star Wars (film series) 38, 49n5
Steele, Leo 58, 59
sword-and-sandal (film genre) 83, 92, 98n54

Tamora (character) 85, 86, 87, 88, 93, 94
Taymor, Julie 9, 82, 83, 84, 85, 86, 88, 89, 90, 91, 92, 93, 94, 95n3, 95n11, 95n12, 97n37, 97n46, 98n65; *Titus Andronicus* (1994) 91, 95n12 97n37; *Titus* (1999) 9, 82, 83, 84, 85, 86, 87, 88, 89, 91, 92, 94, 95n3, 95n11, 97n38; *The Tempest* (2010) 84

Index

Team Deathmatch 145, 153n42
Tennyson, Alfred, 1st Baron Tennyson 37, 54
Terminator (film series) 29, 30, 34n27
Teuta 24, 25, 26, 28, 34n20
Thamyris 24, 25, 26, 28, 34n20
The Assembly of Ladies 22, 24
"The Canterbury Tales" (Tacit Theatre production) 9, 52, 57, 58–9, 60, 64
The Troubles 227, 228, 233, 240
The Tudors (2007–2010) 176, 228, 240
Titus (character) 85, 88, 94, 97n46
Titus Andronicus (1985) 97n37, 97n46
Tofteland, Curt 103, 104
Tolkien, J.R.R. 37, 172, 172, 175, 176
Tresham, Henry 211, *212*
Tumblr 189, 196, 197
Tutan, Defne Ersin 154, 226–7
Twitter 182, 189, 190, 194, 198, 199, 200
Tyler, Anne 10, 99, 104–6, 113; *Vinegar Girl* (2016) 10, 99, 104, 105, 106, 108

Underwood, Frank (*House of Cards* character) see *House of Cards*

video games 1, 5, 6, 11, 67, 107, 108, 137, 147, 150, 151n3, 151n6, 171; visuals 139, 140, 142, 143, 144, 150
Vikings (2013–) 44, 45, 47, 147, 154, 176
Vikings 46, 147, 148, 149, 150
violence 10, 44, 59, 71, 82, 83, 85, 88, 89, 90, 91, 93, 94, 95n13, 111, 125, 129, 146, 150, 159, 171, 176, 177, 178, 179, 194, 233, 234, 240–1, 252; violent behaviour 28, 42, 83, 88, 89, 90, 94, 111, 160, 236
Virgil 1; *Aeneid* 1, 6, 13n3
Voldemort 118, 119, 120, 121, 130

Wales and the Welsh 69, 73, 76, 77 140, 141, 142, 164
Walsingham, Francis 228, 237–8
War of the Roses (2012–2017) 139, 143–4, 145–6, 147
Wars of the Roses 2, 143, 144, 145, 146, 174, 177, 179, 193

Wars of the Three Kingdoms see English Civil War
Weasley (*Harry Potter* characters): Bill 119; Fred 121; George 119, 121; Ginny 119, 120, 121; Mr Arthur 126; Mrs Molly 119, 121, 123; Percy 119, 120, 127; Ron 118, 119, 120, 121, 122, 124, 125, 126, 129, 130
Webster, John 4, 10, 117, 122, 132n39, 132n43; *The Duchess of Malfi* 4, 10, 117, 118, 122, 123, 124, 125, 127, 128, 129, 130, 132n43; *The White Devil* 132n39
Wedgwood, C.V. (Veronica) 245, 249, 251
Weisl, Angela J. 1, 2, 138
Westeros 171, 173–4, 175, 176, 184, 192
Westminster Abbey 53, 54, 256
Wheatley, Ben 13, 244, 251, 253
Whig history 8, 226, 239
William of Newburgh 69, 70, 71, 72, 73, 74, 75, 76, 77
William of Stonham 158–9, 160, 161, 162, 163, 164, 168n27
Winterson, Jeanette 10, 99, 106–8; *The Gap of Time* (2015) 10, 99, 106–8
women warriors, see female warriors
Wonder Woman (2017) see Jenkins, Patty
Wonder Woman (*Wonder Woman* character) 8, 21, 22, 23, 26, 29, 30, 31, 32, 35n30, 35n42
World War Z (2013) 70, 71, 75, 76, 77, 78
worthy, worthiness 8, 23, 24, 25, 26, 28, 29, 30, 31, 33, 47, 54, 77, 130, 158, 200
Wyatt Rebellion 230, 232

young adult fiction 12, 208, 218, 220, 221
Young Lucius (character) 89, 90, 94, 97n46
Young, Helen 166n7, 194, 203n35
Young, Peter 13, 244, 245, 246, 249, 250, 251, 257

zombie 9, 67, 68, 70, 71, 72, 73, 74, 75, 76, 77, 78, 79, 80n9